THE PARADOXES OF IGNORANCE
IN EARLY MODERN ENGLAND AND FRANCE

THE PARADOXES OF IGNORANCE
IN EARLY MODERN
ENGLAND AND FRANCE

Sandrine Parageau

Stanford University Press · Stanford, California

Stanford University Press
Stanford, California

© 2023 by Sandrine Parageau. All rights reserved.

This book has been partially underwritten by the Peter Stansky Publication Fund in British Studies. For more information on the fund, please see www.sup.org/stanskyfund.

No part of this book may be reproduced or transmitted in any form or by any means, electronic or mechanical, including photocopying and recording, or in any information storage or retrieval system, without the prior written permission of Stanford University Press.

Printed in the United States of America on acid-free, archival-quality paper

Library of Congress Cataloging-in-Publication Data

Names: Parageau, Sandrine, author.
Title: The paradoxes of ignorance in early modern England and France / Sandrine Parageau.
Description: Stanford, California : Stanford University Press, 2023. | Includes bibliographical references and index.
Identifiers: LCCN 2022026112 (print) | LCCN 2022026113 (ebook) | ISBN 9781503632561 (cloth) | ISBN 9781503635319 (paperback) | ISBN 9781503635326 (ebook)
Subjects: LCSH: Ignorance (Theory of knowledge)—History—17th century. | Knowledge, Theory of—England—History—17th century. | Knowledge, Theory of—France—History—17th century.
Classification: LCC BD221 .P345 2023 (print) | LCC BD221 (ebook) | DDC 121—dc23/eng/20221104
LC record available at https://lccn.loc.gov/2022026112
LC ebook record available at https://lccn.loc.gov/2022026113

Cover design: Daniel Benneworth-Gray
Cover photo: Unsplash

Contents

Acknowledgments	vii
Introduction	1
PART I: IGNORANCE AS WISDOM	29
1 Fortunes of *Docta ignorantia* in Early Modern England and France	31
2 English Experimental Philosophy and Doctrines of Ignorance	48
PART II: IGNORANCE AS A PRINCIPLE OF KNOWLEDGE	67
3 Ignorance and the Internal Light	71
4 Ignorance, Inspiration, and Religious Knowledge	91
PART III: IGNORANCE AS AN EPISTEMOLOGICAL INSTRUMENT	115
5 Fictions of Ignorance	119
6 Ignorance and Chance Discovery	132
7 John Locke's Anthropology of Ignorance	145
Conclusion	159
Notes	169
Bibliography	221
Index	243

Acknowledgments

I was not entirely convinced, when I first started researching the topic of this book a few years ago, that such a paradoxical project as the intellectual history of early modern ignorance was actually possible. The support of numerous friends, colleagues, and institutions encouraged me to pursue my first insights, and I'm happy to be given the opportunity to express my deepest gratitude to them.

My first thanks go to Line Cottegnies, who first introduced me to research in early modern British history and has remained a constant source of support and counsel over the years.

I am also grateful to the readers of an early version of this book for their suggestions and encouragement, especially Anne Page, the very first reader of the following pages, whose help and support from the beginning of the project have proved essential. Emmanuelle de Champs, Philippe Hamou, Andrew Hiscock, and Pierre Lurbe also greatly contributed to improving the book, and I thank them warmly.

Heartfelt thanks go to Cesare Cuttica and Will Slauter for their advice and guidance throughout the publication of this book. I am also grateful to Erica Wetter at Stanford University Press for being receptive to the manuscript and for taking the project on with such kindness and professionalism. Many thanks to Caroline

McKusick for her support and her help in finalizing the manuscript, and to Katherine Faydash for her impressive and meticulous copyediting. I would also like to thank the anonymous reviewers for their helpful comments and suggestions.

The research for this history of early modern ignorance has benefited greatly from the support of several institutions over the years. In particular, I would like to thank the Institut Universitaire de France, which granted me a five-year *délégation* in 2017, and thus made the research for this book as well as its writing possible in exceptionally favorable conditions. I also wish to thank the Folger Shakespeare Library for a Philip A. Knatchel Fellowship that allowed me to benefit from the library's excellent collections and wonderful community of researchers. I am grateful to the staff of the Huntington Library, California, for their invaluable help during a two-month residency as a Mellon Fellow in 2017. In this idyllic place, I was fortunate enough to meet François Rigolot and the late Howard Weinbrot, who generously shared with me their immense knowledge of the early modern period. There I also met Hélène Demeestere, the best guide to Southern California. Back in France, I would like to thank the members of the Centre de Recherches Anglophones (CREA) of Université Paris Nanterre, of which I was a happy member from 2009 until I joined the Sorbonne in 2021. My research on ignorance was thus largely conducted as a member of the CREA, led at the time by Caroline Rolland-Diamond, who was a great support and inspiration. Finally, I wish to thank my colleagues in the research center Histoire et Dynamique des Espaces Anglophones (HDEA), who welcomed me at the Sorbonne a few months ago.

The support, patience, and humor of many friends have made my task much lighter. My warmest thanks go to my longtime friends Hélène Steinmetz and Fabien Grenèche. Thanks to Karim Fertikh for the inspiring conversations. I also wish to thank Claire Bazin, Luc Benoit à la Guillaume, Fabrice Bensimon, Laurence Dubois, Claire Gheeraert-Graffeuille, Mark Greengrass, Stéphane Jettot, Anne-Claire Le Reste, the Marcucci-Fragneau family, Brigitte Marrec, Emmanuelle Peraldo, Allan Potofsky, Clotilde Prunier, Soizick Solman, Wilfrid Rotgé, Élise Trogrlic, and, of course, "the Bacon girls," Claire Crignon and Sylvie Kleiman-Lafon.

The practice of martial arts has been essential in providing physical and mental well-being all along this project. Special thanks go to my karate instructor Nordine Daoudi. I also wish to thank Hugo Pilkington, Ofer Soussan, Toyoki Nishibayashi and Mathieu François for the many uplifting training sessions.

This book is dedicated to my family, who provide refuge from the turmoil of Parisian life and the restlessness of academia.

THE PARADOXES OF IGNORANCE
IN EARLY MODERN ENGLAND AND FRANCE

Introduction

Lock. *In one word I do not write to the Vulgar.*
Montaigne. *And they are the only People that should be writ to. Not write to the Vulgar? quoth thou; Egad the Vulgar are the only Scholars. If they had not Taught Us we had been Stupid. The Observations made by Shepherds in Egypt and Chaldea gave birth to Geometry and Astronomy. The variety of sound from the Hammers of Smiths striking on their Anville was the Original of their Scale of Music. And some traces on the sand by a poor Cow-herd gave the first Idea of Painting. . . . Was not Gun Powder invented by a poor Monk at Nuremberg; And Printing by an Inferior Tradesman at Haerlem. Look thro your Microscopes and know that Lewinhoeck that brought them to such perfection was a Glazier: and when you next set Your Watch, remember that Tompion was a farrier, and began his great Knowledge in the Equation of Time by regulating the wheels of a common Jack, to roast Meat. . . . In short, I am one of those Vulgar, for whom, you say, You do not write; And in the Name of our whole Community, I take leave to tell You, I think, You have wronged both us and your subject.*[1]

When the English poet and diplomat Matthew Prior (1664–1721) imagined this dialogue between John Locke and Michel de Montaigne in the late 1710s, the latter had been dead for more than a century and the English philosopher for almost fifteen years. Not only had the two men lived in different countries, but also they had known different religious and political contexts, and had thus presumably built their philosophies from different sources. This dialogue of the dead gave Prior the opportunity to celebrate his French champion to the detriment of the English philosopher, but the choice of Locke as Montaigne's interlocutor was not arbitrary. Locke's philosophy was highly praised at the time Prior wrote his dialogue, both in England and in France, but above all, the two thinkers had propounded attitudes to knowledge that Prior deemed contradictory. Thus, Locke was featured as a rationalist in the Cartesian vein while Montaigne was presented as a pragmatic empiricist on the English model. Those relations to knowledge and ways of knowing also implied specific relations to ignorance, as the excerpt here clearly shows, by addressing the learning, or absence thereof, of the two men's intended readerships and the role of ignorance in discovery, invention, and more generally the advancement of knowledge and science. Indeed, in Prior's dialogue, Montaigne rebukes Locke for his contempt of "the vulgar" and mocks his obsession with method and self-knowledge instead. The French Seigneur, however, prides himself on both addressing the ignorant and being ignorant himself, asserting the paradoxical superiority of "the vulgar" over the learned: "the Vulgar are the only Scholars." In other words, the illiterate, understood as men (and possibly women) who have not been educated at school but may possess practical knowledge, such as artisans and peasants, are to be celebrated for the most important discoveries ever made, such as gunpowder and printing, the microscope and the watch, and even geometry and astronomy.[2] Those ignorant people are therefore the legitimate audience of philosophers, and Locke is mistaken in thinking that he should address his writings to scholars. But Montaigne's—or rather, Prior's—accusation is unfair, as the English philosopher did recognize and praise the ingenuity of artisans, as his *Essay concerning Human Understanding* (1690) clearly attests: "It was to the unscholastick Statesman, that the Governments of the World owed their Peace, Defence, and Liberties; and from the illiterate and contemned Mechanick, (a Name of Disgrace) that they received the improvements of useful Arts."[3] Thus, despite Prior's effort to have Locke pass as a philosopher who despised the vulgar and Montaigne as a humble man who identified with the vulgar, the truth is that both thinkers—among many others in the early modern period—celebrated illiterate inventors and discoverers, as if their very ignorance made them more likely than scholars to contribute to the advancement of knowledge.

This paradox is the very subject of this book, which inquires into the conceptions and interpretations of the notion of ignorance that could justify such a reversal of meaning in England and in France from Montaigne to Locke (c. 1580–c. 1700). In other words, the book examines the praises of ignorance expressed in the long seventeenth century and shows that, even though they came under attack, those celebrations were far from marginal, so much so that early modern doctrines of ignorance can be said to have contributed to the emergence of new ways of knowing. Thus, the book claims that the notion of ignorance should be reinstated in the intellectual history of the early modern period as one of the foremost conceptual issues of the time. To make this argument, three main functions or virtues of ignorance conveyed in early modern philosophical and religious discourses are here identified and developed: first, ignorance could be seen as conducive to wisdom and self-knowledge; second, it could be understood as a principle of knowledge, that is, a condition that allowed for a direct access to truth; and third, it came to be construed by a number of natural philosophers as an epistemological instrument that could help elaborate new methods.

Ignorance in Religious, Political, and Intellectual Context

The idea that virtues were attributed to ignorance in the early modern period might seem surprising in the first instance, especially in England, given the Reformation's emphasis on literacy and education. As a matter of fact, a number of defenders of the established church virulently denounced all forms of ignorance, which they associated with the Roman Catholic Church, and promoted education and religious knowledge instead. For those clergymen and theologians, ignorance was a flaw, a distemper, and a major threat to society, as it led to credulity and dangerous or erratic behavior. More precisely, ignorance was defined by most Church of England clergymen as a disability inherited from the Fall.[4] It was also perceived as a worsening and spreading disease, so much so that the preacher William Gearing devoted a whole treatise to the subject in the mid-seventeenth century, *The Arraignment of Ignorance*, in which he lamented the omnipresence of ignorance in England at the time: "What swarms of *ignorant* people are there every where? *ignorant* congregations, *ignorant* families, *ignorant* parents, *ignorant* children, *ignorant* Masters, *ignorant* servants."[5] Yet ignorance was not systematically condemned in the religious and theological discourses of Reformation England. In particular, a number of religious groups celebrated ignorance as a superior mode of knowledge and as the only access to God. Indeed, during the Civil Wars and Interregnum (1640–1660), the emerging religious sects, especially Quakers and Baptists, advocated ignorance and personal inspiration as the way to knowledge of God through the operation of the inner light, rejecting both the useless religious knowledge promoted by the established church and the vain learning of the universities. As a matter of fact, in England, the most vivid debates on the virtues and vices of ignorance occurred in the unstable context of the mid-seventeenth century. In those times of religious and political turmoil, defenders of learning, in contrast, associated ignorance with social and political disorder and sometimes even deemed the general ignorance of the people responsible for the violent outbursts of the time. For them, the ominous and often-quoted verse from Hosea 4.6 justified a ruthless fight against ignorance: "My people are destroyed for lack of knowledge: because thou hast rejected knowledge, I will also reject thee, that thou shalt be no priest to me: seeing thou hast forgotten the law of thy God, I will also forget thy children."[6]

Early modern celebrations of ignorance were also expressed in the context of the emergence of modern science, a development known as the Scientific Revolution. According to this grand narrative of scientific progress, the elaboration of new methods of thinking and knowing led to more effective ways of doing "science," and therefore to numerous groundbreaking discoveries in physics, medicine, anatomy, astronomy, and so on—fields of knowledge that were not yet understood as distinct disciplines with specific methods but as part of the general study of nature and human beings, called "natural philosophy." Of course, as Steven Shapin has famously argued, and as many other sociologists and historians of science have similarly shown, "there was no such thing as the Scientific Revolution,"[7] that is, no sudden move toward modern science in the seventeenth century. But despite this claim, and as Shapin himself admits, there is no denying that a number of important changes (e.g., the mechanization of nature, the progressive emergence of distinct disciplines, the focus on method) leading to modern science did occur in the early modern period. *The Paradoxes of Ignorance* shows precisely how the notion of ignorance contributed to those changes and, generally speaking, to the advancement of knowledge, although this may seem paradoxical at first. Indeed, the book contends that ignorance was not erased or suppressed in the early modern quest for renewed ways of thinking and knowing: it was, on the contrary, assimilated into the philosophical and scientific discourses of the time, although it took different forms in England and in France.

Finally, the argument of a rehabilitation of ignorance in the early modern period must be examined in the intellectual context of antischolasticism and the rediscovery of ancient skepticism at the time. Indeed, most early modern celebrations of ignorance were the result of the growing realization that traditional scholastic learning and methods were an obstacle to the advancement of science. They were also a reaction to the overabundance of (bad) books, as it was perceived, published at the time.[8] Men and women of the early modern period often expressed their distress at the overwhelming amount of knowledge that had been amassed over the centuries and that then, it seemed, grew exponentially in the context of Renaissance humanism and the Scientific Revolution, with the risk of spreading errors and opinions that could jeopardize the advancement of knowledge. Some held that such errors and opinions were spread in particular by past and present scholastic works. To a certain extent, the renewed interest in ancient skepticism at the time was a response to the enduring supremacy of scholasticism, and to the feeling of an overwhelming flood of both invaluable and pointless information. As Richard H. Popkin has shown, several forms of skepticism were rediscovered from the sixteenth century onward: academic skepticism developed from Socrates's recognition of his ignorance and was then taken up by Cicero, Diogenes Laertius, and Augustine, while Pyrrhonism was expounded in the works of Sextus Empiricus, whose *Hypotyposes* were translated into Latin by Henri Estienne in 1562. Those two forms of skepticism were well known in the early modern period, and Popkin argues that they played "a special and different role" in the intellectual crisis caused by the Reformation, especially Sextus's arguments, so much so that the period was characterized by "une crise pyrrhonienne."[9] Popkin gives the "fundamental sense of sceptic" as "one who doubts that necessary and sufficient grounds or reasons can be given for our knowledge or beliefs; or one who doubts that adequate evidence can be given to show that under no conditions can our knowledge or beliefs be false or illusory or dubious."[10] With such a broad definition, a great number of authors of the early modern period can be considered skeptics. The list given by Popkin is indeed very long, including Sanches, Montaigne, Charron, the *libertins érudits*, Mersenne, Descartes, Glanvill, Locke, Leibniz, Bayle, and more, some adopting a form of "constructive or mitigated scepticism," others adhering to "semiscepticism" or "superscepticism," while others yet were "sceptique[s] malgré [eux]," some among them evolving from one of those categories to the other in their lifetime. More recently, other early modern philosophers have been added to the list, such as Francis Bacon. The vast scholarship on early modern skepticism has thus led to the idea that it was omnipresent at the time and that all reactions to scholasticism and attitudes to knowledge in general could find their justifications and expressions in a variety of skeptical attitudes inherited from the conjunction of the rediscovery of ancient skepticism and the religious crisis. *The Paradoxes of Ignorance* does not deny the specificity of the early modern period when it comes to attitudes to knowledge—on the contrary. Nor does it deny the general skepticism of the period: as a matter of fact, the book makes a number of references to forms of skepticism, especially when they were mentioned by the authors themselves, usually to discredit their opponents. But the contention here is that a focus on the notion of ignorance in the writings of some of the authors listed already and others gives a clearer understanding of their attitudes to knowledge than elaborating multiple variations on skepticism.

Moreover, the virtues and functions of ignorance examined here are not all drawn from ancient skepticism. Instead, the book shows that, even though the role of Sextus's skepticism must not be overlooked, other doctrines and intellectual traditions were mobilized by the authors who attributed virtues to ignorance in England and in France, in particular medieval mystical traditions such as negative theology, as expressed in the anonymous *Cloud of Unknowing*, Nicholas of Cusa's *docta ignorantia* and the topos of the illiterate *Idiotus*. According to Popkin, Cusanus, like other "antirational theologians," used skeptical arguments to undermine the rational approach to religious knowledge.[11] *The Paradoxes of Ignorance* contends that the specificity, complexity, and influence of Cusanus's thought are better assessed through an analysis of his doctrine of ignorance and its echoes in sixteenth- and seventeenth-century England and France. Thus, more often than not, intellectual traditions other than ancient skepticism are the sources for the rehabilitation of ignorance studied here. Some of them were admittedly influenced by earlier forms of skepticism, but they nonetheless built their own doctrines of ignorance, which remained influential in seventeenth-century England and France. Therefore, the history of ignorance that is told in this book is also, to a large extent, a reassessment of the history of early modern skepticism or another perspective on the "crise pyrrhonienne."

Ancient, Medieval, and Renaissance Doctrines of Ignorance

SOCRATIC IGNORANCE

Early modern celebrations of ignorance borrowed from a long tradition. Most of them drew in particular upon Socratic wisdom. The idea of knowing one's ignorance as a definition of wisdom can be traced back to *The Apology of Socrates*, where the Greek philosopher famously says that he knows nothing except that he does not know anything.[12] In this passage from his trial, Socrates narrates how he met politicians, poets, and artisans so as to discover whether any of them was wiser than himself, after the Pythia had declared that he was the wisest man. It turned out that none was wiser because, contrary to him, they did not recognize their own ignorance. Forms of Socratic ignorance are also expressed in dialogues such as *Charmides*, which focuses on *sōphrosúnē*, moderation, temperance, or discipline, a virtue that enables one to judge correctly and to experience self-control and wisdom. First identified with the ideal of knowing oneself, it is then defined in the dialogue as "knowledge of knowledge and ignorance," and finally as "knowing what one knows and what one does not know,"[13] which is the very definition of wisdom in the text. The knowledge of ignorance that Socrates and Critias discuss in the dialogue "appears to defy the principle of contradiction, for it is both something and its opposite, both knowledge and ignorance."[14] But more importantly, Socrates shows that knowledge of ignorance is primarily self-knowledge, as ignorance is "not at all a matter *for others* but is integrally 'one's own.'"[15] Thus, the question of ignorance implies "a turn to oneself,"[16] or self-reflection, self-consciousness, self-criticism, and finally, self-knowledge. Socratic ignorance was "a tool of great flexibility" that allowed for many interpretations and uses throughout the early modern period.[17]

PETRARCH ON HIS OWN IGNORANCE

In *De sui ipsius et multorum ignorantia* (1367), a letter addressed to his friend Donato Albanzani, the grammarian, Petrarch responds to four young men who had accused him of being ignorant in philosophy, meaning that he did not know Aristotelianism because he had questioned and even ridiculed some of its theses. Thus, despite his reputation as a learned writer at the time, Petrarch was mocked for his ignorance: "They claim that I am altogether illiterate, that I am a plain uneducated fellow."[18] Drawing mostly upon Cicero and the model of the *honnête homme*, Petrarch discredits learning, or at least some learning, and argues that, for the young men who have accused him, the Aristotelian philosophy has replaced faith, yet ignorant faith is always preferable to proud science: ignorance is indeed a superior mode of wisdom, "as is clearly shown by the long line of illiterate saints of both sexes."[19] In this context, Petrarch uses the expression "learned ignorance" to refer to Aristotelianism or the science of the ancients, who did not know God. It thus means giving precedence to philosophical over divine knowledge, and it is explicitly opposed to humility and awareness of one's ignorance, or the blessed ignorance mentioned by Augustine.[20] Quoting 1 Samuel 2.4, Petrarch claims that the weak and ignorant who believe in God are wiser and happier than the learned who do not know God, emphasizing "illiterate virtue."[21]

Petrarch declares that he prefers God to Aristotle, and he praises humility, awareness of one's ignorance, and weakness. But if he seems to defend ignorance (of Aristotelian philosophy, in particular, and of useless knowledge, in general), he also returns the accusation of ignorance against his detractors, who are said to be blind admirers of Aristotle precisely because of their ignorance, which renders them unable to judge or use their reason correctly. While learning is a useless ornament that "inflates" and "tears down," Petrarch argues, reason is on the contrary an essential part of a human being.[22] He claims, as others did after him in the seventeenth century, that "letters are instruments of insanity for many, of arrogance for almost everyone, if they do not meet with a good and well-trained mind [*idiota*],"[23] underlining the close link between the reflection on ignorance and learning, and on methods or ways of thinking and the mechanisms of the mind. His accusers are the most ignorant because they cannot recognize the inevitable limits to their knowledge and their own imperfection, and as such, they do not know themselves.[24] Thus, as was often the case later in the early modern period, ignorance is given two contradictory meanings in Petrarch's letter: it is the virtue of the humble man who is aware of his ignorance and the intellectual vice of the erudite. Most of the characteristics of later celebrations or discussions of ignorance are found in Petrarch's seminal text, published in the 1554 Basel edition of his *Opera omnia*.

NICHOLAS OF CUSA'S *DOCTA IGNORANTIA*

The German thinker and cardinal Nicholas of Cusa (or Cusanus; 1401–1464) probably found inspiration in Petrarch's *De ignorantia*, of which he owned a copy. Indeed, like Petrarch, Cusanus strongly reacted to the dogmatism and intellectual tyranny of Aristotelianism, which also gave rise in his works to a celebration of some form of ignorance. Another important source for Cusanus's doctrine of learned ignorance, as for Petrarch's claim to ignorance, was St. Augustine, who used the expression in a letter to Proba, a wealthy Roman widow, to refer to the paradox of praying to ask for something that we cannot know, insofar as we should know what we are seeking for in order to desire it.[25] If we were completely ignorant of it, Augustine writes, we would not desire it, but "there is in us . . . a certain learned ignorance, so to speak, but an ignorance learned from the Spirit of God, who helps our weakness."[26] We are ignorant of what we desire, but the Spirit intercedes for us, which is why this ignorance is "learned."

Cusanus's conception of learned ignorance should be understood in the context of a medieval tradition of mysticism, which held that God was beyond all knowing. In the first chapter of the first book of *De docta ignorantia*, entitled "How It Is That Knowing Is Not-knowing," Cusanus expresses his disillusionment at the poor state of human knowledge, regretting that ignorance should proportionally increase with knowledge.[27] He explicitly refers to Socrates, but also to Solomon, for whom words cannot explain things, and to Job 28.21, which says that wisdom and understanding are hidden "from the eyes of all living, and kept close from the fowls of the air." Cusanus also borrows Aristotle's analogy, given in the second book of the *Metaphysics*, between the eyes of the night owl that cannot see the light of day and the human intellect that cannot comprehend the most evident things—yet men still desire to know. Cusanus argues that this natural desire to know cannot be void because nature does nothing in vain, and therefore we desire to know that we do not know (in other words, we desire to know our ignorance). If we understand this, Cusanus concludes, we can reach learned ignorance, which is therefore a form of knowledge: "For a man—even one very well versed in learning—will attain unto nothing more perfect than to be found to be most learned in the ignorance which is distinctively his. The more he knows that he is unknowing, the more learned he will be. Unto this end I have undertaken the task of writing a few things about learned ignorance."[28] The only knowledge that one can get is that of his or her own ignorance. But this is not a form of knowledge that should be rejected. On the contrary, everyone should strive to know that they are unknowing, and the more they know that they are ignorant, the more learned they become.

Cusanus adds that God cannot be known because knowledge implies a comparison or analogy between two objects, and God, or the Infinite, cannot be compared with anything finite.[29] Thus, the knowledge of God can be only "an unknowing." This is an expression of apophaticism or even "a central and exemplary paradigm of the apophatic mode of thought and discourse."[30] Apophaticism, or negative theology, conceives of theology as a practice of unknowing, in the words of the fourteenth-century English mystic who wrote *The Cloud of Unknowing*, a text that proposed a method of contemplation that implied divesting the mind of all knowledge.[31] Love and unknowing were the only means to reach union with God. The text thus promoted a form of apophaticism by encouraging knowledge of God through negation. William Franke has shown that this book was "representative of a turn in fourteenth-century spirituality that divides it from speculative and Scholastic theology and orients it toward a newly emerging experiential dimension":[32] union with God no longer relied on intellectual exercises, but rather on the mystical experience of love and on ignorance or unknowing. The author explicitly inscribed the book in the Dionysian tradition of unknowing that insisted on the limits of human knowledge. But by stating the equation between ignorance and wisdom in a mystical context, it was also a "christianization of the Socratic doubt."[33]

Denys the Areopagite, the author of *Divine Names* and of *Mystical Theology*, is often presented as "the founding father of Western Christian apophaticism,"[34] and also another important source for Cusanus's *docta ignorantia*.[35] His thought became influential in the thirteenth century, when praises of ignorance, simplicity, and genuine piety spread among antischolastic movements. His complete works (*Opera Dionysii*) were then published in Strasbourg in 1502–1503. In Cusanus's *De docta ignorantia*, chapter 26 is devoted to negative theology, which is here identified with *sacra ignorantia*, an expression borrowed from Denys, to convey the idea that God is ineffable because "He is infinitely greater than all nameable things."[36] Thus, nothing can be said about him, but by negation, Cusanus argues: "Therefrom we conclude that the precise truth shines incomprehensibly within the darkness of our ignorance. This is the learned ignorance we have been seeking and through which alone, as I explained, [we] can approach the maximum, triune God of infinite goodness—[approach Him] according to the degree of our instruction in ignorance."[37] If God cannot be known but by ignorance, the erudition of scholars is definitely useless when it comes to knowledge of the highest truths. Like Petrarch, Cusanus criticized the pedantry and arrogance of his Aristotelian contemporaries. But most importantly, his aim in *De docta ignorantia* and in other works was to propose a new method for the acquisition of knowledge. In particular, Cusanus's *De idiota*, which, interestingly, was attributed to Petrarch for some time, features a poor illiterate artisan and illustrates how being unlearned compels one to observe the world, which is preferable to learning from books, as naïve observation is a surer access to both divine and natural truth.[38] This new method, learned ignorance, relies on the recognition of human ignorance and weakness, which itself implies a search for knowledge.

"BETTER BE IGNORANT THAN LEARNED": PARADOXICAL DISCOURSES

In early modern Europe, celebrations of ignorance were often part of a topos, a "paradoxical discourse" that blamed the vain erudition of scholars for the corruption and degeneration of humankind. This humanist "discourse against letters" (*adversus literas et literatos*) emerged in Italy at the turn of the sixteenth century and was then expressed in a great number of texts belonging to a variety of genres (e.g., *sermo, vituperatio, progymnasma*, paradoxes, essays).[39] What these texts had in common was a harsh condemnation of classical learning by authors who were often learned scholars themselves. Most of these texts were characterized by a satirical and declamatory tone. They constantly referred to a small number of biblical passages, in particular Ecclesiastes 1.18 and 1 Corinthians 1.19–20.[40] In keeping with skeptical writing practices, they usually presented catalogs of uncertain knowledge in diverse fields, of mad scholars, or of dangerous consequences of learning. Their ambivalence toward religion was another common characteristic.[41]

But most importantly for an inquiry on ignorance, these "discourses against letters" all used the topos of the superior virtue and happiness of ignorant men and women, which were systematically set against the ridiculous vanity and madness of scholars.[42] Indeed, those discourses very explicitly asserted the superiority of ignorance over learning: "Better be ignorant than learned," Ortensio Lando (1512–c.1555) declared in his *Paradossi cioè, sententie fuori del comun parere* (paradox III),[43] written in the tradition of Cicero's *Paradoxa Stoicorum* against received opinion. Lando's text was soon translated into French, which allowed for a broader dissemination of the work, even though the translator, Charles Estienne, considerably altered the original text to emphasize its witty and facetious dimension rather than the humanist anti-intellectualism that initially characterized the *Paradossi*. It was then published in London in an English translation—based on the French one, not on the original Italian text—in 1593, where it immediately reached a large audience.[44] Lando's paradoxes and their sixteenth-century translations into French and English also contributed to the circulation of the radical and subversive ideas expressed earlier in the sixteenth century by Erasmus and Agrippa.[45] Erasmus's *The Praise of Folly*, a satire of abstruse university theology written in 1509 and first published in 1511 in Paris, is indeed regarded as one of the main inspirations for the paradoxical discourse, and especially for Lando's paradox III on ignorance as Erasmus also praised the poor ignorant man or woman.[46] In *Moriæ encomium*, folly is wisdom, while scholastic theology and philosophy seek to know the unknowable, and despise the very simplicity of the gospel. Drawing upon 1 Corinthians, Erasmus founds his praise of folly on the Pauline *stultitia Dei* and thus expresses a form of paradox. Besides, in other works, Erasmus celebrates the superior virtues of "little women," plowmen and weavers, revealing a *contemptu scientiae* attitude that was also characteristic of the paradox tradition.

Michel Jeanneret has argued that praises of ignorance that took the form of paradoxes were not that common in the "discourse against letters," probably because, for humanists, the idea of the superiority of ignorance over learning was not that paradoxical. Indeed, it was strongly rooted in a double legacy: on the one hand, the revival of skepticism in the Renaissance, and on the other hand, negative theology and Cusan learned ignorance.[47] Whether paradoxical celebrations of ignorance were common or not in the "discourse against letters" can be diversely appreciated, but above all, Jeanneret's comment shows that, at the beginning of the early modern period, authors who asserted the superiority of ignorance over learning could rely on a long and rich tradition that was not limited to forms of ancient skepticism but also included medieval doctrines of ignorance. Moreover, theological and philosophical paradoxes continued to be used as an effective tool to formulate subversive arguments and new ideas all along the seventeenth century.

Ignorance was commonly represented by the figure of an ass or donkey in the early modern period, especially after the publication of Cesare Ripa's famous and often republished *Iconologia* (1593). In the earlier *Emblematum liber* by Andrea Alciato (1492–1550), first published in 1531, ignorance is depicted as a sphinx, with the face of a young woman, the wings of birds, and the legs of a lion, which represent the three evils associated with ignorance: frivolity, pleasure, and arrogance (fig. 1).[48] In Ripa's *Iconologia*, five entries are listed for ignorance. Three of them are titled "Ignoranza," one is titled "Ignoranza in un ricco senza lettere," and one is "Ignoranza di tutte le cose."[49] In the first three allegories, ignorance is represented by a woman: in the first one, the "lascivious" woman has the ears of an ass, the legs and feet of a lion, and the hands of a wolf, calling to mind Alciato's sphinx. In the second one, the blind woman with a deformed face is represented with a bat, to symbolize the blindness of ignorance, as opposed to the light of wisdom (*sapienza*). In the third allegory, the body of the woman is covered with fish scales, the fish being the very symbol of ignorance, according to Ripa, because it is stupid, but the scales can easily be removed from its body, just like the "veil of ignorance" can be removed thanks to the acquisition of classical learning.[50] Finally, the "ignorance of a rich man" is represented by a man riding a sheep, and the "ignorance of all things" is depicted as the head of an ass that looks down to emphasize self-love. The representation of the rich ignorant man, or *dives indoctus*, was probably inspired by Alciato's *Book of Emblems*, which depicts a man riding a sheep across the sea (a reference to Phrixus, who was saved from sacrifice by a flying golden ram). Later French editions of the book explained that the sheep or ram was the stupidest of all animals ("la plus simple, & sotte beste du monde"), hence its assimilation with the rich ignorant man.[51] But it seems that the ass progressively replaced the sheep as the allegory of ignorance. In the 1603 edition of Ripa's *Iconologia*, the first allegory of the 1593 edition was replaced with a different depiction of ignorance, embodied by a naked blindfolded child riding an ass and holding a reed in his hand.[52] The child represents the simplicity of the ignorant, the ass stands for absence of reason and stubbornness, and the reed for the instability and vanity of ignorance.[53] The editions of Ripa's *Iconologia* in Italian throughout the seventeenth century gave a similar allegory of ignorance. This representation was also taken up by most adaptations and translations into English and French of Ripa's book of emblems well into the eighteenth century (fig. 2).[54]

Yet if the association of ignorance with the ass in *Iconologia* was made to emphasize the flaws of ignorant men, it could also be used to refer to the paradoxical

FIGURE 1. Ignorance as a sphinx, in Andrea Alciato, *Emblematum liber*, Augsbourg, 28 February 1531, Emblem 186, folio C3v. Source: University of Glasgow Archives & Special Collections, SM18. Reprinted with permission.

14 *Introduction*

FIGURE 2. Allegory of ignorance. Source: *Cesare Ripa, Iconologie, ou Explication nouvelle de plusieurs images, emblèmes et autres figures hierogliphiques des vertus, des vices, des arts, des sciences, des causes naturelles, des humeurs différentes, & des passions humaines*, ed. Jean Baudoin, Paris, 1643, p. 160.

wisdom of simple and ignorant people. This representation was commonly found in the "discourse against letters" as a tool to discredit and mock the vanity of scholastic learning. The most famous example of a eulogy of the ass in the sixteenth century is that of Henry Cornelius Agrippa at the end of his *De incertitudine & vanitate scientiarum & artium, atque excellentia verbi Dei, declamatio*, written in 1526, first published in Latin in Antwerp in 1530, and then translated into English in 1569 by James Sandford and into French by the Huguenot Louis Turquet de Mayerne in 1582.[55] It was often republished, in several languages, throughout the early modern period and was highly influential in England and in France.

Most of the subsequent translations and editions of the book altered and adapted Agrippa's original work. The purpose of these changes was sometimes to have the book defend specific ideas: the original text was so ambiguous and lent itself to so many contradictory interpretations that it was easily altered in favor of one opinion or another. Yet the aim of those changes and additions was also sometimes to avoid censorship. Indeed, Agrippa's book had been condemned by the Sorbonne immediately after its publication in Paris in 1531, as it was accused of promoting Lutheranism; it was also condemned as heretical by the University of Leuven.

De incertitudine is a violent and radical denunciation of knowledge: "Nothing can happen more Pestilential to Man, than Knowledge: this is that true Plague that invades all Mankind with so much confusion that subverts all Innocence; subjecting us to so many Clouds of Sin and Error, and at length to Death."[56] Knowledge corrupts the understanding of man and makes him lose his innocence. It is also uncertain and vain, as is shown by the accumulation of corrupted knowledge and the diversity of opinions in all the sciences. A radical expression of the "discourse against letters," *De incertitudine* makes a long inventory of the knowledge supposedly acquired in poetry, artificial memory, natural philosophy, medicine, and so on, to which are added chapters on less expected subjects, such as prostitution, temples, and ceremonies. Agrippa's aim in drawing up this long list and emphasizing the endless accumulation of knowledge is to show that this knowledge is nothing but opinions, the very diversity of which proves its vanity. This criticism was aimed primarily at scholastic theology.[57]

Besides the argument of the vanity and uncertainty of knowledge, Agrippa gives five principal reasons ignorance should be preferred to knowledge: first, knowledge leads to the exploitation and manipulation of the vulgar by men who deem themselves learned, and it can even lead to tyranny; second, God prefers ignorant men, as many passages from the Bible prove, as well as Christ choosing illiterate fishermen as his apostles;[58] third, knowledge leads to the admiration of other idols than God, especially Aristotle (as Petrarch had also shown); fourth, when it is associated with folly, in people who are thus "rationally mad,"[59] learning is particularly dangerous; and fifth, knowledge does not save a man—only faith does. The man without knowledge is in a better condition to have true faith than the learned man, who will attempt to know God by demonstration, reason and judgment, all inadequate means to access the divine. As a consequence, Agrippa encourages men to seek for humility and simplicity and take children as models of innocence and purity.[60] Those who celebrate learning are heirs to the serpent, Agrippa argues, reminding the readers several times in the book that the desire for knowledge was Adam's first sin and the cause of the Fall.[61]

Most importantly, in the final chapter (chapter 102) of *De incertitudine*, entitled "Digression in Praise of the Ass" (*Ad encomium asini digressio*), this animal is presented as the symbol of the patient and humble Christian and as a model of simplicity, the very opposite of vain, corrupted, and presumptuous learning. Agrippa lists the qualities of the ass: fortitude, strength, patience, and clemency, but the ass is above all the expression of wisdom, "for he lives by little food, and is contented whatsoever it be."[62] Evidence of the wisdom of the ass is found in the Bible, where it appears in several passages, notably at the Nativity, Jesus's entry into Jerusalem, and with Balaam (Numbers 22.21–38), showing that the ass, and therefore the unlearned simple man or woman it represents here, is the fittest "to carry the Mysteries of Divine wisdom."[63] The ass, also explicitly identified with the idiot (in the sense defined earlier—the illiterate, uneducated man or woman) in the "Digression," can see truths inaccessible to the learned, precisely because its mind is pure and simple: "Thus, I say, sometimes the simple and rude Idiot sees those things oft-times, which a School-Doctor, blinded with the Traditions of men, cannot perceive."[64] The apostles are thus Christ's "silly Asses and rude Idiots," who succeeded in putting to silence "all the Learned Philosophers of the Gentiles."[65]

Another important celebration of the superior wisdom of the ass was found in Giordano Bruno's *Cabala del cavallo pegaseo*, published in 1585 in London (even though the title page indicates Paris), a text composed of three dialogues to which is added, as in Agrippa's *De incertitudine*, a treatise in praise of the ass, "L'asino cillenico."[66] This treatise is itself a dialogue, featuring the Ass, the Pythagorean Fool, and Mercury. The Fool, who is president of the Pythagorean Academy, mocks the Ass when the latter presents himself at the gate of the Academy to apply for admission: "Speaks the ass? . . . O Muses, O Apollo, O Hercules, articulate voices issue from such a head?" The Ass makes his case nonetheless, arguing that he is aware that his appearance might not correspond to the Academy's expectations but that he has qualities that make up for this physical inadequacy, assuring that he has "quickness of the mind" and "efficacy of the intelligence." He gives the example of Socrates, a "dissolute, stupid, dull [and] effeminate man," whose exterior faults were overcome by his study of philosophy. Despite all his efforts, the Ass is denied admission to the Academy, even though the academicians recognize that he is learned. By judging the ass on his external form, they demonstrate their own stupidity, pedantry and vanity, in a reversal that is characteristic of the topos of the ass. At the end of the dialogue, Mercury comes in and declares the Ass "universal academician," which allows him to enter all academies.[67]

But the first three dialogues of the *Cabala del cavallo pegaseo* emphasize even more clearly the superiority of ignorance over learning. In the "Declamation to the Studious, Devoted, and Pious Reader," "saintly ignorance, learned sheepishness, and divine asininity" are praised, while those who mock the ass and reject ignorance and humility are condemned. Celebrations of ignorance and asininity are indeed legion throughout the *Cabala*, for example, in "Sonnet in Praise of the Ass": "Oh holy asininity, holy ignorance, / Holy foolishness, and pious devotion, / Which alone can make souls so good / That human genius and study cannot advance it." A long list of biblical passages mentioning the ass is then given so as to prove that it is a divine animal. The ass is also associated with the prelapsarian condition of Adam and Eve, who "were asses, that is, simple and ignorant of good and evil." Moreover, the time "when humans were asses" was that of an ideal community, characterized by simplicity, equality, and love. The text calls for the return of such a mythical community of humble and hardworking men- and women-asses. Those will be saved because they are truly wise. The three dialogues that follow attempt to demonstrate the paradoxical idea that "ignorance is a most perfect knowledge" and, by extension, that "asininity is a divinity."[68] This paradox cannot but call to mind both Agrippa's praise of the ass and Cusanus's religious philosophy. In Bruno's dialogues, indeed, the ass is clearly the symbol of *coincidentia oppositorum*, learned ignorance or powerful humility: he is at the same time "benevolent and demoniac, powerful and humble, wise and ignorant."[69]

The wise ass was a leitmotif in Bruno's works, but it was more generally a topos in the early modern period, of which Agrippa was seen as the initiator.[70] Many more "minor" texts then took up the eulogy of the ass. For example, the French reformed poet and translator Paul Perrot de la Salle admitted writing his *Le Contr'empire des sciences, et le Mystere des asnes* after reading Agrippa's *De incertitudine*. In "Le Mystere des asnes," written in verse, all the elements of the topos are found: the ass is praised for his virtue, hard labor, courage and goodness, qualities that make him wise enough to arbitrate the quarrels of the Sorbonne.[71] This is why, Perrot de la Salle argues, Plato and the Hebrews used the ass to represent the virtuous man and God chose him to carry his son.[72] The biblical episode of Balaam (Numbers 22) further shows how humility and ignorance bring more knowledge than the learning of scholars.[73] In a word, the ass is a good philosopher and a good worshipper of God, and therefore Perrot de la Salle encourages all his readers to acquire the main qualities of the ass, namely simplicity and humility.[74] But the eulogy of the ass also came under criticism in the early modern period, for example, in the Italian priest and composer Adriano Banchieri's (1568–1634) "The Noblenesse of the Asse," probably a response to Agrippa's "Digression," but more directly to Bruno's praise of asininity.[75] Banchieri also takes up most of the qualities of the ass listed by Agrippa and Bruno, especially his simplicity: "Simplicitie is so naturally proper and given to the Asse, as in one or other kinde of meate, he contends not, or makes any difference at all."⁷⁶ But the irony of Banchieri's treatise leaves no doubt, as it is obviously excessive in its praise and ends with a call to found "the societie or fellowship of the Asse,"⁷⁷ an allusion to Bruno's community of asses mentioned earlier. Despite those criticisms, the ass remained an allegory of the ignorant and virtuous man or woman throughout the early modern period, mostly in France, where this topos was also presented in the seventeenth century as the emblem of the philosopher in the writings of French *libertins érudits* such as François de La Mothe Le Vayer (1588–1672), who wrote about "the mythology of the ass," arguing that human knowledge is an *asnerie*, a word that was then a synonym for ignorance.⁷⁸

Finally, claims of intellectual humility were also expressed through the modesty topos, itself a paradox, whereby authors pretended that they were ignorant of—or at least not expert on—the subject they were dealing with in their books. This practice was often found in the works of one of the most prolific and respected experimentalists of the seventeenth century, Robert Boyle (1627–1691), who also put great emphasis on his "naked way of writing,"⁷⁹ meaning a plain, unadorned, and functional style. His almost systematic disclaimer that he was writing from "loose papers,"⁸⁰ and that the texts he published were therefore necessarily imperfect, was obviously an attempt to undercut accusations of dogmatism. Indeed, experimentalism required that its practitioners be "sober and honest men,"⁸¹ qualities associated with humility and modesty.

The Paradoxes of Ignorance shows that, in seventeenth-century England and France, the doctrines presented here—from Socratic ignorance to Cusanus's *docta ignorantia* and humanist paradoxical discourses—were continued, revived, and adapted in philosophical and religious discourses that gave prominence to the notion of ignorance as a synonym of wisdom, a principle of knowledge, or an epistemological instrument. In all three cases, ignorance was paradoxically understood as a superior way to truth. The antischolasticism of a number of early modern thinkers encouraged a redefinition of ignorance, which may have appeared preferable to vain and excessive erudition in this context. It certainly made learning suspicious (at least certain types of learning, as well as an excess of it) and led to calls for humility and modesty, thus reintroducing ignorance under a more favorable light.

The Argument of the Book

Three main objectives are pursued in *The Paradoxes of Ignorance*. First, the book aims to demonstrate that there was a rehabilitation of ignorance in the long seventeenth century that led to ignorance paradoxically playing an essential part in the emergence of modern science and modern ways of thinking. The main contention here is that, far from being rejected or suppressed in programs for the advancement of knowledge, ignorance—in forms that will be defined and analyzed—was used in the foundation of modern science. The book thus discusses how ignorance, with its underlying theological and mystical connotations inherited from medieval and Renaissance doctrines, was included in the scientific discourse of the time. More precisely, it inquires into the values that were attributed to ignorance so that it became a superior mode of wisdom, a principle of knowledge, and an epistemological instrument. To do so, the book examines the persistence of past doctrines and traditions that inspired the praises of ignorance presented here, arguing that the role of ancient skepticism itself should be qualified and that, instead, the significance of medieval and Renaissance doctrines of ignorance should be reassessed and reinstated as powerful intellectual guides for seventeenth-century philosophers and theologians.[82] When those medieval and Renaissance doctrines did borrow from ancient ones, they transformed and adapted them to the antischolasticism of the time, which led to the emergence of specific early modern doctrines of ignorance that cannot be considered mere variations on ancient forms of skepticism. Consequently, this book strongly argues for a conception of the early modern period that was, to a large extent, the continuation of the Middle Ages in intellectual history, especially in reflections on ways of knowing and thinking. Finally, because it aims to demonstrate the role played by ignorance in the emergence of modern science, the book indirectly examines and develops Peter Harrison's argument in *The Fall of Man and the Foundations of Science* that, contrary to what one might expect and what has often been argued, modern experimental science was founded in the seventeenth century on the recognition and acceptance of the limits of human knowledge, not on a belief that human understanding was all-powerful or that man could become nature's master and possessor.[83]

Second, the book shows that the rehabilitation of ignorance took different forms in England and in France. It demonstrates that, in both countries, ignorance was indeed included in the discourse promoting and fostering the advancement of knowledge, but its definitions and treatments varied. This does not mean that there was a French conception of ignorance that would have been entirely different from the English one,[84] but *The Paradoxes of Ignorance* shows that there were distinct general tendencies, and two proposals to build new knowledge after the rejection of scholasticism, based on different understandings of ignorance. In a nutshell, the book argues that, in France, ignorance was rehabilitated as a personal quality or attribute and a form of wisdom that enabled one to reach truth (as well as happiness). Those who were looking for truth and knowledge were encouraged to make themselves ignorant, to divest themselves of all vain learning and prejudices. In other words, they were prompted to voluntarily induce and experience ignorance personally. In England, such encouragements to make oneself ignorant were rarely found: searchers after knowledge and truth were usually not urged to choose ignorance, even as a preliminary and temporary condition. Instead, strong condemnations of ignorance were actually voiced. But the book argues that, even though ignorance was rarely praised as a personal quality or attribute in England, it was given a positive dimension nonetheless, when the experience of ignorance was used as a thought experiment: one was indeed encouraged to imagine the naked mind and the understanding in a state of complete ignorance in an attempt to shed light on the process of thinking. Imagining the naked mind (a condition that could not be actually realized) enabled one to see the true nature of the understanding and observe its workings. In this case, ignorance was not praised as an attribute, but it became useful as an epistemological instrument. Of course, conceptions that departed from those two general tendencies were found both in England and in France: the example of the Quakers and Baptists, who praised ignorance as a form of personal inspiration in mid-seventeenth-century England, and that of the *libertins érudits*, whose interpretation of ignorance was emphatically distinguished from the Cartesian conception of ignorance as a precondition to knowledge,[85] are also studied in the book, thus complexifying the (too) general binary opposition presented earlier. The comparative perspective is furthermore justified by the significant intellectual exchanges between England and France in the early modern period, as well as by the different religious contexts in the two countries, especially as ignorance remained an important theological issue throughout the period.

Third, the book indirectly inquires into a possible secularization of ignorance in the early modern period. Ignorance had been defined first and foremost along religious lines as a sin and the consequence of the Fall in England, and more often as a mere privation in France. It was obviously more central in the English religious context of the adoption of Protestantism and its subsequent insistence on learning and education, but its theological dimension was not absent from early modern French thought either. Now, if ignorance was progressively included in the scientific discourse and given an epistemological role, as this book argues, does it mean that it was also progressively secularized at the time? This is what Cornel Zwierlein argues in his introduction to the collective volume *The Dark Side of Knowledge*, where he contends that ignorance, which had been perceived as a sin in the Middle Ages, came to be redefined in the early modern period so that it might be included within the epistemological reflection on the new science.[86] A secularization of ignorance would imply that it was progressively no longer considered as a sin or the consequence of the Fall, an evolution that could open a path for ignorance being recognized as an epistemological tool and a heuristic notion in the newly defined processes of scientific inquiry. The contention of *The Paradoxes of Ignorance* is that there was indeed a shift in the understanding and use of ignorance over the period, and that recognition of man's inevitable ignorance did paradoxically lead to the elaboration of modern methods of scientific inquiry. But the book complexifies this picture again by showing that, for most early modern philosophers who elaborated doctrines of ignorance, the notion was not divested of its religious dimension to take on an entirely secular one, even when it came to be defined as an anthropological trait in John Locke's philosophy in the late seventeenth century.

More often than not, in the corpus of texts analyzed in this book, the word *ignorance* is being used, as most of the sources on which this study is based are printed treatises, sermons, pamphlets, essays, and philosophical dialogues explicitly and extensively dealing with the notion of ignorance. But other terms were also understood as synonyms of ignorance, whether made explicit by the author or not. Therefore, the calls for "humility" and "simplicity" expressed in the early modern period can often be interpreted as praises of ignorance, ignorance being actually synonymous with, or at least closely associated to, several other notions, such as simplicity and humility, but also innocence, folly, and foolishness, in early modern dictionaries.[87] Indeed, the definition of the word was fluid and could take different guises (for example, in French, it could be a synonym of *asnerie, erreur, imprudence, inscience, insipience, mescognoissance, niezeté, simplicité*, or *rusticité*).[88] The book elucidates the relations between the term *ignorance* and those notions as the debates on the virtues of ignorance examined here are primarily debates on the meanings and interpretations of the term.

One might object that the celebrations of ignorance examined in this book should not be taken seriously, that they were essentially ironic and devised merely to denounce and mock scholasticism by illustrating and promoting, in an excessive gesture, the exact opposite of vain erudition. As a matter of fact, ironical claims of ignorance were made in the early modern period. Thus, the French author Charles Sorel (1600?–1674) admitted in his encyclopedic work *La Science universelle* (1668) that past promoters of ignorance and doubt had excessively praised ignorance, the better to denounce the arrogance of scholastic doctors. In this passage, Sorel distinguishes between those who were willingly ignorant ("ignorans volontaires")—and therefore aware of their ignorance—and those who were dogmatically ignorant ("ignorans dogmatiques")—and strongly and erroneously convinced that they were learned.[89] This distinction reveals the complex relation of ignorance, knowledge, erudition, learning, and self-knowledge in the early modern period. It shows that detractors of scholasticism boasted of their own ignorance not so much because they actually believed that they were ignorant, but mostly to ridicule the excessive learning of their opponents, which they assimilated to true ignorance. Yet those "ignorans volontaires" also recognized the limits of human knowledge and therefore their own ignorance. Thus, the celebration of ignorance might have been a tool in the fight against scholasticism, not necessarily a statement in favor of ignorance as a superior mode of knowledge, but it was still in this case a call for the recognition of one's ignorance. Among the authors studied in this book, some used the paradox of ignorance as a topos in their denunciation of scholasticism and did not actually call for ignorance, while others undoubtedly used and praised ignorance or recognition of one's ignorance, either because it was held synonymous with wisdom and happiness or because it was an instrument enabling one to devise new ways of thinking.

Ignorance Studies and the History of Ignorance

Ignorance has been the object of renewed interest over the past few years.[90] The most manifest expression of it may be the publication in 2015 of the *Routledge International Handbook of Ignorance Studies*, which recognized and established the existence of a new field of inquiry called ignorance studies.[91] The same year, in the *New York Times*, Jamie Holmes made a "case for teaching ignorance," following scientists like Stuart Firestein, who insisted on teaching a course on scientific ignorance at Columbia University after he realized that the way science was being taught gave students the impression that everything was known about a particular subject and that ignorance did not play any part in the scientific process, apart from representing what should be "erased" by scientific inquiry.[92] Ignorance is now recognized as a legitimate and active part of the scientific process and is therefore also included in university curricula. The recent publication of *The Epistemic Dimensions of Ignorance*, edited by Rik Peels and Martijn Blaauw,[93] confirms the rehabilitation of ignorance as an "epistemic phenomenon" and the attempt to give ignorance its due place in epistemology, an enterprise to which *The Paradoxes of Ignorance* also contributes, but from a historical perspective.

The Paradoxes of Ignorance also grounds some of its arguments on works that have been published in the field of social sciences. Anthropologists and sociologists have long shown interest in the study of the cultural production and social functions of ignorance.[94] A rehabilitation of ignorance was thus attempted in this field as well in the mid-twentieth century by Wilbert Moore and Melvin Tumin, who focused on the social functions of ignorance, arguing that it is often an active and positive element in operating structures and relations.[95] Similarly, in the much more recent 2012 collection *The Anthropology of Ignorance*, Casey High, Ann Kelly, and Jonathan Mair question the assumption that everyone desires knowledge and rejects ignorance, stressing—like Moore and Tumin before them—that ignorance should not be seen systematically as a "purely negative phenomenon." They insist that ignorance is much more than the inverse of knowledge and that it has its own history as "the product of specific practices."[96] Not unlike those anthropological and sociological works, *The Paradoxes of Ignorance* attempts a recognition of the uses, virtues, and functions of ignorance in specific intellectual contexts.

Although it is not the focus here, agnotology, or culturally produced ignorance, popularized by the historians of science Robert Proctor and Londa Schiebinger in 2008, is probably the most dynamic area of ignorance studies today.[97] It has given rise to works that show how states, industries, and other groups hide information, especially scientific knowledge, from citizens and consumers to manipulate them and either make profit or prevent opposition. In this case, ignorance is fostered so as to protect the secrets and status of a few (politicians as opposed to the people, scientists as opposed to laymen, men as opposed to women) and thus preserve a social or intellectual hierarchy. Building on Proctor's agnotology, epistemologies of ignorance have also been articulated in relation to race and to women and feminism. Thus, Shannon Sullivan and Nancy Tuana have shown how ignorance can be actively produced for purposes of domination and exploitation, but they also contradict in their works the assumption that knowledge is always good and preferable to ignorance.[98]

Ignorance studies is undeniably a fledgling field of inquiry involving reflections on science, education, the structures of society and the mind, as well as political and economic practices. What these studies from different disciplinary areas have in common is an emphasis on the idea that ignorance has its own history, is not merely the inverse of knowledge, and should be rehabilitated in some specific forms and contexts. Yet the history of ignorance has not received much attention so far, and in particular, not much has been said about its role in the early modern period, at a time when Renaissance humanism, the Reformation and the emergence of modern science profoundly altered ways of thinking and knowing. In 2016, Cornel Zwierlein called for a history of ignorance in his introduction to *The Dark Side of Knowledge*, emphasizing the relevance of the seventeenth century when it comes to historicizing ignorance.[99] As was mentioned, *The Paradoxes of Ignorance* engages with Zwierlein's thesis that there was a secularization of ignorance from the Middle Ages to the early modern period, and it qualifies this contention, arguing that there was no clear, linear evolution from one conception of ignorance to another, as several—and sometimes contradictory—interpretations of ignorance, inherited from long philosophical and theological traditions, coexisted at any given time in England and in France. Another contribution to the history of seventeenth-century ignorance was made by Joanna Picciotto in her book *Labors of Innocence in Early Modern England*.[100] Although she does not focus on ignorance as such, Picciotto offers an important contribution to its history, as she argues that ignorance, understood as innocence, came to be defined as objectivity by English experimentalists. Contrary to *The Paradoxes of Ignorance*, Picciotto's book focuses exclusively on the English context and ignores the important impact that French philosophers such as Descartes had on seventeenth-century English conceptions of innocence and ignorance.

In 2020, the French historian Alain Corbin also stressed the need for a history of ignorance, which has so far been the blind spot of historians of ideas as well as social historians. In his book *Terra Incognita*, subtitled *Une histoire de l'ignorance*, Corbin focuses on what was not known in eighteenth- and nineteenth-century France, assuming that ignorance can be defined only as absence of knowledge (of the earth, in this case).[101] The aim of Corbin's history of ignorance is to better understand the mental frameworks and decisions of the men and women of the past by focusing on the knowledge that they did not have, but Corbin fails to embrace the complexity of the notion of ignorance and perceives the history of science as a slow regression of ignorance in what very much appears as a teleological approach. Finally, a compelling contribution to the history of ignorance was made in the 2021 special issue of the online *Journal for the History of Knowledge*, edited by Lukas M. Verburgt and Peter Burke, dealing with "histories of ignorance" from the eighteenth to the twenty-first century. In their invaluable introduction, the editors claim that the history of ignorance "makes it possible to tell the story of 'modern, Western science' differently," an argument that *The Paradoxes of Ignorance* also aims to make. Yet even though they claim that ignorance has a history of its own, Burke and Verburgt consider that history as "an opening for the history of knowledge to be more than an expansion of the history of science."[102] In *The Paradoxes of Ignorance*, the history of ignorance is also approached through its relations with that of knowledge, but it is not considered a mere tool in favor of the emancipation of the history of knowledge from the history of science: a call is made here for an interdisciplinary history of ignorance that borrows from the history of knowledge, the history of science and philosophy, and the history of religion. As such, what the book proposes is more aptly defined as an intellectual history of early modern ignorance.[103]

Outline of the Book

The Paradoxes of Ignorance identifies and develops the three main virtues or functions of ignorance expounded in early modern philosophical and religious discourses: it first shows that ignorance could be conceived as a mode of wisdom, mostly a legacy of Socratic ignorance, negative theology, and Cusanus's *docta ignorantia*; it then examines how ignorance was understood as a principle of knowledge, meaning that it was paradoxically required, as a temporary precondition or a permanent state, to reach knowledge; finally, the book argues that ignorance came to be interpreted as an epistemological tool that could be used to better understand the mechanisms of the mind and devise more efficient methods for reaching truth. The book roughly follows a chronological order, starting with Montaigne's and Bacon's interpretations of ignorance, then focusing on Descartes's and the Quakers' conceptions of ignorance in relation to the internal light, and ending with late seventeenth-century English experimentalists, particularly John Locke. Yet parallels with past doctrines are drawn across the book, as it also aims to discover the genealogy of early modern doctrines of ignorance.

The first part examines the claim, often made in late sixteenth- and early seventeenth-century France in particular, that ignorance was a superior mode of wisdom. In this case, ignorance is perceived as a quality or attribute associated with wisdom mostly because it implies humility, simplicity, and self-knowledge, hence the model of the ignorant man or woman as the true philosopher. It is here argued that this interpretation of ignorance was a legacy of Socratic wisdom, but that more importantly, it also significantly drew upon Cusanus's *docta ignorantia* and other medieval doctrines of ignorance. Moreover, this part shows that the praise of ignorance as a mode of wisdom was very much a French phenomenon. Indeed, early modern English assessments of ignorance rarely described it as a quality or as a virtue in itself. Instead, one of the most explicit and powerful expressions of ignorance as wisdom, *docta ignorantia*, was commonly interpreted in England as a mere form of "epistemic restraint." The promotion of "disguised ignorance" by politicians, theologians, and men of letters was denounced by Francis Bacon in the early seventeenth century as the main obstacle to the advancement of learning. Accordingly, followers of Bacon in the Royal Society, who seemed to dread a valorization of ignorance that might jeopardize their scientific endeavor, also took great pains to discredit all forms of ignorance, even the ignorance of Christ's humble apostles. One exception to the English rejection of ignorance as wisdom, it is argued here, is found in the writings of Joseph Glanvill (1636–1680), which the book's first part examines in detail. The propagandist of the Royal Society distinguished himself from other English experimentalists in that he promoted a form of ignorance that borrowed from the Cusan tradition of *docta ignorantia* and its "French legacy."

The second part of the book shows that ignorance could be paradoxically understood as a condition that induced a spontaneous and immediate access to truth. Indeed, in a number of early modern philosophical as well as religious writings, in England and in France, ignorance was assimilated with the internal light or understood as the condition for this inner light to shine. This part therefore focuses on the association of ignorance with personal inspiration or pure immediate or unmediated access to truth. It also shows that the debate on whether one was more likely to reach God by inspiration, without external help, or by acquired learning, led to the controversy on the relevance of a learned ministry that took place in the 1650s in England in the context of the rise of sectarianism. This essentially religious debate on ignorance as personal inspiration took on a philosophical dimension, as the common association in seventeenth-century England (and Holland) of Descartes and the Quakers clearly reveals: their common insistence on the power of the internal light as a way to truth was interpreted as a celebration of ignorance and a promotion of enthusiasm, or some form of ridiculous yet dangerous illumination. This part finally analyzes a significant illustration of ignorance as inspiration in John Bunyan's *The Pilgrim's Progress* (1678), where the character called Ignorance may be considered a representation of the belief by some religious groups of the time that ignorance was a form of inspiration and a sure and immediate way to truth.

In the third and final part, ignorance as an epistemological instrument is the focus. According to this interpretation, ignorance is no longer personally experimented by the seeker after truth; rather, it is presented as a hypothetical state or a tool that enables one to get a representation of human faculties. In this context, the tabula rasa and autodidacticism, in particular, were used to conjure up images of the naked mind, that is, of the understanding in a condition of complete ignorance, stripped of all (unnecessary) knowledge and prejudices. Such representations of the naked mind enabled one to imagine or visualize, as it were, the mechanisms or operations of the mind and the process of discovery. This part shows that the persona of the Idiot as an autodidact and the social figure of the artisan as an objective and truthful observer were often referred to as models of the attitude that one should have to both nature and God in the search for truth. Hence, in the philosophies of both Bacon and Descartes the necessity to imitate the qualities of the illiterate inventor, especially their sagacity. Finally, John Locke's philosophy is here given emphasis, as this book contends that the English philosopher formulated essential theories of ignorance in his works. Indeed, Locke resorted to fictions of ignorance as a means to improve ways of thinking and knowing, but he also founded his argument in favor of toleration on the general ignorance of mankind. His acute attention to ignorance in social and cultural environments, added to a metaphysical definition of ignorance, led to his "anthropologization" of the notion. Last, it is argued here that his *Essay concerning Human Understanding* should be read as an essay on human ignorance, in which the English philosopher precisely shows how ignorance can and must be assimilated into the scientific discourse.

Part I

IGNORANCE AS WISDOM

Intellectual traditions and doctrines such as Socratic ignorance, Cusan learned ignorance and Renaissance paradoxical discourses were very much alive in the early modern period and not at all considered obsolete. On the contrary, the contention here is that most of the philosophical doctrines formulated at the time in England and in France, and that we now tend to define as "modern," were expressions of a rejection or adoption of past—sometimes persisting—doctrines of ignorance and, as such, they should be interpreted as legacies of earlier conceptions of ignorance, an approach that has been neglected so far. Adopting a comparative perspective, this first part analyzes the fortunes of those traditions, and the way they were interpreted, adopted or rejected by late sixteenth- and seventeenth-century French and English authors.

This part first presents the French tradition that explicitly promoted ignorance as a way to wisdom and happiness from the late sixteenth century. Even though it took different expressions from one author to the other, the contention here is that this tradition can be clearly identified and traced back from Nicholas of Cusa in the mid-fifteenth century to Blaise Pascal in the late seventeenth century, with emblematic expressions of it in the works of Montaigne, Charron, and Descartes, which are the focus here. According to this tradition, an ignorant and simple man or woman was more likely to reach truth and happiness than a scholar because they made a better use of their God-given faculties, but also because they were endowed with the qualities that made them prone to divine and natural knowledge, mostly humility and simplicity, understood here as modalities of ignorance. Social models were given to embody this ideal of wisdom, in particular peasants and artisans.

Conversely, in early modern England, one of the most explicit expressions of ignorance as wisdom, namely learned ignorance, was more commonly associated with scholasticism or "epistemic restraint" than with Cusanus's religious philosophy and a state that should be sought out. Indeed, in England, the doctrine of *docta ignorantia* did not give rise to a philosophical tradition as it did in France, although it was influential in some rare cases, such as the works of Joseph Glanvill that are examined in this part. This part finally shows that medieval and Renaissance doctrines of ignorance actually led to a strong opposing reaction on the part of English philosophers from the experimentalist tradition, following Francis Bacon's violent and systematic attack on all forms of ignorance in *The Advancement of Learning* (1605). It is argued here that Bacon precisely aimed at followers of Cusanus and sixteenth-century authors of paradoxical discourses and promoters of ignorance when he wrote his defense of learning. It is thus argued that the examination of the legacy of Cusanus's doctrine in both countries sheds light on two distinct responses to scholasticism and two different proposals to replace scholastic learning with the new philosophy, which therefore stemmed from conceptions of the nature and place of ignorance.

CHAPTER I

Fortunes of *Docta ignorantia* in Early Modern England and France

A French Tradition of Learned Ignorance

This chapter shows that Cusanus's doctrine of learned ignorance, briefly presented in the introduction, gave rise to a long philosophical tradition in France, from Montaigne in the sixteenth century to Pascal a century later, although the focus here is on the three thinkers who most clearly show the legacy of Cusanus in France: Montaigne, Charron, and Descartes. Even though the legacy of *docta ignorantia* took different expressions in the works of those French authors, there was a continuity in their conceptions of knowledge and ignorance, which relied on the idea that ignorance was a superior mode of wisdom, hence their calls for intellectual humility and simplicity.

That Montaigne knew Cusanus's works is not to be doubted. In his *Journal de voyage*, written between June 1580 and November 1581, Montaigne mentions the 1566 edition of the cardinal's works, of which he owned a copy. The important 1514 Paris edition of Cusanus's *Opera omnia* by Jacques Lefèvre d'Étaples (c. 1455–1536), as well as the discussions among Lefèvre's circle of Cusan and Dionysian doctrines, had allowed for the circulation of those works.[1] Even though the precise impact of Cusanus's religious philosophy on the *Essays* cannot be easily assessed, many important characteristics are common to both, for example, the insistence on the impossibility to know God; the references to Socrates, St. Paul, and St. Augustine on knowledge, learning, and wisdom; a particular taste for paradoxes; and the idea that the infinite diversity of things and opinions makes analogy, and therefore science, impossible.[2] But above all, there is in Cusanus's and Montaigne's works a similar doctrine of ignorance. The French philosopher Pierre Magnard has argued that the expression "that ignorance, which knoweth judgeth and condemneth it selfe [is not an absolute ignorance]," found in book 2 of Montaigne's *Essays*, was directly borrowed from Nicholas of Cusa.[3] Moreover, Jan Miernowski has shown that the metaphysics of Nicholas of Cusa provided Montaigne with "an ontological framework that allowed him to escape the rule of noncontradiction," underlining the role of negative theology in the "Apology of Raymond Sebond."[4] Montaigne had also read Agrippa's *De incertitudine*, as appears from the "Apology of Raymond Sebond" again, where a long passage from Agrippa's text is translated. This passage states, among other things, that all presuppositions or prejudices must be questioned because certainty is madness, an assertion that leads to the praise of ignorant "cannibals" who live happily and quietly without the knowledge of physics and of Aristotle's principles.[5] As Miernowski again emphasizes: "There are many studies that confront Montaigne with ancient skepticism, patristic thought or medieval philosophy, but too seldom is he considered the successor of the generation of Rabelais, Erasmus, Lefèvre d'Étaples, Marot and Marguerite de Navarre."[6] Focusing on the notion of ignorance in the *Essays* is a means to precisely assess the legacy of those Renaissance authors, as well as medieval philosophies, in Montaigne's thought.

As was mentioned in the introduction to this book and in Prior's quotation from his dialogue of the dead, Montaigne repeatedly praises the simplicity of the peasant throughout the *Essays*, and more particularly in the "Apology of Raymond Sebond," a long piece, entirely devoted to the place and function of ignorance in one's search for truth. In a word, Montaigne argues that peasants, because their minds are not filled with useless and vain learning, are both wiser and happier than scholars: "I have in my dayes seene a hundred Artificers, and as many laborers, more wise and more happy, then some Rectors in the university, and whom I would rather resemble."[7] Similarly, the inhabitants of Brazil live happily and serenely "in a wonderfull kinde of simplicitie and ignorance,"[8] without any form of learning or even religion. In "Of Cannibals," Montaigne also praises the simple and uneducated sailor, whose reports on the Americas are not distorted by prejudices and classical learning, whereas more "subtile people"—that is, more learned people—tend to "amplifie and glose" things to artificially make their accounts convincing and thus get more credit. In this context, ignorance is the condition of good judgment, as well as of honesty, objectivity and reliability: it is indeed "a condition fit to yeelde a true testimonie."[9]

Three types of ignorance are identified in the *Essays*: one is simple ignorance, or the naïve, natural ignorance of peasants, children, and "savages," who are all uneducated; second, there is the ignorance of "the mongrell sorte of husband-men," who are not completely learned, not utterly ignorant, and sit "betweene two stooles."[10] In this category are found scholars, and Montaigne himself, as he admits. This is the worst form of ignorance, that of dogmatics and pedants, who believe, because they have some knowledge, that they have all knowledge.[11] Some of them, like Montaigne, would like to get back to a state of natural ignorance and thus forgo all the knowledge that they have acquired. Yet leaving this in-between, uncomfortable position seems impossible. Finally, there is learned ignorance, or the ignorance of those who are aware of their ignorance, and therefore wise and unpresumptuous.

Montaigne also argues that ignorance precedes *and* follows science. While engendering some form of "doctoral" ignorance, science annihilates "abecedary" or natural ignorance in the process: "It may with likelyhoode be spoken, that there is a kinde of *Abecedarie* ignorance; preceeding science: another doctorall, following science: an ignorance, which science doth beget: even as it spoileth the first."[12] Under the effect of science, the natural, and therefore pure, ignorance of man is replaced with vain learning, which is another form of (much more negative) ignorance. A similar, yet slightly different typology of ignorance was propounded in the mid-seventeenth century by the French mathematician and philosopher Blaise Pascal (1623–1662) in a famous passage from his *Pensées*: "Sciences have two Extremities that touch each other; the first is pure Natural Ignorance, wherein all Men are involv'd when they come into the World; the other Extream is whereunto great Souls do attain, that having passed through all things 'tis possible for Men to know, they find at last they know nothing, and find themselves in that very Ignorance from whence they first set out. But this is a Learned Ignorance that knows it self."[13] Thus, there is ignorance before and after science, but the ignorance that follows science is nonetheless preferable, according to Pascal, as it is "learned," or self-aware ignorance. In other words, for Pascal as for Montaigne, ignorance precedes and follows science because natural ignorance gives way to learned ignorance. But the latter, defined by Pascal as ignorance "that knows it self," or self-knowledge, is praised as the greatest form of wisdom. Like Montaigne, Pascal believed that there were three types of ignorant people: those who are naturally ignorant, those who are learned but aware of their ignorance, and those who lie in between, Montaigne's "mongrels." The latter are neither naturally ignorant nor "learnedly" ignorant, and they represent for Pascal, as they did for Montaigne, the worst kind of ignorance: they cannot judge rightly and they are pedants, who deem themselves superior to others. Finally, learned ignorance is equated with natural ignorance in the passage from the *Pensées*, an assimilation that Montaigne does not make in the *Essays*, where natural simple ignorance is presented as the ideal human condition.

Indeed, surprisingly perhaps, Montaigne does not wish that he had the learned ignorance or wisdom of Socrates's heirs: he rather aspires to the ignorance of those who follow the natural order of things. They are simple men and women. Simplicity is indeed praised throughout the *Essays* as a condition that implies proximity to nature. Thus, simple men and women have common sense, which appears, for example, in the fact that they recognize and admit the experience of the senses as a legitimate source of information on the world and, contrary to learned men, do not get lost in vain speculations.[14] Besides, they are not slaves to their own imaginations and do not make up fruitless fantasies. On the contrary, they stick to the reality of what they can sense, in the present: "Compare but the life of a man subject to these-like imaginations, unto that of a day-labouring swaine, who followes his naturall appetites, who measureth all things onely by the present sense, and hath neither learning nor prognostications, who feeleth no disease but when he hath it."[15] As a result of their proximity to nature and their rejection of imagination, simple men and women use a straightforward and common language to express themselves. In a word, Montaigne's simple ignorant people have an empirical approach to the world, and as a consequence, they may be mistaken sometimes, but they are always honest and never try to deceive others. What further favorably distinguishes them from the learned is their ability to tell between what is useful and what is vain, although they are unable to distinguish between what is true and what is false. But preeminence is given here to the former quality: being able to distinguish what is useful from what is superfluous is the path to virtue and happiness, according to Montaigne.

In Montaigne's *Essays*, simplicity is also presented as conducive to religious belief. It guarantees the good behavior of Christians, who are more likely to obey the laws, as they do not aspire to a condition that they cannot attain to: "Of simple, lesse-curious, and least-instructed spirits are made good Christians, who simply beleeve through reverence and obedience, and are kept in awe of the lawes."[16] Simplicity is a quality of the good Christian because it implies easy acceptance of authority, both divine and civil. Similarly, in the "Apology of Raymond Sebond," Montaigne states that ignorance is expected from the believer who aspires to divine truth: "ignorance is by our religion recommended unto us, as an instrument fitting beleefe and obedience."[17] Indeed, ignorant simple men and women are not only more inclined to believe in God; they also behave in a more orderly fashion than learned men: "Hee that shall number us by our actions and proceedings, shall doubtlesse find many more excellent-ones amongest the ignorant, then among the wiser sorte: I meane in all kinde of Vertues."[18] Thus, ignorance is not only the condition of good behavior; it also leads to virtue and to knowledge of God, an argument that seems to be taken directly from *De docta ignorantia* or the negative theology of *The Cloud of Unknowing*: "It is more by the meanes of our ignorance, then of our skill, that we are wise in heavenly knowledge."[19] For Montaigne as well, God is known by ignorance.

Montaigne also advocates wisdom and self-knowledge in the *Essays*. Wisdom as an internal and infallible quality is set against learning as external and uncertain knowledge: "Suppose we may be learned by other mens learning. Sure I am, wee can never be wise, but by our owne wisdom."[20] Thus, real knowledge comes from within, it is a form of self-knowledge, which is primarily knowledge of one's own ignorance. For Montaigne, following the Socratic and Cusan traditions of wisdom, ignorance that is not self-known is true or utter ignorance, whereas self-confessed ignorance is not ignorance at all, but knowledge: "That ignorance, which knoweth, judgeth and condemneth it selfe, is not an absolute ignorance: For, to be so, she must altogether be ignorant of her selfe."[21] It seems to follow from this distinction that all kinds of external knowledge or "science" are useless and uncertain and should not be sought. Yet in the "Apology of Raymond Sebond," Montaigne makes an inventory of bits and pieces of knowledge that are deemed certain on a great number of subjects, much as Agrippa had done in his *De incertitudine*. He wonders for example about human behavior, natural phenomena, and the diversity of opinions and customs, showing that the celebration of ignorance does not put an end to the investigation into nature and human beings. But this inquiry, or observation, does not follow a fixed and methodical process; neither does it lead to a definitive conclusion or result. Again, what this inquiry brings is not primarily external knowledge, but self-knowledge or wisdom.

Similar conceptions of ignorance were found two decades later in the theologian Pierre Charron's widely read treatise *De la sagesse* (1601), which was soon given an English translation.[22] Like Montaigne, who was undeniably the main inspiration for his work,[23] Charron (1541–1603) praises the ignorance of peasants and that of simple men and women or idiots, and their superiority over pedants and scholars, whose memory is filled with uncertain and useless knowledge. Ignorant farmers and laborers are therefore presented as paragons of wisdom and virtue: "We see ignorant people, idiots and simple men, leade their lives more sweetly and cheerefully, resist the assaults of death, of want, of sorrow, more constantly and contentedly, than the wisest men and most active. And if a man marke it well, he shall finde among pesants and other poore people examples of patience, constancie, equanimitie, more pure than all those that are taught in Schooles."[24] While simple ignorant men and women are characterized by their wisdom, common sense, and plain language, scholars and pedants have an abundance of useless knowledge borrowed from others, but none of themselves or from themselves: "In euery tongue and nation, *Pedante, Clerke, Master*, are words of reproch. To doe any thing sottishly, is to doe it like a *Clerke*. These are a kinde of people that haue their memories stuffed with the wisdom of other men, and haue none of their owne."[25] Like Montaigne again, Charron insists on the superiority of internal wisdom over external learning. Charron's model of self-knowledge and wisdom is of course primarily Socrates, who is himself explicitly compared to peasants and women, insofar as they all resort to a simple and natural language and to their common sense, like Montaigne's simple ignorant men.[26] Finally, in his denunciation of vain learning, Charron systematically sets wisdom against science in his treatise, arguing that this distinction is analogous to that between memory and judgment. Science is an accumulation of external information, whereas wisdom is "the rule of the soul."[27] Charron assimilates ignorance, innocence, and simplicity, which he opposes to science as superficial and deceitful: "Science serueth not for any thing, but to inuent crafts & subtleties, artificiall cunning, deuises, and whatsoeuer is an enemie to innocencie, which willinglie lodgeth with simplicitie and ignorance."[28]

Although Charron's assertion of *libertas philosophandi* against all kinds of imitators led to the emergence of a *libertin* discourse that was highly critical of Cartesianism, Descartes himself can be included in the tradition of intellectual humility and celebration of learned ignorance described here. Perhaps the best evidence of it is his unfinished dialogue, *The Search for Truth by Means of the Natural Light*, which can be read as an adaptation of Cusanus's own dialogue *De idiota*, first published in 1450. Both dialogues feature the persona of the Idiot, who is presented as the model philosopher because he recognizes and accepts his ignorance, which makes him wiser than scholars.[29] But for Descartes, a man should not only recognize his ignorance, which is indeed the very proof of his wisdom, but also voluntarily make himself ignorant to paradoxically create the condition to reach actual knowledge. So ignorance is not knowledge for Descartes, as it is, to a certain extent, for Cusanus, but it is the way to knowledge or the ground on which true knowledge (as opposed to vain learning) can be built. Yet like Cusanus, but also like Montaigne and Charron, Descartes emphasizes the superior wisdom of simple uneducated people over scholars in several of his writings. In the *Rules for the Direction of the Mind*, an unfinished treatise that largely deals with the theme of ignorance, written in Latin (*Regulae ad directionem ingenii*) and first published in a Dutch translation in Amsterdam in 1684,[30] Descartes emphasizes the common sense and good judgment of the illiterate, as compared to the blindness of the learned: "Experience confirms this, for we very often find that people who have never devoted their time to learned studies make sounder and clearer judgements on matters which arise than those who have spent all their time in the Schools."[31] Descartes is admittedly criticizing the disordered and uncontrolled curiosity of "every chemist, most geometers, and many philosophers" who pursue knowledge without a method, more than he is praising qualities proper to illiterate men.[32] However, he implies in this passage, as he does in other works that are studied in part 2, that uneducated men are more likely to reach truth because their "natural light" or "intelligence" has not been weakened by the repeated and vain practice of looking for truth in the dark, without order or method, simply following the whims of their curiosity.[33] Like Montaigne's simple men and women, Descartes's unlearned people have more common sense and can pass better judgments (even though it does not follow that they can ascribe a method to themselves and follow its rules—at least, Descartes does not affirm that).

If Descartes never mentioned Montaigne in his published works (the only mention at all is in a letter to the Marquess of Newcastle on 23 November 1646), the connection between the two authors is strong and undeniable: many passages from the *Discourse on Method*, for example, echo Montaigne's *Essays*, especially "Of Cannibals," "Apology of Raymond Sebond," and "Of Customs," as Étienne Gilson has shown in his important edition and commentary of the *Discourse*. Descartes's argument against animals being endowed with reason in the fifth part of the *Discourse* can also be read as a response to Montaigne's contrary opinion expressed in the "Apology of Raymond Sebond."[34] Much more recently, Dan Arbib, following Gilson, has also argued in favor of "a strong subtextual presence of Montaigne's *Essays* in the *Discourse on Method*, especially the first part," focusing on the intersections of and differences between the two authors' conceptions of the self.[35] Montaigne and Descartes expressed a similar rejection of authority and critique of erudition—the same *liberté d'esprit*, in a word, that was also found in Charron's *Of Wisdome*—and both attributed a central role to travels and the observation of other cultures and customs, although Descartes discredits the relevance of travels and books in the search for truth, contrary to Montaigne. Indeed, whereas Montaigne accepts the variety of things, Descartes holds that there is only one truth.[36]

Above all, Montaigne and Descartes shared a similar conception of ignorance as a quality of the *honnête homme* and the true philosopher. Indeed, they created a similar persona: that of the well-educated gentleman philosopher who nonetheless disparages established education and learning, and praises ignorance as both a way to knowledge and a posture. It seems indeed that the posture of "the ignorant philosopher"—or learned ignorance—suited a gentleman in early modern France. This is partly confirmed by Furetière in his entry on "ignorance" in the *Dictionnaire universel* (1690), where he states that noblemen commonly boast about their own ignorance.[37] Hence the apparently contradictory behavior of authors, like Montaigne and Descartes, who called for ignorance while displaying impressive knowledge. This is what Malebranche ironically underlined in the late seventeenth century, when he mocked Montaigne's alleged "forgetfulness" and denounced his celebrations of simplicity as a mere posture, arguing that "'twas necessary in the time he [Montaigne] liv'd, to doubt of every thing, to pass for a Man of Parts and a Gentleman."[38] Claims of ignorance in France should therefore also be read from a social perspective as a manifestation of respectability or gentility.

Learned Ignorance, Socratic Wisdom, and Skepticism: The Libertins érudits

In seventeenth-century France, Charles Sorel, like the French *libertins érudits*, was much more distrustful of doctrines of ignorance than the authors mentioned in the previous section. In particular, Sorel strongly condemned those who used the doctrine of learned ignorance to promote ignorance per se. In his book *De la perfection de l'homme* (1655), he proposes a taxonomy of ignorant people, which has a clear social dimension since the ignorant people he describes are first defined by their professional occupation and their status in society, considerations that were also common among the *libertins érudits*.[39] The first category of ignorant people, according to Sorel, is that of laboring men, who have no time for learning and live like beasts. They seem to be endowed with the "sensitive" faculty only. The second category is that of those who would have the time and leisure to become learned but do not want to make the effort and are more attracted to pleasures and debaucheries. In the last category, ignorant people have tried to get knowledge in vain, the worst among them being those who nevertheless believe that they are learned.[40]

Contrary to Montaigne, Sorel does not praise simple ignorant people, and their alleged proximity to nature is not perceived by him as a quality. Yet he does also express the paradox of ignorance, or the superiority of simplicity and ignorance of classical learning over erudition. In particular, Sorel praises craftsmen for their useful and practical activities and experience, which make them more knowledgeable than scholars, who rely on bookish and sterile learning. He thus gives the example of the French Huguenot potter Bernard Palissy (1510–1590), whom he describes as an "uneducated simple man,"[41] admired for his sculptures and enamels. Thanks to his experiments, Sorel argues, Palissy had become more learned than those who have nothing but "the doctrine of books." Besides, he could use his knowledge *and* instruct others in his arts. Yet it appears that Bernard Palissy is not praised by Sorel on account of his ignorance or simplicity per se, but rather because he acquired a form of practical knowledge by himself (Palissy was also the author of three published texts). This celebration of autodidacticism was common in the context of a general criticism of the teaching of the schools. The emphasis here is not on his common sense, good judgment, or even wisdom, but on the acquisition of alternative, self-taught, and useful knowledge, a form of "ignorant knowledge" that experimentalists also came to praise in Restoration England.[42] Actually, what characterizes the knowledge of the uneducated and self-taught Bernard Palissy is its experimental or empirical nature. It is therefore not surprising that Francis Bacon should also show an interest in Palissy's teaching, with which he became familiar during his stay in Paris in 1576–1579. In his lectures, Palissy encouraged his audience to learn natural philosophy from objects and not from theories, an approach that would appeal to Bacon and later English experimentalists.

As a matter of fact, Sorel strongly condemns celebrations of ignorance, especially those that purposefully distort Socratic wisdom, understood as awareness of one's ignorance or self-knowledge. He argues that the example of Socrates is used and abused by those who want to promote or "authorize" ignorance.[43] Indeed, those advocates of ignorance contend that it was "practiced" by Socrates, whose wisdom was evidenced in his assertion that his only knowledge was that he had none. They also argue that the Greek philosopher never wrote anything, precisely because he had nothing to write, having no knowledge whatsoever, as he himself admitted. Sorel replies that Socrates contradicted himself when he claimed that he knew nothing because this claim of ignorance was science, as it meant that Socrates knew the limits of his knowledge. Sorel adds that the Greek philosopher's claim of ignorance merely aimed to show that the knowledge man can reach is nothing compared to universal truth.[44] Sorel is here refuting literal and naïve interpretations of Socrates's claims of ignorance, or maybe dishonest interpretations by people who would feign to believe that Socrates was indeed ignorant, and promoted ignorance, understood as lack of knowledge or vain learning—in any case, not as self-knowledge.[45]

Finally, Sorel often expressed his contempt for the ignorant vulgar, that is, dogmatic people who followed common opinions, and insisted on the necessity for a philosopher to be a learned bibliographer because common sense and reason were fallible. This criticism of ignorance was made in the context of the emergence of an uneducated readership thanks to the printing press, which enabled more people to have access to knowledge and especially to philosophy.[46] But those whom Sorel and the *libertins érudits* like François de La Mothe Le Vayer and Pierre Gassendi denounced as ignorant were not specifically the uneducated vulgar, but rather all those who systematically referred to the authorities, whether they be magistrates, peasants, or philosophers, and who could not think by themselves.[47]

The denunciation of ignorant people—mostly dogmatics who follow common opinions—was a characteristic of the French *libertins*' thought.[48] For example, in a dialogue devoted to "laudable ignorance" (*l'ignorance louable*),[49] La Mothe Le Vayer—or rather Orasius, the author's spokesman—insists on the necessity to become aware of one's ignorance, but he also strongly recommends instruction: self-knowledge or knowledge of one's ignorance is not enough; one should strive as much as possible to become learned.[50] For the *libertins*, learning was a double-edged sword: it might lead one to follow the authorities blindly, but it was also—and paradoxically—required so as to be able to think by oneself and secure the much-cherished *libertas philosophandi* against the vulgar. While he explicitly refuses to borrow the expression "learned ignorance" from "Cardinal Cusan," Orasius praises the "honorable" or "philosophical" ignorance promoted by the skeptics, like himself, against the "gross" ignorance of the Schools. As argued in the dialogue, "philosophical ignorance," a variation on learned ignorance, implies modesty and awareness of the limits of human knowledge, but it is attained through the sciences.[51] La Mothe Le Vayer's declared distrust of the expression "learned ignorance," even while referring to it, may also be accounted for by his wish to distance himself from Cusanus's religious principles.[52]

The examples of Sorel and the *libertins érudits*, compared to those of Montaigne, Charron, and Descartes, are evidence of variations on interpretations of ignorance and learned ignorance, but mostly, they testify to the wide reception in early modern France of doctrines of ignorance, showing that the notion of ignorance was an important object of philosophical reflection. One last important example of a French conception of ignorance is that of the Minim friar Marin Mersenne (1588–1648), who admitted, in his *Questions theologiques*, that searching for knowledge was a "humiliating" experience, as striving to increase one's knowledge merely amounted to "discovering and recognizing one's ignorance."[53] Mersenne added that this was the reason some people argued that perfect science and utter ignorance (he says "extreme science" and "extreme ignorance") met in one point, an argument also found in expressions of the learned ignorance tradition presented above.[54] For Mersenne, the idea that ignorant people were wiser than learned ones was an argument borrowed from the skeptics. Indeed, in *La Vérité des sciences*, a dialogue featuring a skeptic, an alchemist, and a Christian philosopher, Mersenne has the skeptic argue in favor of the superiority of ignorance, which is here illustrated in the topos of ignorant Columbus discovering the New World.[55] The skeptic then draws a list of all the wrong doctrines that have been held by scholars in various fields and thus emphasizes the diversity of opinions. He also quotes Ecclesiastes and the idea that the more one tries to get knowledge, the more one becomes ignorant.[56] For Mersenne, the purpose of these skeptical arguments was to persuade ignorant people that nothing could be known in the world but also, paradoxically, that they were more likely than scholars to make a significant discovery and contribute to the advancement of knowledge. Indeed, even though Mersenne strongly denounced skepticism (especially what he interpreted as Charron's skepticism[57]) in some of his works, it would be a mistake to identify him strictly with one of his characters in this dialogue and to hold that he denounces the skeptic. It is safer to assume that Mersenne himself shared opinions expressed by several of the characters in his dialogue.

Finally, to the question whether an uneducated peasant can become a philosopher without external help, Mersenne replies in *Questions Inouyes* that there are examples proving that good judgment and common sense can suffice to make a philosopher. All men naturally have within themselves what is necessary to philosophize, Mersenne argues, and therefore they need to know only themselves in order to know the others. But even though this statement seems to be in agreement with the doctrine of ignorance described earlier, it actually differs from it, first because Mersenne argues that even ignorant people can become wise, not that they are more likely than learned men to be wise. Moreover, Mersenne also says that ignorant peasants cannot get all kinds of knowledge without help: for example, physics is not accessible to them, as it cannot be known but with the help of other, more learned men.[58] Indeed, Mersenne argues that men need to learn how to observe: this is not naturally given to them, contrary to what Montaigne, for example, assumed. Their inability to observe leads ignorant people, or "villagers," to make use of their imagination instead of their common sense and good judgment, which they are said to be endowed with. Thus, Mersenne concludes on the inequality of knowledge and wits.[59]

Those examples show that there were numerous echoes as well as explicit references to the Cusan doctrine of learned ignorance in late sixteenth- and early seventeenth-century France, where it was used mostly to denounce scholastic and dogmatic knowledge, and to expound a new way of reaching truth, one based on self-knowledge and observation. But the recognition and acceptance of one's ignorance, or wisdom, was not merely the ground for access to knowledge; it also allowed one to live a happy and Christian life. Thus, in Montaigne's and Descartes's philosophies, for example, ignorance had actually two meanings, which these authors had not yet explicitly distinguished: the ignorance that one should become aware of was inadequate or insufficient learning, while the ignorance that was sought, as a way to happiness, wisdom, and truth, was simple ignorance, or the natural ignorance of children, idiots, and the illiterate—an ignorance akin to innocence. Yet the examples of Sorel and Mersenne show that this praise of ignorance was not always received uncritically in France, where it was also sometimes interpreted as a desire to legitimate and spread ignorance, understood as complete absence of knowledge, out of vanity or laziness. However, this reception did not necessarily mean a rejection of the doctrine of learned ignorance; it rather revealed that there were multiple interpretations of this doctrine, as well as misunderstandings between followers of Cusanus's thought that were often due to ambiguous definitions of the notion of ignorance. Those writings on ignorance in the French context also reveal that reflections on ignorance, its definitions, nature, and extent, were closely articulated with the identity of the philosopher and the philosopher's place in society, raising questions on the existence of a natural hierarchy of wits and intelligences, and on the possibility of subverting such hierarchy in the social environment. In the writings of Montaigne, Charron, Descartes, and the *libertins érudits*, ignorance is admittedly a posture of the philosopher and the *honnête homme*, but what distinguishes those authors is how ignorance is also used as a means to knowledge.[60]

The English Reception: Learned Ignorance as "Epistemic Restraint"

If the legacy of Cusanus's learned ignorance can be traced in France in the works of Montaigne, Charron, Descartes, Pascal, and others, as has been argued here, it is not easily found in England, where no such tradition celebrating this doctrine of ignorance seems to have emerged in the early modern period, except perhaps among the religious radicals of the mid-seventeenth century, and for a short period of time.[61] Some have argued that the English physician, astrologer, and mathematician Robert Fludd was "the most important English representative of the school of Nicholas of Cusa, the Christian Neoplatonist, who combined Pythagoreanism and Kabbalah with one another" in seventeenth-century England.[62] Cusanus's Platonism and mystical theology, as well as his astronomical reflections, may also have appealed to a number of Cambridge Platonists, such as John Smith, Henry More, and the Puritan Peter Sterry, for example.[63] As a matter of fact, in his major work on this school of thought, Ernst Cassirer argued that the "Platonic Renaissance in England" was of Cusan provenance,[64] yet Peter Sterry is the only Cambridge Platonist explicitly referring to Cusanus (twice) in his works, and the evidence showing a link between Nicholas of Cusa and those seventeenth-century English theologians and philosophers is slender at best. Nevertheless, there is no doubt that Cusanus's works were known in seventeenth-century England. Some of them were given English translations: his *De visione Dei*, for example, was translated into English (as *The Single Eye*) by the radical preacher John Everard (1584?–1640/41) and published in London in 1646. *De idiota* was also published in an anonymous English translation (as *The Idiot in Four Books*) in London in 1650.

The notion of learned ignorance in particular was known to English philosophers and theologians of the time. Yet it was generally not interpreted as an expression of wisdom. Neither was it attributed to Cusanus for that matter, but to earlier proponents of some forms of *docta ignorantia*, mostly Tertullian and Augustine. Paul Richard Blum has argued that, in England, Cusanus was "much more appreciated as the author of the sermons than as the philosopher of the *De docta ignorantia* and the *De coniecturis*, for instance."[65] More often than not, the expression "learned ignorance" was used as an insult, as it came to be associated with scholasticism and the vanity of learning, or with medical charlatanism. When it was given a more positive interpretation, "learned ignorance" referred to the limits of human religious knowledge, and in this case, it could be praised, not exactly as a form of wisdom, but as the recognition and acceptance by men and women of the limits of their religious knowledge, in accordance with God's wishes. It thus led them to intentionally curb their own curiosity, a virtue that Neil C. Manson has aptly called "epistemic restraint," or "refraining from seeking knowledge."[66] But this acknowledgment of the value of learned ignorance in theological matters was very far from the celebrations of ignorance studied here.

It should first be noted that the expression "learned ignorance" appeared in the sixteenth-century English translation of Calvin's *Christianae religionis institutio*, in a sense that had a great impact on later uses of the expression in England. In a passage on predestination in book 3, chapter 21, Calvin writes (here in Thomas Norton's translation): "First therfore let this be before our eyes, that to couet any other knowlege of Predestination than that whiche is set foorth by the woorde of God, is a poynt of no lesse madnesse than if a man haue a will to go by an vnpassable waie, or to se in darknesse. Neither lett vs be ashamed, to be ignorant of somewhat in it wherein there is some learned ignorance. But rather lett vs willyngly absteine from the serchyng of that Knowlege, wherof the excessyue couetyng is both foolishe and perillous, yea and deadly."[67] The expression "learned ignorance" is here interpreted as a form of ignorance that is good insofar as it implies the recognition of the limits of human knowledge in religious matters. In other words, learned ignorance is the quality of someone who renounces trying to know what God did not want them to know in the first place and who therefore accepts their ignorance and curbs their natural curiosity. Calvin's interpretation of learned ignorance as recognition and acceptance of the limits of human knowledge in divine matters seems to have been most influential in Protestant countries in the early modern period, and not only in England. Thus, Paul Schuurman has shown that the Dutch reformed theologian Gisbertus Voetius (1589–1676), who wrote two scholarly disputations entitled *De docta ignorantia* and was particularly interested in the doctrine of learned ignorance, drew upon Calvin's interpretation of the expression and explicitly rejected Cusanus's. For Voetius, learned ignorance meant knowledge of our cognitive limitations, and therefore recognition of what could and what could not be known, a meaning that he carefully attempted to distinguish from Descartes's own method and the role of ignorance in it.[68]

Calvin's interpretation of learned ignorance as "epistemic restraint" was the meaning most often given to the expression in English religious texts of the early modern period. For example, at the very end of the sixteenth century, the Cambridge theologian William Perkins (1558–1602) repeatedly called for learned ignorance as a way to restrain one's curiosity: "In matters of Religion there is a learned ignorance, whereof this is not the least point, to content ourselves with his wayes, and not curiously to search into those things which he hath not revealed in his word, but though they be against reason to man, acknowledge them as holy & true, with reverence, for all Christs waies be holy. The blind man cannot judge of the light, because he seeth it not: no more can blind man (such as all be) judge of workes hidden with God."[69] Learned ignorance is here defined by Perkins as the quality of someone who accepts God's wish to hide some truths from them. Things that have not been revealed should not be sought. Besides, learned ignorance also leads one to accept as true all that has been revealed by God, even though it may sound irrational. Learned ignorance is thus primarily a submission to revelation.

A few years later, a similar interpretation was given by the Church of England clergyman Thomas Wilson (1562/63–1622), who defined learned ignorance as follows: "When we are willingly ignorant, of that which God would not haue vs know; this is a learned ignorance, as it is a blockish knowledge, when wee are curious to vnderstand things hid from vs, or when we do not apply our knowledge to practise."[70] Here again, learned ignorance is seen as a voluntary inhibition of curiosity, or "epistemic restraint." Wilson attributes the expression to Tertullian, as was often the case at the time in England.[71] Like Augustine, the early Christian theologian from Carthage identified curiosity as a vice and insisted that some knowledge should not be pursued. The reference to Tertullian when it comes to learned ignorance is also made, for example, by the Presbyterian Anthony Burgess (d. 1664), who insists on the distinction between philosophical truths, which can be inquired into, and religious truths, which must merely be accepted: "It is not therefore with divine truths, as it is with philosophical, for with the latter, though we know *Aristotle* saith so, yet we may enquire into the truth of it, but in Theological things, if it appear God hath said this, then we must not judge but believe; so that it is a learned ignorance, when we affect not to know above what is written."[72] As a consequence, learned ignorance is also often associated with modesty and humility in these texts authored by seventeenth-century English theologians: it is "a modest suspense of our judgement," according to Burgess, who adds that we should content ourselves with knowing "*That it is*," and not try to know "*How it is so.*"[73] The modesty that should lead to accepting one's ignorance and renouncing the search for unauthorized divine knowledge was also emphasized, for example, by a certain Richard Whitlock (c. 1616–1672) in a 1654 book devoted to "the manners of the English," and especially to the credulity and ignorance of those in England who were deceived by medical charlatans. There is indeed an "*Acatalepsia*, impossibility of certainty, or full discovery," not only of God and divine matters, but also of nature, according to Whitlock, which is why some inquiries are pointless, and in that case, one should choose ignorance, or the "modest wisdom to be willingly ignorant of some things."[74] As was rarely the case in seventeenth-century English texts, Whitlock explicitly refers to Cusanus, and draws a parallel between the cardinal and the Italian scholar Julius Caesar Scaliger (1484–1558), who had written about the necessity to remain ignorant of many things in his *Exotericarum exercitationum*, a defense of Aristotle's natural philosophy.[75] Finally, to those references on learned ignorance, Whitlock adds Charron and his *liberté d'esprit*, as "the best Temper, a true Patron, and President of this *Independency* of *Reason*, and that *freedome of Spirit*,"[76] showing the important reception of Charron's philosophy, especially his notion of *libertas philosophandi*, in mid-seventeenth-century England, and more importantly, the association of Charron with the doctrine of learned ignorance.[77]

English philosophers also interpreted learned ignorance as some form of "epistemic restraint." Thus, later in the century, John Locke explains, in the opening pages of the *Essay concerning Human Understanding*, that one should accept that not everything can be known, and "sit down in a quiet Ignorance of those Things, which, upon Examination, are found to be beyond the reach of our Capacities."[78] Locke's "quiet ignorance" can be assimilated with the "learned ignorance" of the theologians mentioned already. Interestingly, the notion of a quiet ignorance is also found in England in the writings of the English Puritan Richard Baxter (1615–1691), most explicitly in a manuscript in which he clearly states that men should accept and confess their ignorance of what they are not supposed to know: "When I read many voluminous pretensions of men, that take on them confidently to know what they know not, & call their presumptions by the name of Philosophy & Physicks, I am forced to confess that I am ignorant of what they pretend to know, & am quiet in my ignorance, when I find that I was not made to know it."[79] As in Locke's *Essay*, "quiet ignorance" is here understood as some form of epistemic restraint, while the refusal to confess one's ignorance, that is, "ignorance of ignorance," is perceived as presumption and arrogance. According to Paul Schuurman, "Locke used learned ignorance specifically against the epistemological pretensions of rationalist philosophers,"[80] and therefore the concept of learned ignorance was of great importance to the English philosopher. The ignorance that men should primarily recognize is that of the essence of substances, the knowledge of which is beyond their cognitive faculties, while God has given them faculties that are perfectly suitable to their condition.

But when Locke uses the expression "learned ignorance" itself, he does not mean "epistemic restraint." Rather, he refers to the scholasticism and dogmatic learning of the Schools. In this case, the expression is a criticism of scholars who present themselves as learned but are actually ignorant: "Thus learned Ignorance, and this Art of keeping, even inquisitive Men, from true Knowledge, has been propagated in the World, and hath much perplexed, whilst it pretended to inform the Understanding."[81] In this chapter from the *Essay*, Locke is denouncing "the abuse of words." Those who are most guilty of it, and to whom the expression "learned ignorance" here applies, are "the Schoolmen and Metaphysicians."[82] With their "Art and *Subtlety*," those men managed to prove that "*Snow* was *black*," thus causing confusion among uneducated men, who, to that point, had been perfectly able to express themselves and communicate without difficulty, thanks to their plain but efficient use of language.[83] Then, in book 4 of the *Essay*, when he writes "Of the Improvement of our Knowledge," Locke opposes "learned ignorance" to "profitable knowledge," the latter being what natural philosophers should be looking for: "How little, I say, the setting out at that end, has for many Ages together advanced Men's Progress towards the Knowledge of natural Philosophy, will think, we have Reason to thank those, who in this latter Age have taken another Course, and have trod out to us, though not an easier way to learned Ignorance, yet a surer way to profitable Knowledge."[84] In this section, Locke is also warning against the search for unattainable knowledge, or knowledge that can be had only through revelation, while insisting that *some* knowledge can nevertheless be had.[85] This interpretation of learned ignorance—as the ignorance of men who deem themselves learned because they master the knowledge and language of the Schools—was not found among philosophers only. Earlier in the century, in *The Arraignment of Ignorance*, the churchman William Gearing had written about the human learning of "*Philosophers* and other humane authours," by which he meant advocates of scholasticism: "briefly, we may say of all their speculations, and curious Arts and Sciences, without the saving knowledge of God in Christ, (which none of them ever attained unto by the Moon-light of nature) that it was but *docta quaedam ignorantia, a kind of learned ignorance,* or ignorant kind of knowledge, as *Austin* calleth it."[86] Like Locke later, Gearing accuses traditional scholars and theologians of causing confusion by using dubious means to reach knowledge. But in this passage, he insists in particular on the fact that their knowledge is ignorance because it dispenses with the knowledge of God. Their excessive curiosity leads them to inquire into all the arts and sciences, but since they remain ignorant of divine knowledge, all they attain to is a form of "learned ignorance," an expression attributed to Augustine, and here defined as useless natural knowledge and damning religious ignorance. Learned ignorance for Gearing is more aptly interpreted as "ignorant knowledge."

Thus, it appears that the doctrine of learned ignorance found a very different reception in England and in France. Whereas it inspired a whole philosophical tradition in France, which came to assimilate ignorance with wisdom, as Cusanus had done, it was mostly interpreted in England as "epistemic restraint," in the wake of Calvin's *Institutes*, or as scholasticism, and therefore associated with gross ignorance and vain learning rather than wisdom.

CHAPTER 2

English Experimental Philosophy and Doctrines of Ignorance

Francis Bacon against "Disguised Ignorance"

Even while they praised the qualities of uneducated laymen and artisans, it is argued here that seventeenth-century English experimental philosophers generally showed great distrust toward all forms of ignorance, and in particular toward the idea that virtues might be attributed to ignorance. Some of them admittedly made the distinction between ignorance as dogmatic learning and ignorance as self-knowledge, even sometimes recognizing the possibility of some form of learned ignorance, yet they did not call for ignorance; neither did they praise learned ignorance as wisdom. In other words, most English experimentalists admitted that the absence of traditional learning could be a guarantee of freedom of mind, good judgment, and objectivity, but ignorance itself was not defined positively by them, and it was certainly not attributed the virtues it was endowed with in the eyes of the French authors from the learned ignorance tradition presented in chapter 1.

In particular, the rejection of ignorance was vehemently expressed in Francis Bacon's program for the advancement of learning: the suppression of ignorance was indeed the very aim of Baconian science, and it is argued here that Bacon probably had medieval and Renaissance paradoxical discourses and doctrines of ignorance in mind when he wrote against "disguised ignorance." In *The Advancement of Learning* (1605), a text dedicated and addressed to King James I, Bacon describes the state of knowledge at the turn of the century and puts forth a program for the restoration of learning. This text had a strong impact on conceptions of knowledge and ignorance all along the seventeenth century in England, especially as it was circulated by followers and admirers of Bacon and Baconian science, among whom were the members of the Hartlib circle. As Stéphane Haffemayer has shown, the word *learning* was increasingly common in book titles after the publication of *The Advancement of Learning*, suggesting a wide and favorable reception of this defense of learning. Indeed, after 1605, *learning* met with "increasing historiographical success," both in printed books and in the *House of Commons Journal*.[1]

In the opening pages of the first book of *The Advancement of Learning*, Bacon proposes a systematic defense of learning against what he calls "disguised ignorance," arguing that ignorance is "seuerally" disguised in "the zeale and iealousie of Diuines," in "the seueritie and arrogancie of Politiques," and in "the errors and imperfections of learned men themselues."[2] He then presents the arguments in favor of ignorance put forth by each of these three categories of people—theologians, politicians, and scholars—before he refutes them. He first shows that, according to divines, who claim that they follow Solomon and St. Paul, learning should be limited because knowledge leads to sorrow, the desire for knowledge being indeed the very cause of the Fall. Theologians also argue that learning leads to vanity and arrogance, as well as atheism, because the quest for human learning may take precedence over knowledge of God.[3] Bacon replies that the Fall was caused by man's desire to know good and evil, not by his desire to know the natural world. With knowledge of good and evil, man wished to dispense with God altogether. Natural knowledge, however, has no such aim and therefore is not forbidden by God. This is an important argument in favor of the advancement of learning and against the promotion of ignorance, which is repeated later in the book,[4] as it legitimates the search for natural knowledge against a compelling theological argument. Indeed, the idea that man should renounce searching for knowledge altogether because this search had led to the Fall was common among advocates of doctrines of ignorance. Bacon further argues that God has conceived the mind of man so that it can be filled with the knowledge of the whole universe. He also admits, however, that the search for knowledge should follow certain rules: man should not "place his felicity in knowledge" and forget his mortality; knowledge should have a positive end and not bring "distaste"; and finally, one should not presume to penetrate God's mysteries through the knowledge of nature. Bacon adds that "a little or superficiall knowledge of Philosophie" might lead to atheism, as one may focus on second causes and forget about the highest cause, but if man proceeds further, and strives to know all that there is to know, he will naturally and inevitably be led back to God.[5]

Second, Bacon focuses on the "disguised ignorance" of politicians, who argue that learning makes men unfit for war and more likely to express their disagreement than to obey the rules of the state. Bacon here resorts to "experience" to show that learning and arms do go together. Alexander the Great and Julius Caesar are convincing examples of this "concurrence," he argues. But examples of times are perhaps even more convincing than examples of persons. Thus, in Egypt, Assyria, Persia, Greece, and Rome, the times that are admired for their military victories are also celebrated for the flourishing of learning, showing again that there is a "concurrence" between learning and arms. Bacon adds that the state should not be ruled by "Emperique Statesmen," or men who have experience but no learning, because they will be surprised and at a loss as to how to react each time something occurs that they have no previous experience of. Instead, learning is a cure for indispositions and infirmities of the mind. It furnishes a man, especially a ruler, with examples that will help him avoid errors.[6]

To those who argue that learning disposes a man to leisure, solitariness, and idleness, and diverts him from public employment and action, Bacon replies that "learned men loue businesse as an action according to nature, as agreable to health of minde, as exercise is to health of bodie, taking pleasure in the action it selfe, & not in the purchase."[7] If a learned man is indeed prone to privacy and idleness, it is not because of his learning, but because of his natural disposition. To the idea that learning encourages man to disobey the law, Bacon objects, grounding his argument on experience again: "it is without all controuersie, that learning doth make the minds of men gentle, generous, maniable, and pliant to gouernment; whereas Ignorance makes them churlish, thwart, and mutinous."[8] This idea does not seem to require any justification, according to Bacon, who deems it obvious and undeniable. It is in line with the common association of ignorance with barbarism and learning with refinement and civilization.[9]

Finally, men of letters have also brought discredit to learning, arguing that it led to poverty, retirement, and "meanesse of employments" because they were in charge of the education of young people, an occupation for which they were despised. Bacon replies with a praise of education, in which he expresses his admiration for the "Colledges of the Iesuites." Yet in his refutation of the "disguised ignorance" of learned men, Bacon has to admit that many criticisms can legitimately be made against learning itself and the learned. For example, he condemns the learned men who have become flatterers of rich and powerful people, to whom they dedicate their books, even though he admits that, in some cases, such submissions to rich people should be allowed, when learned men actually need to use the power of their patrons to serve intellectual purposes. Despite the "basenesse" of this submission, it shows "Iudgement truely made."[10]

But Bacon insists above all on the most common reproach against learning (or at least certain types of learning) at the time: its vanity. He lists three "distempers of learning" or "vanities in Studies": "fantastical learning," "contentious learning," and "delicate learning," or "vaine Imaginations, vaine Altercations, & vain affections." The first distemper is when men "hunt more after wordes, than matter." Bacon explains that, thanks to Martin Luther, the writings of ancient authors were reintroduced, schoolmen were harshly criticized, language became the focus, and preaching was fostered. But all this progressively led to an excessive interest in eloquence, and men started to pay more attention to words than to what they actually meant by them. Bacon also denounces the "Copwebs of learning" of scholars who endlessly repeat Aristotle's philosophy and produce fine works without substance. The method of these authors is also to blame—this is the second distemper of learning—since they use not arguments and evidence to prove their assertions, but rather confutations and objections. The third distemper of learning ("vain affectations") is the proneness to deceive and be deceived, or "imposture and Credulitie." The greatest error of learned men, according to Bacon, is that they search for knowledge out of curiosity or to entertain their minds. Instead, knowledge should be sought for the benefit and use of men, and to that end, contemplation and action must always be joined.[11]

Bacon's interpretation of Socrates's attitude to knowledge and ignorance in *The Advancement of Learning* also serves his defense of learning and rejection of ignorance. By arguing that Socrates "vsed to disable his knowledge, to the end to inhanse his Knowledge,"[12] the Chancellor gives a perfectly acceptable interpretation of Socratic wisdom, but he deliberately focuses on Socrates's knowledge and minimizes the role of ignorance, and more particularly, the recognition of ignorance, as the principle of Socratic wisdom. Bacon adds that Socrates's claim (that he did not know anything) was a form of irony, "Scientiam dissimulando simulauit" (an affectation of knowledge under pretense of ignorance),[13] thus taking away any epistemological or heuristic function that could have been attributed to ignorance in this context. Bacon further argues that most of the philosophers who professed the necessity of doubt did not do so "sincerely."

As alluded to earlier, Bacon's condemnation of ignorance also led him to praise the Jesuits as the true promoters of learning, despite their popish superstition.

Indeed, the Chancellor made no mystery of his admiration for Jesuit education and argued in *The Advancement of Learning* that, alongside Protestants, Jesuits had contributed to the "renovation" of knowledge, which in turn had led to the "reparation" of the Church of Rome:

> And wee see before our eyes, that in the age of our selues, and our Fathers, when it pleased God to call the Church of Rome to account, for their degenerate manners and ceremonies: and sundrie doctrines, obnoxious, and framed to vphold the same abuses: At one and the same time, it was ordayned by the diuine providence, that there should attend withal a renouation, and new spring of all other knowledges: And on the other side, we see the Iesuites, who partly in themselues, and partly by the emulation and prouocation of their example, haue much quickned and strengthned the state of Learning: we see (I say) what notable seruice and reparation they haue done to the Romane Sea.¹⁴

Even more striking, in the English context of strong anti-Catholic feelings at the turn of the seventeenth century, Bacon goes so far as to declare in another passage from *The Advancement of Learning* that he wishes the Jesuits were on the side of the reformed church.¹⁵ To a certain extent, Jesuit colleges could serve as a model for Bacon's own conception of Solomon's House as a place devoted to the promotion of knowledge, which he described in his unfinished utopian "novel" *New Atlantis*.

The writing of *The Advancement of Learning* was prompted, as Bacon makes clear, by a dangerous resurgence of arguments in favor of ignorance and by the condemnable idea that limits should be imposed on the search for knowledge. Bacon therefore devoted the entire book to a systematic defense of learning and a refutation of the arguments promoting ignorance. Although he acknowledges that there have been abuses and errors of learning, he never attributes positive values to ignorance as a result. On the contrary, learning should be reformed and fostered to more effectively suppress all forms of ignorance. As a matter of fact, his acknowledging the limits of past learning does not entail the idea that it should be "erased," in an effort to achieve some kind of tabula rasa, as Bacon makes clear in *The Masculine Birth of Time*. Rather, new learning should be engraved upon old opinions and prejudices, so as to replace them, as it were, implying that ignorance is not required as a precondition to the acquisition of knowledge (as it is in Descartes's philosophy, for example), even though doubt is: "on waxen tablets you cannot write anything new until you rub out the old. With the mind it is not so there you cannot rub out the old until you have written in the new."¹⁶

Denunciations of ignorance and condemnations of advocates of doctrines of ignorance are found in yet other texts of the Baconian corpus. For example, in *Valerius Terminus*, where he makes a list of the "impediments of knowledge" (among which the famous "idols of the mind"), Bacon mentions two attitudes to knowledge that have been detrimental to the advancement of learning, he argues, because they have justified putting an end to the search for truth: the obsession with method and the praise of ignorance. Indeed, Bacon deplores that "men have used to discharge ignorance with credit, in defining all those effects which they cannot attain unto to be out of the compass of art and human endeavour."[17] In other words, when men fail to reach knowledge, they not only declare that it is unattainable anyway, but also go so far as to give ignorance a positive value, or some "credit," in the process.

Given the attention to ignorance in the Baconian corpus, it does not seem unreasonable to assume that Bacon's systematic defense of learning was a response to authors like Agrippa and Montaigne, to the "discourse against letters" and its paradoxes, and more generally to the learned ignorance tradition. Indeed, most of their arguments against learning and in favor of doctrines of ignorance were taken up one by one by Bacon and carefully refuted. More precisely, it appears from the study of his conceptions of ignorance that what Bacon actually targeted was the celebration of ignorance as wisdom, an aspect of his thought that has been overlooked by Bacon scholars so far. There is no doubt that Bacon knew Agrippa's works, although a full study of the relations between the two authors remains to be written. Interestingly enough, the Chancellor recommends the reading of *De incertitudine* in his *Letter and Discourse to Sir Henry Savill Touching Helps for the Intellectual Powers*.[18] Yet in *Temporis partus masculus*, Bacon mocks Agrippa, who, despite his being "a modern" like himself, is called "a trivial buffoon, relying on distortion and ridicule."[19] Agrippa is here denounced mostly for his work on magic, *De occulta philosophia libri tres* (1533), which revealed Hermetic and cabalistic influences condemned by Bacon. The Chancellor had also read Montaigne's works, as appears from the numerous echoes in the *Novum Organum* (1620) and the explicit references in the 1625 edition of Bacon's *Essays*, as well as in *De dignitate et augmentis scientiarum* (1623), the expanded Latin version of *The Advancement of Learning*, in which Bacon first cites Montaigne by name.[20] As Pierre Villey (1913) and Kenneth Alan Hovey (1991) have shown, the *Novum Organum* clearly echoes the "Apology of Raymond Sebond," in particular Montaigne's threefold division of philosophy into dogmatists, Academics, and Pyrrhonians, which is taken up and altered by Bacon in his "Praefatio" with no explicit reference to the French philosopher. Bacon here distinguishes his own attitude to knowledge and ignorance from that of Montaigne, claiming that he seeks "to know all we need to know, and yet think our knowledge imperfect," whereas Montaigne seeks "ignorance that knows itself, that judges itself and condemns itself."[21] As Hovey has argued, Bacon interpreted Montaigne's works as embracing human ignorance and accepting it as it were, while he—Bacon—also recognized it but searched for knowledge nonetheless:[22] for Bacon, human ignorance is a fact, but we should not be content with it, let alone celebrate it.

The relation of Bacon to past traditions and doctrines all labeled "skeptical" has been the focus of many studies, some of them arguing that Bacon himself should be included in the category of early modern skeptics, while others qualify this stance and insist instead on the Chancellor's rejection of skepticism. Here again, the difficulty of establishing the legacy of skepticism in Bacon's thought may not be due only to the hesitations or even contradictions found in his works on the subject, but also to the vagueness and broad span of "skepticism," especially when it is applied to texts and traditions as diverse as the humanist paradoxical discourse, medieval doctrines of ignorance, negative theology, and ancient skepticism. Thus, to justify Bacon's denunciation of Agrippa in *Temporis partus masculus*, which appears to contradict his portrayal of Bacon as a skeptic, Luiz Eva suggests that Bacon's criticism might have been modeled on the humanist paradoxical discourse, and that therefore Bacon was not actually criticizing Agrippa in *Temporis*. "Bacon's critique of skepticism would merely be the paradoxical result of a skeptical literary strategy connected with the tradition of paradox," showing how, through a clever mise en abyme, even antiskepticism can be interpreted as skepticism.[23]

Focusing on the exact meaning of what we interpret as the skepticism of an early modern author, Miguel Ángel Granada questions the very definition of skepticism in relation to Bacon's thought and asks whether, in examining Bacon's (alleged) skepticism, one should focus on the legacy of ancient skepticism only, on the skeptical philosophies that Bacon explicitly mentions, or whether one should also include forms of what Granada calls "Renaissance skepticism," for example Agrippa's and Montaigne's philosophies. Like Popkin, Granada wonders whether those "fideistic currents of a relatively anti-intellectualist nature" should be defined as forms of skepticism or not, which raises a crucial question: "If we extend the concept of scepticism to these currents and positions, are we not running the risk of imposing an excessively general denomination on a range of heterogeneous currents which were in fact presented separately at the time?"[24] This very legitimate question underlines the limits and shortcomings of the history of skepticism as it has been written in the wake of Richard H. Popkin's classic work and that tends to include a great variety of philosophies and intellectual traditions without paying much attention to the specificities of each, especially as they were perceived at the time.

Finally, to defend his thesis that Bacon was indeed a skeptic (despite the reservations on the scope of "skepticism" expressed earlier), Granada makes this remark: "Bacon and the sceptics affirm the same thing: 'nothing can be known,' with the difference nonetheless that the sceptics affirm it 'absolutely,' that is as an essential and definitive situation, while Bacon affirms it relatively and conditionally: nothing can be known 'by the way that mankind has followed so far.'"[25] Yet this makes all the difference: the antischolasticism of the authors studied here—Bacon in particular, but not only—meant that they generally rejected existing (scholastic) knowledge and doubted that anything certain could be known by resorting to the methods commonly used at the time. But they did believe that some knowledge could be had, thanks to more effective and reformed methods. Silvia Manzo, who nevertheless argues in favor of Bacon's skepticism, makes a similar remark: "Like many contemporary English authors, Bacon never adopted the sceptical doubt and the provisional suspension of judgement as a permanent state of mind, but as heuristic devices, and necessary tools for the discovery of truth."[26] She adds that Bacon rejected *acatalepsia*, or the idea that nothing can be known, as he makes clear in the *Novum Organum*, in a passage already partly quoted above: "And it is better to know what we need to, and yet not to think that we have complete knowledge, than to think we have complete knowledge, and yet to know nothing that we need to."[27] Expressions of the relations to knowledge and ignorance were primarily attitudes and postures that revealed methodological approaches.

Learned Experimentalists and Ignorant Apostles

Francis Bacon took great pains to ground his promotion of learning in an interpretation of the Scriptures that legitimized the search for natural knowledge. In particular, he responded to the objection that the desire for knowledge had caused the Fall, which implied that ignorance was to be preferred to learning. But he and his followers had to refute another serious theological objection to the advancement of learning: that God himself wanted men and women to remain ignorant, as was evidenced by Christ choosing illiterate apostles to spread the Word. This argument was already found in the sixteenth century in paradoxical discourses and works celebrating ignorance, for example those of Erasmus and Agrippa. Indeed, Erasmus wrote in his *Praise of Folly* that Christ "ministre[d] none other medecines, than the *Folie of the crosse*, by the handes of the *Apostles*, beyng grosse and vnskilled men."[28] Christ expected the apostles to be humble, follow the examples of children, and not pay attention to the words they used or to manifestations of learning. The text then makes a reference to God forbidding Adam to eat the fruit of the tree of knowledge on account that science is "hurtesome and pernicious," as it brings arrogance and "self-glorie."[29] Indeed, "fooles finde so muche grace and favour afore God, as to Folie onely is genuine perdone and forgeveness of trespasses."[30] Thus, fools—or ignorant people here—are saved, but not learned men. Similarly, in *De incertitudine*, Agrippa underlined the relationship between Christ and idiots or illiterate people: "Thus we finde in the Gospel how Christ was receiv'd of Idiots, of the vulgar people, and of the simpler sort, while he was rejected, despised, and persecuted even to death, by the High-priests, by the Lawyers, by the Scribes, by the Doctors and Rabbies. For this cause, Christ chose his Apostles not Scribes, not Doctors, not Priests, but unlearned persons of the vulgar people, void of knowledge, unskilful, and Asses."[31] Agrippa explains that Christ chose illiterate men, "asses," or "idiots" as apostles because he had been well received by the vulgar, whereas learned people rejected him. This tends to show that ignorant people are both naturally and divinely superior to scholars, as they spontaneously welcomed Christ and were then chosen by him as a consequence of their openness. The conclusion is that ignorant people are wiser than learned ones, but more importantly, that God prefers the illiterate and the vulgar, which implies that he disapproves of the search for learning.

Bacon, and after him, most English experimentalists, addressed this objection to the search for knowledge and its subsequent praise of ignorance in their works in order to legitimize their scientific enterprise.[32] The recurrence of this argument in their writings tends to show that this objection to learning was taken seriously and that the promotion of knowledge required responding to those who praised ignorance on the grounds that Christ showed preference for vulgar and illiterate people in the Scriptures. Thus, in *The Advancement of Learning*, Bacon gives a long analysis of passages from the Bible that aims to prove that God encourages the search for knowledge. He insists in particular on the fact that God's support of learning did not change with the coming of Christ: "Neither did the dispensation of God varie in the times after our Saviour came into the world; for our Saviour himselfe did first shew his power to subdue ignorance, by his conference with the Priests and Doctors of the lawe; before he shewed his power to subdue nature by his miracles."[33] In other words, one of Christ's primary aims, according to Bacon, was to fight ignorance and this was evidenced by his conversations with learned men. But Bacon is also forced to comment on Christ's choice of illiterate apostles:

> So in the election of those Instruments, which it pleased God to vse for the plantation of the faith, notwithstanding, that at the first he did employ persons altogether vn-

learned, otherwise than by inspiration, more euidently to declare his immediate working, and to abbase all humane wisedome or knowledge; yet neuerthelesse, that Counsell of his was sooner perfourmed, but in the next vicissitude and succession, he did send his diuine truth into the world, wayted on with other Learnings, as with Seruants or Handmaides: For so we see Saint *Paule*, who was only learned amongst the Apostles, had his penne most vsed in the scriptures of the new Testament.[34]

Bacon admits that God first chose ignorant men and women, but he downplays their role. He also makes clear that they were inspired, emphasizing the fact that they were not the mere vulgar. Moreover, the role of those unlearned men and women was only to settle or "plant" faith in the world—in other words, they played a part only at the very beginning of the introduction of Christianity, and we can assume that they had a short-lived role. Finally, Bacon explains that God chose illiterate men and women with the aim of preventing intellectual arrogance and hubris. And he soon sent his truth as well as "learnings" with learned men, such as St. Paul, and that is when Christianity truly began, with the writing of the Scriptures.[35]

A similar refutation of the argument of the illiterate apostles was given by Joseph Glanvill in one of his essays, "The Usefulness of Real Philosophy to Religion," in which he addresses several objections to the advancement of learning. In particular, he responds to those who argue that the search for knowledge shows excessive curiosity and should therefore be condemned. He admits that there is "blameable curiosity," and that some matters are forbidden and should not be inquired into, but this is not the case of natural knowledge, the search for which is not only allowed by the Scriptures, but even fostered because knowledge of nature leads to the celebration of "our Creator for his *Works*."[36] So that, when Paul says in 1 Corinthians 2.2, "For I determined not to know anything among you, save Jesus Christ, and him crucified," he is not rejecting knowledge, but only rhetorical ornaments and "*affected Eloquence*."[37] What Paul forbids is the superficial knowledge of the words of orators, Glanvill adds. Then, he moves on to the objection of the illiterate apostles, which he expresses thus: "*If Philosophy be so excellent an Instrument to Religion; it may be askt* (and the Question will have the force of an Objection) *why the Disciples and first Preachers of the Gospel were not instructed in it; They were plain illiterate Men, altogether unacquainted with those Sublimities; God chose the foolish things of this World, to confound the wise.*"[38] The objection to the search for knowledge and the celebration of ignorance based on the choice of illiterate apostles by Christ is here clearly rendered. If Christ wanted men to be philosophers, he would have chosen philosophers to receive and spread the Word in the first place. Instead, he chose ignorant men, which emphasizes his disapproval of human learning and his preference for ignorance in men. Glanvill responds that God gave preference to "such seemingly unqualified Instruments," not exactly to prevent arrogance and hubris, as Bacon had argued, but to show that "the contrivance of *Wit, Subtilty* and *Art*," which are all superficial qualities used to deceive people, should be avoided in the search for knowledge.[39] Reaffirming one of the main principles of the Royal Society, the necessity of a plain unadorned language, Glanvill argues that the "simplicity" of the first promoters of Christianity should be a model for the natural philosopher: "To which I add this; It might be to shew, That God values *Simplicity* and *Integrity* above all *Natural Perfections*, how excellent soever. So that there being such special Reasons for the chusing plain Men to set this grand Affair on foot in the World, it can be no disparagement to the *Knowledge* of *Nature*, that it was not begun by Philosophers."[40] In other words, Christ did not choose ignorant men, but simple and plain ones, or more precisely "innocent" men, as the word *integrity* indicates: those men were free from moral corruption and had therefore an honest relation to truth.[41] This choice did not imply that Christ condemned philosophy or the search for knowledge. Rather, it was an indication about *how* this inquiry should be made and which moral qualities were expected from the natural philosopher: honesty, modesty, and an uncorrupted mind.

Like Glanvill, the respected experimentalist and prominent fellow of the Royal Society Robert Boyle also resorted to physico-theological arguments to defend the search for knowledge, asserting that natural philosophy enabled one to know and admire God's works, and therefore to worship him in the right way. Boyle insists that knowledge is "a gift of God, intrusted to us to glorifie the Giver with it."[42] Thanks to his good and diligent curiosity, as well as his reason, the learned man knows exactly why he should worship God, and what divine truth he cannot attain to, whereas the unlearned observer is led to "wonder" out of ignorance, not knowing therefore if the cause of his admiration is the beauty of God's works, or his own ignorance: "And certainly, Gods Wisdom is much less glorifi'd by the vulgar astonishment of an unlettered Starer (whose ignorance may be as well suspected for his Wonder, as the excellency of the Object) then from their learned Hymns, whose industrious Curiosity hath brought their understandings to a prostrate Veneration of what their Reason, not Ignorance, hath taught them not to be perfectly comprehensible by them."[43] In *The Christian Virtuoso*, Boyle insists again on the idea that the search for knowledge was encouraged by God, who endowed human beings with reason for this purpose.[44] To the objection that God wants men and women to remain ignorant, otherwise Christ would have chosen learned people as his apostles, Boyle replies that those illiterate fishermen were more likely to convince people as they did not resort to rhetorical and superficial tools, but instead used a plain and simple language, an argument already found in Glanvill's essay, which nicely echoed the principles of the Royal Society. But Boyle also argues that God chose those men because he did not *need* learned men; the truth of his message was so evident and unquestionable that it did not matter whom he sent to spread it: "To which may be added, that ten or twelve Fishermen (called the *Apostles*) were sent to convert all Nations to the Worship of a Crucify'd Person; which would have been a strange Commission to be given such Men at that time, if their Master, who sent them, had not Foreseen the Success, as well as Known the Truth, of the Doctrine he sent them to Preach."[45] In this case, Boyle denies the unlearned apostles any quality linked to their ignorance or even to their innocence. Their being illiterate might have enhanced the truth of God's message, as it showed that nothing could diminish its power, not even the ignorance of the messengers. But those were not chosen because their ignorance gave them qualities making them more worthy of God's Word.

"The Knowledge I Teach Is Ignorance": Joseph Glanvill and Learned Ignorance

That the doctrine of learned ignorance was mostly interpreted by English philosophers and theologians as "epistemic restraint" and attributed to other authors than Cusanus does not mean that there was no legacy of Cusan religious philosophy in seventeenth-century England, only that his doctrine of learned ignorance in particular did not permeate a whole tradition of thought, as it did in France. In particular, the Cusan doctrine of learned ignorance did not have a favorable reception among English experimentalists, although it could easily have been interpreted by them as a philosophy supporting their own scientific practices and beliefs.[46] Yet Joseph Glanvill, who was not exactly an experimental philosopher himself, but an ardent supporter of the Baconian program in Restoration England and a propagandist of the Royal Society, stands as an exception. The contention in this section is that Joseph Glanvill expressed views that were strikingly similar to those held by authors of the Cusan tradition, despite his defense of learning in a Baconian sense. It could even be argued that Glanvill was one of the very few, in the context of experimentalism, who promoted a form of Cusan learned ignorance in Restoration England.

Right from the beginning of his treatise *The Vanity of Dogmatizing* (1661), Glanvill makes this highly paradoxical assertion: "The *knowledge* I teach, is *ignorance.*"⁴⁷ If this declaration can probably be read as a typical expression of the modesty topos, or maybe of the "mitigated" skepticism that has been attributed to Glanvill in the wake of Popkin's history, it is also directly reminiscent of the paradoxical treatment of ignorance and knowledge in the Cusan tradition, which assimilates knowledge and ignorance. With this expression, Glanvill underlines the general ignorance of mankind, as well as his own, a disclaimer that aims to show that, although he is writing a treatise on knowledge, or rather on the danger of dogmatism, he does not pretend to be learned himself. Like Agrippa and Montaigne a century earlier, but more especially like the authors of paradoxical discourses, Glanvill insists on the uncertainty of knowledge and on the extent of human ignorance through long lists of "sciences," or fields in which a lot remains to be known, and what is already known remains uncertain.

In *The Vanity of Dogmatizing* first, and then in the revised version of this text, entitled *Scepsis Scientifica* (1665), Glanvill gives a systematic account of the causes of human ignorance. He first underlines the extent of human ignorance, described as "a great darkness," in the "Ad[d]ress to the Royal Society" that opens *Scepsis scientifica*. This "*intellectual* Deficience" is obviously the result of the Fall, which caused the "Decay and Ruines" of "our Intellectual Powers,"⁴⁸ according to the Augustinian-Calvinist interpretation, but this does not mean that an inquiry into the causes of ignorance is not needed: "And therefore beside the general reason I gave of our intellectual disabilities, The *Fall*; it will be worth our labour to descend to a more particular account: since it is a good degree of *Knowledge* to be acquainted with the *causes* of our *Ignorance*."⁴⁹ Glanvill thus distinguishes between the general cause of ignorance, namely the Fall, and particular causes of ignorance, which are to be found in the very workings of the mind.

The first cause of human ignorance is "the depth of verity": Glanvill explains that truth is hard to reach because it is often mixed with opinion and because the knowledge of one truth requires the knowledge of others, as truths are interdependent.⁵⁰ The second cause of ignorance is that we perceive the world through limited and imperfect senses, and thus a large part of nature cannot but escape us, the weakness of our senses being here presented as "an infirmity beyond prevention."⁵¹ The third cause of ignorance, which is closely linked to the previous one, is the deception of our senses: not only are they limited, but also they deceive all of us, "common Heads," as well as "more refined *Mercuries*."⁵² Glanvill here gives the usual examples of a staff that will appear crooked in water or a square tower that will seem round from a distance. Only Descartes's method can offer a solution to the contagion of reason by the senses, Glanvill argues, although he immediately adds that divesting the reason of all sensitive prejudices, as

Descartes recommends, is a very difficult task.[53] Yet the senses themselves do not really deceive us, as they faithfully transmit what they perceive to the principal faculties: our judgment or understanding is at fault when it draws hasty conclusions from sensory perception.[54] Neither is the imagination deceptive in itself, yet it is the fourth cause of our ignorance, according to Glanvill. Imagination is indeed the faculty we resort to when we perceive an object that is absent, and that therefore cannot be perceived through the senses. This faculty engenders prejudices and ungrounded opinions because it persuades without evidence.[55] The last two causes of our ignorance are "the *praecipitancy* of our Understandings," and the role played by our affections, such as the will or passion, in forming a judgment. They both underline the weakness of our understanding. Indeed, Glanvill explains that the understanding tends to draw hasty conclusions without the necessary preliminary observations and meditations. This leads to ignorance, as we are easily convinced that what seems unlikely is downright impossible, and we are prompt to establish links between causes and unrelated effects.[56] Moreover, our affections mislead us because they are prejudiced by custom and education (in particular by reverence to the authorities), by interest, and by the "Love to our own Productions."[57] But Glanvill also admits that the understanding as well as the other faculties have their "idiosyncrasies." In other words, there are individual differences, as well as regional or national ones, which can be accounted for by "the conflicts of the humours," or the influence of bodily dispositions on mental faculties.[58] Moreover, Glanvill explicitly associates ignorance and error, arguing from the start that what he has to say about ignorance "equally concern[s] our *misapprehensions* and *Errors*."[59] Therefore, the causes of ignorance that he lists are also causes of error.

More interestingly, Glanvill argues that recognition of one's ignorance (or "confest ignorance") is the first step in the search for science: this is expressed in the very title of his 1665 treatise *Scepsis Scientifica: Or, Confest Ignorance, the Way to Science*, but it was already present in the earlier version of the text, *The Vanity of Dogmatizing*, where Glanvill writes, "'Tis the first step of Knowledg to be sensible that we want it."[60] Glanvill effects the reversal of the meaning of ignorance and contends that those who are truly ignorant are those who believe that they are learned, or those who are ignorant of their ignorance: "He is the greatest *ignorant*, that knows not that he is *so*: for 'tis a good degree of *Science*, to be sensible that we *want it*."[61] Natural ignorance is preferable to presumptuous and arrogant knowledge because it can be cured more easily: "*Ignorance* is far sooner cured, than *false conceit* of *Knowledg*: and he was a very wise Man that said, *There is more hope of a Fool, than of him that is wise in his own Eyes.*"[62] Glanvill here quotes Proverbs

26.12, one of the favorite biblical passages of the learned ignorance tradition, to underline the superiority of ignorance over "ignorance of ignorance" or presumptuous knowledge.

What Glanvill proposes through his call to awareness of one's ignorance is a method to science. His model is Descartes, whose "method [is] the only way to Science,"[63] just as confessed ignorance is the way to science. Indeed, Descartes's philosophy is here explicitly associated with ignorance, in a positive way that recognizes its role as a principle of knowledge: "For I am apt to think, that Mankind is like to reap more advantage from the *Ignorance* of *Des Cartes*, then perhaps from the greatest part of the *science* was before him."[64] Yet Glanvill does not praise simple ignorant people, as Montaigne did, for example. He refers to them, much as the *libertins érudits* did, as "the Rabble," "the inconsiderate Vulgar," or "common heads," to show that, just like presumptuous scholars, those vulgar, illiterate people are ignorant of their own ignorance, and therefore cannot avoid error because they will follow others' opinions or "*science*," understood here as traditional learning, whereas "the *Ignorance* of *Des Cartes*," in contrast, is conducive to truth.[65]

Another requirement of Glanvill's method, besides the recognition of one's ignorance, is the necessity to divest oneself of all false knowledge and opinions, which result from a flawed education and an uncontrolled use of the senses. Glanvill often regrets in his works that divesting oneself of all prejudices should be so difficult a task, especially when they were acquired at an early age: "That which is early received, if in any considerable strength of *Impress*, as it were grows into our tender natures, and is therefore of difficult remove."[66] In a similar discourse to that of Descartes (or at least to Descartes's philosophy as interpreted at the time), Glanvill encourages all seekers for science to "*unlive* [their] former *lives*, and (inverting the practice of *Penelope*) undo in the *day* of [their] more advanc't understandings, what [they] had spun in the *night* of [their] *Infant-Ignorance*."[67] This kind of ignorance is all the more difficult to overcome as prejudices and opinions are "impressed" on the mind, which is conceived here as a tabula rasa, on which anything can swiftly be written, but from which nothing can as easily be erased: "For our initial age is like the melted wax to the prepared Seal, capable of any impression from the documents of our Teachers. . . . [W]e may with equal facility write on this *Rasa Tabula*, Turk, or Christian."[68] A similar passage was found later in Glanvill's essay "Against confidence in philosophy, and matters of speculation," where he writes that the soul is not "truly" "an unwritten table in it self," but custom and education do impress things on it, making it incapable of receiving other impressions afterward.[69] Yet one must make all the efforts necessary to forgo those prejudices in the search for science.

The attitude that has been defined here as one of learned ignorance could be interpreted as a form of skepticism in seventeenth-century England and criticized for that reason, which is why Glanvill needed to justify his claims about ignorance. In *Scepsis Scientifica*, in particular, he replies to accusations of skepticism made against *The Vanity of Dogmatizing*, especially by the Catholic priest and philosopher Thomas White (1592/93–1676).[70] Interestingly, Glanvill here refers to Charron's "*Universal Liberty*" or *liberté d'esprit* (underlining the favorable and widespread reception of Charron's works in seventeenth-century England, already mentioned[71]) and to Montaigne's "*Je ne sçay*," to make it clear that the doctrine he promotes is not a rejection of knowledge or even a refusal to search for knowledge, but merely the recognition of the uncertainty of all knowledge and the acknowledgment of the central role of ignorance in the search for truth. His call for ignorance is thus not a renunciation; on the contrary, it is conducive to wisdom: "in a sense *Je ne scay*, is a justifiable *Scepticism*, and not mis-becoming a Candidate of *wisdom*."[72] The ignorance that Glanvill praises is the condition for the acquisition of knowledge, not the inverse of knowledge. He makes clear that he uses the word *scepticism* reluctantly: it is the term that the enemies of Cartesianism, who defend "*Dogmatical Ignorance*," according to Glanvill, are most likely to use when they refer to Descartes's method. But Glanvill insists again that this "scepticism" (as they call it) is "the only way to *Science*."[73] Indeed, a skeptic is "a *Seeker*,"[74] and moreover, a skeptic in philosophy is not necessarily a skeptic in religion, Glanvill argues.

As a matter of fact, later in the seventeenth century, the English Puritan Richard Baxter recommended reading Glanvill's *Scepsis Scientifica* precisely to prevent one from falling into skepticism: "As *Cornelius, Agrippa*, who is one of his chief commentators, yet freely confesseth in his *lib. De Vanitate Scientiarium*, which now I think of; I will say no more of this, but desire the Reader to peruse that laudable book, and with it to read *Sanchez* his *Nihil scitur*, to see uncertainty detected, so he will not be led by it too far into Scepticism. As also Mr. *Glanviles Scepsis Scientifica*."[75] Thus, to Baxter, Agrippa's *De incertitudine*, Sanches's *Quod nihil scitur*, and Glanvill's *Scepsis Scientifica* belong to the same tradition: not the skeptical one, but a tradition that praises the recognition of ignorance and at the same time emerges as a bulwark against skepticism. Because they acknowledge uncertainty and ignorance, those texts are effective guarantees against radical skepticism.

Yet Glanvill's skepticism might actually seem more radical than what he is ready to admit, or what Baxter implies, especially when he legitimizes the attitude of those who, being acutely aware of their own ignorance, renounce searching for knowledge altogether: "But many of the most accomplish't wits of all ages, whose modesty would not allow them to boast of more then they were owners of, have resolv'd their knowledge into *Socrates* his summe total, and after all their paines in quest of *Science*, have sat down in a professed *nescience*."[76] Those people who have eventually renounced searching for science have not chosen "ignorance" exactly, but rather "nescience," which, in the seventeenth century, was usually given the meaning of "nothing,"[77] or a form of ignorance devoid of moral dimension. It was also, more often than not, a form of unconscious ignorance.[78] But in this passage from *Scepsis Scientifica*, "nescience" is "professed": it is thus a morally "neutral," noncondemnable ignorance, of which people are aware. Glanvill compares those people favorably to the "shallow unimprov'd intellects" who are convinced to be learned and to be right.[79]

What was specific to Glanvill's discourse, compared to that of most fellows of the Royal Society, was the insistence on ignorance, the recognition and acceptance of it, as well as its role in the search for truth and the idea that it should be advocated in some contexts. The recurrence of the word *ignorance* is also characteristic of Glanvill's philosophical discourse among Restoration English experimental philosophers. A close examination of the occurrences of the term in *Scepsis Scientifica* shows that *ignorance* could be associated with different and even contradictory values in the very same text: thus, "*Confest Ignorance*" is praised as the way to science; "*Primitive Ignorance*" is merely stated as a fact, or the condition of man before the Fall; "*Dogmatical Ignorance*" is attributed to philosophical opponents, especially those who reject Descartes's method that they wrongly interpret as a form of skepticism; "*Fatal Ignorance*" is the consequence of prejudices and opinions; "*Antique* ignorance" is the ignorance of ancient philosophers, whose legacy is still largely present in man's tendency to interpret all natural phenomena irrationally in the seventeenth century, and "*Infant-Ignorance*" is the natural ignorance of credulous children.[80] This insistence on ignorance and the complexity of Glanvill's interpretation of the dialectic of knowledge and ignorance make his thought an interesting exception in the context of English experimental philosophy, where he stands as one of the very few followers of the learned ignorance tradition.[81]

To conclude this part on ignorance as wisdom and on the fortunes of *docta ignorantia* in early modern England and France, an important remark should be made: even though a French tradition of learned ignorance has been identified here, which originated in Cusanus (who himself borrowed from Socrates, Denys the Areopagite, and Augustine, among others, as has been shown) and persisted at least until the mid-seventeenth century with Pascal, after being appropriated and adapted by Montaigne, Charron, and Descartes, it goes without saying that there were major differences in all these philosophies' promotion of ignorance. Some of these differences have been discussed here already. They were often due to the fact that the same words, especially *ignorance* and *learned ignorance*, did not have the same meaning for all the authors mentioned here. And more often than not, contradictory assertions about ignorance were found within the same book. These apparent contradictions were the consequence of the polysemy of ignorance, and of the fact that a number of the texts studied here were written following the tradition of the "discourse against letters," which made paradoxes its favored mode of expression. These differences also revealed various attitudes to skepticism and to the power of reason to lead to knowledge.

Despite these qualifications, a tradition can be identified that, in order to denounce the vanity of scholasticism, promoted another relation to divine and natural knowledge through ignorance as wisdom. In this tradition, peasants and craftsmen, or poor uneducated people, became the model of the good philosopher, and simplicity was made an essential virtue, mostly because those uneducated people were more likely to avoid dogmatism. The Cusan tradition of learned ignorance advocated the recognition of one's unavoidable ignorance, an awareness that would bring self-knowledge and wisdom. In some of its manifestations, it also encouraged efforts to come back to a state of natural ignorance or simplicity— on the grounds of which new knowledge could be built, according to Descartes, while others believed, on the contrary, that the state of ignorance should not be the premise for a new (dogmatic) philosophical system. For Descartes, in particular, this voluntary or chosen ignorance would both allow for the expression of qualities such as modesty and humility and enable one to start again the search for knowledge, with the mind free from erroneous opinions and prejudices. For the *libertins*, the chosen ignorance had to be learned in a more literal sense as well, not as a way to build a new intellectual system, but as the means to free themselves from common opinions. Learned ignorance, as the *libertins* understood it, was exactly the paradox that the expression apparently conveyed: the association of doubt and erudition.

Thus, *docta ignorantia* was given various interpretations in France, but it was undeniably a doctrine that appealed to a number of authors. The important Paris edition of Cusanus's *Opera* by Jacques Lefèvre d'Étaples in 1514 might at least partly account for the French interest in learned ignorance in the sixteenth and seventeenth centuries. On the contrary, as was also shown in this part, Cusan learned ignorance did not exactly take root in early modern England. In many works, the expression "learned ignorance" was given a negative interpretation, as it came to be associated with the erudition of scholars, and most of the time it was attributed to Tertullian and Augustine rather than to Cusanus. It also has been argued here, though, that a few English authors did expound philosophies that expressed the doctrine of learned ignorance, even though the phrase itself was not always used. Joseph Glanvill was one of them.

Indeed, despite the general imperviousness to Cusan *docta ignorantia* and its avatars among English philosophers and theologians of the Church of England, some religious groups—often labeled "radical"—elaborated their own doctrine of ignorance. Part 2 shows that, in the mid-seventeenth-century context of religious and political unrest, Quakers and other nonconformists attributed virtues to ignorance as a condition for the internal light to shine, and as an intellectual and moral state or attitude favored by God, echoing the argument of the illiterate apostles examined earlier and the learned ignorance doctrine. The second part thus demonstrates that doctrines of ignorance were not entirely absent from the English context—but they were promoted and shared by religious groups who were often silenced at the time and who have not been included in the early modern intellectual canon. But part 2 also reveals that the English detractors of those doctrines often associated them with French philosophy, confirming the idea that celebrations of ignorance in seventeenth-century England were viewed, often with much disapproval, as a French phenomenon.

Part II

IGNORANCE AS A PRINCIPLE
OF KNOWLEDGE

A number of seventeenth-century philosophies and theologies held that ignorance should be induced and fostered in one's mind as a means to reach truth. More precisely, for the authors studied in this part, ignorance was either a condition that enabled the internal light to shine and lead to knowledge, or it could be inspiration itself, and therefore an unmediated and spontaneous access to truth. In both cases, ignorance was considered a principle of knowledge rather than a form of wisdom, as studied in part 1. For the detractors, those calls for ignorance were dangerous, as they more likely led to madness and enthusiasm than knowledge. Also examined in this part is a consequence of the idea that ignorance and the internal light—not learning—led to divine truth, namely the belief that intermediaries between the believers and God were superfluous, or at least that those intermediaries had to be ignorant and inspired themselves so as to better lead their flocks to religious knowledge and to God.

In the traditional imagery, ignorance is generally assimilated to blindness and darkness, whereas knowledge is associated with light and transparency.[1] But this analogy could also be reversed in the early modern period, when some—philosophers and theologians alike—argued that learning obscured the light present in all men and women, a light that therefore shone all the more vividly in ignorant people. For them, the internal light was indeed a mode of knowledge, which guaranteed an immediate and spontaneous access to truth through inspiration. Thanks to the light, one could therefore dispense with external knowledge acquired from books or teachers. In the seventeenth century, the internal light took different forms: it could be related to reason and common sense, as in Descartes's philosophy, or to "Christ within," some kind of divine revelation, as in the Quakers' theology—two conceptions of the internal light that actually came to be assimilated in the seventeenth century, mostly in England and the Netherlands, as this part shows.[2]

The notion of an internal light was nothing new in the early modern period.[3] Many expressions of it were found in ancient philosophy, as well as in the Old and New Testaments. Fathers of the church, such as Tertullian and Augustine, had also developed a theory of the inner light. Augustine held that there were two kinds of light, an external bodily light and an internal light that was a means of knowledge. This does not imply that learning was superfluous for Augustine; it was on the contrary recommended as "provoker, encourager and sign."[4] Another important doctrine of the internal light before the seventeenth century, which remained influential throughout the early modern period, was that of Thomas Aquinas, which played an essential role in the scholastic theory of knowledge. Aquinas held that an idea was formed in man—in other words, knowledge was acquired—through, first, the apprehension of the object by the senses, followed by a process of abstraction thanks to the natural light.[5] Descartes's, but also the Quakers', conceptions of the internal light were precisely built against this form of scholastic empiricism. For Descartes, the senses could not be the basis of knowledge, as they were more often than not the source of prejudices and error. But Aquinas also claimed, in his commentary on Aristotle's *De anima*, that the natural light gave man knowledge of the "first principles," upon which his reasoning is based. This knowledge cannot be mistaken and is not the result of a rational process.[6] It is rather some form of infallible, evident knowledge, like Descartes's natural light and the Quakers' inner light.

The principal purpose of this part is to examine and compare early modern conceptions of the internal light, and analyze their relation to ignorance: was ignorance required (or was it a necessary condition) for the internal light to shine? In other words, could the internal light shine only in ignorant people? Or was ignorance ever conflated with the light itself? Moreover, one can wonder what kind of truth was reached via the internal light: was it knowledge of God, of nature, or of oneself—or of all three together? This reflection raises another question: were men or women who had reached truth thanks to their internal light "omniscient," or were they still ignorant, in the sense that they did not possess classical human learning but had reached a whole new level of divine or metaphysical knowledge? In other words, did such men or women get back to the perfect science and innocence of Adam, or did they reach some form of "learned ignorance," a state in which they would remain ignorant of human learning but become endowed with superior knowledge or wisdom? For the opponents of the idea that there was an internal light in human beings, which granted an immediate access to truth that made learning superfluous or even harmful, such natural light was first and foremost a manifestation of enthusiasm. It was nothing but "the ungrounded Fancies of a Man's own Brain" being mistakenly used as a guide for opinion and action.[7] Thus, the promotion of the internal light as direct and sufficient access to truth was interpreted by its detractors as a form of illumination or madness, the expression of enthusiasm and melancholy, and therefore mental disorder. This part thus examines the arguments against ignorance as inspiration and shows what roles the opponents of the existence of a self-sufficient light in man attributed to ignorance in one's access to divine and natural truth.

Finally, the focus on the internal light raises the essential question of the possibility and dangers of an *unmediated* access to truth, which was at the heart of the Reformation in England. Could a man or a woman reach perfect divine knowledge and secure salvation merely through the use of his or her internal light, without the help of external agents, such as preachers? In other words, could an ignorant man or woman have a direct and spontaneous access to God? Claiming that the internal light was sufficient in itself to reach God amounted to no less than a radical questioning of the relevance and usefulness of the clergy. It could therefore be seen as a radical implementation of a major principle of the Reformation: the distrust of intermediaries—other than the Scriptures—between the believers and God. Conversely, this stance could also be seen as a threat to the Church of England and as a strong criticism of the English clergy, perceived as an intolerable legacy of the old religion. Immediately after the Civil Wars, in the context of the rise of sectarianism in England, a debate opposed the promoters of divine inspiration, who argued that external knowledge was unnecessary and even detrimental to proper worship of God and to Christian salvation, and the defenders of a learned clergy, who insisted on the contrary that the flocks needed to be taught the right doctrine in order to become good Christians in a fully reformed church. Two related aspects were at stake in this debate: first, the preservation of the reformed church through knowledge of God, and second, salvation.[8] To better illuminate the relation between ignorance, inspiration, and the inner light, this part finally focuses on the allegory of ignorance presented in John Bunyan's widely read *The Pilgrim's Progress* (1678) and the surprising fortune of Mr. Ignorance in the book.

CHAPTER 3

Ignorance and the Internal Light

The Quakers' Inner Light

The Scottish Quaker George Keith (1638?–1716) may not be representative of seventeenth-century Quaker theology as a whole, given that he disagreed with other Friends on several important subjects, notably the recognition of the historic Christ, which led to his disownment by the London Yearly Meeting of the Society of Friends in 1694. Besides, Keith converted to Quakerism around 1665 and thus belonged to the second generation of Quakers, whose ideas admittedly differed from those of early Quakers. But his writings are worth quoting for several reasons: first, Keith did play a significant role in the definition of Quaker principles; and second, his writings are particularly relevant here, as they emphasize ignorance and simplicity in one's access to knowledge. Third, Keith had relationships with the English natural philosophers of his time, and he was involved in the projects for the advancement of learning which are essential to this history of early modern ignorance.

In *The Woman-Preacher of Samaria* (1674), a text that attempts to demonstrate women's ability to preach as well as men, Keith shows how a simple ignorant woman can get to know Christ better than doctors of the university with all their divine erudition. He points out that, in John 4, the woman of Samaria receives knowledge directly from Christ: "She learned more of Christ from himself, in that small time, (perhaps not one hours length) than your Doctors, and University men have yet learned, for all their many years studying, laboring, reading, and hearing."[1] The knowledge imparted to the woman of Samaria is both unmediated—coming directly from Christ—and immediate—without delay. Keith further explains that what she gets from Christ is the knowledge of "all things," which is obtained through the very presence of Christ in her heart. This knowledge may have been some kind of omniscience, or, more accurately, the knowledge of Christ himself and of his being the Messiah: "So first of all, she was taught Christ by Christ Himself."[2] In other words, if this perfect knowledge is indeed immediate—taught "in the twinkling of an Eye"—it is not exactly unmediated since Christ, "the Word, the Life, the Light in her heart,"[3] plays the role of the teacher: he is both the teacher and the thing taught. Thus, according to Keith, Christ is the internal light, and that light brings knowledge of all things and of itself. In other words, the internal light—Christ—is both knowledge and the purveyor of it.

Keith also argues that the example of the woman of Samaria demonstrates that "Letter Learning" is not required of a good preacher—only faith and piety are.[4] This is precisely the main thesis of his book and one of the essential principles of Quaker theology. But Keith goes even further and asserts that being unlearned, and having the light of Christ in one's heart, is the only guarantee of good preaching. Learning is thus not only not necessary; it is actually an impediment to good preaching: "Again the Method of this Womans Preaching was not like their School Method, who make a Tale of an hours length, and yet never come to the matter itself; who take a text from some place of Scripture, and raise from it so many points of Doctrine, which they have studied so long before hand."[5] In this passage, the fairly common denunciation of scholastic method and erudition is meant to underline the originality and spontaneity of the inspired knowledge of the woman of Samaria, which is deemed far superior to the vain learning of theologians and their endless repetitions of what previous authors have said. Because she has no learning and is therefore guided by her faith (or "Christ within") only, her preaching is more efficient, she gets to the point, and she does not stray from God's Word.

In *The Universal Free Grace of the Gospel Asserted*, published two years before *The Woman-Preacher of Samaria*, George Keith had given a more precise definition of the internal light: "When we speak of the *Light*, as given unto all Men that they may be saved, and as being sufficient unto all for salvation: by *Light* we do not simply understand a thing, that hath but this *one property or quality*, of enlightening or manifesting, as only to give a true understanding of things, and to work out ignorance and error from out of the minds of men, but this *Light* hath *Life* in it."[6] Several characteristics of the Quakers' inner light are made explicit in this passage: first, all men (including women, as is made obvious from *The Woman-Preacher of Samaria*) are endowed with it; it is not the privilege of a few elected people, and as a consequence, it is not dependent on acquired characteristics, such as learning; second, the inner light is that which ensures salvation, nothing else is needed to be saved (and therefore, again, no external element is required); third, the inner light has life. But most importantly, in the context of this inquiry on ignorance and its relation to the internal light, Keith explains that the light within brings truth and "understanding of things" and, in the process, suppresses ignorance and error from the human mind. In other words, the inner light "corrects" the understanding, as it were, and replaces ignorance, understood as excessive erudition, with knowledge, understood as ignorance of scholastic learning, a reversal of the meanings of ignorance and knowledge that was characteristic of the paradoxical discourses on inspiration and the internal light.

One of the most influential early Quakers, the founder of the Society of Friends George Fox (1624–1691) expressed an apparently similar conception of the internal light, but in Fox's theology, the presence of the inner light led to an identification of human beings with Christ. Like Keith, Fox held that Christ had come to teach men himself; therefore, they should not listen to earthly professors, who instead would try to keep them away from the inner light. In his *Epistle to All People on the Earth* (1657), Fox describes Christ as "the Teacher, who saith, Learn of me, I am the way to the Father."[7] Christ is also presented in Fox's works as the light and truth.[8] What the inner light brings is knowledge of God through Jesus Christ, who is "the word of life which became flesh."[9] In his obscure and repetitive prose, Fox invariably insists that "the light . . . enlighten[s] every man that cometh into the world," but a man who does not "hear" the light, or who hates it, is condemned and cannot know God: it "is the light . . . which is given to all men to believe in the light, which who do not believe in the light, is condemned already."[10] It thus seems that, for Fox, the internal light is both the teacher and what is taught, or what is given to all men and women so that they believe in the light, that is, in God, a similar interpretation to that found in Keith's works mentioned earlier.

Like Keith again, Fox claims that the light saves a man from darkness, understood here as Satan, evil, or ignorance: "Now such as are turned to the light, the eye comes to be opened, and from the darkness these comes, and from the power of Satan, the god of the world, that hath blinded their eye."[11] In another text, *A Word to the People of the World* (1659), Fox explicitly associates darkness and ignorance: "wait in the true light, that you may come out of your thoughts and darkness, and unstableness and ignorance."[12] Fox argues that men tend to love darkness and ignorance, and to hate the light, because the light compels them to admit that they are doing evil and therefore requires from them that they give up sinning. The idea that men prefer to remain ignorant so that they may indulge in their sins was also commonly found in the sermons on ignorance, but while Church of England clergymen deplored the lack of religious knowledge, Fox denounced the chosen ignorance of the inner light.

Yet the exact nature of the inner light, as Fox understood it, is not clearly defined in his works, although he mentioned it obsessively. But he did insist that it was a *spiritual* light, and not a natural light, as learned men would have it. Neither was it a "natural conscience," but it did shine in one's conscience and encouraged one to do right by guiding one's actions.[13] Thus, Fox claims, the light shows the drunkard that he should not be drunk and the swearer that he should not swear, and so on.[14] In other words, the inner light is a spiritual and moral guide; the knowledge it brings is that of good and evil. In Fox's works, Christ, the inner light, the spirit, and truth are one entity that teaches and guides men: "the Spirit is light, and the light is the truth."[15] Christ is indeed the true light, and he is, as Keith also stated later in his own works, the life itself in one's heart.

If the inner light was essential to Quaker theology, it was not given the same interpretation by all seventeenth-century Friends. Besides, conceptions of the inner light evolved between the time of the early Quakers and the late seventeenth century. Thus, in their chapter "Quakers, Philosophy, and Truth," Jeffrey Dudiak and Laura Rediehs argue that "over time, some Quakers increasingly identified the Light Within with the Light of enlightenment reason. Friends inclined to see Christ in terms of a fulfillment of an inherent human potential (and not as divine intervention) increasingly adopted this position," whereas the early Quakers had made a clearer distinction between the light of reason and the light of Christ.[16] It is certainly true of Fox, for example, who insisted on the spiritual or supernatural dimension of the light and explicitly rejected the idea that it might be a natural light.[17] Keith's conception of the nature of the inner light was more ambiguous and could, in some of its expressions, be assimilated to a natural light or the light of reason.

Descartes's Natural Light

Descartes's natural light was presented and defined in his unfinished dialogue *The Search for Truth by Means of the Natural Light*, written in French, but first published posthumously in a Dutch translation in 1684.[18] It also appears, in relation with reason or common sense, in the more widely known *Discourse on Method*, also written in French and first published anonymously in Leiden in 1637.[19] What those two texts, which are the main focus here, have in common, apart from dealing with the natural light, is that they were written in the vernacular for a nonacademic audience. It should be noted, though, that the expression *lumière naturelle*, in its various forms (*lumen naturale, lumen rationis, lux naturalis*) appears throughout Descartes's works.[20] Besides, the French philosopher did not only resort to metaphorical uses of the light: "physical" light and scientific accounts of light were also of interest to Descartes, as is shown, for example, in his essay "On Light" in the *Dioptrics*.[21]

The Search for Truth by Means of the Natural Light features Epistemon, the traditional scholar; Polyander, the uneducated gentleman; and Eudoxus, the true philosopher, who, throughout the dialogue, guides Polyander toward the truth thanks to some form of Socratic method. The preamble to the dialogue states that Eudoxus—like Descartes himself—has been taught classical learning as a young man, and he has traveled and met with the scholars of his time, before eventually choosing to retire to his country home to meditate and rely on his reason only in his search for truth. Eudoxus thus represents the disengaged sage who has mastered his insatiable curiosity thanks to the method of doubt and who can now think by himself.[22] The dialogue, though unfinished, demonstrates that the natural light alone, without any external help from philosophy or religion, leads one to truth on all matters, even to "the secrets of the most curious sciences," as the title indicates. Consequently, to make perfect use of his natural light and reach truth, a man must first divest himself of all the learning, false knowledge, and prejudices that he has acquired since childhood, or, in other words, he should first make himself ignorant. But this chosen ignorance is not sufficient to reach truth: a good use of reason, once the mind is divested of useless learning and prejudices, is also required, as is demonstrated in other works by Descartes, especially the *Discourse on Method* and the *Rules for the Direction of the Mind*. The process through which man deliberately puts himself in a state of ignorance is also explicitly described at the beginning of Descartes's *Third Meditation*: "I will now shut my eyes, stop my ears, and withdraw all my senses. I will eliminate from my thoughts all images of bodily things, or rather, since this is hardly possible, I will regard all such images as vacuous, false and worthless. I will converse with myself more deeply; and in this way I will attempt to achieve, little by little, a more intimate knowledge of myself."[23] In the *Discourse on Method*, Descartes shows both the role of the natural light and how it should be employed. Although the expression "natural light" occurs only twice in the text, it is referred to through its relation to common sense and reason, or "right understanding," as the seventeenth-century English translation has it.[24] The expression *lumière naturelle*, or "natural light," appears at the end of the first part of the *Discourse*, when Descartes explains that, after his course of study, he decided to forgo classical learning and look for science or knowledge in himself and in the great book of the world. He thus started traveling and discovered the diversity of other peoples' mores and opinions, but he soon realized that this knowledge was as uncertain as the one he had acquired in his education. Indeed, the multiplicity of opinions led him to believe that they must all be equally doubted. Therefore, he "learn'd to beleeve nothing too firmly," and "so by little and little . . . freed [him]self from many errors, which might eclipse our naturall light, and render us lesse able to comprehend reason."[25] In this regard, his travels were highly beneficial, although not in the way he expected, as they made him realize that all knowledge was uncertain. The things that he had learned and believed to be true were actually errors that obscured his natural light and made him less likely to be guided by reason, as memory naturally tends to dim the internal light.

Another explicit and relevant mention of the light is found in the third part of the *Discourse*, when Descartes asserts that God has given everyone "a light to discern truth from falsehood," which is also how he defines reason and common sense at the very beginning of the text: "the faculty of right-judging and distinguishing truth from falshood (which is properly call'd, Understanding or Reason) is naturally equal in all Men."[26] But the ability or faculty to tell between truth and falsehood, which is presented here as a light, is also linked to innate ideas, or principles that all men are naturally endowed with. Indeed, Descartes explains in the *Meditations* that innate ideas, for example the idea of God or the idea of oneself, are "obvious to everyone."[27] Contrary to "adventitious ideas" (ideas coming from outside) and ideas "invented by me," innate ideas are self-evident, cannot be doubted, and are present in everyone's mind.[28] In his replies to the objections against the *Meditations*, Descartes insists again on the fact that innate ideas are common to all: "the idea of God is implanted in the same way in the minds of all," and "we all have the same ability to conceive of the idea of God."[29] The philosopher also makes it clear that innate ideas are not "pre-existing ideas," or ideas that are "always there before us": saying that we have innate ideas means that "we have within ourselves the faculty of summoning up the idea."[30] So it appears that not all have the same innate ideas, but all have the same faculty—natural light or reason—to summon those innate ideas.

Moreover, in the *Rules for the Direction of the Mind*, Descartes explains that we can have science only through intuition and deduction, and not through opinions, whether they be our own or others'. In Rule III, he defines intuition as "the indubitable conception of a clear and attentive mind which proceeds solely from the light of reason."[31] Thus, the natural light, or light of reason, makes possible and guarantees the operations of intuition and deduction. Besides, about intuition, Descartes adds: "Because it is simpler, it is more certain than deduction."[32] Deduction, or inference from true and known principles, is a valid mode of knowing, but it implies a long chain of thought, or sequence, and therefore, it must rely on memory, which makes it more complex and less efficient than intuition.[33] And indeed, Rule III is a plea in favor of simplicity of argument, which should always be preferred to obscurity, despite what those who rely only on classical learning might think. Descartes dismisses erudition in the search for knowledge as something that leads to history and not science. On the contrary, what enables one to reach knowledge and truth is one's "intellectual aptitude."[34] The knowledge obtained by intuition is self-evident and certain. If the internal light is here presented as what makes intuition possible, in other texts, Descartes seems to assimilate the two, for instance in a letter to Mersenne, dated 16 October 1639, where he writes of "the natural light or *intuitus mentis*" as if they were equivalent.[35] What is clear, though, is that, for Descartes, intuition and innate ideas are modes of knowledge that do not require learning or any external addition to the intellect.

Ignorance, Inspiration, and Enthusiasm

The similitudes between the Quakers' inner light and Descartes's natural light did not escape contemporaries, especially in England and the Netherlands. Both conceptions of the internal light seemed to imply an immediate and (apparently) unmediated access to truth, which therefore did not require external knowledge.[36] At first sight, and for their detractors, it appeared that Descartes and the Quakers similarly perceived learning as an obstacle to inspired knowledge, and therefore praised ignorance as a preconditional state necessary to reach truth. Like the Quakers, Descartes believed that all men had the same internal light. He thus made it clear that, in lunatics and children, for example, the natural light was obscured but not extinguished. Besides, some people may refuse to acknowledge the presence of the light, or use it properly, but they are still endowed with it in Descartes's philosophy. Similarly, early Quakers insisted that, thanks to the inner light, everyone—even people who had not been preached the Gospel, for example, inhabitants of the "New World" as well as ancient Greek philosophers—could have (had) access to truth, or Christ.

Yet in Descartes's philosophy, contrary to Quaker theology, the internal light is very clearly a *natural* light, not a supernatural or spiritual one. It is not "Christ within," but a faculty, even though Descartes makes it clear that God is the creator of man's natural light. Early Quakers, in contrast, distrusted natural reason, as discussed earlier. Descartes insists on the good use of the natural light through method, meditation, and experimentation, while acceptance of the inner light is understood by the Quakers as a matter of belief and faith. This is probably what leads to the most important difference between Descartes's and the Quakers' conceptions of the internal light: while Descartes believed that one should first divest oneself of prejudices in order to free the natural light from all hindrances, and thus make the search for truth possible, early Quakers believed that the light was sufficient in itself to reach truth or God. In other words, the radical doubt or chosen ignorance that Descartes recommended was only the first step on the path to science, and he did not encourage anyone to persist in a state of ignorance (contrary to a common seventeenth-century interpretation and criticism of Cartesianism that is presented later). For the Quakers, recognition and acceptance of one's inner light as "Christ within" were sufficient to know God. Finally, and consequently, as the full titles of *The Search for Truth* and the *Discourse on Method* indicate, the truth that Descartes's natural light leads to is "scientific truth," or "truth in the sciences," whereas the Quakers' inner light brings knowledge of God.

Despite those fundamental differences, Cartesianism and Quakerism came to be associated—and even sometimes assimilated—in the seventeenth century as doctrines that recommended and praised inspiration and ignorance in one's access to truth.[37] More precisely, the association of Cartesianism and Quakerism often revolved around their alleged common consequence and manifestation: enthusiasm. Indeed, detractors argued that the celebration of ignorance allegedly induced by the sufficiency of the internal light in Descartes's philosophy and in Quaker theology—that is, deliberate ignorance—could not but lead to madness and enthusiasm, or be a sign of madness and enthusiasm. The association of Cartesian philosophy and Quaker theology was thus rooted in a close articulation between ignorance and enthusiasm that was often expressed in seventeenth-century England.

THE RELATION BETWEEN IGNORANCE AND ENTHUSIASM

The relation between ignorance and enthusiasm was given explicit attention in *A Treatise concerning Enthusiasme* (1655) by the scholar and divine Meric Casaubon (1599–1671). Although Casaubon does not focus in this work on the association of Cartesianism and Quakerism, as he did later in the 1660s, this treatise prepares, as it were, for this assimilation by making explicit the articulation of ignorance, enthusiasm and the internal light. Right from the beginning, indeed, when he presents the contents of the book, Casaubon shows that enthusiasm and ignorance are closely linked: "Politick pretensions to *Enthusiasme*, or Divine Inspiration, very usual in all Ages: But mistaken, through ignorance of natural causes, (our only Subject and aime in this Treatise) as more frequent, so more dangerous."[38] Indeed, the principal aim of the book is to discover the natural causes of enthusiasm, which, Casaubon claims, are generally not known.[39] These natural or medical causes are melancholy and "distempers of the brain."[40] For Casaubon, it is essential to have them known because the ignorance of natural causes leads to mistaken explanations and to representations of enthusiasm and inspiration as supernatural manifestations.[41]

In this text, Casaubon thus puts forward a medical interpretation of enthusiasm, and he founds his criticism of inspiration on a defense of classical learning. He explains that there are two different forms of enthusiasm, which imply two different relations to ignorance. Indeed, claims to inspiration can be a genuine belief or a deliberate lie: "By the opinion of divine Inspiration, I mean a real, though but imaginary, apprehension of it in the parties, upon some ground of nature; a real, not barely pretended, counterfeit, and simulatory, for politick ends."[42] When people are genuinely—although wrongfully—convinced of their being inspired, it is often because they fail to recognize the real cause of their condition, and ascribe supernatural causes to what is actually a natural, or medical, manifestation. When they pretend to be inspired, knowing perfectly well that they are not, they are merely trying to exert some control over others by attributing to themselves supernatural powers and a direct access to God.

Claims to inspiration as an "imposture," and the relation between enthusiasm and ignorance in this context, are examined mostly in chapter 3 of the *Treatise concerning Enthusiasme*, entitled "Of Contemplative and Philosophicall Enthusiasm."[43] Here, Casaubon introduces the enthusiasts' celebrations of their own ignorance by focusing on Denys the Areopagite's *De mystica theologia*, in which is presented "a new kind of practical *Divinity*" that implies renouncing one's understanding and intellectual faculties in one's access to God.[44] The idea is that one might better reach God "through elevation of mind," which requires forgoing all passions, affection, and knowledge.[45] According to this doctrine, which comes from Plato, and not from the Gospel of Christ, Casaubon argues, "*a mist of ignorance in man*" is conceived as "the readiest way to the knowledge of God." Casaubon immediately states that he does not know the ground, "either in reason, or Scripture," for "this strange doctrine," or "mystical theology."[46] To refute it, he "goes by authority," and relies on the criticism of inspiration by Synesius of Cyrene, a fourth-century Greek bishop. In Synesius's time, "some illiterate Monks" used the doctrine of "*absolute ignorance*" for their own benefit, "pretending by that ignorance, to have nearest accesse unto God, and most of God in themselves."[47] Thus, paradoxically, their ignorance made them pass as wise and godly men, which gave them power over people.[48] Synesius refuted this doctrine and wrote in defense of human learning and philosophy, even though he admitted that a very small number of ignorant people might have been able to access God. Casaubon explains that the "professors of ignorance" whom Synesius refuted, and the enthusiasts whom he is himself denouncing in his treatise are the same. Following Synesius, he admits that God is indeed present in man, but in his reason only: "*God forbid*, saith he [Synesius] there in a place, *that we should think that if God dwell in us, he should dwell in any other part of us, then that which is rational: which is his proper Temple. It cannot be certainly, that Truth should be found in Ignorance; or that he should be wise truly, which is irrational.*"[49] Casaubon repeatedly argues in his treatise that reason is the faculty that leads to God because it is God's gift to man, and choosing to be ignorant means denying the power of reason. This argument thus relies on the assumption that reason and knowledge are related, or even identified, and that ignorance is therefore opposed to both knowledge and reason.

Casaubon then focuses on particular cases of "fools" who allegedly experienced visions and ecstasies. He shows that these were due to distempers of the mind: those visions were "the effect of pure melancholie," not the signs of an elevation of the mind caused by ignorance.[50] He gives several arguments against the mystical theology that would have ignorance be the surest way to God: first, this doctrine comes from heathen philosophers, which accounts for the fact that it completely ignores the Scriptures, and even goes against them, as it recommends neglecting one's reason; second, this way of divinity might be tolerated in philosophers, but certainly not in ordinary men and women, whom it will lead to madness and make prey to the devil; finally, this mystical theology is typical of the Jesuits, who thus attempt to manipulate people, as is well known.[51] Casaubon also draws an analogy between the mystical theology and Descartes's "new method," laying the first stone of his assimilation of Cartesianism and radical religion a few years later: Descartes and mystical theologians encourage ignorance because they define it as a superior mode of divine knowledge.[52]

Casaubon's criticism of enthusiasm is particularly interesting in the context of an inquiry into the early modern uses and conceptions of ignorance as it shows that, at least in the eyes of the defenders of classical learning (and not only in those of Francis Bacon, as was already argued), there was a dangerous attack against knowledge coming from different sources or enemies of learning, who all wished, as it seemed, to herald the reign of ignorance. Whether they be honest—yet mistaken—believers in the superiority of ignorance as a direct way to divine knowledge or deceivers who aimed to manipulate people for their personal benefit, enthusiasts were a threat to learning, which they merely wanted to replace with ignorance, by reversing the very meanings of ignorance and learning. This theologico-philosophical stance jeopardized the true religion and the success of the Reformation, but also the very order of the state.

Just one year after the first publication of Casaubon's treatise against enthusiasm, the Cambridge Platonist Henry More (1614–1687) expressed his ideas on the subject in *Enthusiasmus triumphatus*. Like Casaubon, More gave a medical interpretation of enthusiasm, arguing that it was a disease and a consequence of melancholy, or of "the enormous strength of Imagination."[53] And it should be noted that imagination is all the stronger in people with a weak reason or understanding. If not exactly presented as a cause of enthusiasm by More, ignorance is nevertheless seen as the reason fanatics cannot realize that they are mistaken, or that they are fanatics. Indeed, ignorance makes them self-conceited and certain that they are right: "their setled and radicate ignorance ma[k]e them so Enthusiastically confident in their own Errour."[54] A few years later, in *An Explanation of the Grand Mystery of Godliness* (1660), More denounced enthusiasm again and made a plea in favor of learning as a way to curb claims to inspiration. He first recognized that the Quakers and the Familists might be sincere in the expression of their faith, but he argued that they were wrong in rejecting all external manifestations of Christ. As a response to their insistence on "that Mystical Christ within us," More attempted to demonstrate the necessity to recognize "*Christ without*," or the historical Christ, as well as "*Christ within*," thanks to reason and the Scriptures, thereby showing that the inner light is not a sufficient means to access divine truth.[55] More also called for the erection of "*publick Schools of Learning*" because "the more knowing [the] Subjects are, the more certainly will they keep to Christianity," and stay away from all kinds of enthusiasm.[56] As a matter of fact, More argues, Christianity was born in the most civilized regions of the world, which proves that learning makes not only good Christians, but also obedient subjects. Moreover, learning is necessary because an ignorant man or woman is unable to interpret the Scriptures correctly:

> Besides that it is a piece of unspeakable madness to think that any man can be a fit Interpreter of Scripture without that which some in contempt call *Humane Learning*, as *Logick* or the known Principles of *Reasoning*; I will adde *Mathematicks* and *Philosophy*, and *skill in Tongues* and *History*: no man without the knowledge of these can make good the Truth of those holy Oracles to knowing and understanding men. And therefore they that decry these helps, are either very ignorant, or out of their wits, or have a treacherous plot against the flourishing of *Christianity*, and would bring in some *Fanatick Religion*, or else are enemies to all Religion whatsoever.[57]

The idea that someone could understand the Scriptures and therefore know God without any human or classical knowledge is the result either of ignorance, or of madness, or, worse, of a desire to replace Christianity with some form of fanaticism, according to More. Later, in *A Plain and Continued Exposition of the Several Prophecies or Divine Visions of the Prophet Daniel* (1681), he condemned both Roman Catholics and Fifth Monarchists on the grounds of their ignorance. While Fifth Monarchists were described as "an ignorant and fanatical sort of men that cannot see wood for trees," Catholics were said to "wallow in the black mire of ignorance and the filth of idolatry."[58] Even though ignorance was mostly used in these instances as an insult that may not have had a profound and specific meaning, it still revealed the dangerous consequences of a lack of knowledge, especially when it was actively pursued. For More and others, the solution to the threat posed by all forms of enthusiasm was the development of education and places of learning, and therefore the organized fight against ignorance.

Although Locke's philosophy is more closely examined in part 3, it is pertinent to mention here briefly that the English philosopher also emphasized the link between ignorance, the internal light, and enthusiasm in his *Essay concerning Human Understanding*. More precisely, Locke condemned enthusiasm as the belief that the internal light was "its own proof," and therefore could dispense not only with external knowledge, but also with demonstrations of its own existence and efficiency, the internal light being self-evident. Locke laments the fact that those who believe in the self-sufficiency of the internal light to reach truth cannot possibly be convinced otherwise since there is no discussing, let alone questioning, the light: "the Ease and Glory it is to be inspired and be above the common and natural ways of Knowledge so flatters many Men's Laziness, Ignorance, and Vanity, that when once they are got into this way of immediate Revelation; of Illumination without search; and of certainty without Proof, and without Examination, 'tis a hard matter to get them out of it."⁵⁹ Locke also uses arguments that were made earlier in the century against the internal light and Descartes's conception of it, in particular the idea that positing the existence of an internal light that is sufficient in itself to reach truth encourages men's laziness, as it exempts them from making the effort of looking after truth, an attitude that keeps them in ignorance. For Locke, the search for truth was on the contrary a painstakingly long process. Another danger of believing in the self-sufficiency of the internal light, according to Locke, was that it made both reason and revelation useless, even while attempting to replace reason with revelation.

THE ASSOCIATION OF CARTESIAN PHILOSOPHY AND QUAKER THEOLOGY AS CHAMPIONS OF IGNORANCE

The articulation of ignorance and enthusiasm served as the intellectual foundation or background for the assimilation of Cartesianism and Quakerism from the mid-seventeenth century, in England mostly, but also in the Netherlands. Indeed, this assimilation was expressed in the context of the 1640s "Utrecht quarrel," when the Dutch philosopher Martin Schoock (1614–1669) claimed that Descartes had "waged a war on books and reading," encouraging young people to give up their education and indulge instead in laziness and meditation.⁶⁰ Schoock argued that Descartes deceived and manipulated young people, by urging them to forget all that they had previously learned. To ensure their obedience, Descartes first "broke them" with the harshest offenses and portrayed them as the most ignorant of men. Being thus humiliated and convinced of their ignorance, they were manipulated into believing anything, eventually becoming disciples of the French philosopher.⁶¹

In his virulent attack, Schoock associated Descartes with other alleged enemies of the Christian religion, including Nicholas of Cusa, Cornelius Agrippa, and Francisco Sanches (1551–1623).⁶² A Portuguese philosopher and doctor, the latter had published in 1581 *Quod nihil scitur*, a systematic refutation of Aristotelian philosophy, which ran through six editions until 1665. Even though Sanches's book title stressed the general ignorance of mankind, his aim was mostly to destroy the Aristotelian system of knowledge and its use of the syllogism, not to demonstrate that nothing *could* be known. Aristotelianism did result in complete ignorance, but another way to knowledge was possible. In this regard, a parallel between Descartes's and Sanches's works could legitimately be made. As a matter of fact, Descartes had read the 1618 Frankfurt edition of *Quod nihil scitur*; besides, the prologue to Sanches's text and the *Discours de la méthode* bear similarities. But above all, what they had in common was an interpretation of their philosophies in the seventeenth century as radical celebrations of ignorance. As mentioned earlier, in the late seventeenth century, Sanches was still associated with Agrippa as a thinker who stressed the inevitability of human ignorance, but their philosophies were seen as a protection against radical skepticism, for example in Richard Baxter's works.

Schoock insisted that Descartes's method of "radical doubt" implied that one should forget all the knowledge that one had previously acquired, that is, make oneself ignorant, and that this was more likely to lead them to a mental institution than to wisdom or truth. In his book *Admiranda methodus* (*The Admirable Method*), published in 1643, Schoock explicitly assimilated complete ignorance (which he argued Descartes promoted as the very principle of his philosophy) with mental disorder, because choosing ignorance amounted to voluntarily putting off the light of reason: "A grown man who forgets everything is ignorant of everything, and where there is ignorance of everything, there is mental disorder. Because what is, by nature, absolutely evident, can be ignored only if one extinguishes the light of reason, so that a candidate to wisdom actually becomes a preacher of foolishness."[63] Schoock argues that there is some knowledge that a man cannot choose not to know because it is naturally inscribed, as it were, in his reason. Renouncing this self-evident knowledge would mean extinguishing the light of reason or going against nature, and therefore becoming mad. A man who is completely ignorant is a mad man.

As a matter of fact, in the mid-seventeenth century, ignorance was often described as a disease and a form of madness, as was already alluded to in the commentary on Casaubon's treatise on enthusiasm. This idea was also found in the religious discourse. John Gauden (1599/1600?–1662), for example, presented ignorance as a contagious disease that could easily spread and "infect" other people. He thus denounced the ignorance of all kinds of heretics: "*Indians* in barbarous idolatry; or *Turks* in ridiculous Mahometry; or . . . the *sillier* sort of Papists in saplesse superstitions; or . . . the wilder generation of *Enthusiasts* in their various fancies and most incongruous *dreams*; all which grossely erre, and covet to infect others through *ignorance* even in the matters of right Reason as well as Religion."[64] But he also explicitly associated, and even assimilated, ignorance with a mental infirmity or madness itself. Drawing upon Plato, he categorized ignorance and madness as two "diseases of the Soul," or mental disorders: "There are, saith *Plato*, two diseases of the Soul of man madnesse and ignorance; Madnesse is from the abounding with pride and passion; Ignorance from the want of knowledge and instruction: Ignorance is but a tamer madnesse: mad men have lost their wits; and ignorant men never had them. Learning and Religion cure both. The highest and most *incurable* madnesse is, an *ungracious hatred* of learning, and an irreligious love of ignorance."⁶⁵ Plato's *Timaeus* explains that there are two kinds of diseases or dementia: folly or madness and ignorance, which are the results of excessive pleasure and excessive pain, respectively. Plato showed how bodily dispositions, or the relation between body and soul, in particular the imbalance between the two, was the cause of diseases of the soul. Thus, ignorance was caused by the body overpowering the soul, and as such, it was the most serious mental disorder. To avoid these diseases of the soul, one should seek a perfect balance between body and soul.⁶⁶ In this passage, Gauden explicitly borrows from Plato's *Timaeus*, but he adapts the Greek philosopher's account of ignorance. The main difference is that Gauden does not articulate the two kinds of dementia with the relation between body and soul. For Gauden, ignorance is indeed a disease of the soul and a form of madness, even though he holds that madness proceeds from an excess (of passions), and ignorance from a lack (of instruction). Moreover, madness is described as the result of a process whereby one comes back to an original state of complete ignorance, while ignorance itself is a condition that affects one from their birth but becomes a disease when it is prolonged. Both madness and ignorance can be cured, Gauden adds, thanks to learning and religion, but not thanks to the preservation of a balance between body and soul, as is the case in the *Timaeus*. Gauden also argues that love of ignorance and hatred of learning—that is, the association of ignorance and madness with the passions, as opposed to mere ignorance and madness—cannot be cured.

Besides his association of Cartesian philosophy, ignorance, and madness, Martin Schoock also mocked the idea that knowledge could be found within one's mind. According to the Dutch philosopher, claiming that there is an inner light or spirit that leads to truth is paramount to saying that God himself is present in one's mind, and if Cartesians admit that God is within themselves, they might as easily be led to believe that they are in God.⁶⁷ Such assertions were expressions of enthusiasm, a form of illumination shared by Cartesians and Quakers alike, Schoock argued. Enthusiasm, according to the Dutch philosopher, manifested itself in the belief that one's mind was the only judge on everything, so that one could dispense with the Scriptures altogether. In other words, Cartesians replaced the authority of the Scriptures with that of their own minds. Schoock's conclusion is clear: by encouraging one to forget all previous knowledge and use one's natural light only in the search for truth, Descartes's method "led directly to enthusiasm."⁶⁸ It is manifest here again that ignorance, the internal light, and enthusiasm are closely linked: the internal light excludes learning and requires a state of ignorance in order to shine, and belief in the self-sufficiency of the internal light or inspiration is the very definition of enthusiasm.

Descartes's reply to Schoock is interesting as it gave the French philosopher the opportunity to articulate his conception of the role of ignorance in the search for truth. Descartes thus argued, as he often repeated, that he had never encouraged anyone to forget all their knowledge, but only to get rid of their prejudices. Yet he did also insist that relying on erudition and the authorities led one to neglect their natural reason, which is why all previously acquired knowledge had to be doubted before one could proceed on the way to science.[69] In the article "Descartes and the Problem of Culture," Denis Kambouchner inquires about the exact meaning of the French philosopher when he encouraged his readers to make themselves ignorant: did he actually intend to discredit all learning and praise complete ignorance, as *The Search for Truth*, the *Regulae*, and the *Discourse on Method* might imply? Was Schoock right in believing that, for Descartes, schools and books could not teach anything useful and that therefore all acquired knowledge was an obstacle to accessing truth? Kambouchner replies that this interpretation is obviously a caricature, and he gives three reasons to dismiss it: first, Descartes himself was extremely learned; second, he wrote very favorably of his own studies and of his masters in La Flèche; finally, and more importantly, there are nuances or "subtle modulations" in Descartes's discourse on ignorance and learning in all the above-mentioned works. Indeed, "those who have never studied" are never opposed to "those who have studied" in Descartes's works, but always to "those who have spent *all their time* in the schools," or those who, like Epistemon, know *all* that is taught at school, revealing a distinction between *docti* and *eruditi*, and underlining therefore the idea of an excess of knowledge. Descartes, like most contemners of knowledge at the time, did not condemn knowledge as such, but the excess of knowledge. Those who have not studied can grasp the simplicity of Descartes's philosophy, but it requires knowledge to fully understand it. Kambouchner argues that to replace the scholastic philosophy with a more certain and a more exact one, Descartes could not but reject all the instituted culture in the first place—selecting some acceptable elements within it would have been a delicate and confusing enterprise.[70]

In England, the most telling example of the association of Cartesianism and Quakerism is probably that of Meric Casaubon again, who, in a manuscript epistolary treatise of 1668 on the subject of "general learning," insists that learning reached perfection around 1600, and has declined since then, mostly because method now plays too great a part in intellectual endeavors, and because the recent development of printing allows for the publication of too many worthless books that spread ignorance instead of knowledge.[71] In this text, Casaubon explicitly accuses Descartes, English religious radicals (whom he identifies as Quakers and Puritans), and Jesuits of making ignorance a virtue by insisting on the necessity to divest oneself of all knowledge in order to reach truth. In particular, Casaubon describes the Jesuits' strategies of conversion and argues that their modus operandi is also that of Descartes and of English "Puritans":

> Wherein the man [Descartes] seems to me to take the same course with disciples, as many Jesuited Puritans doe with theirs; which is, first to cast them downe to the lowest pitt of despaire; and then with such engins of persuasion, they are commonly [well] stored with, to rayse them up againe, to the highest pitche of confidence: but soe that they leave themselfes a power still, to caste downe, & to raise againe, when they see cause; which must needs oblige the credulous disciple, as he hath found the horror of the one, & the comfort (whether reall or imaginarie) of the other, to a great dependencie. Soe Descartes, after he hath obliged his disciples, to forgett & forgoe all former præcognitions & progresses of eyther senses or sciences; then he thinks he hath them sure; they must adheare to him tooth & nayle, or acknowledge themselfes to have beene fooled, (which of all things in the worlde, though nothing more ordinarie in the world;) with most men, is of hardest digestion.[72]

Casaubon's ranting can also be read as testimony to the revival of anti-Catholic feelings in the Restoration and to the "moral panic" caused by the perceived invasion of England by God's Soldiers, who came to be associated with English religious radicals at the time. Actually, in a similar passage from his book *Of Credulity and Incredulity*, published two years later, Casaubon claims that Puritans got their conversion "methods" from the Jesuits.[73] But more importantly here, Casaubon attempts to describe how exactly the Jesuits and Descartes are suspected of using and encouraging the ignorance of the people: they first manage to convince them to give up the knowledge they possess (in accordance with Descartes's "radical doubt"), which is presented to them as corrupted and wrong thanks to "engins of persuasion," probably casuistry, mental reservation, and equivocation. As a consequence, people find themselves in a state of utter ignorance and therefore of despair, vulnerability, and credulity, and are thus made to believe that only those who have plunged them into such darkness can get them out of it. In other words, Casaubon argues, "radicals," whether they be Cartesians, Puritans, or Jesuits, use the feelings of loss and weakness, and the credulity that accompanies ignorance (imagined or real), to convert people to their own beliefs, by presenting themselves as the only saviors and consolers in a painful situation that *they* themselves have caused.

Casaubon did not merely denounce the use of ignorance by Descartes, he also asserted that Cartesianism was the very cause of Quakerism. In other words, by encouraging people to give up their knowledge and make themselves ignorant,

Descartes "turned" them into Quakers: "What a mysterie doth he make of his *Ego sum: ego Cogito,* to attaine to the excellencie whereof, a man must first strip himselfe of all that he hath ever knowne, or beleeved. He must renounce to his naturall reason, & to his senses: nothing but caves and solitudes will serve the turne, for such deepe meditation, such profound matter: rare inventions to raise the expectation of the credulous, & in the end to send them away pure Quacks, or arrand Quakers."[74] Casaubon's criticisms in this passage are admittedly based on exaggerations of and confusions about Descartes's philosophy—interpretations of Cartesianism that were common in seventeenth-century England. Yet Casaubon is also being disingenuous when he identifies Descartes's radical doubt with the idea that a man should renounce his reason, his senses, his social life, and basically retreat into a cave, with Descartes's method as only company.[75] Casaubon adds that the ignorance and solitude in which the followers of Descartes are thus plunged is not a fortuitous consequence of Cartesian principles; it is actually the result that Descartes actively seeks to better control and manipulate the minds of these people: "Soe Descartes, after he hath obliged his disciples, to forgett & forgoe all former præcognitions & progresses of eyther senses or sciences; then he thinks he hath them sure; they must adheare to him tooth & nayle, or acknowledge themselfes to have beene fooled, (which of all things in the worlde, though nothing more ordinarie in the world;) with most men, is of hardest digestion."[76] The association of Cartesianism and Quakerism as two similar forms of enthusiasm, on account of their common praise of ignorance and inspiration, was reaffirmed after the publication of Adrien Baillet's *Vie de Monsieur Descartes* (1691), in which the biographer narrated Descartes's famous dreams of November 1619, a story that had never been told before. Baillet writes that, on the evening of 10 November 1619, Descartes went to bed "*Brimfull of Enthusiasm,*" the word *enthusiasm* appearing several times throughout the relation of the three dreams, thus giving new arguments to those who assimilated Cartesianism and Quakerism in the late seventeenth century.[77] One of them was the English Catholic convert and priest John Sergeant (1623–1707), who explicitly associated Descartes's philosophy and Quaker theology in his works, although the focus was no longer on ignorance as such. Instead, Sergeant emphasized the danger of Descartes's innate principles, rather than deliberate ignorance and its role in the search for truth. Indeed, while Schoock and Casaubon had focused mostly on the absurdity of chosen ignorance and how it was used to control people's minds, Sergeant argued instead that the French philosopher could not possibly have a "clear and distinct idea" of his first principle, *ego cogito*, and therefore had no knowledge of anything:

> No man can have a Clear and Distinct *Idea*, (in which, according to him [Descartes], all knowledge consists) of any thing *following* out of a First Principle, unless he have a Clear and Distinct Knowledge of that Principle *it self*. But *Cartesius*, when, in the progress of his Thoughts, he came to the settling *Ego cogito* (or *Ego sum*) for his First Principle, had *no* Clear and Distinct Idea of that Principle *it self*; therefore he could have *no* Clear and Distinct *Idea* of any thing which *follow'd* out of that Principle; and, consequently, all that *Method to Science* laid by him is Useless to that End, and Fruitless.[78]

Describing what has sometimes been called "the Cartesian circle," Sergeant argues in this passage that, to establish a first principle, one needs a clear and distinct idea, which itself requires knowledge of the first principle, so that nothing can be known by following Descartes's method. In his refutation of skeptics and "ideists" more generally, Sergeant also underlines the impossibility of finding knowledge within oneself since knowledge or truth is defined as the conformity of our judgment to the object.[79] The notion of the internal light leads him to explicitly associate Cartesianism and Quakerism, as well as philosophy and religion, when he exclaims about Descartes's ideas, "Was ever such *Quakerism* heard of among Philosophers!"[80]

To conclude, this chapter on the articulation of ignorance, inspiration, and enthusiasm in seventeenth-century interpretations of Cartesianism and Quakerism shows, first, that ignorance was a central preoccupation of philosophers and theologians who wished to define new ways of thinking. Second, it reveals that doctrines interpreted as praises of ignorance were seen as a serious threat to the religious and political order by their detractors, who took great pains to refute those doctrines, which they saw as forms of radicalism. Third, this chapter sheds new light on the definition of madness in the early modern period, and this deserves more attention here.

Indeed, when arguing that until the mid-eighteenth century, there was "no such thing as diseased mind" because madness was interpreted in bodily terms, Akihito Suzuki may have underestimated the role played by interpretations of Cartesianism (if not Descartes's philosophy itself) and radical religious doctrines in the conceptions of madness in philosophy and theology, but also probably medicine, even though Suzuki does stress the role of dualism in the shift from a definition of madness as a disease of the body to the conception of a diseased mind.[81] Indeed, Suzuki argues that a shift of focus from the body to the mind occurred in the eighteenth century only, with François Boissier de Sauvages, who, in his *Nosologie méthodique* (1763), showed that the mind is active in madness, or "actively commits errors."[82] The role played by the mind was also determined by ignorance and learning: Sauvages took the example of a peasant and a philosopher and claimed that if they had hallucinations, the peasant was likely to believe in the reality of what he saw, whereas the philosopher would be able to recognize and avoid the delusion. A cultivated and learned mind was thus more able to be preserved from madness, which was here understood as "a disease essentially caused by vitiated will."[83] But the reactions to Cartesianism and to the theology of English religious sects, which all supposedly called for voluntary ignorance, show that madness could be seen as a disease of the mind as early as the mid-seventeenth century, precisely when it was the result of *chosen* ignorance. One should perhaps understand that this conception of madness as a disease of the mind emerged in metaphysical and theological discourses before it did in the medical language. In any case, the idea that ignorance could be actively sought for considerably altered the interpretation of madness, by underlining the role played by the mind and the will ("what the mind did") in what was already perceived as a disease of the mind. The choice of ignorance was a manifestation of madness because it was "an opposition to reason."[84]

CHAPTER 4

Ignorance, Inspiration, and Religious Knowledge

That Ignorance Cannot Lead to Knowledge

Early modern detractors of Cartesianism in England and in France deduced from Descartes's call to divest oneself of all prejudices in order to reach truth that ignorance was supposed to lead directly to knowledge in his philosophy. They argued that if one was to forget everything one knew so as to be able to reach science, then ignorance did not only precede knowledge chronologically, but also was a necessary and logical precondition for the acquisition of knowledge.[1] The paradoxical idea that ignorance could engender science was refuted in seventeenth-century England and France. For example, the polygraph Charles Sorel asserted in *De la perfection de l'homme* (1655) that "ignorance engenders neither science, nor admiration."[2] The aim of the book was to demonstrate that all men were naturally capable of "perfection," and therefore of science and knowledge, and that it was expected of them by philosophers and by God that they seek that perfection.[3] Sorel argued that ignorance was caused by the absence of instruction or by bad teachers, who had themselves been taught inadequately, hence the dissemination of ignorance. For many authors in early modern England and France, instruction was the most efficient cure for ignorance, but it could also have the opposite effect if left to teachers who applied wrong methods or were themselves ignorant. Yet Sorel and others warned that studying on one's own would not make one more learned: masters were needed to cure ignorance.[4]

Against those who (apparently) defended ignorance as a means to science, Sorel argued that it was nothing but an "infertile mother," who could not possibly engender knowledge: "Some Sophists who wished to defend the wrong party and make sure that Ignorance would not be entirely despised, have turned it into a principle of knowledge, as if something could engender its opposite."[5] Sorel explains that the promoters of ignorance in the search for truth (those who belong to "the wrong party") claim that ignorance causes admiration, and admiration is itself the cause of philosophy and knowledge, so that, according to them, an ignorant man or woman is essentially a philosopher. But they forget that "those who are completely ignorant admire nothing, so let us not ask such an infertile Mother as Ignorance to bring us Science."[6] Sorel is here refuting the classical idea that philosophy and knowledge begin with wonder, admiration, or *thaumazein*, a conception expressed in the *Theaetetus* and in Aristotle's *Metaphysics*, and taken up by a number of authors promoting doctrines of ignorance, especially from the learned ignorance tradition.[7] This idea was indeed adapted and used as an argument in favor of "a science of ignorance," for example in Nicholas of Cusa's works, or in Montaigne's essay "*Of the Lame or Cripple*," where he writes: "*Iris* is the daughter of *Thaumantis*. *Admiration is the ground of al Philosophie: Inquisition the progresse: Ignorance the end.* Yea but there is some kinde of ignorance strong and generous, that for honor and courage is nothing beholding to knowledge: An ignorance, which to conceive rightly, there is required no lesse learning, than to conceive true learning."[8] Just before this passage, Montaigne had explained that children should be encouraged to ask questions, not taught how to answer them. Those questions are obviously an admission of ignorance, but as he explains in the quotation, this ignorance is much more commendable than learning, because conceiving it requires as much "science" (the word used in the French text) as does conceiving science itself. Other sixteenth-century authors resorted to the assimilation of admiration and ignorance in more ambiguous texts, where it is not clear whether the aim was to defend or to ridicule ignorance. For example, in his paradoxical *Lode dell'Ignoranza*, Giulio Landi (1498–1579) had used the idea in a burlesque syllogism, whereby he tried to show that ignorance was knowledge: admiration, which Aristotle should have called ignorance, Landi wrote, was the cause of curiosity, and curiosity leads to knowledge, hence ignorance leads to knowledge.[9] Sorel's response to such arguments in defense of ignorance is that a difference should be made between men who are completely ignorant, and therefore in no position to admire anything, and those who claim that they are ignorant while incessantly seeking for knowledge. The former kind of ignorance should be despised, Sorel argues, whereas the latter, also called "learned ignorance" ("Ignorance sçavante"[10]), is a friend of science. This rejection of both ignorance (understood here as mere want of learning that should nevertheless lead to knowledge) and scholastic erudition in Sorel's works echoes the writings of the *libertins érudits*, as well as those of Francis Bacon.

Three decades later in England, the Puritan Richard Baxter also endeavored to refute the idea that ignorance might lead to knowledge, testifying to the persistence of this interpretation of Descartes's philosophy until late in the century. Baxter wrote in his *Treatise of Knowledge and Love Compared* (1689) that Descartes's call for ignorance was inadmissible for two reasons: first, because men know some things *necessarily* and cannot choose to ignore them, even if they want to, and second, because ignorance cannot lead to knowledge, its very opposite. According to Baxter, men should not forgo their previous knowledge because knowledge is what leads to more knowledge, and therefore the acquisition of knowledge cannot be based on ignorance: "Some things, we know *necessarily*, and cannot chuse but know: For the Intellect is not *free* of it self, but only as *quoad exercitium actus*, it is *sub imperio voluntatis*. And it is vain to bid men *not to know* what they cannot chuse but know: And it is vain to tell them that they must suppose (falsly) that they *know not* what they *know*, as a means *to know*. For ignorance is no means to knowledge, but knowledge is: One act of *knowledge* being necessary to more, and therefore not to be denied."[11] Baxter took great care to distinguish his thought from Descartes's philosophy, as if talking about ignorance, more precisely calling for the recognition by men and women of their own ignorance in the late seventeenth century, would inevitably lead the reader to suspect some form of Cartesianism in the text. As the analysis of the association of Cartesianism and Quakerism has shown (as well as Glanvill's interpretation of Descartes's method), the disclaimer was far from superfluous since the notion of ignorance was commonly associated with Descartes's method in seventeenth-century England. If some critics of Descartes's thought believed or feigned to believe that the French philosopher called for ignorance as an end in itself, others, like Baxter, understood that ignorance, for Descartes, was merely a temporary self-induced condition of the mind meant to produce knowledge. But then, as the passage quoted emphasizes, provoking ignorance to get knowledge seemed paradoxical, to say the least. And anyway, Baxter argued, this state of ignorance could not be artificially produced, as men are not able to forget what they know: their intellect will simply not allow it. Besides, it seemed both useless and unsound to contend that ignorance would lead to knowledge or was, as it were, a precondition to knowledge.

With this criticism of Descartes, Baxter was actually trying to demonstrate that he was not a Cartesian himself. The previous quotation was indeed his reply to an objection that he made to his own arguments: "*You talk like a Cartesian that must have all that would know, suppose first that they know nothing, no not that he feeleth and liveth.*"[12] If Baxter deemed it necessary to make a distinction between his ideas and those of Descartes when it came to ignorance, it was mainly because he was aware that some readers might find similitudes between those ideas. Indeed, in his treatise, Baxter warned against "pretended knowledge" or "ignorance of ignorance," and made a plea for the recognition of one's ignorance, arguing that presumption, or ignorance of ignorance, was the main cause of religious divisions: "O happy the World, happy Kingdoms, but most happy the Churches of Christ, if we could possibly bring men but to *know their Ignorance.*"[13] If he did not exactly encourage men to divest themselves of all previous knowledge, Baxter did warn them against vain and corrupted erudition, which led those who possessed it to believe that they knew everything there was to know. Their presumption was an obstacle to their own salvation and to the preservation of the true church, as it brought division and conflict. As a consequence, Baxter asked them to doubt their knowledge and question what they held as undeniable truths, a stance that might have appeared similar to that of Descartes, although Baxter explicitly rejected what he interpreted as Descartes's praise of ignorance.

Given the importance of ignorance in Baxter's works, a short review of his treatment of the notion is here required. Indeed, ignorance is a central theme in Baxter's numerous writings, probably because he thought that lack of religious and classical knowledge was the main cause of division in the church, and in the aftermath of the British Civil Wars, division or factionalism was very much dreaded. Like other defenders of learning, Baxter associated ignorance with barbarism or heresy, arguing that "the ignorantest countreys [were] the most ungodly."[14] He also insisted that ignorance served the devil: "I must confess that *Ignorance* is the great Enemy of Holiness in the world; and the Prince of Darkness, oppugneth the Light, and promoteth the works of Darkness by it."[15] Baxter thought that the devil needed people to remain ignorant so he could secure his power over them. Yet Baxter's conception of the roles of ignorance and knowledge in the Christian's life was complex as he seemed to believe that ignorance was both the worst sin that caused all the other sins and a condition that guaranteed the good Christian's humility and sincerity. In Baxter's writings, indeed, ignorance of ignorance, and the presumption it implied, were harshly criticized, but at the same time, the ignorance, simplicity, and humility of the innocent man and woman were praised.[16]

In *The Saints Everlasting Rest*, an early publication of 1649, Baxter denounces "the Pride of Ignorant Zealots," which leads to "the dissolution of all Churches."[17] He therefore encourages men to become learned, for their own salvation and for the survival of the church. Written when Baxter was very ill and feared for his life, this sermon is actually a guide or a series of advice on the acquisition of knowledge, the only protection against error, addressed to his flocks, and more specifically to those whose "povertie and labors will not give . . . leave to read so much as others may do."[18] Although he was aware of the difficulties met by laborers and poor people in their access to learning, Baxter insisted that there were many sources of knowledge available to all in their search for God, such as books and ministers: even when people had no leisure, Baxter believed, like John Locke for example, that they should find a way to learn the principles of religion because "a willing minde will finde some time."[19]

A few years later, in *The Arrogancy of Reason against Divine Revelations Repressed* (1655), Baxter again emphasized the danger of ignorance for the unity of the church. He denounced the "self-conceited ignorant Souls," who, being unaware of their ignorance, were convinced that what they did not know did not exist: "They are like an ignorant fellow in a Watch-maker shop, that thinks no body can set all the loose peeces together, and make a Watch of them, because he cannot."[20] Because ignorant people are not aware of their own ignorance, they believe that they know all there is to know and deny the existence of anything else: "And this Arrogancy is much increased by the very nature of ignorance, which is, to be even ignorant of it self. He that never saw the light knows not what light is, nor what darkness is as differing from light."[21] Since they have no idea or conception of knowledge, those utterly ignorant men and women cannot realize that they want it. Therefore, making ignorant people aware of their own ignorance is a difficult, if not impossible, task, just as it is impossible to have an enthusiast doubt the self-sufficiency of the internal light. But it should be tried, according to Baxter, because ignorance of ignorance leads to unbelief, doubt, and skepticism, which are great threats to religion.

Baxter came back at length to the danger of "ignorance of ignorance" or "pretended knowledge" as the main cause of division in the church in *A Treatise of Knowledge and Love Compared*, which is entirely devoted to the "calamity" of ignorance.[22] This text, already mentioned, shows the complexity of Baxter's attitude to ignorance and learning, or to inspiration and acquired knowledge, or more precisely, it shows the ambiguity of the meanings given to ignorance and learning.

Ignorance is here condemned when it takes the form of excessive erudition or unawareness of one's ignorance and inspiration, but it is encouraged when it is defined as the opposite of vain learning, and the synonym of innocence and humility. Baxter explains that the reason why ignorance of ignorance is so dangerous is that ignorant people, who, as a rule, are not aware of their own ignorance, are too confident, and therefore prone to judge, based on nothing more than their own erroneous opinions: "I conclude again that this is the Plague and misery of mankind and the cause of all Sin and Shame and Ruines, that *Ignorant unhumbled understandings will be still judging rashly before they have thoroughly tried the case, and will not suspend till they are capable of Judging*, nor be convinced that they know not what they know not, but be confident in their first or ungrounded apprehensions."[23] Perhaps again a reference to Hosea 4.6, this passage underlines that the overconfidence and presumption of ignorant people lead to no less than the destruction or "Ruines" of the church and of mankind because contradictory opinions and judgments are expressed by people who are all convinced that they are right. On the contrary, Baxter advocates caution and suspension of judgment until one has acquired the knowledge needed to be able to pass judgment.

The arrogance of ignorant people is a particularly serious problem, Baxter argues, first because it jeopardizes the unity of the church, and second, because there seems to be no remedy to it, given that ignorant people are not easily made aware of their own ignorance, and therefore will not attempt to cure it, an idea he had already expressed in *The Arrogancy of Reason*: "The first and grand cause is the very Nature of *ignorance* it self; which many ways disableth men, from *knowing* that which should abate their *groundless confidence*. For 1. An ignorant man knoweth but little *parcels* and *scraps* of things: And all the rest is unknown to him: Therefore he fixeth upon that *little* which he *knoweth*, and having no knowledge of the rest, he cannot regulate his narrow apprehensions by any conceptions of them."[24] Like Locke in the *Essay concerning Human Understanding*, published at around the same time as *The Treatise of Knowledge and Love Compared*, Baxter deplores men's tendency to focus on what they know, instead of attempting to span the extent of what they do not know.[25] This attitude reinforces their presumption that they know a lot, whereas they are ignorant, possessing only bits of knowledge. These people are not aware of the fact that this little knowledge is nothing compared to the vast immensity of what they do not know.

Baxter explains that the plague of ignorance in England is mostly due to the inadequate education that children are given: among the "faults of our common learning" are indeed the insistence on words and memory, as well as the teaching of false notions.[26] In a word, ignorance is caused mainly by scholastic methods of teaching and learning. These methods engender the "ignorant-learned crowd" that populates late seventeenth-century England.[27] The growth of ignorance, according to Baxter, is also fueled by the great number of printed books which spread false and arbitrary notions.[28] But as already mentioned, because his criticism of vain and scholastic learning might be interpreted as a rejection of knowledge and a celebration of ignorance, Baxter anticipates and answers objections that would associate him with Descartes and with the papists, more generally. To those who would object that the consequence of his denunciation of vain learning is that men should be kept away from knowledge as papists are by the Roman Church, Baxter replies that he does not encourage men to avoid all learning on the grounds that it might be corrupted, or to renounce using one's reason on the grounds that it can be wrong.[29] By keeping people away from knowledge, the Roman Catholic clergy try only to reinforce their control over them. Baxter insists that he does not "*favour the Popish Doctrine of Ignorance*," nor does he think that all knowledge is corrupted: what he denounces is merely *pretended* knowledge.[30]

Even though he insists on the difficulty of making ignorant people aware of their own ignorance, Baxter provides means to cure ignorance (of ignorance). He shows indeed that ignorance is not a fatality, and that it is not completely impossible for an ignorant man to realize that he does not know:

> But it is not impossible 1. For an *ignorant man* to know that he is ignorant, (nor for a man without light or sight to know that he *seeth* not; though he cannot see that he *seeth* not). For though *Nescience* be *Nothing*; and *Nothing* is not properly and directly an *Object* of our *Knowledge*, no more than of our *Sight*: Yet as we *see* the *limited quantity* of substances, and so know little from big, by concluding that it hath *no more quantity* than we see; so we *know* our *own knowledge*, both as to *Object and Act*, and we know the degree of it, and to what it doth extend: And so can conclude, *I know no more*. And though *Nescience* be nothing, yet this Proposition, [*I know no more*] is not *nothing*. And so *nothing* is usually said to be known *Reductively*; but indeed it is not properly known at all; but this proposition *de nihilo* is known, which is something.[31]

In this important philosophical development, Baxter explains that nescience cannot be known since one cannot know nothing, but a man can know that he does not know more than he actually knows, which is in itself a form of knowledge. Man's sense of proportions or degrees can help him realize that his knowledge is limited and that he could know more. The attitude to knowledge and ignorance that Baxter encourages is thus: "*To know as much as we can; but withal to know how little we know, and to take on us to know no more than we do know, nor to be certain of our uncertainties.*"[32] In other words, men should search for knowledge while always keeping in mind that they are ignorant, whatever the extent of their learning, and they should not try to know what they cannot know or believe that uncertain knowledge is certain.

In Baxter's typology of ignorance, there is a distinction between four categories of people: (1) those who are utterly ignorant, (2) those who have studied a little and thus wrongly believe that they are learned, (3) those who have studied a lot and have turned skeptics, and (4) those who have studied a lot and become learned but nevertheless remain aware of their ignorance. The fourth category is obviously the one that everyone should wish to belong to: "They that study a little, know little, and think they know much: They that study very hard, but not to maturity, oft become Scepticks, and think nothing certain. But they that follow it till they have digested their studies, do find a certainty in the great and necessary things, but confess their ignorance in abundance of things which the presumptuous are confident in."[33] Like Socrates, those who "have digested their studies" know that they are ignorant and that the acquisition of knowledge is a difficult task. But they are not skeptics (or at least not radical skeptics): they know that some knowledge can be had. Baxter insists on this point because he fears that his criticism of scholastic erudition might be interpreted as a promotion of skepticism. Besides, when men realize that what they have been taught is but vain learning, they are likely to doubt or reject *all* knowledge. To avoid this, Baxter recommends reading authors who denounced the corruption of vain learning and promoted true knowledge, such as Cornelius Agrippa (*De vanitate scientiarum*), Francisco Sanches (*Quod nihil scitur*), and Joseph Glanvill (*Scepsis Scientifica*). In these texts, readers are told which learning is uncertain, and they are thus prevented from being led too far into skepticism, Baxter claims.[34] As a matter of fact, although he insistently warns against skepticism, Baxter is pessimistic about men's capacity to cure the plague of ignorance, not only because it is essentially a difficult task, but also because a man who would like to overcome his ignorance has no way of knowing if the teacher he has chosen will guide him toward true knowledge or toward vain learning: "O how much ado have I to keep up from utter despondency under the consciousness of so great ignorance, which no study, no means, no time doth overcome."[35]

His criticism of vain learning and pretended knowledge also led Baxter to argue paradoxically that unlearned simple people were often more likely to reach God than presumptuous scholars. In the second part of his *Treatise of Knowledge and Love Compared*, where he focuses on the relation between knowledge and love mentioned in the title, Baxter argues that knowledge is to be "valued, sought and used," because it makes us "Lovers of God," and in return, we are "known with Love by him."[36] However, Baxter does not merely oppose love and knowledge to hate and ignorance: he admits that some people know God enough to love him, although they remain ignorant. As long as these people are aware of their ignorance, they will be saved. But Baxter goes even further and asserts that their love of God makes those ignorant people wiser and more knowledgeable than learned men: "so he that hath wisdom enough to love God and be saved, shall quickly be in that World of light, where he shall know more than all the Doctors and subtile disputers upon Earth, and more (in a moment) than all the Books of men can teach him, or all their Authors did ever (here) know."[37] The allusion to the immediacy of the knowledge obtained directly from God ("in a moment"), as opposed to the learning of "the Doctors," cannot but call to mind the Quakers' conception of the inner light, and George Keith's example of the woman of Samaria. Although he does not defend the internal presence of Christ, Baxter does argue that knowledge is not necessary to love God, and an ignorant man or woman who loves God sincerely is wiser and more likely to be saved than a scholar. Drawing upon 2 Corinthians 11.3, Baxter opposes the corruption of vain learning to the "simplicity which is in Christ."[38] Baxter also quotes 1 Corinthians 3.18 to show that a man must become a fool (understood here as a man aware of his own ignorance) so that he may be wise: St. Paul does not encourage ignorance per se, but true and profitable learning, or humble and simple knowledge.[39] Humble ignorant people (who do not pretend to be learned) are among the "little ones" whom Christ protects: "But if really you see a poor Neighbour whom you count ignorant, live as one that loveth God and Goodness, take heed that you proudly despise not Christs little ones; but Love and Cherish those sparks that are kindled and Loved by Christ: The *least* are called by Christ, his Brethren, and their interest made as his own."[40] For Baxter, love and ignorance can go together, but only when it is ignorance of unnecessary truths, that is, truths that are not required for salvation. As a consequence, papists or heretics can be saved if they truly love God and hold "the essentials of Christianity," despite their otherwise false opinions.[41] Thus, ideally, for Baxter, men would be learned, yet aware of their inevitable ignorance at the same time. If this form of wisdom, which requires time as well as humility, is not accessible, then it is preferable for men to be totally ignorant, as long as they do not pretend to be learned, the worst condition being that of people who possess vain erudition and assume that they know all there is to know.

Ignorance, Learning, and Knowledge of God

One of the practical consequences of the belief that there was an internal light in man and (for some authors) woman, which enabled them to reach truth without the help of external agents, such as teachers or books, was the idea that religious ministers and preachers did not need to be learned. On the contrary, their learning might even represent an obstacle to their audience's and their own access to God, as it naturally tends to obscure the internal light. Thus, some argued that learning was not a condition of good preaching and that anyone, even the most ignorant woman, could preach, as the example of the woman of Samaria aptly showed. This questioning of the role, the attributes, and even the necessity of ministers led to a debate in mid-seventeenth century England between those who defended the necessity of a learned ministry (mostly members of the Church of England and Presbyterians) and those who argued that learning was not required from a minister and that anyone should be allowed to preach (mostly Quakers and Baptists). If this debate on the role played by learning and ignorance in preaching and access to God arose in England with the emergence of Puritanism in the sixteenth century, it was particularly vivid in the aftermath of the Civil Wars with the spread of sectarianism.

An important early contribution to the debate on a learned ministry was made by the Baptist Samuel How, a cobbler, in *The Sufficiencie of the Spirits Teaching without Humane Learning*, first published in 1639. In this treatise, which ran through at least six editions in the seventeenth century, How insists that Christ himself was unlearned, in the sense that he was never taught anything. Asserting that he had human learning, and therefore that he had been taught, is blasphemy, according to How, as it amounts to questioning the perfection of Christ's manhood.[42] Moreover, Christ chose "*babes and sucklings*" to spread his Word, not learned men, which is proof enough that God wants foolish ministers.[43] Above all, How argues that human learning is superfluous because men are endowed with a "Spirit of God," which gives them all the knowledge that they need. Like all enthusiasts, if one is to adopt Locke's definition of "enthusiasm" given previously, How claims that no evidence of the Spirit of God is needed because it is "*a sufficient witnesse to it selfe.*"[44] It is to be known only by its operations, which are spiritual:

> And so our *learning* comes to us, being taught of the Father, Sonne, and Spirit, for all our Instructers and Councellors, and this is all the *learning* that we need, to know the things that are of *God* by, agreeable to his will: so from these words thus interpreted, the Conclusion comes to this, *That such as are taught by the Spirit of God, destitute of Humane-Learning, are the Learned ones that truly understand the Scriptures according to* Peters *mind.* I say, such as are taught by the Spirit, without *Humane-Learning*, are such persones as rightly understand the Word.[45]

How argues that unlearned men and women—that is, those who are deprived of human learning but taught by the Spirit of God—are those who understand God's

Word. In other words, learning is not sought out: it is spontaneously granted by God through the Spirit. But one understands that there are two different forms of learning in How's discourse: "*Humane-Learning*," or the external erudition of scholars, which he rejects as unnecessary, and the learning of ignorant people, which comes from the teaching of the Spirit of God within. The human learning that How deems superfluous or even harmful is defined as "the knowledge of Arts and Sciences, divers Tongues, and much reading, and a persisting in these things."[46] It is also described as "fleshy and carnal," and it causes vanity, How argues, contrary to knowledge of God through the Spirit.[47] As a consequence, one should "avoyd and beware of Science, that is, all knowledge naturall" (as opposed to knowledge spiritual), because this learning does not perfect men and women, it is of no use in understanding the Gospel, and it leads them to err from their faith.[48]

This is why, following the apostle (1 Corinthians 3.18), How urges men and women to make themselves fools so that they may be wise. This implies awareness of the limits of external, acquired knowledge: "Now what is more foolish to a man then to know that there is nothing that all the wits of man can reach unto, that can benefit him: and if nothing, then not this thing in question, but that it must needs be that we must be fooles to it."[49] Foolishness, or recognition that human learning is detrimental to one's access to God, is knowledge, and this is what leads one to the love of God. So as to make oneself a fool, one must become ignorant, and How argues: "and what is the true marke of a foole but to be ignorant, and without knowledge, therefore we call them fooles in the world, and so is it here: the best way for a man not to deceive himselfe, is to know nothing of this *learning*, nor any other fleshly excellencie that so he may learn true *wisdom*."[50] That God wants men and women to be ignorant is confirmed by the fact that the Gospel itself is "simplicity" and "foolishness," therefore there should be only foolish, or ignorant, ministers in the Church of Christ.[51] Indeed, the demonstration of the superiority of ignorance applies to all believers, including ministers, and it implies that any man who has the Spirit of God, regardless of his social status, can preach: "if a Man have the *Spirit of God*, though he be a *Pedler*, *Tinker*, *Chimneysweeper*, or COBLER, he may be the helpe of *Gods spirit*, give a more *publique interpretation*, than they all."[52]

The social consequences of the promotion of ignorance in one's access to God were found in other Baptist texts of the period, such as Thomas Collier's *The Pulpit-Guard Routed* (1651), a reply to Presbyterian Thomas Hall's *The Pulpit Guarded* (1650), which argued against lay preaching. In his text, Collier (d. 1691) defended the ability of "men of Callings" ("a *Nailer*, a *Baker*, a *Plough-right*, a

Weaver, and a *Bokers-boy*"⁵³) to preach the Gospel and be ministers of God. Indeed, those who want learning "have more natural Philosophy, Logick, Rhetorick in their heads," thanks to the Spirit of the Lord, than learned men, Collier argued (although he also condemned the Quakers, whose "light within" led to disregard of the Scriptures).⁵⁴ Ironically, Collier denounced the ignorance of those who claimed that ministers should be learned, accusing them of not knowing that there were many examples of unlearned ministers in the Scriptures.⁵⁵

In his study of the literature and language of English radical religion between 1640 and 1660, Nigel Smith has insisted on the essential role of "lay 'mechanic preachers'" like Samuel How in denouncing the inadequate education of the clergy, and claiming personal inspiration instead. Interestingly, Smith stresses the influence of "continental mystical and spiritual works," especially those of Nicholas of Cusa, on the discourse and thought of those radical preachers and writers, who were not put off by the Catholicism of those mystical texts. Nor should this influence sound surprising or paradoxical. As seen earlier, Francis Bacon also expressed his admiration for Jesuit education and learning. Radical preachers and writers merely ignored what they perceived as the dogmatic parts in the writings of Catholic authors and retained the reflection on personal inspiration and illumination, which appealed to them—Cusanus's works could easily be adapted and appropriated. As Smith underlines, radical religious networks played a great part in the dissemination of those continental mystical works in mid-seventeenth-century England: they were translated into English by John Everard and Giles Randall, among others, and made available by publishers who were themselves radicals or had close links with radical networks.⁵⁶ Moreover, Thomas Wilson Hayes has argued that some features of Cusanus's works, especially the character of the Idiot, represented the "democratization of learning" that was occurring in the mid-seventeenth century as vernacular literacy gained momentum. Thus, according to Hayes, the translation of the cardinal's works by English religious radicals was part of the effort to promote popular literacy. Everard, for example, believed that those works "would help liberate working people from the intellectual hegemony of university-trained bishops, ministers, and lawyers."⁵⁷ Here again, what appears is that the reflection on ignorance and its role in intellectual "systems" was also steeped in social considerations. Indeed, mid-seventeenth-century English religious radicals were probably sincere in their belief that ignorance gave the surest access to God, but their celebration of ignorance was also a way to make social claims. In other words, the role of ignorance in their thought ensured the coherence of their religious and social stance.

Conversely, defenders of a learned ministry in the English Church warned against the enthusiasm of those who claimed a special gift or inspiration as the only condition of good preaching. A particularly interesting example, in the context of the new English republic, is that of Bishop Gauden, whose book *Hieraspistes* (1653) was meant as a systematic defense of the Church of England ministry, as the subtitle clearly indicates: *A Defence by Way of Apology for the Ministry and Ministers of the Church of England.* This text gives most of the arguments against ignorance and in favor of learning that were also found in other treatises of the time. Gauden first argues, like Baxter, that it is the devil's plan to have all men become fools, so as to ensure that they remain unaware of his evil doings: "How willing is he [the devil] to have all men as ignorant, weak, and unlearned, as these *Objectives* are, that so none might discern his *snares*, and gins, of which these *Ignato's* are to be his setters."[58] The devil, who caused the first sin, continues to encourage ignorance in order to jeopardize the establishment of reformed churches.[59] By promoting ignorance, he takes away the best weapon and defense against heresy and wrong doctrines: learning.[60] An important argument in favor of a learned ministry was indeed the necessity to have intellectual weapons that would help win the "warre in Christian Religion,"[61] in the context of the post-Reformation. Gauden admits that there are learned Jesuits, Papists, Socinians, Pelagians, and so on, and thus, for Church of England ministers to be able to defend their religion and measure up to their opponents, learning is needed. Being learned is also a way to honor one's adversaries, as well as the Christian religion itself, Gauden argues. If all are learned, the debates can remain fair and civil, even though Church of England ministers obviously need to be more learned than their opponents if they are to win the religious fight: "It would ill become us while we see the adverse partie *daily arming* themselves, with all possible *compleatnesse*, in languages, arts, and sciences, in Fathers, councels, and histories, for us to sit still on our *lazy*, and *unlearned ignorance*: expecting either *miraculous illuminations* and *assistances*, (as idle, vain, and proud mindes do) or else, most *inevitable ruine*, and certain overthrow of that truth and reformed Religion, which we professe to maintain."[62] Here again, as in the criticism of Descartes and the Quakers, ignorance is presented as a symptom of laziness and vanity, and not as a principle of knowledge or the condition of the internal light or spirit, which is derogatorily described in this passage as one of the "*miraculous illuminations* and *assistances*." Gauden may also implicitly be referring here to Hosea 4.6, where ignorance is said to lead to destruction ("My people are destroyed for lacke of knowledge"). Ignorance in the Church of England would lead to no less than the destruction of the reformed religion, according to Gauden, since unlearned ministers would appear unarmed in the fight against learned religious adversaries. Moreover, the future bishop argues that the church had been ignorant for many centuries, until the onset of the Reformation, and that long reign of ignorance brought nothing but "barbarity" and superstition. In other words, religious ignorance was already tried in the church, and the results were not satisfactory, as the degenerate state of the Roman Church demonstrates.[63]

In *Hieraspistes*, the detractors of the Church of England are mocked as silly asses:

> And what is it that these mens *brutish simplicity* would have? Namely this: That the *purer Religion* among the *Protestant and Reformed Churches*, should have no *learned Champions*, or able *defenders*; but onely such silly *Asinellos*, or *Massinellos*, who think it enough to trust to their rude and irrationall confidences; to their *hard heels*, and *harsher brayings*, for the defence of true *Religion*, when as the *large and luculent* eares of these animals doe give so great advantage to any crafty error, or grosser heresie to get hold of them, that they will as easily be led to any *damnable opinion*, and desperate faction, as an *Oxe is to the slaughter*, and a *fool to the stocks*.[64]

In this passage, Gauden ridicules the stupidity of the defenders of ignorance and inspiration in the church. They are given the characteristics of the ass, such as silliness and simplicity, but they are also given more general characteristics of animals, namely brutishness and irrationality. These flaws lead Gauden's enemies to believe anything, he argues, and therefore fall into error and heresy. On a more serious tone, they are also accused of being a threat to the order of the country, through the association of "Asinellos" and "Massinellos," the latter being probably a reference to Tomaso Aniello (1620–1647), also called Masaniello, an Italian fisherman who had been the leader of the rebellion against the rule of Spain at Naples in 1647. The revolt of Naples inspired several publications throughout Europe soon after it occurred, and especially in England, where Masaniello embodied both a popular hero, and the political and social danger posed by the illiterate masses.[65]

In keeping with their brutishness, the "faction" of "*Antiministeriall adversaries*" want civility and politeness, Gauden argues. Appropriating analogies that were common at the time, he explicitly associates learning with virtue and civilization, and ignorance with immorality and barbarism:

> We finde, by daily experience, that the *unlearned sort* are either grosse, dull, and very *inducible*; or else they are rough, impolished and *insolent*, prone to a *rustick impudence*, and clownish *untractablenesse*. . . . Nothing is sacred, nothing is civill among those, that carry all by ignorant confidence and *brutish strength*; we see in those of the *Antiministeriall faction*, that by want of learning (whereof they are generally guilty) men onely learn this *Indian* or *Turkish* quality, to hate, contemne and seek to destroy all good learning, which is nothing else, but the good husbandry and great *improvement of the reasonable soule* in it self to God and to others.[66]

In another similar passage from *Hieraspistes*, Gauden adds that ignorant men are violent: because they cannot argue, being unable to use their reason, they necessarily resort to violence as their only weapon.[67] The association of learning with civilization and Christianity, and ignorance with barbarism and the Muslim religion, found in the previous passage, was common in the debate on a learned ministry, as well as, more generally, in defenses of learning. It was also found in the 1660s, for example, in Meric Casaubon's letter on general learning, already mentioned, in which he defends the Church of England against "fanatics" who would have only one book left, the Bible: "when all light of Historie, sciences, & languages, by which the credit of the Scriptures & Christian religion hath beene by learned men soe happily upheld, against all human forgeries & delusions, is taken away, (which God forbid should ever happen) there will be but little difference between the *Bible*, & the *Alcoran*."[68] By encouraging ignorance, fanaticism might lead to a situation in which the difference between truth and error, or between the true religion and heresy, is no longer clear.

Ignorance leads to barbarism, Gauden argues, because unlearned men, who despise learning, also despise reason, which is God's gift and what makes men human (an argument also found in Casaubon's *Treatise concerning Enthusiasme*,[69] where reason and knowledge are associated): "The *despisers of good learning* are not onely *spitefull enemies* to the Christian reformed Religion (whose *perfection* disdaineth not to use those good *gifts*, which come from the *Father of lights*, (any more than a *gracious soul* doth its eyes, and other senses of the body:) but they are also *silly abusers* and degraders even of *humane nature*, whose *divine excellencie, Reason*, no man above the degree of *brutish stupidity, Bedlam madnesse*, or *divellish envy*, ever sought to deprave, or depresse."[70] Throughout the text, Gauden takes the association of reason and learning or knowledge for granted. This is based on the common assumption—also linked to the association of ignorance with barbarism and brutishness mentioned above—that ignorance is characteristic of animals, whereas humankind is endowed with reason, and therefore the possibility of knowledge: thus, ignorant people "*degenerate* to *brutish sensualities*" and give preeminence to the body over reason.[71] While Samuel How accused learning of being "fleshy and carnal," those characteristics are here applied to ignorance by Gauden, who argues that refusing knowledge means refusing to acknowledge the presence of reason in man and choosing to live like an animal. This is why, by rejecting learning in the church, "antiministerial" factions also degrade human nature itself. On the contrary, learning cultivates and nourishes the "*innate vertues and properties* of mans nature (*Reason*, and *Religion*)."[72]

Moreover, in several passages from his defense of the Church of England ministry, Gauden remarks on the laziness of the advocates of ignorance, who merely save themselves the effort to acquire learning, an accusation that was often made against enthusiasts and Cartesians, as was seen earlier (for example, in Locke's *Essay concerning Human Understanding*). Positing inspiration, or the internal light, as an immediate and spontaneous access to God, exempts one from studying, and justifies idleness:

> For what would not these *Illiterate Furies* give to have indeed, *such an Inspiration*, as might in one night make them every way as learned and able in all points, as those *Ministers* and other men have been and still are, who daily *pare* the ruder *nails*, and *muzzle* the *bolder jaws* of these degenerate and desperate men; who like *horse and mule*, being without understanding, are ready to fall upon those, that are fit to be their *Masters and rulers*, both in Church and State; who in stead of sound and healthfull learning have only the three distempers which Sir *Francis Bacon* observed to be in most men; Fantasticknesse, Contention, and Curiosity, by imagination, altercation, and affectation.[73]

Here again, Gauden compares ignorant people to animals ("horse and mule") lacking reason and understanding. He also insists on the social and intellectual hierarchy between learned and ignorant men, the former being the "masters and rulers," precisely on account of their learning. Thus, learning does not only render one able to preach, it brings to those who possess it a social and intellectual superiority over those who do not. Finally, Gauden borrows from Francis Bacon's own defense of learning to show that enthusiasts are unable to correct their mental disorders, "Fantasticknesse, Contention, and Curiosity," which were presented by the Chancellor as the three distempers of learning.[74] The reference to the *Advancement of Learning* in a defense of a learned ministry against claims of ignorance and inspiration tends to show that Bacon's work was indeed read along the seventeenth century primarily as a refutation of doctrines of ignorance, as was argued in part 1.

As a consequence, "*good learning*" must be encouraged in ministers so that they might be able to defend the reformed church and the true religion. But according to Gauden, learning is not only a weapon in the religious wars; it is also the best way to worship God and to reach happiness on earth, as well as salvation: "[Learning is] a *grand Magazine*, and Catholick *Storehouse* of all divine and intellectuall excellencies, affording to all men, upon all occasions, happy advantages, by which to glorifie the wise and *admirable Creator*, and also to furnish both a mans self & others with what may most conduce to his temporall and eternall felicity."[75] For Gauden, "good learning" is not only *religious* learning, and it can be had from different sources. The knowledge ministers must have is defined by

Gauden as "all *Truths*, both humane and divine, naturall, politick, morall and Theologicall; usefull either for *speculation*, or practice," as well as knowledge of grammar and orthography, and skill in the languages, which are essential to understand and interpret the Scriptures.[76] The learning required of a minister, according to Gauden, is thus particularly broad and touches on almost all fields of knowledge. Those expectations were shared by most defenders of a learned ministry in the 1650s. William Gearing, for example, also believed that a good minister should be learned in natural philosophy and astronomy, cosmography, geography, typography, logic, and history.[77] Gearing argued that this learning was "very useful and necessary to a Minister of the Gospel" if he was to interpret the Scriptures. This was actually a major argument in favor of a learned ministry: learning was required to give a correct interpretation of the Scriptures and avoid "*damnable errors.*"[78]

Gauden admits that too much learning can be harmful to religion. But it does not mean that it should be abandoned altogether: "no more may the *abuse of learning* take away the *use of it.*"[79] Indeed, learning is like the "light of the world," but it must be guided. Human reason can help find and keep "the middle way" between enthusiasm or the celebration of ignorance, on the one hand, and excessive learning or vain erudition, on the other.[80] Another danger is to be neither utterly ignorant nor perfectly learned, and to be kept "on the shore of ignorance, or but on the borders of knowledge."[81] This category of people, who take learning as a mistress, and not as a wife, as Gauden puts it, echoes Montaigne's "mongrell sorte of husband-men," this mixed breed of people who are no longer ignorant, yet still not wise, and who, in their unstable condition, are "dangerous, peevish, foolish, and importunate, & they which trouble the world most." But contrary to Montaigne, Gauden does not encourage men to come back to simple ignorance, neither does he praise the simplicity or the "*Abecedarie* ignorance" of the peasant or artisan,[82] even though he insists that he does not despise the humble illiterate Christians who do not enjoy the leisure necessary to acquire learning.[83] However, these concessions and nuances do not contradict Gauden's general argument presented earlier: there is no doubt for him that learning is expected from all Christians, and more particularly from ministers of the church.

The controversy over the ignorance of the clergy, which prompted the publication of Gauden's *Hieraspistes*, was revived in the early 1660s in England, in a different religious and political context. Interestingly enough, this later controversy revived the allegory of the ass to denounce the English ministry's ignorance. In 1661, Lewis Griffin (on whom there seems to be no biographical information) first published *The Doctrine of the Asse*, listing the rules that should guide the good Christian. The book starts with a praise of the ass that underlines his noble functions in the Bible: "Remember (I beseech thee) that however contemptible the *Asse* is in this *age*, yet in the days of the Prophet *Isaiah* he was a great *Rabbi* in *Israel*: insomuch that *Heaven* and *Earth* were called to witness how far he excelled the very *people of God* in Knowledge."[84] But then, in *The Asses Complaint against Balaam*, included in the work, Griffin explicitly denounces the ignorance of the ministers of the church. By resorting to the topos of the ass, Griffin probably wished to insist on the wisdom and modesty that the ministers of his time wanted, as well as on their lack of classical learning. Contrary to the paradoxical uses of the ass in the "discourse against letters," where his very ignorance made him of superior wisdom, Griffin's reference to the ass is not aimed at celebrating ignorance: he makes a clear distinction between favorable depictions of the ass in the Bible and his condemnable ignorance. As he had anticipated, Griffin was harshly mocked for his use of the topos of the ass, which launched a "controversy of the ass" through a whole series of responses published in the early 1660s.[85]

Ignorance and Damnation

Finally, the interpretation of ignorance as inspiration is explicitly addressed in John Bunyan's *The Pilgrim's Progress* (1678), which features an interesting and puzzling character called Ignorance. The contention here is that, in this book, Bunyan precisely assesses the idea that ignorance might be equated with a direct access to God through the internal light, or some form of inspiration. The severe punishment of Ignorance at the very end of the book offers an irrevocable answer: ignorance is not a form of inspiration, but rather the erroneous belief that one is absolutely right, beyond a doubt.

Introduced as "a very brisk Lad," who comes out of the country of conceits, Ignorance is an intriguing character and "a particularly troubling case" in *The Pilgrim's Progress*.[86] While he is heading toward the celestial city, he announces to Christian and Hopeful, whom he meets on the way, that he has nothing to show at the gate, only the knowledge of his Lord's will. Besides, he did not come through the wicket gate like them, but through a "crooked lane," presented as an easier and shorter route. Yet he insists that he has always had the behavior expected from a good Christian—praying, fasting, paying the tithes, and giving alms—and he is convinced that this will be enough to open the gate to heaven.[87] Christian doubts that Ignorance will be admitted into the celestial city when the time comes, but Ignorance brushes his objections aside and replies that he has followed his own path or religion, which is admittedly different from Christian's, but he believes that he will be saved nonetheless because he has faith and obeys Christ's law.[88] Judging that the man is "wise in his own Conceits" and worse than a fool, Christian and Hopeful leave him, and decide to meet him again later and see whether he is then more inclined to listen to them.[89]

When they meet again, Ignorance walks some distance behind them, and when asked why, replies that he prefers to be alone, to ponder upon God and heaven—his predilection for solitude is indeed often mentioned throughout the text.[90] In his short conversation with Christian and Hopeful at this stage, he explains that what he knows, he knows from his heart, and his heart is good.[91] This is his answer to most of the questions that Christian asks him: in other words, Ignorance has no knowledge of anything, apart from knowledge of God, which is spontaneously present in his heart, and which he deems sufficient for his salvation. When he has left them again, Christian and Hopeful talk about Ignorance's condition and wonder whether he sometimes has "convictions of sin" and thus realizes that he might not be saved. About ignorant people in general, Christian says: "*Then I say sometimes (as I think) they may, but they being naturally ignorant, understand not that such convictions tend to their good; and therefore they do desperately seek to stifle them, and presumptuously continue to flatter themselves in the way of their own hearts.*"[92] Christian explains that ignorant people do not realize that convictions of sin are not an obstacle to their salvation, but rather an assistance. Instead, they are convinced of their behaving as God wishes, and of acting in keeping with His Word, and therefore cannot be brought to realize that they are wrong. As Christian's comment implies, this presumption is both a consequence of their natural ignorance and a decision or act of the will since they *choose* not to question or doubt their own goodness.

According to Christian, the main danger is that ignorant people have no fear, whereas "the fear of the Lord is the beginning of wisdom" (Proverbs 9.10). Christian adds that ignorant people think that fear is caused by the devil, who thus tries to undermine their faith, and therefore, by resisting fear, they believe that they resist evil and protect their faith. They also want to preserve their "self-holiness," which might be jeopardized if they accepted fear. But most importantly, the consequence of this absence of fear is that ignorant people become presumptuous and self-confident,[93] an attitude that was also strongly criticized by Richard Baxter, as shown earlier. As a matter of fact, it can be argued that the ignorant people represented by Ignorance in *The Pilgrim's Progress* are the same as the "ignorant zealots" denounced by Baxter in *A Treatise of Knowledge and Love*

Compared, who are not aware of their own ignorance and who are therefore convinced that they are always in the right.

Ignorance eventually reaches the gates of heaven without difficulties, as again, he takes a shorter and easier route than the one followed by Christian and Hopeful. Besides, he receives the help of Vain-Hope, a ferryman, to cross the River of Death: the allusion to vanity here again reinforces the idea that Ignorance is but a presumptuous zealot with pretended knowledge. Ignorance then arrives alone at the gates of heaven and knocks, assuming, as he has all along, that he will be admitted without difficulty or delay. But instead, he is asked for a certificate, looks for it, and is unable to provide it, since he never possessed one, as he had admitted to Christian and Hopeful earlier in the book, claiming that his good behavior would be sufficient to have him accepted into heaven. Ignorance does not even try to justify himself or explain why he does not have the certificate: he "answered never a word."[94] His hands and feet are then tied, and he is taken to another gate, which is a way to hell. Immediately after the scene in which Ignorance is sent to hell, the narrator awakes, so that the whole book and the whole pilgrimage end on the image of the damnation of Ignorance.

As Anne Dunan-Page has shown, Ignorance is probably "the character who has attracted the most commentaries, other than Christian himself."[95] This may be due to the reader's mixed feelings upon discovering Ignorance's fate at the end of the book. Since the character reappears several times and makes it until the end of the pilgrimage, contrary to other characters whom Christian and Hopeful meet on their way, the reader progressively comes to expect Ignorance to be saved, or in any case, treated less harshly than he actually is. Besides, Ignorance is presented as a harmless and, to a certain extent, innocent character (after all, he is said to be "naturally ignorant"), who does not try to impose his ways on others and who generally keeps to himself, so that he does not seem to be particularly evil. As Vincent Newey has put it, readers inevitably feel "sympathy for Ignorance's misunderstanding of the words above the Gate, his misconceived hope, his fumbling helplessness,"[96] and they recognize their own shortcomings in his errors and vulnerability. Ignorance's damnation thus comes as a surprise, if not a shock. Admittedly, as Thomas Luxon has argued, Ignorance "never believed sufficiently in the invisible things," and he represents the flesh, or Christian's and Hopeful's "sinful carnality,"[97] which accounts for his damnation. More convincingly perhaps, Luxon contends that there are two kinds of ignorance in *The Pilgrim's Progress*: the ignorance of Ignorance, who does not know that he does not know, hence his self-confidence, and that of Christian and Hopeful, who are strongly aware of their ignorance, hence their fear.[98] Ignorance is given the chance to repent twice, become aware of his own ignorance, and turn it into some form of humble piety, but he refuses to be enlightened, which reinforces the idea that his ignorance is not merely natural, but also chosen, and therefore a sin.[99]

Another reason Ignorance has drawn so much attention is the difficulty of determining with any certainty whom exactly he personifies. Scholars have generally assumed that Bunyan had a specific religious group in mind when he drew the portrait of Ignorance, who has thus been interpreted, for example, as "a disciple of Natural Religion" (by John Draper), as a Latitudinarian (by Henri A. Talon), as a Quaker (by Richard Hardin, who sees in Ignorance "the same unwavering self-confidence that is found in George Fox"), and even as a "sophisticated Boy Scout" (by James Forrest).[100] John Stachniewski has argued that Ignorance "obeys Anglican imperatives" (e.g., praying, fasting, paying the tithes) but "lacks a continuous sense of himself,"[101] as is evidenced by the fact that he cannot describe his own spiritual experience, contrary to Christian and Hopeful. The difficulty of interpreting those allegories, especially in the case of Ignorance, is reinforced by the fact that assigning a clear religious affiliation to Bunyan himself is problematic. He was probably perceived by his contemporaries as "an extreme Anabaptist," and he himself was accused of being ignorant and fanatical, for example, in 1672, in the context of the controversy on baptism, when the anonymous author of *Dirt Wip't Off* mocked his "Ignorant Fanatic Zeal."[102] The common use of ignorance as an insult in the religious strife further complicates the interpretation of its uses and meanings. Yet it seems safe to argue that Bunyan did not have one specific religious group in mind when he portrayed Ignorance, but rather targeted all those who presumptuously claimed that they held the one right doctrine. Their overconfidence and inner conviction that they would be saved was a consequence of their remaining unaware of their ignorance. James Forrest is thus probably right when he states: "The fault of which Ignorance conclusively proves himself guilty is not confined to Latitudinarians or Quakers, though admittedly on a sectarian view these souls are more in jeopardy than others; it is rather a sin so potentially universal and grievous that even the sanctified pilgrims, and particularly Christian, could only be forgiven for it."[103] Bunyan merely intended to warn the reader to fear God and never take salvation for granted. Good behavior is not sufficient to be saved: doubt and awe are also expected from the good Christian. If the punishment of Ignorance might be interpreted as a defense of religious learning,[104] it is also, and more importantly, a plea in favor of fear and doubt, as well as a strong criticism of pretended knowledge, or "ignorance of ignorance." Ignorance's fate in *The Pilgrim's Progress* underlines the fact that ignorance for Bunyan should not be mistaken for inspiration. The ignorant man has no way of realizing that he is wrong, precisely because he is ignorant, and ignorance, or rather ignorance of ignorance in this case, inevitably leads to the belief that one is absolutely right. As a consequence, the ignorant man cannot be persuaded out of the belief that he is inspired and has spontaneous knowledge of God.

As appeared several times throughout this part, the main difficulty in interpreting the relation between ignorance and different forms of access to truth, such as the internal light, often lies in the ambiguity of the meanings attributed to the notion of ignorance by those who used it, either to defend it or to condemn it. In the early modern period, the very same word could indeed refer to mere lack of knowledge, whether it was recognized or not by the ignorant man or woman, or to an excess of learning, likely to engender self-confidence and presumption. *Ignorance* could thus mean one thing and its opposite, and those who used the word did not necessarily define it, perhaps considering that the sense of such a common notion was obvious to all. As a consequence, depending on the meaning it was given in a religious context, ignorance could be the worst sin or the safest guarantee of salvation.

With the Reformation and the emergence of radical religious groups that claimed inspiration, the subject of ignorance became central in England, where it was also deemed to be at the heart of Descartes's philosophy. A future bishop of the Church of England, John Gauden strongly defended learning against the promoters of the inner light—and ignorance—as the safest way to knowledge of God. Quakers and Baptists rejected with equal force the idea that learning gave access to God and instead praised a form of ignorance and reliance on the inner light, or the wisdom of the fool. Finally, Puritans like Richard Baxter and John Bunyan took presumptuous knowledge or ignorance as inspiration as one of the most serious threats to religion and social order, and they recommended as an antidote, not exactly learning per se, but recognition of one's ignorance. In their criticisms of ignorance, John Gauden and Richard Baxter, and to a certain extent, John Bunyan as well, voiced a common concern that doctrines of ignorance, sometimes borrowed from the continental traditions studied in part 1, might be spreading in England, and they obviously feared that this rehabilitation of ignorance might discredit all learning. In this context, those doctrines were not interpreted as expressions of "mitigated" or acceptable skepticism, but as celebrations of ignorance here understood as a legitimate—though paradoxical—principle of knowledge.

The last part of this book examines the third main function attributed to ignorance in the seventeenth century: its use as an epistemological instrument in the methods of the nascent sciences. Its purpose is to assess the extent to which the conceptions of ignorance previously studied, and the reflection on its role in the acquisition of divine and natural knowledge analyzed in the first two parts of this book, served as the basis for the recognition of the use and value of ignorance in science under certain conditions and in specific contexts. The contention here is that even though ignorance (in science) was not praised as such, that is, as a personal quality or attribute that should be fostered, it could be seen as an epistemological instrument and a legitimate object of the scientific discourse. In other words, in England and in France during the seventeenth century, ignorance was progressively no longer defined as what science should be built against, or what it should strive to erase, but as a limit of the understanding that one needed to admit into scientific discourses and methodologies to build the new science. The introduction of ignorance into the scientific discourse seems to imply, as a corollary or as a cause, a secularization of ignorance. Yet the analysis of ignorance as an epistemological instrument presented in part 3 shows that this function remained deeply rooted in the religious and mystical interpretations of the notion.

Part III

IGNORANCE AS AN EPISTEMOLOGICAL INSTRUMENT

If ignorance was perceived as a form of wisdom and as a principle of knowledge in the early modern period, it could also be used as a tool to promote the advancement of science. In this case, ignorance was understood as a legitimate object of the scientific discourse. It is here argued that this conception was the result of the philosophical and theological debates about the dialectic of ignorance and knowledge presented in foregoing chapters. More precisely, ignorance is here interpreted as an epistemological instrument that can help the natural philosopher encompass the real nature of human understanding: through fictions, myths, or personae featuring ignorant men and women, natural philosophers could imagine and convey a representation of the naked mind that would enable them to grasp the mechanisms of the understanding, the process whereby it acquires knowledge, and how it discovers and invents. Only when it was divested of all acquired knowledge could the understanding reveal its workings. Accordingly, the process whereby an ignorant man or woman made a discovery by chance was observed by natural philosophers, who could then try and reproduce the conditions in which the discovery was made. Finally, a study of John Locke's philosophy and epistemology is here proposed as it is arguably the most relevant illustration of ignorance being introduced into the scientific discourse of the late seventeenth century.

The epistemological role of ignorance is first evidenced in the different myths of the blank slate, that is, forms of complete ignorance imagined by the philosophers of the time in England and in France. They used fictions of ignorance or representations of an ignorant man's understanding to assess its nature, qualities, and limits, as well as the process through which it discovers the truth and acquires or produces knowledge. By imagining a blank understanding or naked mind, ignorant of all forms of knowledge, natural philosophers could indeed get an image of this faculty. This led to a renewed interest in the tabula rasa, as well as a focus on autodidacticism, as the perfect illustrations of the process whereby the understanding progressively acquires and produces knowledge. The "conceptual persona" of the Idiot,[1] as well as the social persona of the artisan, were depicted as models of the natural philosopher in England and in France. It was believed that, thanks to their ignorance of classical learning, those personae knew how to observe nature better than scholars. In this context, complete ignorance was thus used as a fiction to get an accurate representation of the understanding in its purest form, prior to the acquisition of knowledge, which enabled philosophers to grasp its mechanisms and thus improve the methodologies of discovery. This use of ignorance is different from that propounded by Descartes in the *Discourse on Method*, as it does not encourage the searchers of truth to make themselves ignorant, even temporarily. Neither does it necessarily imply that ignorance, or awareness of one's ignorance, is knowledge, as in the Cusan-Socratic tradition.

As a matter of fact, the rejection of learned ignorance, or at least the indifference to the Cusan doctrine of ignorance among seventeenth-century English experimentalists, might seem all the more surprising when one examines Cusanus's persona of the Idiot, for whom experimentation was the way to natural knowledge and who could easily be seen as a perfect illustration of the experimental philosopher. The fourth dialogue of *De idiota*, on "statick Experiments," might even be read as the very manifesto of experimentalism, in which the Idiot shows his exceptional skill for observing the natural world. The translation of Cusanus's dialogue into English and its publication in London in 1650 seem to point to an interest in England in the themes of the book, but there is not much evidence of this interest in the works of English experimentalists themselves, whereas it was, as is argued here, the model for Descartes's dialogue *The Search after Truth*.

This part also focuses on another "fiction of ignorance" or manifestation of ignorance in science: the myth of the uneducated inventor. It shows that discoveries made by chance were often attributed to illiterate and obscure figures, who were supposed to have accidentally stumbled upon something new and important while they were merely attending to their own affairs. The question that this myth of the illiterate inventor raises is, Were ignorant men and women attributed specific qualities that made them more likely (than learned men) to make important discoveries by chance? The fact that the discovery was made by an ignorant person admittedly reinforced the unexpectedness of such discoveries, and this might have been the main purpose of insisting on the illiterateness of the discoverer. But this part argues that, in this case, ignorance implied an important quality, which played an essential role in both Descartes's and Bacon's philosophies, namely sagacity, the natural knowledge, or proximity with nature typical of ignorant people. This part thus contends that chance discoveries made by ignorant people became a model of scientific discovery, meaning that natural philosophers tried to understand and even reproduce—artificially, as it were—the natural and spontaneous process whereby these discoveries occurred. Indeed, it is argued that ways were devised to allow for the introduction of ignorance and chance in the highly regulated process of scientific discovery.

Finally, the epistemological use of ignorance in John Locke's works is presented. It is argued here that his conception of ignorance, while building on previous doctrines (presented in parts 1 and 2), represented a paradigmatic shift in the history of science. His interpretation of ignorance in relation with notions like enthusiasm has already been tackled above, showing that he did contribute to the debates on doctrines of ignorance, but this part emphasizes on the extensive treatment of ignorance in his works. Like other philosophers, Locke resorted to fictions of ignorance in order to conjure up images of the understanding, and he was indeed particularly interested in the tabula rasa and autodidacticism, but the contention here is that the notion of ignorance actually played a crucial role in Locke's philosophical, political, and social thought, a role that has been underestimated so far.

CHAPTER 5

Fictions of Ignorance

The Tabula Rasa and Autodidacticism

The concept of the tabula rasa holds that human understanding should be conceived as a blank paper or an "empty tablet" on which knowledge is progressively inscribed through observation and experience.[1] If this concept was often used in the seventeenth century as a refutation of Cartesian innate principles, it insisted, not unlike Descartes in *Discourse on Method*, for example, on the necessity to come back to the purity of the mind and divest it of all prejudices and false knowledge so as to understand how the mind works when it is not burdened with useless information or stifled by memory. This operation could also help determine how "good" knowledge should be acquired. As a matter of fact, Cornelius Agrippa himself had claimed that ignorant people were superior to scholars because their hearts were purer and because their minds were a tabula rasa, by which he meant that, being ignorant, they were free from the corruption of the sciences. In chapter 101 of *De incertitudine*, Agrippa explicitly describes the mind of the ignorant people he praises, and whom Christ chose as the recipients of his message, as a tabula rasa, in the original Latin edition.[2] Interestingly enough, the expression was faithfully translated into French by Turquet de Mayerne as "un beau papier blanc, auquel n'a encor esté escrit aucune chose des traditions humaines,"[3] while the English versions of the text had this reference to the tabula rasa altogether disappear from the book. The sixteenth-century English translations replaced the reference to ignorant people's minds as a tabula rasa with the idea that they were "peacemakers, not followers of other men, to the intent to learne,"[4] so that the passage insisted more on the ignorant people's desire to learn than on their absence of learning, although it was the very focus of the original text.

The early modern philosopher most commonly associated with the concept of the tabula rasa is evidently John Locke. At the beginning of book II of the *Essay concerning Human Understanding*, Locke assumes that the mind is like "white paper" in order to explain that knowledge comes from experience and not from innate ideas: "Let us then suppose the Mind to be, as we say, white Paper, void of all Characters, without any *Ideas*; How comes it to be furnished? . . . To this I answer, in one word, From *Experience*."[5] In the *Essay*, Locke takes great pains to refute the theories of innate principles, which held that man is born with mathematical notions, eternal truths, and the idea of God, and which were widely shared at the time.[6] But it should be noted that, as the passage indicates (with the verb *suppose*), the tabula rasa is here used as a hypothesis, not a description of the mind. It merely serves Locke's demonstration: the empirical explanation of the origin of our ideas—the tabula rasa—should be preferred to the theory of innate ideas, not because it has been demonstrated, but because it is the most simple explanation and because it is a "sufficient" one insofar as it can account for the origin of all of our ideas.[7] Thus, Locke's tabula rasa should probably be read as some kind of heuristic analogy. In the earlier *Essays on the Law of Nature* (1664), the English philosopher had referred more explicitly to the concept of the tabula rasa, when he explained that he aimed "to inquire whether the souls of the newly-born are just *rasas tabulas*, afterwards to be filled in by observation and reasoning, or whether they have the laws of nature as signs of their duty inscribed on them at birth."[8] In other words, Locke's inquiry aims to find out whether there are innate moral propositions in the mind (an idea which, of course, he refutes), the tabula rasa being the device that helps him determine this. The fiction of the tabula rasa, conceived as a representation of a naked mind or an understanding devoid of knowledge, is a tool used by Locke to determine how the understanding "comes to be furnished," that is, to reveal the process whereby the understanding acquires knowledge.

The tabula rasa and innate principles were a common but divisive subject among late seventeenth-century English experimentalists. For example, in his famous *Christian Virtuoso*, published in 1690, Robert Boyle expressed doubts as to the "truth" of the tabula rasa:

> We may observe then, that, whether or no it be True, which is taught by *Aristotle*, and commonly receiv'd in the Schools, that the Understanding is like Blank Paper; and that it receives no Knowledge, but what has been convey'd to it through the Senses: Whether, I say, this be or be not admitted, 'tis plain, that the Notions which are either Congenite with the Understanding, or so easily and early Acquir'd by it, that divers Philosophers think them Innate, are but very few, in comparison of those that are requisite to Judge aright, about any one of a multitude of things, that occur, either in Natural Philosophy, or Theology.[9]

Boyle admits that he does not know whether the understanding is like blank paper or not, but he certainly casts doubt upon that hypothesis. The reason is that, contrary to Locke, Boyle did believe that there were some forms of innate principles in man: the only thing he *can* say, he confesses in this passage, is that the notions that are from the beginning or from an early stage in human understanding—"congenite notions" for Boyle, "innate principles" for Descartes and others—are "very few." So, in spite of his claim that he suspends his judgment on the reality of the tabula rasa, Boyle does recognize that the understanding is not exactly like a blank paper: there are indeed—even though in a very small number—innate ideas. As a matter of fact, the idea that there were innate principles was widely shared in the seventeenth century, and Locke's refutation did not aim at Cartesianism only or even primarily, despite a common interpretation of book I of the *Essay*. Yet Locke's rejection of innate principles did not imply that he believed in a tabula rasa or the possibility of a naked mind, either at birth or as a consequence of some form of chosen ignorance. Rather, the blank slate was for him a fiction or a hypothesis that allowed for the representation of a naked or original understanding.

The fiction of the tabula rasa was also illustrated at the time in the persona of the self-taught philosopher.[10] Autodidacticism was indeed of interest to Locke in particular, as well as to other Restoration English experimentalists. This interest was manifest in the reception of *Philosophus autodidactus*, or *Hayy Ibn-Yaqzan*, a treatise written by the Andalusian philosopher Abu Bakr Ibn-Tufayl in the twelfth century. It was first translated from Arabic into Latin by the Oxford Orientalist Edward Pocock and published in Oxford in 1671. It was then translated into English by the Quaker George Keith (whose interest in the text is not surprising given his conception of ignorance and divine knowledge studied in part 2), and published in London in 1674, and then again by Church of England clergyman George Ashwell (London, 1686). This philosophical treatise tells the story of a boy who grows up on an uninhabited island in the Indian Ocean. He is taken care of and protected by a gazelle. Thanks to a careful observation of nature and his own experiments (for example, the dissection of the body of the gazelle when she dies), the boy eventually gets knowledge of the world and of himself, so much so that he actually becomes a natural philosopher, the author says, without the help of teachers or books. By trial and error only, he discovers the fundamental laws of nature. The story thus illustrates how knowledge can progressively be written on the blank slate of the mind through experience and observation. Ibn-Tufayl's text emphasizes the process or operation whereby Hayy gets knowledge, not so much his wisdom. Only at the end of the story is there mention of some form of introspection or self-knowledge when Hayy confines himself in a cave to meditate. Yet what he actually discovers through meditation and introspection is not his own ignorance, but the fact that he has the same essence as God.[11]

It is not surprising that autodidacticism should be of interest to seventeenth-century English experimental philosophers. As Avner Ben-Zaken has argued, it "represented the rejection of traditional intellectual authorities but also marked the rise of European experimentalist practices that diverged from transcendent medieval authorities."[12] Ben-Zaken adds that the English translation of Ibn-Tufayl's treatise "highlighted autodidacticism as a central component of experimentalism."[13] By illustrating an unmediated access to knowledge (insofar as it dispensed with teachers and books), this text showed that being ignorant of the learning of the schools did not prevent one from acquiring knowledge. If anything, illiterateness made one's access to knowledge easier and safer because the mind was not corrupted by prejudices. But contrary to the conception of ignorance presented in part 2, Hayy's story also showed that the "right" acquisition of knowledge was not the result of the intervention of an internal light: knowledge was obtained primarily through the operation of the senses. Finally, Hayy could be seen as the model experimental philosopher because he was humble and honest, qualities that had been preserved in him thanks to his keeping away from other men. Interestingly enough, if Ibn-Tufayl's text received a lot of attention in Restoration England, as well as in the Netherlands, it seems that it was not the case in France—the text was actually not translated into French in the early modern period.[14] As a matter of fact, the idea that a child growing up away from all human society would become wiser and more learned was criticized for example by the French *libertin érudit* François de La Mothe Le Vayer in his *Opuscule ou petit traité sceptique*,[15] in which he writes that children raised in the woods like beasts would become even more stupid than the beasts themselves on account of the weakness of human reason. The purpose of the treatise was to demonstrate that there is no such thing as common sense.

Hayy's story was perceived by Locke and others as an illustration of empiricism and the tabula rasa, which shed light on the workings of the understanding.[16] Indeed, autodidacticism, or the slow and progressive acquisition of knowledge by oneself, without interference from external agents, showed how the process of the acquisition of knowledge was made. In other words, this fiction gave an image of the naked mind and its mechanisms. Yet this interest in the naked mind did not entail a celebration of ignorance. For example, in the *Essay concerning Human Understanding*, Locke insists on the purity and virginity of the understandings of children, idiots, and savages—people whose minds have not been corrupted by learning—yet he does not do so to praise their ignorance. Those types of ignorant people are summoned by Locke as in an experiment to enable him to draw a conclusion that cannot be drawn from the observation of people who do have knowledge: ignorant people are testimony that there are no innate principles. The observation of learned people cannot prove this because it would be impossible to tell between the knowledge they have acquired and the knowledge that is "preexisting" in them. On the contrary, if there were innate principles, they would be apparent or perceptible in the people who have no acquired knowledge and who are therefore closer to nature, with a pure and unaltered understanding: "For *Children, Ideots, Savages,* and *illiterate* People, being of all others the least corrupted by Custom, or borrowed Opinions; Learning, and Education, having not cast their Native thoughts into new Moulds; nor by super-inducing foreign and studied Doctrines, confounded those faire Characters Nature had written there; one might reasonably imagine, that in their Minds these innate Notions should lie open fairly to every one's view, as 'tis certain the thoughts of Children do."[17] Locke continues: "alas, amongst *Children, Ideots, Savages,* and the grosly *Illiterate,* what general Maxims are to be found? What universal Principles of Knowledge? Their Notions are few and narrow."[18] Besides, those few notions are not the abstract or speculative maxims of innatism: they are the result of experience, and more particularly of what has most impressed those ignorant people. Yet there is no indication that their ignorance makes them wiser than learned men, as was the case of Montaigne's simple men, for example. Here again, as in the case of the tabula rasa and autodidacticism, the ignorance of certain groups of people is used by Locke experimentally, as it were, to demonstrate the vanity of the theory of innate principles. They give an image of the understanding in itself and reveal that it has no innate principles, otherwise children, savages, idiots, and illiterate people would have more notions than they actually do.

The "Conceptual Persona" of the Idiot

The autodidact can be compared to another apparently similar persona, already alluded to: the Idiot. When Locke refers to "idiots" in the *Essay*, he means people who are "deficient in reasoning powers,"[19] more precisely, those who "make very few or no Propositions, and reason scarce at all."[20] But the Idiot—or *morio, stultus, stupidus, futuus, insulsus*, and so on[21]—also embodied a positive representation of ignorance and can be described as a trope. Gilles Deleuze and Félix Guattari have argued that the Idiot is a "conceptual persona," found in diverse contexts throughout the history of philosophy, which emerged in a Christian environment as a reaction against scholasticism. They defined the Idiot as the private man, as opposed to the public thinker, or the technician as opposed to the scholar: while the latter resorts to concepts he has been taught, the former invents his own concepts. Thus, the Idiot thinks by himself and says "I." He is the one who "launches the cogito," according to Deleuze and Guattari.[22]

A famous example of the Idiot in seventeenth-century France is that of the Jesuit professor Jean-Joseph Surin's encounter with "the young man on the coach." In a letter to his community at La Flèche, dated 8 May 1630, Surin gives a precise account of his encounter with a poor illiterate young man on his way to Paris.[23] This letter was then largely circulated throughout Europe and published in Paris, Lyon, and Rouen, and abroad, in Brussels, Antwerp, and Cologne, among other places.[24] The young man is described as an eighteen-year-old with no formal education who has spent most of his life serving a priest. But Surin writes, he has been instructed in the mysteries of the spiritual life by God himself. His soul shows simplicity, humility, and purity,[25] the qualities that are required to reach truth, and Surin insists that the young man's simplicity helped him (Surin) discover many wonders. Although his language is simple and crude,[26] the young man shows prudence and efficiency, and he claims that he can see everything he needs to see thanks to God's supernatural light in his soul.[27]

According to Michel de Certeau in his edition of Surin's correspondence, the story told by the Jesuit is the reinterpretation of an old theme, that of "the illiterate and illuminated *Idiotus*," a topos illustrated in the episode of the conversion of a theologian by the (maybe fictitious) "Friend of God from the Oberland" around 1345.[28] This fable was often mentioned in the works of fifteenth-century German mystics, and it found prominent expression in Cusanus's *De idiota*. It relates the story of a humble layman who teaches divine knowledge to a great preacher.[29] He shows him in particular how to apply in his everyday life the virtues and principles he preaches so that he might quit his pedantry and arrogance. The theologian is ashamed to be taught by an Idiot, but he cannot but recognize the superior wisdom and knowledge that the Idiot got directly from God, who found in him the humility and sincerity required from the good Christian.[30] This fable has taken different forms throughout history, but it invariably features a poor and illiterate man or woman, often a peasant, who has not read a single book in life but is nonetheless wiser than scholars because the peasant's mystical science or personal experience of God greatly surpasses the learning of the schools.

Deleuze and Guattari have suggested that Cusanus was the author who gave "full status" to the "conceptual persona" of the Idiot in his dialogue *De idiota* (1450).[31] As mentioned in part 1, the text was anonymously translated into English and published in London in 1650.[32] It is composed of four dialogues featuring the Idiot, a spoon carver; the Orator, who represents the humanist scholar; and the Philosopher, or the "institutional representative of philosophical culture."[33] The Idiot is presented as "utterly ignorant"—he is the ordinary, uneducated man, or the "private man."[34] It soon appears that he is paradoxically more likely to reach truth than his learned interlocutors, and he is accordingly the one who leads the dialogue. There are several reasons for this. First, his knowledge comes from observation, not books, and therefore he is not persuaded of wrong opinions or deceived by authorities. An opposition, largely emphasized in the first dialogue, is made by the Idiot between "the food of bookes" and "a naturall nourishment," to show that the former does not engender truth because "*wisdome cryeth out in the streets.*"[35] Second, the Idiot is aware of his own ignorance: "I know my self an Idiot; and hereupon am more humble, and in this peradventure more learned."[36] This is clearly an expression of Socratic wisdom or learned ignorance. Third, the Idiot is not afraid of making mistakes, and is therefore happy to discuss any subject with anyone: "for being that I confesse my self an ignorant Idiot, I never fear to answer any thing. Learned philosophers, and such as have the reputation of knowledge, deliberate carefully, because they have need to fear failing."[37] The Idiot is not expected to have knowledge, and his social status makes him free to think and express his ideas as he wishes, and even to be wrong. His failure would easily be excused as he is not supposed to take part in intellectual activities in the first place.

The social dimension of the dialogue has rarely been studied or even noticed so far, although it is largely insisted upon in the text: the Idiot is indeed presented several times as "a poore Idiot, or private man," and his manual activity is often mentioned. For example, when the Philosopher is first introduced to him in book 3, the Orator says: "I am ashamed, Idiot, that thou shouldest be found by this great Philosopher, thus busied about these rusticall workes; he will never beleive that he shall hear any speculations from thee."[38] The manual or technical nature of the Idiot's activity is here clearly set against the intellectual or speculative nature of the Philosopher's. But the social position of the Idiot is also set against that of the Orator, who is presented as "very rich."[39] The insistence on the social status of the Idiot obviously aims at emphasizing the unexpectedness of his wisdom and the paradox of learned ignorance, but it also shows that his particular place in society and the very "rusticity" of his activity favor his access to truth.[40]

Yet the Idiot soon forgets his humble status and takes on the role of the (learned) teacher. The fourth book is particularly striking in this regard, as it tackles complex experimental knowledge and aims to show that everything can be expressed in quantitative terms, with the help of instruments, such as the balance mentioned in the title of this dialogue: "The fourth Booke, concerning statick Experiments; Or, Experiments of the Balance."[41] It also shows that wisdom, which was defined in the first three dialogues, must lead to practical knowledge. In this last part, it appears that, because the Idiot is an artisan, he is better suited to deal with experimental knowledge and mathematics. A legacy of the idea that the truths of mathematics were open to the minds of unlearned men was found in the circle of Jacques Lefèvre d'Étaples, a professor of arts in Paris, who edited Cusanus's works in 1514. Richard Oosterhoff, who has examined the theme of the "untutored mind" in the Fabrist circle, argues that Lefèvre and his circle were influenced by Ramon Lull, a thirteenth-century mystic, who presented himself as an *idiota*.[42] They also read the natural theology of Raymond de Sebonde, a medical professor at Montpellier in the 1430s, who emphasized the superiority of naïve wisdom (and inspired Montaigne his famous essay on ignorance). But above all, they borrowed from Cusanus, who himself "took up the Lullian theme of the unlearned knower 'inventing' truths from the book of nature" in *De idiota*, Oosterhoff argues. Cusanus's Idiot is indeed more likely to master the truths of mathematics precisely because he is an artisan: "By virtue of being an artisan, the *idiota* emerges as a special authority in measuring and governing rough material, since by performing such activities in daily life he more deeply understands the basis of the Divine Artisan's creation in number, weight, and measure."[43] In a word, the art of making spoons is analogous to God's creative art. Besides, man being the measure of all things (an idea also found in Cusanus's *De docta ignorantia*), there is no need to be learned so as to be able to measure: this ability is naturally given to all men. Oosterhoff adds that, in Lefèvre's circle, the *idiota* was an important character that "linked late medieval hunger for the experience of God and objects on the one hand, with the rising interest in experience of nature on the other."[44] In other words, the character of the Idiot illustrated a move from religious experience to scientific or philosophical experience. This can mean that there was some kind of secularization of experience, or at least that experience was progressively no longer restricted to divine matters, but it also entails that the character of the Idiot played a part in the emergence of movements that gave preeminence to observation and experimentation. In seventeenth-century England, Cusanus's dialogues were read, for example, by John Dee, who was particularly interested in the fourth dialogue on experiments and thought that this reference gave authority to "Experimentall Science."[45] But surprisingly enough, the dialogue does not seem to have had a particularly favorable reception among English experimentalists themselves, even though it illustrated most of their principles.

Conversely (and in accordance with the argument of part I above on the reception of *docta ignorantia* in England and in France), the legacy of the Cusan Idiot was found in seventeenth-century France. It is argued here that this persona not only illustrated the conception of ignorance as wisdom, presented above, but also was a fiction employed to reveal the use of ignorance as an epistemological instrument. The character of the Idiot is indeed prominent in Descartes's *The Search for Truth*, a dialogue—already mentioned—between Eudoxus, the Idiot or true philosopher; Polyander, the uneducated gentleman who eventually adheres to the method of doubt taught by Eudoxus; and Epistemon, the traditional scholar. Because he has questioned and rejected all the knowledge that he was taught in his youth, Eudoxus has no prejudices and is therefore more likely to avoid error by making good use of his reason, a faculty that is thus not encumbered by the false and vain learning of the schools. The aim of the dialogue, as its (long) title indicates, is indeed to show that one can have access to the secrets of "the most curious sciences," but more importantly perhaps, that one can determine the opinions that should be held on diverse subjects, without resorting to external—and therefore uncertain—knowledge, such as religion and philosophy.

If Eudoxus is the true philosopher, Polyander may be perceived as another embodiment of the Idiot, and even as the character who is at the center of the dialogue. Indeed, Eudoxus and Epistemon compete to demonstrate that each one's method to truth is the best, Eudoxus relying on the natural light only and Epistemon on scholastic erudition. They use Polyander's mind as an object of experimentation: Polyander is a character on whom one can experiment precisely because of his ignorance and his naked mind. Because he has never studied, he is presented by Eudoxus as "a neutral person," who is "not preoccupied," that is, who is unprejudiced.[46] The fiction of ignorance is here used by Descartes as a tool to get a representation of the naked understanding, and to conduct an experiment that confronts two methods to access truth: through the natural light and through learning. What the dialogue expectedly demonstrates is that the method of the scholar inevitably misses the truth because it relies entirely on memory and on the authority of previous authors. On the contrary, Eudoxus's method dispenses with learning and opinion, and relies on the only sure way to truth: reason or the natural light. Thus, Polyander soon becomes Eudoxus's disciple, and the (unfinished) dialogue ends on his recognition of the necessity of doubt, while Epistemon expresses his fear that general doubt might lead to Socratic ignorance or Pyrrhonian uncertainty. In other words, the dialogue demonstrates that the natural light alone, without any external help from philosophy or religion, leads one to truth on all matters, even to "the secrets of the most curious sciences," as the title indicates. The experiment on the mind of the ignorant Polyander conducted in the dialogue shows that, in order to make perfect use of his natural light and reach truth, a man must be naturally ignorant or divest himself of all the learning, false knowledge, and prejudices that he has acquired since childhood—in other words, he should first make himself ignorant, and then learn how to use and trust his natural light. Descartes's dialogue is particularly interesting for the study of early modern fictions of ignorance as it displays two forms or representations of ignorance: the natural ignorance of those who have never studied and the chosen ignorance of those who have studied but then doubted all their previously acquired knowledge to rely on their natural light only. Both forms of ignorance win the day in this contest against scholastic learning and pedagogy. Besides, Descartes also relies in this dialogue on the fiction of ignorance of the tabula rasa when he features the character of the ignorant Polyander, on whose mind nothing has been inscribed yet, presenting him as a "neutral person" and his mind as a blank slate.

Despite obvious similitudes, *De idiota* and *The Search for Truth* do not draw the exact same portrait of the Idiot. *De idiota* teaches that truth is accessible to anyone, as long as that person is not deceived by vain learning, through the observation of the world or "God's books." Indeed, the Idiot in Cusanus's dialogues insists, much more than Eudoxus in Descartes's *Search for Truth*, on access to knowledge through the senses. The fourth dialogue on "static experiments" also confirms the "empiricist" bias of *De idiota*. Knowledge is brought by observation of the world, not so much by the workings of an internal natural light.[47] Admittedly, there is within human beings "a certaine fore-taste of the eternall wisdome," which makes them desire wisdom because "there is nothing desired that is utterly unknowne"[48]—a "foretaste" that might be understood as some kind of innate principle. But contrary to Descartes's dialogue, which aims at the truth of the sciences, as the title indicates, *De idiota* focuses mostly on knowledge and understanding of God. A large part of the book is indeed devoted to demonstrating negative theology, which was also expounded in *De docta ignorantia*, as shown in the introduction to this book. For example, in book 2, the Idiot says to the Orator, after long developments on the subject: "for in that Divinity which denies all things of God, we must speak otherwise; because there the truer answer is to every question, a negation: yet, by that means or manner, we are not led to the knowledge what God is, but what God is not."[49] It also appears from Cusanus's dialogues that the Idiot is a better worshipper of God precisely because of his ignorance, calling to mind Montaigne's assertion that ignorance is "an instrument fitting beleefe, and obedience."[50] The idea is that the simple unprejudiced man or woman will follow his or her heart, giving precedence to love over learning.[51] In this regard, the topos of the Idiot could be set against medieval and early modern representations of the ridiculous "fool" as an illiterate man who lacks self-knowledge. In emblematic writings such as Sebastian Brant's *Narrenschiff* (1494) and Jacob Locher's *Stultifera navis* (1497), the "fools" are indeed presented as sinners blinded by their ignorance and self-love. In these cases, simplicity and illiterateness do not bring wisdom, but stupidity and irreligious behavior.[52]

Cusanus's and Descartes's Idiots show the persistent interest, from the late Middle Ages to the seventeenth century, in philosophical personae that could illustrate the virtues of ignorance. Focus has been placed here on the use of this persona in an experiment aimed to understand the workings of the understanding by imagining the "neutral" mind of a fictional character, but the Idiot most evidently combines the three virtues of ignorance presented in *The Paradoxes of Ignorance*. Indeed, the ignorance of the Idiot makes him wise, or at least wiser than learned men; he reaches truth thanks to his natural light or reason alone, and he can be conceived of as a fiction of ignorance. Moreover, it should be underlined that the Idiot, as Cusanus and Descartes understand this persona, is not merely an ignorant man. He is also a free man: because he belongs to the lowest classes of society or because he has retired to a secluded area of the countryside, he is not expected to display learning, contrary to the scholar. What might have appeared as a social and intellectual disadvantage at first is actually the guarantee of his being a good philosopher, first because he is not corrupted by false knowledge (to which he does not have access or which he rejected), and second, because he is free to think by himself (being subjected to no social expectations in intellectual matters). In other words, to the moral, psychological and epistemological qualities expected from the model philosopher, one should add a place in society that ensures intellectual freedom. Yet if Cusanus's and Descartes's Idiots are free, their social positions are actually very different: the Cusan Idiot is a poor artisan, while Eudoxus and Polyander are leisurely gentlemen and *honnêtes hommes*. In other words, the former did not choose his ignorance and freedom, while the latter did, which is why in this case ignorance appears as a mere posture. But both cases are examples of philosophical personae that made possible a reflection on ways of knowing and thinking, and on the role of ignorance in them.[53]

One might wonder whether idiots are commended for their ignorance or their innocence. Indeed, when idiots such as children, savages, or the illiterate were praised in seventeenth-century England, it was mostly on account of their innocence, while their ignorance was usually considered as a fault or a deficiency, and rarely as a quality conducive to wisdom or knowledge. The importance of the distinction between innocence and ignorance was emphasized in Glanvill's *The Vanity of Dogmatizing*, in particular. In the title of the first chapter, the perfections of prelapsarian Adam are presented as "*the Perfections of Innocence*"[54]—in other words, Adam was both innocent and knowledgeable before the Fall. This association of innocence and knowledge was then confirmed in the second chapter of *Scepsis Scientifica*: "While Man was *innocent* [before the Fall] he was likely *ignorant* of nothing, that imported him to know."[55] Glanvill here makes it explicit that innocence does not imply ignorance and that they are distinct notions. As a matter of fact, the title of the first chapter of *Scepsis Scientifica*, "A General Description of the State of *Primitive Ignorance*, by way of *Introduction*," was later corrected, as the list of errata preceding the text shows. Indeed, it is here indicated that instead of *ignorance* in the title of chapter 1, one should read *innocence*.[56] As mentioned, *innocence* was the word used in the title of the first chapter of *Vanity of Dogmatizing* ("*the Perfections of Innocence*"), but for whatever reason, it was changed to *ignorance* in the revised version of the treatise, *Scepsis Scientifica*, before Glanvill had it mentioned in the errata that it was a mistake and should be read *innocence*. These hesitations and corrections reveal both the distinction between innocence and ignorance in Glanvill's mind and their close relation. Yet this distinction or opposition was not systematic in the seventeenth century. For example, Charron, who was accidentally one of Glanvill's sources, stated in his treatise *Of Wisdom* that innocence "willinglie lodgeth with simplicitie and ignorance,"[57] three qualities that he opposed to the artifice, deceitfulness, and cunning of science.

Finally, the relation between innocence and ignorance in seventeenth-century England is given an interesting interpretation by Joanna Picciotto in her book *Labors of Innocence*. Picciotto argues that innocence, though traditionally associated with ignorance, came to be defined as objectivity and seen as "an epistemological privilege" in the context of English experimental philosophy.[58] Adam's innocent curiosity became a model for the experimental philosopher, who was thus encouraged in his pursuit of knowledge through observation.[59] Picciotto argues that innocence became a method in itself,[60] insofar as the pursuit of innocence required from experimental philosophers or the truth seekers that they divest themselves of the prejudices they had acquired through education and custom.[61] The insistence on innocence and objectivity is also what led the fellows of the Royal Society to try and imitate "laborors," who were seen as embodying some of the qualities of prelapsarian Adam.[62] Like Adam, they were innocent and read the book of nature only, which made them free from prejudices and the temptation to submit to intellectual authorities. In other words, Picciotto's contention is that the experimental philosophers' praise of artisans was founded on their association of "laborors" and "mechanics" with Adam, a contention that is discussed in this next chapter. The emphasis on innocence, which very ostentatiously replaced ignorance in Glanvill's *Scepsis Scientifica*, supports Picciotto's assessment of the epistemological role of innocence in experimental philosophy and its dissociation from ignorance. Glanvill thus associated in his writings a conception of ignorance as wisdom borrowed from the Cusan tradition, as argued in part 1, and a praise of innocence characteristic of seventeenth-century English experimental philosophy, although the hesitations and errata might also point to Glanvill's difficulty to fully endorse the Cusan heritage in an English context.

CHAPTER 6

Ignorance and Chance Discovery

It was argued in the previous chapter that ignorance could be used in myths, fables, or fictions to give a representation of the naked mind and thus expose its workings. The aim of these fictions of ignorance was to understand the nature, limits, and mechanisms of the understanding, by imagining it in itself, divested of all learning, in order to devise efficient methods for acquiring knowledge based on the observed workings of the mind. This chapter focuses on another use of ignorance in the scientific context: it examines the chance discoveries made by illiterate men and women, a topos in the early modern period, and inquires whether ignorant people were deemed to have specific qualities that rendered them more likely than scholars to make those discoveries by chance. The chapter argues that one of those qualities was sagacity, which played an essential part in the philosophies of both Bacon and Descartes in particular. It also contends that the Baconian program devised means to imitate or experimentally reproduce the conditions that led to chance discoveries by illiterate men, with the aim to appropriate this kind of discovery and introduce it into the scientific discourse.

Artisans and the Myth of the Illiterate Inventor

That chance discoveries were made primarily by ignorant people and not by scholars or natural philosophers was a topos in the early modern period. The discovery of the New World by Columbus, while he was actually looking for another land, was often given as an example of such discoveries, even though Columbus was not illiterate, but merely ignorant of the continent where he had landed.[1] Although the distinction between illiterateness or general lack of knowledge on the one hand, and specific ignorance on the other is important, it was often overlooked in this topos, and the discoverers were called "ignorant" even when they were actually educated. In *La Vérité des sciences*, the skeptic in Mersenne's dialogue argues that "the most ignorant people were wiser and more learned than those who were deemed the wisest and most learned," emphasizing that "ignorant Columbus found the New World" and that the magnet, the cannon, and the printing press were invented by "weak artisans." All this proves, according to the skeptic, that "fools and ignorant people work quantities of marvels that the most learned scholars cannot even begin to understand."[2] But the idea that many important discoveries had been made by ignorant people was not the opinion of the skeptics only, or a fallacious argument they used to discredit learning. A famous example of a crucial chance discovery made by an illiterate man was found in Descartes's essay on the *Dioptrics* included in the *Discourse on Method*. In this text, the Dutch artisan Jacques Métius is presented by Descartes as the inventor of the first perspective glass or telescope:

> But to the shame of our sciences, this invention, so useful and so admirable, was found in the first place only through experiment and good fortune. It was about thirty years ago that a man named Jacques Métius, of the city of Alcmar in Holland—a man who had never studied, although he had a father and a brother who made a profession of mathematics, but who particularly enjoyed making mirrors and burning glasses . . . having on that occasion many lenses of different shapes, happened by chance to look through two of them, one being slightly thicker in the middle than at the edges, and the other, on the contrary, much thicker at the edges than in the middle. And happily he hit upon the idea of placing them in the two ends of a tube, so that the first of these telescopes of which we are speaking was thereby made.[3]

Métius was used to making mirrors and lenses for his pleasure, and one day, "by chance," he "happily hit upon the idea" of placing his lenses in a way which resulted in the making—or invention—of the first perspective glass.[4] This discovery was thus made "only through experiment and good fortune." In other words, Descartes indirectly admits that the invention of the first perspective glass was not due to chance only, but to experience as well, since Métius was manipulating all kinds of glasses when the discovery unexpectedly occurred. Therefore, it was not a miracle: it did not occur out of the blue, so to speak, but when the artisan was actually using glasses for a particular purpose, even though he was not looking for what he eventually discovered, just as Columbus discovered the New World while he was looking for another place. Finally, Descartes does credit Métius with making an important discovery, but he also clearly states that the sciences, and in particular mathematics, should have led to this discovery, not an illiterate artisan, "a man who had never studied."

A few decades later, in England, Robert Boyle, an assiduous reader of Descartes's works, also underlined that the telescope had not been discovered by mathematicians or philosophers, but by a man named Métius, and only by chance or "casually": "On which occasion I shall mind you, that to hide Pride from Man, divers others of the chief Discoveries that have been made in Physicks, have been the Productions, not of Philosophy, but Chance, by which Gunpowder, Glass, and, for ought we know, the Verticity of the Load-stone, (to which we owe both the *Indies*) came to be found in these later Ages; as (more recently) the Milky Vessels of the Mesentery, the new Receptacle of the Chyle . . . were lighted on but by Chance, according to the Ingenious Confession of the Discoverers themselves."[5] Thus, according to Boyle, chance discoveries made by people who were not natural philosophers, such as the discoveries of gunpowder, the microscope and telescope, and parts of the human body, aim at—or at least result in—"hiding Pride from Man," in particular the pride of philosophers and scholars, who are then forced to admit that they are not the only ones with the ability or opportunity to make essential discoveries. They can also be made by artisans like Métius, who are characterized by their "*ingenuity*," a quality that, in the context of the emergence of modern science, was associated with innocence, honesty, common sense, and the faculty of invention.[6]

Those qualities were often attributed to artisans in the early modern period. For example, John Locke acknowledged the artisans' invaluable contribution to the promotion of the sciences in book III of the *Essay concerning Human Understanding*, arguing that "it was to the unscholastick Statesman, that the Governments of the World owed their Peace, Defence, and Liberties; and from the illiterate and contemned Mechanick (a Name of Disgrace) that they received the improvements of useful Arts."[7] He then immediately set the illiterateness of artisans against the "artificial Ignorance" or "learned ignorance" of scholastics, whose learning is described as vain and useless. Artisans are here praised both because their minds are not corrupted by prejudices, opinions, and sterile erudition, and because they possess practical knowledge or skills, usefulness being an essential quality in the experimental program.

But artisans were not merely personae in the early modern fables of chance discoveries, they were also scientific actors of the Royal Society. They were needed to make or improve the instruments that the fellows then used to conduct experiments, and they also sometimes conducted experiments themselves. As a result, close relationships—sometimes based on trust—were established between artisans and fellows who worked together. One example is the collaboration between Robert Hooke (1635–1703) and the clockmaker Thomas Tompion (bap. 1639–1713), one of the artisans of lowly birth who nonetheless made exceptional discoveries, according to Prior's Montaigne in the quotation given at the very beginning of this book. As curator of experiments for the Royal Society, Hooke was a paid employee and often treated as such by the fellows. Yet he was an irreplaceable member of the society, and as Rob Iliffe has shown, the interaction between Hooke and Tompion was "possibly unparalleled by any other combination between a British craftsman and natural philosopher in this period."[8] Hooke first commissioned Tompion on behalf of the Royal Society to make a quadrant that would demonstrate the limits of naked-eye astronomical observation. Tompion then made a number of sophisticated barometers and clocks that Hooke had devised. They also worked together on the conception and making of a watch for King Charles II, which is said to have been signed "Robert Hooke invent. 1658. T. Tompion fecit 1675," showing the distribution of the roles as well as the collaboration between the two men. At a time when the competition between clockmakers all over Europe was fierce, and secrets of design and fabrication well preserved, it seems that Hooke and Tompion trusted each other, as their long-lasting relationship demonstrates. Hooke's diary shows that they exchanged precise technical information on diverse subjects, without reservations, not fearing, as it seems, that the other might exploit this information for his own personal credit. In the entry for 2 May 1674, for example, Hooke writes that he met Tompion in Water Lane and had "much Discourse with him about watches. Told him the way of making an engine for finishing wheels, and a way how to make a dividing plate; about the forme of an arch; about another way of Teeth work; about pocket watches and many other things."[9] Moreover, Hooke very often mentions spending time at Tompion's home, or simply writes "Tompion" without further detail, suggesting that he saw the clockmaker or wrote to him.[10]

In the context of seventeenth-century English experimental philosophy, the artisans' ignorance of classical learning was perceived as a guarantee of their trustworthiness. Because they would (or could) not rely on intellectual authorities, but only on their own "unbiased" perception of the world, their observations were deemed objective and reliable. The most significant example—the very epitome, perhaps—of the illiterate artisan, who showed qualities lacking in "professional" experimentalists, was Antoni van Leeuwenhoek (1632–1723), an uneducated Dutchman who made his own microscopes, another example of a great discoverer among the illiterate vulgar, according to Prior's Montaigne. As Philippe Hamou has argued, Van Leeuwenhoek corresponded to Hooke's model of the "faithful eye" because his modest social origins (he was a draper) and his ignorance of authorities and languages guaranteed the virginity and purity of his mind, as well as his ability to "recognize" a discovery when he saw one: "Van Leeuwenhoek's ignorance preserved him both from blindly submitting to the authority of the Ancients, which was condemned by the Royal Society in its motto '*nullius in verba*,' and from getting lost in the vain speculations of the Moderns."[11] Van Leeuwenhoek was therefore credited with some form of honesty: he would merely describe what he observed without trying to conform to the authorities, whether ancient or modern, or ascribing what he observed to a particular theory. In many regards, Van Leeuwenhoek was an autodidact in experimental philosophy. If he was ignorant and a layman when first introduced in the Royal Society, he then became an experimental philosopher himself and was officially recognized as such when he was made a fellow in 1680. He may not have read as many books as the natural philosophers he worked alongside, but he did gain unique knowledge through experience and observation, described by Pamela H. Smith as "artisanal literacy."[12]

Yet the trust between fellows and artisans illustrated here through the example of Hooke and Tompion was far from universal, and moreover, it did not extend to technicians, those men whose role was to assist the fellows and carry out the experiments they had devised. Steven Shapin has shown that technicians, who were perceived as servants, often did most of the work without getting much recognition for it, as they were rarely mentioned in the essays that presented the observations *they* had made.[13] Besides, the work of technicians was often used as an excuse by fellows when the experiment they had devised happened to fail: in such cases, both skill and reliability of the technician were questioned.[14] One reason the fellows did not spontaneously trust their assistants was that, in seventeenth-century England, servants were suspected of being prone to deceiving their masters, out of envy, as well as resentment over their inferior social status.[15] Because of their financial dependence on others, technicians were also often despised by the fellows for whom they worked. This was reinforced by the persistent belief in the distinction between theoretical knowledge and practical knowledge, and the alleged superiority of the former, well into the seventeenth century.[16] The openness of seventeenth-century English natural philosophy, which has often been underlined, may thus have "tempered" the "traditional gentlemanly disdain for the mechanical arts and contempt for those who remuneratively practiced them,"[17] but it certainly did not put an end to this attitude. It might even be argued, following Pamela H. Smith, that natural philosophers felt even more strongly the need to distinguish themselves from artisans, as they shared interests and practices with them.[18]

Shapin gives the example of Boyle, yet one of the main advocates of the openness of natural philosophy, who, in the mid-1640s, said that he enjoyed conversations with his gardener, but three decades later, emphatically wished that he did not have to deal so often with artisans and technicians.[19] In his essay *The Excellency of Theology*, Boyle explains that experimental philosophy is "a very troublesome and laborious Imployment" precisely because of the great number of objects that the philosopher must study, for which he will inevitably require the help of assistants:[20] "[The great variety of objects] will put [the experimental philosopher] upon needing, and consequently upon applying himself to such a Variety of Mechanick People, (as Distillers, Drugsters, Smiths, Turners, &c.) that a great part of his time, and perhaps all his Patience, shall be spent in waiting upon Trades-men, and repairing the losses he sustains by Their disappointments, which is a Drudgery greater than any, who has not try'd it, will imagine, and which yet being as inevitable as unwelcome, does very much counter-ballance and allay the Delightfulness of the Study we are treating of."[21] Boyle's harsh judgment shows that "mechanicks" were not always portrayed as the men who had improved "useful arts," as Locke put it. Above all, it seems that there was a contradiction between the Royal Society's official discourse on experimental philosophy as open to all, especially innocent and ignorant laypeople, and the reality of the everyday practice of science.[22]

Distrust and contempt were not the preserve of the Royal Society or of English natural philosophers. They were also expressed in France in the same period, as Paola Bertucci has shown in her study of the *artistes*' contribution to enlightened projects. Bertucci quotes André Félibien (1619–1695), a member of the Académie des Inscriptions and secretary of the Académie d'Architecture, who, in his *Des principes de l'architecture, de la sculpture, de la peinture, et des autres arts qui en dépendent*, testified, just like Boyle, to his difficulty of communicating with artisans: "very often one finds ignorant or bizarre people who, instead of answering the questions one asks and talking honestly about the craft they practice, say things that are opposite to what one wishes to know, and often disguise the truth one searches with mischievousness,"²³ even though Félibien added that those were not the best kind of artisans, implying that others might be more receptive. The success of Félibien's work may indicate that this opinion on artisans was common in France at the time.²⁴

Interestingly, it seems that the distrust and resentment were reciprocal: Van Leeuwenhoek, for example, expressed his own contempt for natural philosophers, and even showed "a superior anti-academic attitude," often suggesting in his correspondence that the learning of university-educated fellows made them less competent than him despite (or thanks to) his lack of academic training.²⁵ Van Leeuwenhoek implied that his abilities and skills stemmed from his illiteracy. This reciprocal distrust partly accounts for the failed "history of trades" project of the Royal Society. Inspired by Francis Bacon, the project aimed to describe all the trades and their history, but as it happened, fellows and artisans could not collaborate, and the project was abandoned. To conclude, Pamela H. Smith has shown that the divide between learned scholars and illiterate artisans was questioned in the seventeenth century, with the emergence of the laboratory as the place where science was made (instead of the library),²⁶ but this development shows that this divide persisted under different forms, and morphed into a complex and ambivalent relation between the actors of the "new science."

Illiterateness, Method, and Sagacity

Paradoxical though it may seem, given what was said about his relations with artisans, Robert Boyle often emphasized the qualities of craftsmen as well as peasants that made them a great help to the experimental philosopher. In particular, he insisted on their proximity to nature and their direct access to the true nature of things in *The Christian Virtuoso*: "I shall not on this occasion altogether overlook this Circumstance, That an Experimental Philosopher *so* often increases his Knowledge of Natural things, by what He learns from the Observations and Practises, even of Mean, and perhaps of Illiterate, Persons, (such as Shepherds, Plowmen, Smiths, Fowlers, &c.) because they are conversant with the Works of Nature."²⁷ Thus, "mean" and "illiterate" artisans and peasants are "conversant with the Works of Nature," and as such, they are of great help to the experimental philosopher. The contention here is that the proximity with nature described by Boyle manifested a specific quality of the illiterate: their sagacity, which was often presented as some kind of instinct by natural philosophers, and which was believed to lead ignorant people to significant chance discoveries.²⁸

In the early modern period, sagacity was commonly attributed to people and groups of people who were (supposedly) closely linked to nature through their way of life, their occupation or their illiterateness, as if learning, on the opposite, had the effect of driving someone away from nature, or of making them less able to know it.[29] Thus, for example, early modern navigators and colonists often underlined the indigenous populations' knowledge of nature—of its operations and creatures—which they described as empirical knowledge or sagacity.[30] Sagacity was also commonly considered as the main quality of a man who made important discoveries by chance. Thomas Hobbes, for example, defined sagacity as the "faculty of invention" in *Leviathan* and associated it with *solertia*, or ingenuity, a form of practical wisdom.[31] Besides, *sagacitas*, according to Hobbes, was some kind of discursive thought, a hunt or pursuit triggered by an appetite that urged one to follow a track or a scent. In his earlier treatise on *Human Nature*, sagacity refers to the process or the successive steps that lead from the birth of the appetite to its being satisfied.[32]

A detailed presentation of sagacity is found in the works of the Calvinist theologian Theophilus Gale (1628–1679), for whom it plays an essential role in the relation between human beings and God. In *The Court of the Gentiles*, a work in four volumes first published in Oxford between 1669 and 1678, Gale defines sagacity as a form of prudence.[33] He also associates it with *phronesis*, some kind of practical wisdom or disposition, and with *agkinoia* (ἀγχίνοια), which is close to intuition. Gale explains that sagacity enables one to spontaneously and immediately penetrate the essence of things; it is therefore compared to Adam's ability to name all the animals in Genesis.[34] In other words, sagacity is "*philosophick penetration*" into the nature of things.[35] Because it is akin to instinct, sagacity is a quality often attributed to dogs in particular, with their sharp sense of smell.[36] But it also refers to human wisdom. Following Plato, Gale argues that sagacity is "This *perspicacitie* of finding out things . . . or a *natural Invention*, which direct the Reason to find out things wrapt up in Nature."[37] Sagacity is thus distinguished from reason, which it assists in its search for knowledge. Its role is more precisely to direct reason toward what is hidden in nature: it is therefore an ability to sense (or smell) and spontaneously perceive what is hidden. Being thus closely linked to perception, it is not surprising that sagacity should be so often mentioned in the works of early modern English experimentalists, for whom it was a quality that the natural philosopher should strive to acquire and foster.

Despite the recognition and praise of the illiterate's sagacity, a quality that enabled them to make important discoveries, it was often made clear in the seventeenth century that such discoveries by chance should remain exceptions as the new science was not to be founded on a series of mere accidents. Francis Bacon in particular was very critical of this mode of discovery, which he assimilated to archaic practices and modes of knowing that were in high need of reformation in the early seventeenth century. Thus, in the *Novum Organum* (1620), he regrets that "everything has been left to the blindness of traditions, the swirling bluster of arguments, or the turbulent waves of chance, and experience undisciplined and ungrounded."[38] In another aphorism, Bacon wishes that the invention of the printing press, gunpowder, and the magnet did not have such "dark and inglorious origins," although he recognizes that those three discoveries considerably improved human life: "Again it helps to observe the force, virtue and consequences of what has been discovered, and that is nowhere more apparent than in those three things which were unknown to the ancients and whose origins, though recent, are dark and inglorious: namely the *Art of Printing*, *Gunpowder*, and the *Mariner's Compass*. For these three have altered the whole face and state of things right across the globe: the first in things literary, the second in things military, and the third in navigations."[39] In the unfinished *Temporis partus masculus*, or *The Masculine Birth of Time*, written in the early years of the seventeenth century, Bacon had already been critical of chance discoveries, not because of what they brought to the world, but because of the way they were made, arguing that their occurring by accident may have led humanity to miss other potential discoveries. Indeed, Bacon wished that the discovery of gunpowder had occurred not by chance, but methodically, arguing that if gunpowder had been discovered "not by chance (as they say) but by good guidance,"[40] or by following a "scientific" mode of inquiry or a "masculine" (i.e., an active as opposed to passive) approach to knowledge, it would have been accompanied by many more innovations and inventions. Because it was discovered instead by ignorant people who did not know what they were doing, mankind missed an opportunity for more improvements. To a certain extent, this "wrong" way of discovery spoilt the discovery itself. The same idea is found in the *Novum Organum* as well: "if many useful things have been discovered as if by chance or circumstance when men were not looking for them or had their minds on other things, no one can doubt but that if they were looking for them and had that as their business, and pursued it systematically by the right route, and not fitfully and in a desultory fashion, many more things by far would necessarily have come to light."[41] Those discoveries made by chance should not be celebrated because they are also a loss for humanity: the loss of the other discoveries that would have been made had the adequate rules been followed in the first place. Bacon makes clear that one should prefer methodical discoveries made by learned and conscious philosophers to accidental or chance discoveries made by ignorant men.

A similar attitude to chance discoveries was found a few years later in Descartes's works. The French philosopher was indeed equally critical of discoveries that did not occur as a result of a progression and an ordered mode of thinking, even though, just like Bacon, he acknowledged the importance of those discoveries. In the *Regulae*, Descartes condemned "those who study mechanics apart from physics," who skip stages of the process of discovery, and "without any proper plan, construct new instruments for producing motion."[42] Descartes argues that discoveries by chance should not be sought after because they are made without the help of reason, which is consequently rendered useless. In the case of such discoveries, reason is not given the opportunity to practice and therefore reinforce itself: "Above all, we must guard against wasting our time by making random and unmethodical guesses about similarities. Even though problems such as these can often be solved without a method and can sometimes perhaps be solved more quickly through good luck then through method, nevertheless they might dim the light of the mind and make it become so habituated to childish and futile pursuits that thereafter it could always stick to the surface of things and would be unable to penetrate more deeply."[43] So as to be able to advance knowledge, reason must be trained to discover things, which implies that it get used to following rules. In the case of a discovery by chance, reason does not follow those rules, so that it misses an opportunity to become stronger and more efficient through practice. Descartes insists that it is essential to train reason, as it is the faculty whereby most important discoveries are made. It appears from this criticism, as it appeared from the excerpt on Métius quoted earlier, that Descartes, like Bacon, did admit the importance of chance discoveries such as the telescope, but he nonetheless advocated progressive and organized discoveries, methodically made by reason.

As a matter of fact, training one's reason, for Descartes, actually means becoming more "sagacious," and therefore more likely to make discoveries, thanks to the appropriate method. This tends to show again that sagacity may have been first and foremost the quality of the illiterate, but it could nonetheless be acquired and developed by philosophers and learned men. Sagacity is not presented in the *Regulae* as an instinct that allows one to make spontaneous and immediate discoveries (as it was for some of the English authors discussed, especially Gale), but as a quality of the mind that can be trained and developed through exercises, as the title of Rule X makes clear: "In order to acquire [sagacity] we should exercise our intelligence by investigating what others have already discovered, and methodically survey even the most insignificant products of human skill, especially those which display or presuppose order."[44] In other words, so as to improve one's sagacity, one must *imagine* or figure out the path taken by discoverers and carefully follow in their steps. Descartes adds that he himself had often tried to discover whether, "perchance," thanks to "some inborn sagacity,"[45] he could find out what the title of a book announced: the aim was to try and imagine the progression of the discoverer toward his discovery before even reading the book. For Descartes, this way to proceed toward truth is in itself a method, which enables him to establish rules, as opposed to what others usually do, whose research is made "by vague and blind investigations, aided by luck rather than by skill."[46] Moreover, Descartes associates sagacity with perspicacity and intuition, the former being defined as a deduction (of the relations between things), made with art, or methodically. It should be noted here that the meaning of *sagacity* in Descartes's *Regulae* is close to that found in Hobbes, as it implies following a path or a scent. It also calls to mind the role played by the myths of the tabula rasa and the self-taught philosopher, described here as fictions of ignorance: in all those cases, there is a focus on the workings of the understanding and the processes that lead to knowledge, either by imagining a "virgin" mind that would move from complete ignorance to knowledge or by reconstituting the mechanisms of another man's mind to reach knowledge. Finally, just like Bacon, Descartes rejects the "blind investigations" that may lead to chance discoveries but do not contribute to the advancement of science.

Although Bacon considered discoveries by chance as an archaic mode of knowledge, which prevents humanity from making more discoveries, it is argued here that he nonetheless introduced chance into his program for the advancement of learning and tried to devise a way for the natural philosopher to appropriate the sagacity of the illiterate inventor. The exact nature of the relation between experimentation and chance, as well as the definition of the role played by chance in the Baconian program, has given rise to various interpretations by Bacon scholars. The one examined here argues that Bacon endeavored to imitate or reproduce, through experimentation, the process by which an ignorant man makes a discovery by chance.[47] More precisely, the contention is that *experientia literata*, or "literate / learned experience," is the instrument that makes possible the introduction of chance into the Baconian program for the advancement of knowledge. It is defined by Bacon as one of the two parts of the art of indication, the other being the interpretation of nature. *Experientia literata* is presented as some kind of experimental protocol that allows for variations on an experiment so that it might lead to other experiments (and not to axioms).[48] In *De augmentis scientiarum*, Bacon explains that *experientia literata* is not a method per se, neither is it a part of philosophy. It is rather "a kind of sagacity" and of "hunting by scent,"[49] which is why it is assimilated to the hunt of Pan in *The Wisdom of the Ancients* (1609):

"the discovery of things useful to life and the furniture of life, such as corn, is not to be looked for from the abstract philosophies, as it were the greater gods, no not though they devote their whole power to that special end—but only from Pan; that is from sagacious experience and the universal knowledge of nature, which will often by a kind of accident, and as it were while engaged in hunting, stumble upon such discoveries."[50] Useful discoveries are made by chance, through sagacious experiments (i.e., *experientia literata*) and "the universal knowledge of nature," a way of knowing that is here opposed to "abstract philosophies." One might be tempted to deduce from this quotation that *experientia literata* is a mode of knowing that dispenses with rules and method altogether to rely on an instinctive search only, leading the naturalist from experiment to experiment, without a specific aim or order, with the hope of stumbling upon something interesting along the way. But Bacon insists that moving from one experiment to another without following a predetermined path or process yields very few interesting results. This is how empirics proceed, he argues:

> For all inventions of works which are known to men have either come by chance and so been handed down from one to another, or they have been purposely sought for. But those which have been found by intentional experiment have been either worked out by the light of causes and axioms, or detected by extending and transferring or putting together former inventions; which is a matter of ingenuity and sagacity rather than philosophy. And this kind, which I noways despise, I will presently touch on by the way, when I come to treat of *learned experience* among the parts of logic. . . . But they who pursue these studies do but creep as it were along the shore, *premendo litus iniquum*. For it seems to me there can hardly be discovered any radical or fundamental alterations and innovations of nature, either by accidents or essays of experiments, or from the light and direction of physical causes, but only by the discovery of forms.[51]

The kind of experimentation described here, that of empirics, initially seems to be a true description of *experientia literata*, or "learned experience," which consists in "extending and transferring or putting together former inventions." This kind of experimentation, "purposely sought for," yet submitted to chance, and therefore without a predetermined path, does not yield satisfactory results, according to Bacon.

But *experientia literata* does not operate this way, without order or method. The contention here is that, as *literate* experience, it has its own principles and rules that aim to systematically associate chance with the process of experimentation and discovery. Indeed, chance discovery appears for Bacon as an experimental model, which means that the experimentalist should try to reproduce the conditions that allowed for the occurrence of the discovery. This is what Michael

Witmore explains in his work on "unexpected knowledges" in early modern England: "Bacon's method is designed to bring about deliberately those conditions that nature and ignorant investigators bring about spontaneously."[52] As a matter of fact, Bacon draws a parallel between experiment and accident when he distinguishes—and associates at the same time—spontaneous experience, also called accident, and deliberate experience, also called experiment.[53] He adds that the former is "nothing more than an unbound broom, and just the groping of benighted men trying steadfastly to feel their way to the right road by luck."[54] Accordingly, accidents are experiences that occur by chance, while experiments are experiences deliberately sought out. But neither accident nor experiment follows the course of nature: they both result from irregular natural conditions or "an unusual disposition of circumstances."[55] In other words, Pan's hunt or *experientia literata* is a way to simulate chance, and experiments are made in imitation of the conditions that caused the accident.[56] *Experientia literata* gives the experimentalist or naturalist the means to artificially reproduce, through deliberate experience or experiment, the conditions that allowed for the chance discovery made by an ignorant person to occur.

It appears from those remarks that part of the experimentalist program since Bacon consisted in enabling naturalists to appropriate the mode of discovery by chance, instead of leaving it to ignorant men and empirics; in this regard, *experientia literata* is indeed literate. The aim was to put an end to unconscious, spontaneous, and blind contributions to the advancement of knowledge,[57] and replace them with *literate* experience, that is, multiple and various experiments methodically and "self-reflectively" conducted. In this context, natural philosophers were encouraged to acquire and develop the sagacity of the illiterate inventors. Thus, following Bacon, the observation by English experimentalists of ignorant people making chance discoveries led, not to the idea that one should make oneself ignorant in order to reproduce the feats of the illiterate, but instead to the idea that the process whereby an ignorant man made a discovery unknowingly should be understood and imitated in one's own deliberate experimentation.

CHAPTER 7

John Locke's Anthropology of Ignorance

The main purpose of this chapter is to show that the notion of ignorance is central to Locke's philosophy, perhaps more than it was to other English experimentalists' thought, and definitely more than has been discussed by Locke scholars so far. Moreover, this chapter shows that Locke's conception of ignorance articulates several aspects of his philosophy. It also demonstrates that ignorance was indeed introduced into the scientific discourse of the late seventeenth century, and shows how it was done. It was argued in chapter 5 that Locke used representations of complete ignorance in the myths of the tabula rasa and the self-taught philosopher as instruments to apprehend the mechanisms of the understanding. This chapter focuses on Locke's conception of ontological ignorance—its nature, extent, causes, and consequences—and how it could be remedied or even made useful, depending on the social, political and religious environment.

The Measure of Ignorance

Although seventeenth-century English experimentalists did not all share the exact same philosophical and theological principles and beliefs, most of them interpreted human ignorance from a religious point of view as a punishment for

Adam's sin or the legacy of the Fall: Adam had all the knowledge he needed, but he wanted more, "& hence springs our ignorance . . . the soul hath been darkned and dimsighted."[1] This Augustinian-Calvinistic approach to ignorance, though apparently very pessimistic as to man's ability to reach knowledge, was actually a boon to the experimentalist project as it provided the premise on which the whole enterprise could be firmly founded—in particular, instruments designed for the observation of nature could be construed as correctives for postlapsarian human deficiencies. Thus, far from jeopardizing the experimental project—by showing that men could not reach knowledge, their faculties being corrupted from the start—the Augustinian-Calvinistic interpretation of ignorance actually helped reinforce and legitimize the empiricist approach of the Royal Society.[2] Evidently, this interpretation was also in keeping with the personal religious beliefs of most English experimentalists.

Yet among seventeenth-century English experimental philosophers, John Locke had a singular conception of ignorance. What primarily accounts for this singularity is that ignorance was not for him a corruption inherited from Adam as a consequence of the original sin. While his interpretation of the Fall may have evolved over time, it is clear that, to him, ignorance and other mental disabilities or distempers were *natural* defects or anthropological limits, and not the legacy of Adam's sin.[3] Relying on a close reading of the Bible, rather than on commentators, Locke held that the Fall had admittedly suppressed mankind's chance for immortality, but it had not caused an inherent corruption and depravity.[4] Locke was nonetheless acutely aware of human deficiencies, which he describes at length in the *Essay concerning Human Understanding*. But those deficiencies were to him of human origin, a stance that also preserved the responsibility of human beings for their actions. Indeed, they could not justify their doing evil—or their choosing to remain ignorant, for that matter—by invoking an uncontrollable legacy that would have been imposed on them, or some form of "invincible ignorance."

In the *Essay concerning Human Understanding*, Locke emphasizes the extent of human ignorance before listing its main causes. The explicit marginal title for IV, 3, 22 reads "*Our ignorance great,*" and indeed, Locke shows here that human ignorance is much more extended than human knowledge:

> Our Knowledge being so narrow, as I have shew'd, it will perhaps, give us some Light into the present State of our minds, if we look a little into the dark side, and take a view of *our Ignorance*: which being infinitely larger than our Knowledge, may serve much to the quieting of Disputes, and Improvement of useful Knowledge; if discovering how far we have clear and distinct *Ideas*, we confine our Thoughts within the Contemplation of those Things, that are within the reach of our Understandings, and lanch

not out into that Abyss of Darkness, (where we have not Eyes to see, nor Faculties to perceive anything), out of a Presumption, that nothing is beyond our Comprehension. But to be satisfied of the Folly of such a Conceit, we need not go far. He that knows any thing, knows this in the first place, that he need not seek long for Instances of his Ignorance. The meanest, and most obvious Things that come in our way, have dark sides, that the quickest Sight cannot penetrate into.[5]

This passage is obviously reminiscent of Socratic wisdom (insisting on the necessity of acknowledging our ignorance) and calls for intellectual humility, as it is folly to believe that one is capable of reaching any kind of knowledge, and that nothing is completely and definitively hidden. This folly leads to sterile controversies and vain disputes, a danger that Locke often emphasizes in his works, as will be shown again. But the excerpt also underlines the possibility of *some* knowledge. By looking into ignorance, defined here as "the dark side" of knowledge, one might become aware both of the limits and of the extent of human knowledge, whereas man naturally tends to look into his knowledge only, which gives him the false impression that all things can be known or that he already knows everything there is to know.[6] The conscious and chosen experience of ignorance is thus an experience of humility—as our ignorance is much more extended than our knowledge—but also of lucidity, insofar as it sheds light on the state of one's knowledge (a statement that was also clearly made in Mersenne's works in the early seventeenth century, for example). In other words, looking into one's ignorance and measuring it allows to construe a reasonable and balanced conception of one's knowledge. If Locke encourages everyone to observe their ignorance, he certainly does not encourage them to make themselves ignorant. Here again, as with the myths of the tabula rasa and the self-taught philosopher, the aim is to *observe ignorance* or to *experiment on ignorance*, and not to adopt the posture of the (learned) ignorant man.

Locke also lists the main causes of our ignorance in the *Essay*. The first one is the want of ideas, due to the disproportion between the ideas that we can have thanks to our faculties and the things themselves. We can have ideas only through sensations (in the case of corporeal objects) or through the operations of the mind (in the case of intellectual objects), and these are insufficient to apprehend the vast extent of beings; as a result, what we know is nothing in comparison to what we do not know.[7] Thus, Locke argues, we can perceive but a negligible part of the world because our senses are not acute enough to grasp what is very small or what is far away in the material world, and they also miss the whole intellectual world: "When we consider the vast distance of the known and visible parts of the World, and the Reasons we have to think, that what lies within our Ken, is but a small part of the immense Universe, we shall then discover an huge Abyss of Ignorance."[8] To this statement on the want of our ideas, Locke gives the seemingly pessimistic conclusion that universal and certain knowledge might not be attainable, even though we are capable of experimental knowledge or observation.[9] The second cause of human ignorance, according to Locke, is the want of a discoverable connection between our ideas: there is indeed no obvious correspondence or affinity between the properties of the body that we perceive and the ideas or sensations that they produce in us. Again, Locke concludes that we can therefore have no certain or philosophical knowledge of these bodies, only experimental knowledge.[10] The third and last cause of our ignorance is the "want of *tracing* our *Ideas*": Locke explains that we cannot find intermediate ideas that could show us the relations (of agreement or disagreement) between those ideas, and that could enable us to compare the ideas that we have. He adds that the reason for this want of tracing and examining our ideas is probably "the ill use of *Words*."[11]

Should the insistence on ignorance in Locke's works be read as a form of pessimism or skepticism? Locke's supposed skepticism has been largely dealt with, in the early modern period and in the secondary literature. His position toward skepticism is actually very clear: Locke argues that a man who would refuse to search for truth because he cannot know everything is like a man who would refuse to walk because he cannot fly.[12] It does not ensue from man's unavoidable ignorance of some things that he should renounce searching for knowledge altogether. Indeed, Locke insists that "a little knowledge is still knowledge and not scepticism." In other words: "This state of our minds, however remote from the perfection whereof we ourselves have an idea, ought not, however, to discourage our endeavors in the search of truth, or make us think we are incapable of knowing any thing, because we cannot understand all things."[13] He makes it clear that ignorance is merely a characteristic of the human condition, a manifestation of man's mediocrity;[14] as such, it should neither be condemned nor praised. In other words, ignorance should not lead to despair; neither should it be celebrated: "For what need have we to complain of our ignorance in the more general and foreign parts of nature, when all our business lies at home?" Our mind is indeed "well fitted" to know and discover what we need, and therefore bring us happiness, which, for Locke, "consists in pleasure whether of body or mind, according to everyone's relish."[15]

For Locke, awareness of one's ignorance is neither knowledge nor wisdom in itself, although it is the basis for science, so to speak, because "taking a view of our ignorance" allows us to determine what can be known. But it is not so much awareness of one's ignorance that matters for Locke as the measure of that ignorance, which is based on an examination of "the present state of our minds" and is precisely the aim of the *Essay concerning Human Understanding*: "Whereas were the Capacities of our Understandings well considered, the Extent of our Knowledge once discovered, and the Horizon found, which sets the Bounds between the enlightned and dark Parts of Things; between what is, and what is not comprehensible by us, Men would perhaps with less scruple acquiesce in the avow'd Ignorance of the one, and imploy their Thoughts and Discourse, with more Advantage and Satisfaction in the other." The measure of ignorance is thus the first step toward knowledge, but the search for knowledge also implies for the understanding "to stop, when it is at the utmost Extent of its Tether; and to sit down in a quiet Ignorance of those Things, which, upon Examination, are found to be beyond the reach of our Capacities."[16] As mentioned in part 1, this approach to ignorance is in keeping with the principle of "epistemic restraint" shared by a number of English theologians. But Locke makes a doctrine of this principle, on which he builds his own scientific method. Once the extent of "unavoidable" or "invincible" ignorance has been established, it should be accepted and even declared, and man should then focus on knowing what can be known and enjoying the discoveries that he can make: "For the Understanding, like the Eye, judging of Objects, only by its own Sight, cannot but be pleased with what it discovers, having less regret for what has scaped it, because it is unknown."[17] The recognition of the inevitable ignorance of some things is a necessary first step in the search for truth and happiness. It also means getting a better knowledge of oneself, namely of one's "abilities and defects," so that we might be "the better enabled to find out remedies for the infirmities."[18] Yet Locke is aware of the difficulty of the task: determining how far our faculties can reach, that is, assessing the extent of our ignorance, "is an inquiry of as much difficulty as any we shall find in our way of knowledge, and fit to be resolved by a man when he is come to the end of his study, and not to be proposed to one at his setting out."[19] But it can be said from the outset that things infinite and the nature of substance are beyond the reach of our understanding. What can be known falls within two categories: natural philosophy, for improvement of this life, and moral philosophy, for preparation of the life to come.

The observation and measure of ignorance are thus an essential part of Locke's discourse on method, and ignorance is here clearly and consciously introduced into the search for knowledge. Indeed, the *Essay* makes it clear that the study and measure of ignorance are the preamble to all search for knowledge. The central role of ignorance in the *Essay* is further confirmed by the fact that, from the fourth edition onward (1700), Ecclesiastes 11.5 was quoted on the title page: "As thou knowest not what is the way of the Spirit, nor how the bones do grow in the Womb of her that is with Child: even so thou knowest not the works of God, who maketh all things," reinforcing the idea that the *Essay* is primarily about human ignorance and its function in the search for knowledge. Locke scholars have interpreted this quotation, as well as the Ciceronian epigraph also quoted on the title page of the *Essay*, as evidence of Locke's skeptical approach or as calls for humility.[20] More importantly, they indicate a rehabilitation of ignorance, not as a virtue or a quality, but as a legitimate object of the scientific discourse and an important component of scientific method. Given the role and importance attributed to ignorance in the *Essay*, the text is as much an essay concerning human understanding as an essay concerning human ignorance.[21]

The Argument from Ignorance

In addition to the measure of ignorance as an essential part of Lockean method, ignorance is given another important function in Locke's philosophy, which is actually a consequence of the recognition of its ontological and universal dimension. Since ignorance is shared by all, Locke argues that no one should endeavor to convince others that they are wrong, when they themselves have no sure way of knowing who is right: "We should do well to commiserate our mutual ignorance, and endeavour to remove it in all the gentle and fair ways of information; and not instantly treat others ill, as obstinate and perverse, because they will not renounce their own, and receive our opinions."[22] Indeed, since all men are ignorant, no one can claim that they are right, and the opinions of others must be deemed as legitimate and relevant as one's own, in the first place, before any evidence can be given, or if no evidence can be given. This is the foundation of the "argument from ignorance," first defined by Locke in the *Essay concerning Human Understanding*.[23] Ignorance was thus given yet another function in Locke's philosophy since he founded a call for religious toleration upon human ignorance or universal fallibility, which implied that no one could prove and assert without a doubt that a religion was the right one and that all the others were erroneous. As a consequence, Locke argued, several churches should be tolerated or accepted in the state, as long as they do not jeopardize the social order of the country.

The argument from ignorance, or *argumentum ad ignorantiam*, has often been classified as a fallacy in logic textbooks because it implies that a proposition should be accepted on the grounds that it cannot be disproved, thus making ignorance or negative knowledge an argument in favor of the assertion of a proposition. The most obvious illustration of the argument from ignorance is the conclusion that there must be ghosts (or other similar immaterial entities) because no one has ever proved that there are no ghosts.[24] The argument from ignorance is also commonly used in a context in which it is not held as a fallacy, a court of law, where a person is presumed innocent until proven guilty. Here again, the conclusion—even though it may be temporary—is based on ignorance, or absence of certain knowledge or proof. In Locke's *Essay concerning Human Understanding*, the *argumentum ad ignorantiam* is described as "a way that Men ordinarily use to drive others, and force them to submit their Judgments, and receive the Opinion in debate." It consists in requiring "the Adversary to admit what they allege as a Proof, or to assign a better."[25] It is presented as one of four sorts of arguments "that Men in their Reasonings with others do ordinarily make use of, to prevail on their Assent, or at least so to awe them, as to silence their Opposition."[26] Even though the argument from ignorance is here defined as a means to impose one's opinions on others in the absence of positive knowledge or proof, and is therefore potentially suspicious, Locke does not clearly state that it is inherently fallacious. As the logician Charles Hamblin puts it, Locke "stands poised between acceptance and disapproval."[27] The *argumentum ad ignorantiam* is described by the English philosopher as a method or a sort of argument, used by one party in a dialogue. Although it does not establish knowledge directly, it can "prepare the way for knowledge."[28]

In his book *Arguments from Ignorance*, Douglas Walton demonstrates that the *argumentum ad ignorantiam* can have nonfallacious uses and can thus be a reasonable kind of argument. Its being presumptive and inconclusive does not imply that it is necessarily fallacious or erroneous. Walton claims that this argument is considered fallacious by those for whom only knowledge is worth having, but one can reply to this objection that knowledge of one's ignorance is also a relevant and legitimate basis for action or reflection.[29] Interestingly enough, Walton contends that the argument from ignorance can be traced back, even before Locke, to Socratic wisdom or knowledge of one's own ignorance, and to Nicholas of Cusa's doctrine of learned ignorance. In this context, learned ignorance is a form of knowledge.[30] One can understand how the argument from ignorance can then be used as a nonfallacious argument. Walton further states that, with the rise of foundationalism, ignorance came to be excluded from science. It was especially the case with Descartes, for whom scientific reasoning should be based on "axiomlike bedrock first principles that can be absolutely and indubitably known to be true."[31] As a consequence, the argument from ignorance came to be seen as a fallacy. According to Walton, the rejection of the *argumentum ad ignorantiam* by foundationalists was based on a misunderstanding of this argument, which should not be interpreted as a positive, knowledge-based kind of argument, which it clearly is not.[32] Instead, the argument from ignorance is "a presumptive kind of argument that has the function of pointing the way in reasoning in certain frameworks of conversational argument, subject to retraction and correction in the future, should new information come in."[33] Finally, as the positivistic view of science came to be criticized, ignorance was reintroduced as an important dimension of scientific reasoning, Walton argues.

Walton's developments on the origins and historical uses of the argument from ignorance show the relevance of the notion of ignorance to seventeenth-century French and English philosophy, as well as the important role of Cusanus's thought in this history. But his conception of foundationalism and of Descartes's philosophy in particular echoes erroneous interpretations of Cartesianism as a form of dogmatism that were common in the early modern period.[34] More importantly, and this is the focus here, in the context of seventeenth-century religious debates, the *argumentum ad ignorantiam* was used as a nonfallacious type of argument by Locke in his defense of religious toleration, which was partly founded on human fallibility or universal ignorance. Indeed, in 1661, Locke wrote an essay on infallibility, entitled "An necesse sit dari in Ecclesia infallibilem Sacro Sanctae Scripturae interpretem? Negatur" ("Is it necessary that an infallible interpreter of Holy Scripture be granted in the church? No"), in which he refuted the claim of the Roman Catholic Church that the pope was an infallible interpreter of Scriptures. One of Locke's arguments was that, even if there existed such an infallible interpreter, they could never prove their infallibility: "How anxiously you must anticipate a cure for vice and ignorance from someone, when you do not know whether the man to whose trust you comit yourself is a doctor or a charlatan."[35] Moreover, Locke argued that, as men, magistrates did not have more certain or infallible knowledge than anyone else, contrary to what was commonly assumed: "religious coercion rests on an assumption, explicit or implicit, of the legislator's infallibility."[36] Because no one has infallible knowledge, or at least can demonstrate that they have such knowledge, no one should be allowed to impose religious opinions on others. Similarly, in the *Essay concerning Human Understanding*, Locke rejected innate principles on the grounds that they were claims of infallibility allowing men in office to govern as they wished.[37] For similar reasons, Locke also rejected the enthusiasts' inner light, defined as certain knowledge above reason, as was shown in part 2. Like innate principles, the inner light, which is no more than its own proof, could be used to impose opinions on others.[38]

In Locke's *Letter on Toleration*, written at about the same time as the *Essay*, the argument from ignorance plays again a central part in the defense of toleration, as G. A. J. Rogers has demonstrated.[39] In this text, Locke asserts again that magistrates are not superior to other men and that the ignorance of all when it comes to religious matters should lead to liberty in "speculative opinions" (opinions that do not have consequences on the lives of others):

> I have a weak Body, sunk under a languishing Disease, for which (I suppose) there is one only Remedy, but that unknown: Does it therefore belong unto the Magistrate to prescribe me a Remedy; because there is but one, and because it is unknown? . . . Those things that every man ought sincerely to enquire into himself, and by Meditation, Study, Search, and his own Endeavours, attain the knowledge of, cannot be looked upon as the peculiar Possession of any one sort of Men. Princes indeed are born superior unto other Men in Power, but in Nature equal.[40]

Princes are as ignorant in religious matters as other men. They have no certain knowledge of what will ensure the salvation of their subjects, and they are probably less concerned by that salvation than the subjects themselves, who should therefore be allowed to follow their consciences: "The one only narrow way which leads to Heaven is not better known to the Magistrate than to private persons; and therefore I cannot safely take him for my Guide, who may probably be as ignorant of the way as my self, and who certainly is less concerned for my Salvation than I my self am."[41] Since there is no reason magistrates should be allowed to decide what religion is the true one, all the churches that do not threaten the order and peace of the country should be admitted. Thus, human ignorance or universal fallibility was used by Locke to serve and support an important principle of his philosophy, that of religious toleration.

Ignorance and Habits

It has been argued so far that, for Locke, ignorance was an epistemological tool that enabled him to get an image of the naked understanding and its workings, an anthropological limit that philosophers needed to measure in order to found the new science, and an argument used to justify religious toleration. One last aspect of the treatment of ignorance specific to Locke's philosophy should be mentioned here: in keeping with his vision of the original sin presented above and with his rejection of innate principles, Locke interpreted ignorance in relation with the social and cultural environment of individuals, which also had an impact on his conception of education. He was very much aware that the distempers and weaknesses of the faculties had a natural and a social or cultural origin: "There are several

Weaknesses and Defects in the Understanding, either from the natural Temper of the Mind, or ill Habits taken up, which hinder it in its progress to Knowledge."[42] Locke was indeed particularly attentive to the social and cultural dimensions of knowledge and ignorance. In *Conduct of the Understanding*, for example, he asserts that there is no natural hierarchy of men's understandings, although there is a great variety of them, and knowledge is variously advanced among people: "The *Americans* are not all born with worse Understandings than the *Europeans*, tho' we see none of them have such reaches in the Arts and Sciences. And among the Children of a poor Country-man, the lucky chance of Education and getting into the World, gives one infinitely the superiority on Parts over the rest, who continuing at home, had continued also just of the same size with his Brethren."[43] The variety of social conditions results in inequalities between men and groups of men, some being more ignorant than others because they do not have access to education or because they want time and leisure to dedicate themselves to the search for knowledge: "the difference so observable in Men's Understandings and Parts, does not arise so much from their Natural Faculties as acquired Habits."[44] Locke insists in several of his works on the difficulty for laborers to get out of ignorance for lack of leisure and opportunities. This is explicitly stated in the *Essay concerning Human Understanding*, for example, where, using a very striking imagery, Locke first describes those men "given up to Labour, and enslaved to the Necessity of their mean Condition; whose Lives are worn out, only in the Provisions for Living," whose time is spent silencing "the Croaking of their own Bellies, or the Cries of their Children." Those men are "unavoidably given over to invincible Ignorance of those Proofs, on which others build, and which are necessary to establish those Opinions."[45] Yet just as all are nevertheless required to get religious knowledge, all must learn to use their understandings properly, Locke insists, even though expectations from a gentleman and from a peasant cannot be the same: "No body is under an Obligation to know every thing. Knowledge and Science in general, is the business only of those who are at Ease and Leisure. Those who have particular Callings ought to understand them; and 'tis no unreasonable Proposal, nor impossible to be compass'd, that they should think and reason right about what is their daily Imployment."[46] Men who have "particular Callings" can thus make the most of "the one Day of seven, besides other Days of Rest," to improve their knowledge of religion. There is no reason why they should not be able to do so as "the Original make of their Minds is like that of other Men."[47] They must make the effort to search for knowledge and be encouraged to do so. Locke adds that there are examples of poor people who have succeeded in "clear[ing] that Condition of Life from a necessity of gross Ignorance," such as "the Peasantry lately in *France*... of the Reformed Religion,"[48] even as they were in a far worse situation than the day laborers in England.

With a good use of the understanding, improvement of a man's faculties, whatever his role in society, is possible and ignorance can be overcome, but men tend to neglect this faculty, out of laziness, belief that it cannot be improved, or want of leisure: "And it is easie to perceive that Men are guilty of a great many Faults in the Exercise and Improvement of this Faculty of the Mind, which hinder them in their Progress, and keep them in Ignorance and Error all their Lives."[49] Those who refuse to get the knowledge that is expected from them are "in love with Ignorance and ... accountable for it,"[50] hence Locke's interest in education as a means to perfect the human mind and overcome social limits. The aim of education is therefore not so much to acquire knowledge, but to learn how to reason properly, which is why, in *Conduct of the Understanding*, Locke insists so much on the model of mathematics, whereas he judges reading and learning severely.[51] In a 1677 entry to his journal, Locke also stresses the danger of reading bad books, which is not only a loss of time but also a step back in one's studies, as "he that has his head filled with wrong notions is much more at a distance from truth than he that is perfectly ignorant."[52]

Locke adds that, given their different social environments, men are bound to have very different intakes on particular subjects, and he encourages them to talk and exchange their views as a way to gain knowledge. In his *Thoughts concerning Education*, Locke explains that children as well as adults always need to be helped out of ignorance by others, thus underlining the collective dimension of the acquisition of knowledge: "happy are they who meet with civil People, that will comply with their Ignorance, and help them to get out of it."[53] Locke takes the example of a man traveling to Japan and asking "a thousand Questions" to the indigenous population, who would probably find them irrelevant. In this case, Locke explains: "we should be glad to find a Man so kind and humane, as to answer [those questions], and instruct our Ignorance."[54] Besides, all men have but partial views of the world: consulting others, especially people from a different social background and with a different role in society, is a way to have a more comprehensive view of the world, and therefore build knowledge.[55] Locke regrets that "some Men of Study and Thought, that reason right, and are Lovers of Truth, do make no great Advances in their Discoveries of it" because they consult only with people of a similar social and cultural condition, so that they remain ignorant of a whole part of the world.[56]

In other words, "men of study" presume that other people, who have not studied as they have, are ignorant and have therefore nothing to contribute to the search for knowledge. But this is a mistake, and the consequence of this assumption or prejudice is that general knowledge is not increased as it could be. Social divisions are therefore a hindrance to the advancement of knowledge.[57] But these remarks also imply that the assimilation of ignorance and wisdom is erroneous: ignorant men who think themselves wise are mistaken. They are merely representative of "those who live thus mued up within their own contracted Territories, and will not look abroad beyond the Boundaries that Chance, Conceit, or Laziness has set to their Enquiries."[58] Locke takes the example of the inhabitants of the Mariana Islands, who knew nothing of other nations and cultures before the arrival of the Spaniards and thus lived "in the want and ignorance of almost all things."[59] They thought that they were "the happiest and wisest People of the Universe," while they were actually like those "men of study" who love truth but never progress in their discovery of it because they refuse to open up to other people and places. It is fair to say that Locke did not share Montaigne's admiration for the inhabitants of Brazil, who lived "in a wonderfull kinde of simplicitie and ignorance."[60] For Locke, simplicity and ignorance may have brought happiness to those people, but they also prevented them from contributing to the discovery of truth, while it is very clear that, for Locke, all men (and perhaps women), whatever their origins or conditions, are expected to search for truth and increase their knowledge, or rather the general knowledge of mankind, which can be improved only through a collective endeavor.

Douglas John Casson has argued that Locke imitated Montaigne and Charron in drawing upon ancient sources as well as contemporary travel literature to emphasize the importance of customs and habits. Locke often referred to foreign traditions, which he discovered in the numerous travel books that he owned and that were then used in his anthropology as a source for understanding human nature or human dispositions. Thus, in book I of the *Essay concerning Human Understanding*, for example, Locke draws a long list of customs to refute innate principles.[61] It should be added though that references to travel literature were also a Baconian practice, shared by other fellows of the Royal Society, such as Robert Boyle. But it is interesting to come back to Montaigne at the very end of this inquiry on Locke and reflect again on Prior's imagined dialogue between the two philosophers, quoted at the beginning of this book. Montaigne's and Locke's philosophies are obviously very different, even when it comes to their conceptions of ignorance. Yet focusing on interpretations of ignorance according to both authors also shows what Locke's *Essay* owes to Montaigne's *Essais*. Locke owned copies of Montaigne's work, both in French and in Florio's translation; he also owned numerous works by Charron (among them *Of Wisdom* in English and in French), which echoed Montaigne's, as was mentioned earlier. Locke's debt to Montaigne in terms of pedagogy has been widely acknowledged, but the similarities between the works of the two men on other subjects, as well as on their styles of writing philosophy, deserve more attention. Like most English readers of Montaigne's *Essais* in the late seventeenth century, Locke probably interpreted the text as presenting a form of empiricism and a *liberté d'esprit* that suited his own philosophy.[62] He may also have found in the *Essais* the language and resources to encourage amateurs' participation in philosophy. Casson adds that Locke shared with Montaigne and Charron "a similar skepticism."[63] But rather than a skeptical outlook, it has been shown here that a continuity can be traced from Montaigne's *Essais* to Locke's *Essay* in the central role attributed to ignorance in the search for knowledge and truth: what Montaigne and Locke have in common is the conviction that ignorance as an anthropological trait should not be ignored but instead carefully understood and assimilated into discourses and methods promoting the advancement of knowledge. Both authors developed doctrines of ignorance that put this notion to the forefront of reflections on human nature and human science.

To conclude, this part has shown that ignorance could be used as an epistemological instrument in the context of the emergence of modern science. Representations of complete ignorance through myths of the tabula rasa, autodidacticism, and the persona of the Idiot served to shed light on the workings of the understanding and, as a result, devise more efficient methods to search for truth. Moreover, the processes whereby chance discoveries made by illiterate men occurred were appropriated by the experimentalists who tried to reproduce their conditions of occurrence and foster in themselves the sagacity of ignorant discoverers. Finally, Locke's treatment of ignorance shows that it was fully introduced into the scientific discourse of the late seventeenth century in England, not as an obstacle to knowledge, but as an anthropological limit that needs to be measured as a preamble to all search for truth. This was made possible thanks to the dissociation of ignorance and the original sin.

Because ignorance is not perceived as a deficiency, as a sin or a disease that should be cured in Locke's philosophy, it can be part of the search for truth. Moreover, as was seen earlier, universal ignorance or fallibility was used by Locke to promote toleration—yet another important function of ignorance, with a strong legacy in the eighteenth century. This part has shown that, despite its novelty, Locke's enduring doctrine of ignorance drew upon a great number of traditions and conceptions of ignorance studied in parts 1 and 2, regardless of their religious or intellectual origins: it borrowed from Montaigne's and Charron's anthropologies of ignorance, from Calvin's interpretation of learned ignorance, and from the emphasis of Restoration authors—especially Joseph Glanvill and Richard Baxter—on the role of ignorance in religious and political divisions.

Conclusion

There will always be half-wise men to say that this posture is an illusion, that ignorance is only a ruse of the learned, or a mere rhetorical stratagem. Admittedly, there is no erasing knowledge, one cannot start again from scratch. But this ruse is stimulating and sometimes necessary. . . . The postulate of ignorance aims to free the intelligence and give new impetus to the search. . . . There are occasions when, in order to save the mind, a tabula rasa is a salutary ruse. The topos of ignorance may be naïve, but it is also a spiritual necessity and, for the intelligence, a vital reflex.[1]

In this fervent plea for the recognition of the virtues of ignorance, the historian of literature Michel Jeanneret goes beyond the observation and exposition of the essential role of ignorance in the early modern period to celebrate "the postulate of ignorance" in our lives as an invigorating ruse that enlivens the mind. It is but a stratagem because complete ignorance cannot be realized and is thus never found; it is also a posture usually held by learned men and women—and often by early modern gentlemen, as was shown earlier. Yet it is required for the advancement of learning, for new discoveries to be made, for the elaboration of new ways of thinking, as well as for the welfare and vigor of the mind. The idea of divesting oneself of all previous knowledge, emptying or liberating one's mind, to make a new birth (of knowledge and of the self) possible, is admittedly a myth, but it is, Jeanneret argues, "the founding myth of modernity."[2]

Jeanneret's call for the recognition of the essential role of ignorance in the workings of the mind is also central to *The Paradoxes of Ignorance*. This inquiry into the fortunes of ignorance in early modern England and France shows that it played a pivotal role in the emergence of modern science as a quality or an attribute that implied self-knowledge and wisdom, as a promoter of reason and the inner light, and as an epistemological instrument. In other words, ignorance has been reinstated in this book as one of the foremost conceptual issues of the early modern period. The notion of ignorance was examined by theologians and philosophers well before that time, but it became particularly relevant in the context of humanism, the Reformation and the emergence of the new science that all entailed rethinking the dialectics of ignorance and knowledge, and elaborating new ways of thinking and knowing. If the counterintuitive celebrations of ignorance studied in this book show the importance played by this notion in the early modern period, the objections to those praises and the debates that often ensued confirm this role.

Three virtues of ignorance have been presented in the book. It was first argued that ignorance could be identified with wisdom. In the paradoxical tradition of learned ignorance, peasants, artisans, "savages," and generally the illiterate were seen as model philosophers. Their humility and the recognition of their own ignorance made them wiser and happier than scholars. They could reach divine and natural truth through a naïve but lucid observation of the world, and a greater proximity to nature. It is argued here that this conception of ignorance as wisdom was not so much a legacy of different forms of ancient skepticism as evidence of an appropriation of medieval mystical doctrines, especially Nicholas of Cusa's *docta ignorantia*, the anonymous *Cloud of Unknowing*, and other praises of negative theology, underlining the persistence of medieval traditions throughout the early modern period, especially in France. This favorable reception of learned ignorance was indeed largely found in writings by French authors, those who have been considered as the promoters of the new science, like Descartes, but also his adversaries at the time, in particular the circles of the *libertins érudits*. In England, on the contrary, such doctrines of ignorance did not permeate the main intellectual traditions and were rarely found. They admittedly received attention from groups of thinkers or individuals in seventeenth-century England, in particular the Cambridge Platonists, Joseph Glanvill, and radical preachers, but this influence was limited and marginal. Instead, it was shown here that virulent refutations of those doctrines of ignorance were expressed in England, in particular by Francis Bacon and some of his followers in the experimental tradition.

The second conception of ignorance studied in this book assimilates it to a principle of knowledge, meaning that it was supposed to offer a spontaneous access to natural and divine knowledge. In this case, ignorance was defined as the inner light or as a condition that allowed for the inner light to shine. Ignorance was thus interpreted as a precondition to knowledge because learning was suspected of hindering the operations of the faculties, especially those of reason. Promoters of ignorance argued that learning confused and stifled or obstructed the understanding and, conversely, ignorance liberated the mind, which could then spontaneously access truth. Thus, according to this conception (or at least the interpretation it was given at the time), ignorance was understood as paradoxically leading to knowledge. This conception of ignorance as a principle of knowledge caused many reactions, especially in England, where it was deemed dangerous both for the order of society and for the advancement of learning, essentially because it was associated with radical theology. In France, it was accused of being an inefficient method to reach truth as well as a threat to religion.

Finally, this book has shown that ignorance was rehabilitated in the early modern period as an epistemological instrument. In this case, it was not an attribute or a condition of the mind that should be self-induced, but a tool enabling philosophers to imagine the naked understanding to better comprehend its inner workings. The aim of fictions of ignorance such as the tabula rasa, autodidacticism, and the Idiot was to devise new ways of thinking and knowing based on the observation of the mechanisms of the human mind. Their purpose was thus to improve the methods for the acquisition and production of knowledge. In this reflection on method, a particular quality of ignorant people was praised: their sagacity, which enabled them to make chance discoveries, as the topos of the illiterate inventor went. Their ignorance itself was not considered a quality, as it was in the learned ignorance tradition presented here, but their sagacity was recognized as an efficient tool for knowledge of nature. Therefore, even though English experimental philosophers did not exactly recommend fostering sagacity in oneself (whereas Descartes did, for example), they devised ways to *imitate* sagacity, as well as methods that would deliberately cause the occurrence of accidents by imitating the process whereby ignorant people made discoveries by chance. Ignorance was thus clearly introduced into the scientific discourse of the time. This epistemological role of ignorance was found mostly in the Baconian program and in the works of a number of his followers. In the late seventeenth century, ignorance was also an epistemological tool and an object of the scientific discourse in the works of John Locke, where it was given a prominent role. However, Locke's conception of ignorance was different from that of Bacon and from most of his fellow experimentalists. In particular, this book underlines the comprehensive treatment of ignorance in Locke's works, where it is defined as a logical and epistemological tool, as an anthropological trait, and as a social reality that implies a reflection on its potential remedies and not only on its causes. If there was a form of secularization in Locke's treatment of ignorance, it cannot as easily be affirmed for other early modern conceptions of ignorance, even in the context of experimentalism, where condemnations of ignorance, based mostly on its religious interpretation, remained common.

The comparison between England and France has shown that there were different tendencies in the understanding of the function of ignorance in one's access to truth. Those tendencies can be summed up as follows: in France, a tradition that can be traced back to Cusanus and his appropriation of Socratic wisdom, and that also bore the legacy of the "discourse against letters," celebrated ignorance as a condition conducive to wisdom and happiness. In this tradition, ignorance should be sought for and even deliberately provoked in the quest for knowledge as the truth can be discovered only to the unprejudiced mind. Access to truth therefore required awareness of one's ignorance as a form of knowledge. In England, an influential tradition, which may be traced back to Francis Bacon in the early seventeenth century, strongly rejected ignorance as such, which was understood as an obstacle to the advancement of learning and, for some experimentalists, the mark of the Fall on the human mind. If some of the fellows of the Royal Society who later implemented the Baconian program for the promotion of science insisted on the necessity to accept and define human ignorance before science could actually be advanced, they did not celebrate ignorance per se. They held artisans in high esteem, mostly because of their innocence and integrity, as their minds were not corrupted by the vain learning of the schools, but innocence did not imply ignorance, as the model of prelapsarian Adam well showed. Yet English experimentalists were also interested in ignorance, as a tool that enabled one to have a clearer image of the understanding, and thus better grasp the process of knowledge acquisition, which could then be improved thanks to more efficient methods of inquiry. One might have expected advocates of experimental philosophy to support or judge favorably the doctrine of learned ignorance because the Cusan philosophy, especially as it was expounded in *De idiota*, could easily be used to their advantage in their effort to legitimize the experimental program, and because it echoed their own calls for humility and modesty. On the contrary, it appears that all forms of ignorance as a personal quality or attribute were condemned. As has been argued here, Bacon may very well have been responding, in *The Advancement of Learning*, to those who had given ignorance some credit in the previous decades, in particular Agrippa and Montaigne. Hence his systematic refutation of the doctrines of ignorance.

Thus, it seems that, apart from a few exceptions, English philosophers remained largely impervious to doctrines that would attempt to praise and foster ignorance. However, philosophies and theologies that attributed a positive role to ignorance per se were found in seventeenth-century England as well, for example among religious sects, such as the Quakers and Baptists, and among the Cambridge Platonists. Moreover, it is shown in this book that English doctrines of ignorance were developed in the context of experimentalism, by Joseph Glanvill, in particular, who probably drew upon the learned ignorance tradition even while he adopted a Calvinistic interpretation of ignorance as a consequence of Adam's sin. In France, most *libertins érudits* condemned celebrations of ignorance, and insisted instead on learning, which was required, they argued, in order to formulate one's own opinion. Contrary to most criticisms of learning as a burden that merely filled the memory with useless notions and prevented one to think by themselves, the *libertins* argued that learning was the basis of personal and independent thinking. Given this praise of learning, the numerous references to Francis Bacon in the *libertins'* works and their radical condemnation of Cornelius Agrippa are no surprise. Yet the *libertins'* skepticism also led them to celebrate some form of learned ignorance, understood as the alliance of erudition and doubt. But ignorance for them was not a mode of wisdom, and it could not be used as a premise to the elaboration of a new philosophical system, as it was for Descartes. It thus appears that there were not only two different or "national" attitudes to ignorance in the early modern period, but variations on those general tendencies within each country. It also appears that underlying those contradictory debates on the role of ignorance was an important reflection on ways of thinking and knowing.

It has been assumed throughout the book, for simplicity's sake, that knowledge, science, wisdom, and truth were all more or less equivalent when they expressed the end of mankind's quest, that is, what early modern philosophers and theologians were searching for. Those notions were often used interchangeably and loosely by the authors themselves. But it is obvious, at the end of this inquiry, that a distinction should be made between science and wisdom in particular. A more precise analysis of the relations between those terms in England and in France is needed, but a few remarks can be made here, based on the writings studied in this book. First, it is safe to say that, in the learned ignorance tradition, wisdom fared favorably compared to science. Thus, Charron's systematic opposition between wisdom (*sagesse*) and science (*science*) showed that he conceived of the two as mutually exclusive: "he that hath much knowledge or arte is seldome wise, and he that is wise hath not much knowledge."[3] Science, which is here assimilated with "art" and "knowledge,"[4] is a mere collection of things heard or read, therefore obtained from others, and gathered in one's memory. Wisdom, in contrast, is "the rule of the soule,"[5] which is managed by judgment—in other words, wisdom is the good government of the soul. As mentioned earlier, a similar opposition between science or learning and wisdom was found in Montaigne's *Essays*, where the former is also defined as something obtained from others, whereas wisdom is superior precisely because it comes from within one's soul: "Suppose we may be learned by other mens learning. Sure I am, wee can never be wise, but by our owne wisdom."[6] Wisdom is self-engendered, which makes it more invaluable. It can be defined as self-knowledge or knowledge of one's ignorance, as a necessary prerequisite to any form of divine or natural knowledge.

In Bacon's *The Advancement of Learning*, which presents his systematic rejection of ignorance analyzed here, the opposition between knowledge and wisdom is made along religious lines. Bacon distinguishes between learning, defined as "knowledge acquired"—the equivalent of "science," according to Montaigne and Charron—and wisdom or "sapience," presented as spontaneous knowledge of God: "all learning is knowledge acquired, and all knowledge in God is originall. And therefore we must looke for it by another name, that of wisedome or sapience, as the scriptures call it."[7] Natural knowledge or learning is here distinguished from religious wisdom, a distinction that enabled Bacon to exclude religion from the activity of the natural philosopher.[8] It has been argued that Bacon's thought ushered a transition from wisdom to science as the primary aim of the philosopher, who stopped being a moral sage to become a natural philosopher.[9] Indeed, what is also at stake in this inquiry into early modern conceptions of ignorance is the very figure or persona of the philosopher and his qualities, as well as his relation to religion. The relevance of conceptions of ignorance to the definition of the good philosopher is also evident in the early modern authors' interpretations of Socrates's attitude to knowledge and ignorance reported in this book. The history of ignorance presented here draws a multifarious portrait of Socrates, the greatest philosophical paradox.

But the opposition between wisdom and science should be qualified as well, and no clear line can be drawn between the two, or between two traditions, a tradition of learned ignorance that would favor wisdom and a tradition stressing the fight against ignorance that would favor science. The vanity of attempting to distinguish between the two was underlined in the mid-seventeenth century by Charles Sorel, who first pointed to the difference between wisdom and science, arguing that wisdom was superior to all other virtues and to science itself as it was defined as knowledge of God, which also implied knowledge of oneself.

More precisely, wisdom is conceived in *De la perfection de l'homme*, much as it is in Charron's *De la sagesse*, as "the disposition of a man to order his thoughts, his words, and his actions."[10] Wisdom needs no other science than the science of God. But then Sorel adds that learning is useful and can guide one toward wisdom. After those hesitations and a long list of oppositions between science and wisdom, the conclusion reveals the difficulty of distinguishing between the two: "Let us no longer make these distinctions between Science and Wisdom: The Man who enjoys true Science also has Wisdom, and the one who has Wisdom has true Science."[11] Despite irresolution on the subject, such reflections, which involved considerations on knowledge and ignorance, show a common desire to establish a clear distinction between science and wisdom. This distinction was closely linked with the reflection on interpretations of ignorance: if wisdom, understood as the government of the soul, was the aim, then ignorance was the way, whereas if science was the aim, then ignorance was an obstacle, except when it was conceived as a principle of knowledge, in philosophies of the internal light.

Finally, an important contention of this book is that ignorance played a central role in John Locke's philosophy, an aspect that has been largely overlooked so far. If Locke was not a skeptic, he did focus on ignorance, its definition, its causes, and its consequences, stressing that the measure of ignorance was the first necessary step in the search for knowledge. Unlike Descartes, Locke did not encourage men and women to make themselves ignorant by rejecting all previous knowledge, but only to observe their natural ignorance and assess its extent, even though, in both cases, considerations of ignorance are the way to knowledge. Locke built upon past doctrines of ignorance, in particular those of Montaigne and Charron, as well as those of Joseph Glanvill and Richard Baxter, to elaborate his own anthropology of ignorance, which, this book argues, marked a turning point in the history of this notion. Indeed, even though Locke's "anthropologization" of ignorance and his insistence on the observation and measure of this human trait may seem unremarkable at first, partly because it borrowed from previous thinkers, it did have a great impact on ways of knowing and thinking as ignorance became entirely included into the scientific discourse—without being deprived of its theological dimension, as the verse from Ecclesiastes on the title page of the *Essay* also attests. It became the main source for conceptions of ignorance all along the eighteenth century in England and in France.

That Locke's philosophy was a common reference in eighteenth-century encyclopedias is well known, but a closer look at the treatment of ignorance, in particular, in those volumes is instructive: in Diderot and d'Alembert's *Encyclopédie* (1765), the first entry on ignorance, namely "metaphysical ignorance," is, for the most part, a translation of Locke's definition of ignorance and list of its causes given in the *Essay* (IV, 3, 23), while the presentation of "moral ignorance" in the *Encyclopédie* relies on medieval theological treatments of the notion.[12] The very distinction between metaphysical and moral ignorance may be an effect of Locke's philosophy. In the first edition of the *Encyclopaedia Britannica* (1771), explicit reference is made to Locke's presentation of the causes of ignorance, which is found again in the article on "metaphysics," where the passage on the definition and causes of ignorance in the *Essay* is reproduced, with only a few adjustments or reformulations.[13] Again, if those references to Locke in eighteenth-century English and French encyclopedias are not surprising as such, they do testify to the fortune and enduring relevance of Locke's conception of ignorance in the decades following his death in both countries.

Even more interestingly, there is evidence that some of Locke's works were read in eighteenth-century France as treatises dealing specifically with human ignorance. Scholarship has shown that two main aspects of Locke's philosophy received attention across the Channel in the decades following his death: his refutation of innate ideas and his conception of thinking matter.[14] But Locke's notion of ignorance was also an important dimension of his reception in France, especially in the writings of Voltaire. As is well known, Voltaire was a great admirer of Locke, whom he mentions in several of his works from 1733 and the publication in London of the *Letters concerning the English Nation*, especially Letter XIII, which draws a flattering portrait of the English philosopher that was instrumental to the favorable reception of his ideas in France. But very few scholars have noticed that Voltaire had perceived the crucial role of ignorance in Locke's works: the comparatist Charles Dédéyan may be the only one to have underlined that Voltaire was particularly receptive to Locke's notion of ignorance.[15] This favorable reception appears in the *Letters concerning the English Nation*,[16] but also in less well-known works, such as *Poème sur la loi naturelle* (1752), for example, where Voltaire emphasizes Locke's essential and positive role in defining the limits of knowledge and restricting its extent: "Et ce Locke, en un mot, dont la main courageuse / A de l'esprit humain posé la borne heureuse."[17] The reference to the "happy boundaries" of the mind that Locke charted reveals what is essential in his philosophy, according to Voltaire: a philosophical and anthropological conception of ignorance that, to a certain extent, frees humankind.

Le philosophe ignorant (1766) is, among Voltaire's texts, the treatise that most clearly reveals the importance of Locke's conception of ignorance. Not only does Voltaire in this text stress the central role of ignorance in Locke's epistemology—the model "ignorant philosopher" being Locke—but he also shows how the notion of ignorance was to him closely linked to calls for toleration. Voltaire argues in this text, following Locke, that universal ignorance and fallibility mean that no one should feel entitled to impose their ideas on others. Thus, the 1779 English translation of Voltaire's text by Reverend David Williams was unsurprisingly published alongside the philosophe's *Treatise on Toleration* (1763), in a volume entitled *A Treatise on Toleration; The Ignorant Philosopher; and a Commentary on the Marquis of Becaria's Treatise on Crimes and Punishments*, emphasizing the relation between ignorance and toleration.[18] Moreover, Voltaire's very learned *Philosophe ignorant* does not merely echo Locke's *Essay concerning Human Understanding*: it is for a great part a rewriting and adaptation of the text, with an insistence on the main themes of the *Essay* in relation to ignorance, namely man's weakness (II), innate ideas (V), the limits of human understanding (IX), discoveries that cannot be made (X), and the despair of not knowing anything perfectly (XI). Then, three sections are devoted to Locke himself, who is presented as "a modest man, who never pretends to know what he is really ignorant of."[19] Finally, four sections deal with ignorance per se, insisting again on the extent of human ignorance and listing its main objects. Following Locke's call for the observation and measure of our ignorance prior to our search for knowledge, Voltaire writes when addressing "impossible discoveries": "In the small circle where we are confined, let us see therefore what we are condemned to be ignorant of, and what we may have a little knowledge of."[20] As for Locke, those reflections on ignorance are not merely epistemological and anthropological considerations: they lead to vehement calls for toleration at the end of "A Short Commentary by the Ignorant Philosopher, on the Eulogium of the Dauphin of France," appended to the main treatise, with an eloquent conclusion drawn by the ignorant himself: "*Let us persecute no man.*"[21]

Notes

Introduction

1. Matthew Prior, "A Dialogue between Mr. John Lock and Seigneur de Montaigne" (1721), in *Dialogues of the Dead and Other Works in Prose and Verse*, ed. Alfred R. Waller (Cambridge: Cambridge University Press, 1907), 223–46, here 231–32.

2. On ignorance and the myth of the illiterate inventor in the early modern period, see part 3 and Sandrine Parageau, "'Colomb ignorant trouva le nouveau monde': Ignorance, découverte fortuite et expérimentation à la première modernité," *Revue d'Histoire des Sciences* 74, no. 1 (2021): 41–62. Although the relation between women and ignorance is broached several times throughout this book, it is not the focus here. On this subject, more specifically on early modern English women philosophers, their conception of their own ignorance, and how they used the modesty topos, see Sandrine Parageau, *Les Ruses de l'ignorance: La contribution des femmes à l'avènement de la science moderne en Angleterre* (Paris: Presses de la Sorbonne Nouvelle, 2010).

3. John Locke, *An Essay concerning Human Understanding* (1690), ed. Peter H. Nidditch (Oxford: Clarendon Press, 2011), III, 10, 9, 495. Montaigne's praise of artisans and the illiterate, which is further examined in part 1, is corroborated by several passages from his *Essays*, especially in the "Apology of Raymond Sebond," for example: "I have in my dayes seene a hundred Artificers, and as many laborers, more wise and more happy, then some Rectors in the university, and whom I would rather resemble." In Michel de Montaigne, "*An Apologie of* Raymond Sebond," in *The essayes or morall, politike and millitarie discourses of Lo: Michaell de Montaigne* (1580), trans. John Florio (London, 1603), II,

12, p. 281. The word *artificers* translates *artisans* in the original French version. Note that, whenever possible, references given in *The Paradoxes of Ignorance* are to early modern editions and translations, which give an indication of how a text was read and received at the time. The choice of words is often meaningful, especially in this inquiry on the conceptions and uses of ignorance, which implies retracing the genealogy of ideas and concepts. In the case of English translations, the original French is given in note when the passage is particularly important for the argument being made or when the original words deserve notice.

4. On religious interpretations and uses of ignorance in the context of the English Reformation, see Sandrine Parageau, "'Papists Make a Direct Profession of This Shamefull Sin': Denouncing Catholic Ignorance in Seventeenth-Century England," in *Anti-Catholicism in Britain and Ireland, 1600–2000: Practices, Representations and Ideas*, ed. C. Gheeraert-Graffeuille and G. Vaughan (London: Palgrave Macmillan, 2020), 93–108. On the difference between early modern English and French interpretations of the Fall and its consequences, see Peter Harrison, *The Fall of Man and the Foundations of Science* (Cambridge: Cambridge University Press, 2007).

5. William Gearing, *The Arraignment of Ignorance: Or, Ignorance. With the Causes and Kinds of it, the mischiefes and danger of it, together with the Cure of Ignorance: as also, the Excellency, Profit, and Benefit of Heavenly Knowledge, largely set forth from Hos. 4.6* (London, 1659), 28–29. As the title page of the book indicates, Gearing was minister at Lymington in the 1650s, but otherwise little is known about him. He was the author of texts that were often republished at the time, such as *The History of the Church of Great Britain* (London, 1674).

6. All biblical quotations are from the King James Bible, unless otherwise specified.

7. Steven Shapin, *The Scientific Revolution* (Chicago: University of Chicago Press, 1996), 1.

8. On the feeling that there was an unprecedented flood of information and on the contemporaries' attempts at finding solutions to manage such information, see Ann Blair, *Too Much To Know: Managing Scholarly Information before the Modern Age* (New Haven, CT: Yale University Press, 2010).

9. Richard H. Popkin, *The History of Scepticism from Savonarola to Bayle* (Oxford: Oxford University Press, 2003), xx. On Academic skepticism in the Renaissance, see Charles Schmitt, *Cicero scepticus: A Study of the Influence of* The Academica *in the Renaissance* (The Hague: Martinus Nijhoff, 1972).

10. Popkin, *The History of Scepticism, op. cit.*, 94.

11. *Ibid.*, xix.

12. Plato, *The Apology of Socrates*, trans. and ed. Thomas G. West (Ithaca, NY: Cornell University Press, 1979), 21a–23b, 25–27.

13. Plato, *Charmides*, trans., with introduction, notes, and analysis, Christopher Moore and Christopher C. Raymond (Indianapolis: Hackett Publishing, 2019), 167a, 23. In this translation, *sōphrosúnē* is rendered as "discipline."

14. David Lawrence Levine, *Profound Ignorance: Plato's* Charmides *and the Saving of Wisdom* (New York: Lexington Books, 2016), 214.

15. *Ibid.*, 222.

16. *Ibid.*, 223.

17. Jean-Pierre Cavaillé, *Les Déniaisés: Irréligion et libertinage au début de l'époque moderne* (Paris: Classiques Garnier, 2013), 244 (my translation).

18. Francesco Petrarca, *On His Own Ignorance and That of Many Others*, trans. Hans Nachod, in *The Renaissance Philosophy of Man*, ed. Ernst Cassirer, Paul Oskar Kristeller, and John Herman Randall Jr. (Chicago: University of Chicago Press, 1948), 47–133, here 54. Interestingly, Hans Nachod notes here that Petrarch uses the word *idiota* to refer to an illiterate or uneducated man, that is, "a man without higher education, in contrast to *literatus*" (n. 15, 54). This acceptation of *idiot, idiota,* and *idiotus* is also the one adopted in this history of ignorance. Nachod adds that the word *idiot* was becoming more pejorative in Petrarch's time and progressively equated with *simpleton*, but it will appear here later that the former meaning of the word remained common throughout the early modern period, allowing for a praise of ignorance understood as simplicity and humility as opposed to the vanity of scholastic erudition.

19. *Ibid.*, 79 and 127. Petrarch quotes at length from Cicero's *De natura deorum*, a text that was unsurprisingly a common reference to early modern praises of ignorance.

20. *Ibid.*, 64.

21. *Ibid.*, 65. Also, 1 Samuel 2.4 reads: "The bows of the mighty men are broken, and they that stumbled are girded with strength."

22. *Ibid.*, 62 and 72.

23. *Ibid.*, 56–57. On the centrality of method and the processes of the mind to the history of early modern ignorance, see in particular parts 2 and 3. This statement is in keeping with Descartes's approach to knowledge and reason, for example.

24. *Ibid.*, 67. On Petrarch's letter, see, for example, Michel Jeanneret, "Éloge de l'ignorance," in *La Philologie humaniste et ses représentations dans la théorie et dans la fiction*, ed. Perrine Galand-Hallyn, Fernand Hallyn, and Gilbert Tournay (Geneva: Droz, 2005), 2:637–651, here 2:640–642; and Zygmunt G. Barański, "The Ethics of Ignorance: Petrarch's Epicurus and Averroës and the Structures of the *De Sui Ipsius et Multorum Ignorantia*," in *Petrarch in Britain*, ed. Martin McLaughlin, Letizia Panizza, and Peter Hainsworth (Oxford: Oxford University Press, 2007), 39–59.

25. See Nicolas de Cues, *De la docte ignorance*, ed. Jean-Claude Lagarrigue (Paris: Éditions du Cerf, 2010), 73, n. 1, and 48, and St. Augustine, Epistle 130, in *The Works of Saint Augustine, Letters 100–155 (Epistulae)*, trans. Roland Teske, SJ, ed. Boniface Ramsey (New York: New City Press, 2003), pt. II, 2:183–199. See also *Confessions*, trans. F. J. Sheed (Indianapolis, Hackett, 1942), IX.x.xxiii–xxv, 199–201, and *De Trinitate*, 10.1.3, where Augustine focuses on self-knowledge. The question he asks is, How can we desire to know something that we are ignorant of, whether it be God or ourselves?

26. Augustine to Proba, in *The Works of Saint Augustine, op. cit.*, Epistle 130, 197.

27. See Nicolas de Cues, *La docte ignorance*, trans. and ed. Hervé Pasqua (Paris: Payot, 2011), 14. See also the English translation by Jasper Hopkins, *Nicholas of Cusa on Learned Ignorance: A Translation and an Appraisal of De Docta Ignorantia* (Minneapolis: Arthur J. Banning Press, 1981). *De docta ignorantia* is composed of three books: the first

one is about God (in himself), the second is about nature (God's manifestation), and the third one is about Christ (God's revelation).

28. *Nicholas of Cusa on Learned Ignorance*, op. cit., 6.

29. Cues, *La docte ignorance* (ed. Pasqua), *op. cit.*, 28. This idea is developed in chapter 3 of *De docta ignorantia*.

30. William Franke, "Learned Ignorance: The Apophatic Tradition of Cultivating the Virtue of Unknowing," in *Routledge International Handbook of Ignorance Studies*, ed. Matthias Gross and Linsey McGoey (London: Routledge, 2015), 26–35, here 28. See also William Franke, ed., *On What Cannot Be Said: Apophatic Discourses in Philosophy, Religion, Literature, and the Arts*, vol. 1 of *Classic Formulations* (Notre Dame, IN: University of Notre Dame Press, 2014). This book is an anthology of texts on apophaticism from Plato to Silesius Angelus in the seventeenth century, with commentaries by Franke. On apophaticism, learned ignorance, and negative theology, see also Denys Turner, *The Darkness of God: Negativity in Christian Mysticism* (Cambridge: Cambridge University Press, 1995).

31. *The Cloud of Unknowing*, ed. Patrick J. Gallacher (Kalamazoo: Western Michigan University Institute Publications, 1997), also available at Robbins Library Digital Projects, University of Rochester, https://d.lib.rochester.edu/teams/publication/gallacher-the-cloud-of-unknowing. See also Turner, *The Darkness of God*, op. cit., chap. 8 "*The Cloud of Unknowing* and the Critique of Interiority," 186–210, and the introduction to the text by John Clark (Universität Salzburg, 1995).

32. Franke, ed., *On What Cannot Be Said*, op. cit., 333.

33. Bram Kempers, "The Fame of Fake, Dionysius the Areopagite: Fabrication, Falsification and the 'Cloud of Unknowing,'" in *How the West Was Won: Essays on Literary Imagination, the Canon, and the Christian Middle Ages for Burcht Pranger*, ed. Willemien Otten, Arjo Vanderjagt, and Hent de Vries (Leiden: Brill, 2010), 301–311, here 309.

34. Turner, *The Darkness of God*, op. cit., 268. Franke also argues that the concept of apophatic theology was first formulated by Denys the Areopagite (see *On What Cannot Be Said*, op. cit., 159). Denys or Dionysius the Areopagite was long erroneously identified with the Dionysius converted by St. Paul on the Acropolis at Athens (Acts 17.34), but the author of *Mystical Theology* was actually a Syrian monk writing at the turn of the fifth to the sixth century. He was known as the promoter of a doctrine of ignorance well into the seventeenth century, as appears from his being the target of Meric Casaubon's criticism of enthusiasm and ignorance (studied in part 2). But the origin of apophaticism can be found in Plato's *Parmenides*, and the idea that the One cannot be named without being divided into two, itself and its name. See *Parmenides*, trans. and analysis by R. E. Allen (Oxford: Blackwell, 1983), 137b–144e, 15–27. Other Socratic dialogues such as *Timaeus* (28c) were also referred to by later apophatic authors. See also Thomas Aquinas, who wrote that we cannot know what God is, in *Summa Theologica*, trans. Fathers of the English Dominican Province (Westminster, MD, Christian Classics, 1981), pt. 1, question 3 "On the Simplicity of God": "Now, because we cannot know what God is, but rather what He is not, we have no means for considering how God is, but rather how He is not."

35. On sources for *De docta ignorantia*, see Dermot Moran, "Nicholas of Cusa (1401–

1464): Platonism at the Dawn of Modernity," in *Platonism at the Origins of Modernity: Studies on Platonism and Early Modern Philosophy*, ed. Sarah Hutton and Douglas Hedley (Dordrecht, Netherlands: Springer, 2008), 9–29.

36. *Nicholas of Cusa on Learned Ignorance*, op. cit., 45.

37. *Ibid.*, 46. See also Cusanus's *Dialogue on the Hidden God* (*De deo abscondito*, 1444–1445), trans. H. Lawrence Bond, in Nicholas of Cusa, *Selected Spiritual Writings* (New York: Paulist Press, 1997), 209–213. This text follows the *Parmenides* tradition in arguing that knowledge of God can be only a finite conception of the infinite.

38. Nicholas of Cusa's *De idiota*, a dialogue in four books, was first published in 1450.

39. For an analysis of these texts and the evolution of the genre, see Nicolas Corréard, "Discours, invectives et autres paradoxes 'contre les lettres,'" *Réforme, Humanisme, Renaissance* 86, no. 1 (2018): 117–153; and Jeanneret, "Éloge de l'ignorance," *op. cit.* This paradoxical discourse has also been extensively studied by Hiram Haydn in *The Counter-Renaissance* (New York: Charles Scribner's Sons, 1950). See also Jan Miernowski, "La littérature anti-scientifique à la Renaissance comme réflexion sur les limites d'une culture," *Nouvelle Revue du XVIe siècle* 14, no. 1 (1996): 91–100, on Marguerite de Navarre and Agrippa in particular.

40. Corréard, "Discours, invectives et autres paradoxes 'contre les lettres,'" *op. cit.*, 128 and 130. Ecclesiastes 1.18: "For in much wisdom is much grief: and he that increaseth knowledge increaseth sorrow." 1 Corinthians 1.19: "I will destroy the wisdom of the wise."

41. *Ibid.*, 149–152.

42. *Ibid.*, 135 and 137.

43. Ortensio Lando, *Paradossi cioè, sententie fuori del commun parere novellamente venute in luce* (Lyon, 1543). Nicolas Corréard convincingly argues that paradox III should be read literally in his article "Le paradoxe landien: Une poétique pour la dissidence," *Bruniana & Campanelliana* 22, no. 1 (2016): 541–552, here 547.

44. Ortensio Landi, *Paradoxes, ce sont propos contre la commune opinion*, trans. Charles Estienne (Paris, 1553); and *The Defence of Contraries: Paradoxes against Common Opinion*, trans. Anthony Munday (London, 1593).

45. Corréard, "Le paradoxe landien," *op. cit.*, 552. In this article, Corréard also shows the link between Lando's text and Agrippa's digression on the ass as a portrait of the Christian *Idiotus*. On the "epidemic of paradoxy" in the Renaissance, see also Rosalie L. Colie, *Paradoxia Epidemica: The Renaissance Tradition of Paradox* (Princeton, NJ: Princeton University Press, 1966). Colie distinguishes rhetorical, logical, and epistemological paradoxes. On the reception of Lando's *Paradossi* at the Elizabethan Inns of Court and the use of the paradox genre in the seventeenth century, see Patrizia Grimaldi-Pizzorno, *The Ways of Paradox from Lando to Donne* (Florence, Olschki, 2007).

46. *Moriæ encomium* was translated into French (Paris, 1520) and into English (London, 1549). Many new editions were then published throughout the early modern period. See also *The Praise of Folly and Other Writings*, ed. and trans. Robert M. Adams (New York: Norton, 1989). For a short survey of the sixteenth-century reception of the work and the contention that it differs from other paradoxes, see M. Geraldine, CSJ, "Erasmus and the Tradition of Paradox," *Studies in Philology* 61, no. 1 (1964): 41–63. For an analysis of

The Praise of Folly in relation to Socrates, St. Paul, and the topos of *docta ignorantia*, see Colie, *Paradoxia Epidemica, op. cit.*, introduction, 22-26. See also, in relation to the paradoxical discourse, the influence of Paulinism and of the theology of foolishness in the sixteenth century. E.g., Kirk Essary, *Erasmus and Calvin on the Foolishness of God: Reason and Emotion in the Christian Philosophy* (Toronto: University of Toronto Press, 2017), esp. chap. 2 "Foolishness as Religious Knowledge."

47. Jeanneret, "Éloges de l'ignorance," *op. cit.*, 637 and 639.

48. Andrea Alciato, *Emblematum liber*, Augsbourg, 28 February 1531, "Submovendam ignorantiam" ("Ignorance must be done away with"), Emblem 186, [sig. C4ʳ]. The illustration was slightly modified in the following editions of the book, but it remained a sphinx. See the Glasgow University Emblem Website, which gives access to the twenty-two editions of Alciato's book, from 1531 to 1621: https://www.emblems.arts.gla.ac.uk/alciato/index.php.

49. Cesare Ripa, *Iconologia overo descrittione dell'imagini universali cavate dall'Antichita et da altri luoghi* (Rome, 1593), 124–126.

50. *Ibid.*, 126.

51. Andrea Alciato, *Emblemes* (Lyon, 1549), 235.

52. Cesare Ripa, *Iconologia overo descrittione di diverse Imagini cavate dall'Antichità, & di propria inventione trovate & dichiarate da Cesare Ripa Perugino* (Rome, 1603), 222.

53. *Ibid.*, 222.

54. See, for example, the French editions of the text by Jean Baudoin, *Iconologie, ou Explication nouvelle de plusieurs images, emblèmes et autres figures hierogliphiques des vertus, des vices, des arts, des sciences, des causes naturelles, des humeurs différentes, & des passions humaines* (Paris, 1643 and 1698). In the 1636 edition by Baudoin, there was no entry on ignorance—it was introduced in the 1643 edition. Neither was it mentioned in the first English edition: see *Iconologia: Or, Moral Emblems, by Cæsar Ripa. Wherein are express'd various images of Virtues, Vices, Passions, Arts, Humours, Elements and Celestial Bodies. As designed by the Ancient Egyptians, Greeks, Romans, and Modern Italians*, ed. Peirce Tempest (London, 1709). It was introduced later in the eighteenth century. See *Iconology, or a Collection of Emblematical Figures*, ed. George Richardson (London, 1779), 2:93: "The bandage over [the child's] eyes, shows intellectual blindness, Ignorance, and want of knowledge. The ass is emblematical of unintelligent minds, and inelegance of manners; and the reed is significant of an ignorant person being void of understanding."

55. Henrie Cornelius Agrippa, *Of the Vanitie and Uncertaintie of Artes and Sciences, Englished by Ja. San. Gent.* (London, 1569); and Henry Corneille Agrippa, *De l'incertitude, vanité, & abus des Sciences, traduit en français par Louys de Mayerne Turquet* (Geneva, 1582). The edition used here is that of 1676, entitled *The Vanity of Arts and Sciences, by Henry Cornelius Agrippa*, published in London.

56. Agrippa, *The Vanity of Arts and Sciences, op. cit.*, 7.

57. Note that Cornelius Agrippa, who plays a great part in this history of ignorance, was first considered by Richard H. Popkin as an example of a "fundamentalist anti-intellectualism" that does not deserve to be labeled skeptical because it does not provide "a genuine philosophical argument" or "a serious epistemological analysis," but Popkin

nevertheless presents it as "a facet of the revival of ancient scepticism," in *The History of Scepticism, op. cit.*, 29.

58. This argument in favor of ignorance was often found in the sixteenth and seventeenth centuries. It is further studied, as well as its refutations by English experimentalists, later in part 1.

59. See Agrippa, *The Vanity of Arts and Sciences, op. cit.*, 8: "To a Commonwealth there can be nothing more pernitious than Learning and Science, wherein if some happen to excel the rest, all things are carried by their Determination, as taking upon them to be most Knowing; who thereupon laying hold upon the simplicity and unskilfulness of the Multitude, usurp all Authority to themselves." and 5.

60. *Ibid.*, 359.

61. *Ibid.*, 6. On the association of knowledge with the serpent, see also, for example, 3: "Let him therefore glory in this Serpent, who boasts himself in knowledge."

62. *Ibid.*, 360.

63. *Ibid.*, 361. See also 363: "it is now as clear as the Sun, that there is no Beast so fit and proper to retain Divinity as the Ass; into which creature if ye be not transform'd, ye shall not be able to carry the Divine Mysteries."

64. *Ibid.*, 362.

65. *Ibid.*, 363. The "Digression" is reminiscent of Cusanus's celebration of humility and simplicity in his dialogue *De idiota*. On the influence of Cusanus on Agrippa, see, for example, Charles G. Nauert, *Agrippa and the Crisis of Renaissance Thought* (Urbana: University of Illinois Press, 1965), 145–146. Nauert argues that Agrippa's allegory of the ass directly echoes Cusanus's Idiot. Marc Van Der Poel, on the contrary, writes that "there is no indication that [Agrippa] was directly influenced by [Nicholas of Cusa]," even though there is no doubt that he knew the works of Cusanus and made similar criticisms of scholastic theology, in *Cornelius Agrippa, the Humanist Theologian and his Declamations* (Leiden: Brill, 1997), 11. The seriousness of Agrippa's praise of ignorance has also been discussed. Van Der Poel, for example, argues that Agrippa's declamations were serious (*ibid.*, 8). There is a similar hesitation about the interpretation to be given to Erasmus's *The Praise of Folly*, in which it is not clear whether the narrator, *Stultitia*, who was nursed by *Methe* (drunkenness) and *Apaedia* (ignorance or privation), should be seen as the embodiment of wisdom or of stupidity (in a negative sense). Those hesitations are characteristic of paradoxical discourses.

66. [Giordano Bruno], *Cabala del Cavallo Pegaseo. Con l'aggiunta dell'Asino Cillenico. Descritta dal Nolano*, [Paris] London, 1585), "A l'asino cillenico," [D2ᵛ], and "L'asino cillenico del Nolano," [D3ʳ]. See also Giordano Bruno, *The Cabala of Pegasus*, ed. and trans. Sidney L. Sondergard and Madison U. Sowell (New Haven, CT: Yale University Press, 2002), "The Nolan's Cillenican Ass" is at 82–90; and Giordano Bruno, *Œuvres complètes*, vol. 4, *Cabale du cheval pégaséen*, ed. Giovanni Aquilecchia and Nicola Badaloni, trans. Tristan Dagron (Paris: Les Belles Lettres, 1994); on the theme of ignorance in the text, see the introduction to volume 4.

67. Bruno, *The Cabala of Pegasus, op. cit.*, 83, 86, 86–87, and 90.

68. *Ibid.*, 16, 14, 26, 27, 29, and 51.

69. Eugenio Garin, preface to Nuccio Ordine, *Le Mystère de l'âne: Essai sur Giordano Bruno* (1987), trans. F. Liffran and P. Bardoux (Paris: Les Belles Lettres, 2005), xiv (my translation).

70. Bruno himself seemed to believe that Agrippa's digression on the ass mocked asininity, as is mentioned in the "Declamation to the Studious, Devoted, and Pious Reader," and, consequently, he (or the narrator?) feared that his own praise of the ass might also be interpreted as a satire, in *The Cabala of Pegasus, op. cit.*, 17.

71. P. P. P. P. [Paul Perrot de la Salle], *Le Contr'empire des sciences, et le Mystere des asnes* (Lyon, 1599), 86–92, here 86.

72. *Ibid.*, 87.

73. *Ibid.*, 88: "(Ainsi l'humble cognoit / Ce que le mondain sage à toute peine voit)." See also: "Je vous renvoye à luy [the ass] vou. Docteurs curieux, / Qui cherchez a tastons les mysteres des Cieux: / Je vous renvoye humains à sa simple nature, / Et vous impatiens au labeur qu'il endure, / Car sa tardiveté monstre tacitement / Que qui fait bien un faict le fait prou vistement."

74. *Ibid.*, 91 ("Il est bon Philosophe").

75. [Adriano Banchieri], *La nobilità dell'asino* (Venice, 1592). An anonymous English translation was published in London in 1595 under the title *The Noblenesse of the Asse. A Work rare, learned, and excellent*. The quotations here are taken from this edition.

76. [Banchieri], *The Noblenesse of the Asse, op. cit.*, the first part, [C2^v].

77. *Ibid.*, the second part, [D3^r].

78. François de La Mothe Le Vayer, *Cincq dialogues faits à l'imitation des Anciens, par Oratius Tubero* (1630), vol. 1 (Frankfurt, 1716), "Lettre de l'autheur" (unpaginated). La Mothe Le Vayer also wrote a dialogue on the ass: *Dialogue sur les rares et eminentes qualitez des asnes de ce temps, entre Philonius et Paleologue*, in *ibid.*, 241-326. On the word *asnerie* as a translation of the English *ignorance*, see Randle Cotgrave, *A Dictionarie of the French and English Tongues* (London, 1611).

79. Robert Boyle, *Certain Physiological Essays* (London, 1661), 35–36.

80. Robert Boyle, *A Free Inquiry into the Vulgarly Receiv'd Notion of Nature Made in an Essay, Address'd to a Friend* (London, 1685), The Preface, [A4^{r-v}]. The passage insists on the imperfection of the book: "I shall not only be content, but must desire, to have this Rhapsody, of my own loose Papers, look'd upon but as an *Apparatus*, or Collection of Materials, in order to [what I well know this maim'd and confus'd Essay is not,] a compleat and regular Discourse." The whole preface of *A Free Inquiry* is a perfect example of Boyle's usual claims of modesty.

81. Boyle, *Certain Physiological Essays, op. cit.*, "A proemial essay," 5. On modesty as an important trait of the trustworthy experimenter, see part 3; see also Steven Shapin, *A Social History of Truth: Civility and Science in Seventeenth-Century England* (Chicago: University of Chicago Press, 1994).

82. See also Cecilia Muratori and Gianni Paganini, eds., *Early Modern Philosophers and the Renaissance Legacy* (Dordrecht, Netherlands: Springer, 2016), for a reassessment of the common periodization that distinguishes between the Renaissance and the early

modern period. *The Paradoxes of Ignorance* also questions this distinction, as well as that between the Middle Ages and the Renaissance.

83. Harrison, *The Fall of Man, op. cit.*, 258: "The birth of modern experimental science was not attended with a new awareness of the powers and capacities of human reason, but rather the opposite—a consciousness of the manifold deficiencies of the intellect, of the misery of the human condition, and of the limited scope of scientific achievement."

84. That there were two national traditions regarding knowledge and ignorance was the thesis defended by Karl R. Popper in the famous paper he gave to the British Academy in 1960 that was then published under the title *On the Sources of Knowledge and of Ignorance* (Oxford: Oxford University Press, 1961).

85. Yet most of the French *libertins érudits* presented a positive conception of ignorance as well. But contrary to Descartes, they did not think that it should be self-induced as a first step in the process of founding new knowledge, a conception that they interpreted as another form of dogmatism. Instead, the *libertins érudits* praised awareness of one's ignorance and denounced common prejudices, which were for them true ignorance. Learning was also celebrated as a way to promote free thinking.

86. Cornel Zwierlein, ed., *The Dark Side of Knowledge: Histories of Ignorance, 1400 to 1800* (Leiden: Brill, 2016), introduction, 35: "The empiricist shift made morally indifferent ignorance—what would have been Thomas's *nescientia* in which he was largely disinterested—an object of its own concern. Now, the questions of its shape, its size, the proportion of its development and potential growth in relationship to its twin, knowledge, emerged. This entailed a methodology of distinguishing between kinds of ignorance, delimiting and crafting the frame of ignorance(s). One therefore had to devote distinct chapters to 'ignorance' in theories of cognition and methodologies of how reason can progress. In so doing, empiricism reified 'ignorance'—in different terminologies—as subject and object of knowledge production itself. . . . the increase and possible decrease of knowledge/ignorance was thought of in secular terms and, first implicitly, only later explicitly, as open-ended."

87. See, for example, John Baret, *An Alveary or Triple Dictionary, in English, Latin, and French* (London, 1574). Baret also associates ignorance and error.

88. See Cotgrave, *A Dictionarie of the French and English Tongues, op. cit.*

89. Charles Sorel, *La Science Universelle* (Paris, 1668), 265.

90. Not all recent publications on ignorance can be listed in this brief bibliographical essay. Insistence is made here on those that are related to the object and methodologies of *The Paradoxes of Ignorance*. See also the bibliography at the end of the book for further references.

91. Matthias Gross and Linsey McGoey, eds., *Routledge International Handbook of Ignorance Studies* (London: Routledge, 2015). The editors of the collection mostly focus on the uses of not knowing, as well as on decision-making in situations of ignorance.

92. See Jamie Holmes, "The Case for Teaching Ignorance," *New York Times*, 24 August 2015; and Stuart Firestein, *Ignorance: How It Drives Science* (Oxford: Oxford University Press, 2012).

93. Rik Peels and Martijn Blaauw, eds., *The Epistemic Dimensions of Ignorance* (Cambridge: Cambridge University Press, 2016).

94. See, for example, Mark Hobart, ed., *An Anthropological Critique of Development: The Growth of Ignorance* (London: Routledge, 1993); and Roy Dilley, "Reflections on Knowledge Practices and the Problem of Ignorance," *Journal of the Royal Anthropological Institute* 16, suppl. 1 (2010): 176–192. See also the works by Michael Smithson on ignorance, uncertainty, and risk; for example "Toward a Social Theory of Ignorance," *Journal for the Theory of Social Behaviour* 15, no. 2 (1985): 151–172; *Ignorance and Uncertainty: Emerging Paradigms* (Dordrecht, Netherlands: Springer, 1989); and "Ignorance and Science: Dilemmas, Perspectives, and Prospects," *Science Communication* 15, no. 2 (1993): 133–156.

95. Wilbert E. Moore and Melvin M. Tumin, "Some Social Functions of Ignorance," *American Sociological Review* 14, no. 6 (1949): 787–795.

96. Casey High, Ann H. Kelly, and Jonathan Mair, eds., *The Anthropology of Ignorance: An Ethnographic Approach* (Basingstoke, UK: Palgrave Macmillan, 2012), 3 and 15. The role of ignorance in the methodologies of sociology was discussed in 1987 by Robert K. Merton in an article from the *Annual Review of Sociology* through the notion of "specified ignorance" as problem finding: specifying ignorance (or recognizing what is not yet known, and needs to be known) is the role of social scientists, Merton argues, as much as the advancement of knowledge. See "Three Fragments from a Sociologist's Notebooks: Establishing the Phenomenon, Specified Ignorance, and Strategic Research Materials," *Annual Review of Sociology* 13 (1987): 1–28.

97. Robert Proctor and Londa Schiebinger, eds., *Agnotology: The Making and Unmaking of Ignorance* (Palo Alto, CA: Stanford University Press, 2008). See also the special issue of *Critique* "Fauteurs de doute" (2014) with an interview of Robert Proctor by Mathias Girel. In 2016, Girel launched a research project on science and ignorance at the Centre d'Archives en Philosophie, Histoire et Édition des Sciences of the École Normale Supérieure—PSL (Paris). Since then, many conferences have been held on agnotology, ignorance, and doubt; a bibliographical database has been created and a review of the latest publications on ignorance is posted each month on the website (https://caphes.ens.fr/science-and-ignorance-online-bibliographic-database).

98. Nancy Tuana and Shannon Sullivan, eds., "Feminist Epistemologies of Ignorance," special issue, *Hypatia* 21, no. 3 (2006); and id., *Race and Epistemologies of Ignorance* (Albany, NY: SUNY Press, 2007).

99. Zwierlein, *The Dark Side of Knowledge*, op. cit. See also Zwierlein, *Imperial Unknowns: The French and British in the Mediterranean, 1650–1750* (Cambridge: Cambridge University Press, 2016). In this monograph, Zwierlein deals mainly with what early modern historical agents did not know, and how people acted or made decisions in situations of ignorance, especially how they built empires. So far, the history of ignorance has been conceived as a history of what people did not know at a particular time, not as a history of the notion of ignorance, as in *The Paradoxes of Ignorance*.

100. Joanna Picciotto, *Labors of Innocence in Early Modern England* (Cambridge, MA: Harvard University Press, 2010).

101. Alain Corbin, *Terra Incognita: Une histoire de l'ignorance, XVIIIe–XIXe siècle* (Paris: Albin Michel, 2020). An English translation by Susan Pickford was published in 2021: *Terra Incognita: A History of Ignorance in the Eighteenth and Nineteenth Centuries* (London: Polity).

102. Lukas M. Verburgt and Peter Burke, "Introduction: Histories of Ignorance," *Journal for the History of Knowledge* 2, no. 1 (November 2021): 1–9, here 1 and 3 (https://doi.org/10.5334/jhk.45). The seven essays in this collection deal with a wide variety of subjects and assume many different definitions of ignorance that are not directly related to the conceptions of ignorance studied in *The Paradoxes of Ignorance*. Moreover, the essays deal with a later period than the one that is the focus here.

103. On methodological considerations, see also Lukas M. Verburgt, "The History of Knowledge and the Future History of Ignorance," *KNOW: A Journal on the Formation of Knowledge* 4, no. 1 (2020): 1–24 (https://doi.org/10.1086/708341). For a plea in favor of an intellectual history of early modern ignorance, see Sandrine Parageau, "Pour une histoire intellectuelle de l'ignorance. Représentations, usages et valeurs de l'ignorance à la période moderne, XVIe-XVIIIe siècles," *Revue d'Anthropologie des Connaissances* 15, no. 4 (December 2021): http://journals.openedition.org/rac/23570.

Chapter 1

1. For a study of the parallels between Cusanus's ideas on ignorance and Lefèvre's, see part 3. See François Rigolot, ed., *Journal de Voyage de Michel de Montaigne* (Paris: Presses universitaires de France, 1992), 71.

2. On the idea, held by both Cusanus and Montaigne, that there is an infinite diversity of things, which may result in the impossibility of science, see Raymond Esclapez, "Montaigne et Nicolas de Cuse: Le thème de la 'docte ignorance' dans les *Essais*," *Littératures* 18 (1988): 25–40, here 29–32. Esclapez concludes that there is no textual evidence of Montaigne appropriating Cusanus's ideas, but there are affinities between *De docta ignorantia* and the *Essays*. If Cusanus is never explicitly mentioned in the *Essays*, Esclapez argues, it may be because he did not have the prestige of antiquity in the eyes of the humanist Montaigne (*ibid.*, 38–39). There are also obvious differences between the two texts, mostly because Montaigne was not a mathematician, contrary to Nicholas of Cusa, according to Esclapez (*ibid.*, 32).

3. See Montaigne, "*An Apologie of* Raymond Sebond," in *The essayes, op. cit.*, II, 12, 281; and Pierre Magnard, "Une ignorance qui se sait," *Montaigne Studies* 21, nos. 1–2 (2009): 183–189, here 183.

4. Jan Miernowski, "Montaigne on Truth and Scepticism," in *The Oxford Handbook of Montaigne*, ed. Philippe Desan (Oxford: Oxford University Press, 2016), 544–561, here 557.

5. Montaigne, "*An Apologie of* Raymond Sebond," in *The essayes, op. cit.*, II, 12, 303.

6. Miernowski, "Montaigne on Truth and Scepticism," *op. cit.*, 561.

7. Montaigne, "*An Apologie of* Raymond Sebond," in *The essayes, op. cit.*, II, 12, 281.

8. *Ibid.*, 274.

9. Montaigne, "*Of the Caniballes*," in *ibid.*, I, 30, 101.

10. Montaigne, "*Of vaine subtilties, or subtill devises*," in *ibid.*, I, 54, 170.

11. Montaigne, "*An Apologie of* Raymond Sebond," in *ibid.*, II, 12: "that which we thinke to knowe, is but a parcel, yea and a small particle of our ignorance," 280.

12. Montaigne, "*Of vaine subtilties, or subtill devises*," in *ibid.*, I, 54, 170.

13. Blaise Pascal, *Monsieur Pascall's Thoughts, Meditations, and Prayers, touching matters moral and divine as they were found in his papers after his death . . . done into English by Jos. Walker* (London, 1688), 207.

14. On common sense and its history, see Sophia Rosenfeld, *Common Sense. A Political History* (Cambridge, MA: Harvard University Press, 2011). Rosenfeld writes "the intellectual history of [this] fundamentally anti-intellectual construct that signifies an assortment of pre-rational, tacit presuppositions" (8). She argues that in the seventeenth century, because it was "a moment of crisis in other forms of legitimacy," the idea emerged that ordinary people shared "unquestioned notions" based on their "common natures and experiences" (15, 4). In the context of seventeenth-century philosophy, common sense was defined as "the rudimentary ability to form clear perceptions, make elementary judgements, and engage in simple reasoning about everyday, practical matters without falling into bald-faced contradictions and inconsistencies," a skill "within the capacity of all humans" (22). Yet the idea of common sense also came to be criticized in the early modern period, especially by the *libertins érudits* (see chap. 3, "The Radical Use of *Bon Sens*").

15. Montaigne, "*An Apologie of* Raymond Sebond," in *The essayes, op. cit.*, II, 12, 284.

16. Montaigne, "*Of vaine subtilties, or subtill devises*," in *ibid.*, I, 54, 170.

17. Montaigne, "*An Apology of* Raymond Sebond," in *ibid.*, 272.

18. *Ibid.*, 282.

19. *Ibid.*, 279.

20. Montaigne, "*Of Pedantisme*," in *ibid.*, I, 24, 63.

21. Montaigne, "*An Apologie of* Raymond Sebond," in *ibid.*, II, 12, 281.

22. Pierre Charron, *De la sagesse. Livres trois* (Bordeaux, 1601); and Pierre Charron, *Of Wisdome. Three Bookes Written in French by Peter Charron, Doct of Lawe in Paris*, trans. Samson Lennard (London, 1608). The book is divided into three parts: the first one deals with self-knowledge, the second one gives rules of wisdom, and the third one discusses wisdom in relation to the four moral virtues. A revised edition appeared in Paris in 1604, and the book was published many times in France in the seventeenth century. It was a major reference of the French *libertins érudits*, but it was also widely read in England, where it was reprinted twelve times in the seventeenth century.

23. On Charron and his relation to Montaigne, see Emmanuel Faye, *Philosophie et perfection de l'homme, de la Renaissance à Descartes* (Paris: Vrin, 1998), pt. 4, "La 'Vraye science de l'homme' selon Pierre Charron," 259. On Charron and Montaigne, as well as Charron's influence on Gassendi, Descartes, Pascal, and La Mothe Le Vayer, see also José R. Maia Neto, *Academic Skepticism in Seventeenth-Century French Philosophy: The Charronian Legacy 1601–1662* (Heidelberg: Springer, 2014), chap. 2.

24. Charron, *Of Wisdome, op. cit.*, second book, 259.

25. *Ibid.*, 152. See also: "To become truly wise, and to leade a life more regular and pleasant, there needs no other instruction but from our selues: and doubtlesse, if we were good scholars, there are no books could better instruct vs, than we teach our selues" (3).

26. See *ibid.*, 260: "*Socrates* by simple and naturall discourses, by vulgar similitudes and inductions, speaking like a country swaine, did furnish vs with precepts and rules of good life, and remedies against all euils, so substantiall and strong, that all the arte and science of the world could not deuise better or the like." In the original French edition (332), Charron compares Socrates not only to peasants, but also to women, a mention that was omitted by the English translator.

27. *Ibid.*, 468 ("La sagesse est un maniement doux & reglé de l'ame," in *De la sagesse, op. cit.*, 643).

28. *Ibid.*, 468. Despite this apparently harsh criticism of "science," what Charron actually denounces is the way science was taught at the time, not science or knowledge per se.

29. The two dialogues are analyzed at length and compared in part 3, which examines the persona of the Idiot. There is evidence that Descartes had read some of Cusanus's works. He commented on his astrological conceptions, for example, in a letter to Father Chanut from 6 June 1647. See Moran, "Nicholas of Cusa (1401–1464)," *op. cit.*, 11–12.

30. Like *The Search for Truth*, the *Rules for the Direction of the Mind* were then published in the *Opuscula posthuma* of 1701. On ignorance in the *Regulae*, see part 2; and Gianni Paganini, "Socrate, Montaigne, Descartes: Sur l'utilisation de l'ignorance socratique dans les *Essais* et dans les *Regulae*," *Montaigne Studies* 21, nos. 1–2 (2009): 169–182.

31. René Descartes, *Rules for the Direction of the Mind*, in *The Philosophical Writings of Descartes*, trans. John Cottingham, Robert Stoothoff, and Dugald Murdoch (Cambridge: Cambridge University Press, 1985), 1:16 (Rule IV).

32. *Ibid.*, 16.

33. *Ibid.*, 16.

34. René Descartes, *Discours de la méthode*, introduction and notes by Étienne Gilson (Paris: Vrin, 1964), in particular 57, 63, 66, and 122–123.

35. Dan Arbib, "Le moi cartésien comme troisième livre: Note sur Montaigne et la première partie du *Discours de la méthode*," *Revue de métaphysique et de morale* 74, no. 2 (2012): 161–180, here 162 (my translation).

36. *Ibid.*, 170.

37. Antoine Furetière, *Dictionaire universel* (The Hague, 1690): "Il y a bien des Nobles qui font vanité de leur *ignorance*." On Descartes's and Montaigne's personae, see also Michael Moriarty, "Montaigne and Descartes," in *The Oxford Handbook of Montaigne*, ed. Ph. Desan, *op. cit.*, 347–363, especially 351 (Moriarty also lists the differences between Montaigne and Descartes).

38. Nicolas Malebranche, *Father Malebranche his Treatise concerning the Search after Truth, To which is added the Author's Treatise of Nature and Grace: being a consequence of the Principles contained in the Search. All translated by T. Taylor* (London, 1700), 95. For a study of the links between Montaigne, Descartes, and Pascal, see also the classic work by Léon Brunschvicg, *Descartes et Pascal lecteurs de Montaigne* (1945; Paris: Pocket, 1995).

39. Sorel's relation with the *libertins érudits* was ambiguous. He is sometimes considered as an "imperfect *libertin*" himself; he knew the *libertins* of his time, and some of his works are clearly reminiscent of French *libertinage*, such as *L'Histoire comique de Francion* (1623). Yet Sorel could also be critical of the *libertins*, for example in *La Science universelle* (*op. cit.*, 255–256), where he assimilates them with the skeptics, whom he strongly refutes. Moreover, in his attack against skepticism, Sorel was influenced by Mersenne, in particular by the Minim's *La Vérité des sciences* (1625). On this relation, see also Popkin, *The History of Scepticism, op. cit.*, 107.

40. Charles Sorel, *De la perfection de l'homme ou les vrays biens sont considerez, et specialement ceux de l'ame* (Paris, 1655), 81–82.

41. *Ibid.*, 358 ("un simple homme qui n'avoit aucune estude").

42. On autodidacticism, see part 3. On Bacon and Palissy, see also Benjamin Farrington, *The Philosophy of Francis Bacon* (Liverpool: Liverpool University Press, 1964), 33. On Palissy, see also Pamela H. Smith, *The Body of the Artisan: Art and Experience in the Scientific Revolution* (Chicago: University of Chicago Press, 2004), 100–102.

43. Sorel, *De la perfection de l'homme, op. cit.*, 171 ("autoriser l'ignorance").

44. *Ibid.*, 171–172.

45. See the similar restoration of the "true" meaning of Socrates's profession of ignorance by Francis Bacon, discussed later.

46. On the *libertins*' contempt for ignorant people, their elitism and distrust of common sense, see also Isabelle Moreau, *"Guérir du sot": Les stratégies d'écriture des libertins à l'âge classique* (Paris: Honoré Champion, 2007), especially 947–949 on Sorel, and 1025–1029 on ignorance and common sense according to the *libertins*.

47. La Mothe Le Vayer, *Cincq dialogues faits à l'imitation des Anciens, op. cit.*, "Lettre de l'autheur" (unpaginated) and Pierre Gassendi, *Dissertations en forme de paradoxes contre les Aristotéliciens* (*Exercitationes Paradoxicæ Adversus Aristoteleos*), bks. I and II, trans., ed., and with notes by Bernard Rochot (Paris: Vrin, 1959), 11–12: "Mais par 'vulgaire' je n'entends point ici les gens du peuple (qu'est-ce qu'un âne aurait à faire d'une lyre?) mais le gros des Philosophes, qui ont l'esprit si bas qu'à la façon du vulgaire ils traitent de Barbare tout ce qui va à l'encontre de leurs opinions préconçues une fois pour toutes."

48. See Sophie Feller, "De l'ignorance des doctes à la docte ignorance: le savoir selon les libertins érudits," in *Sottise et ineptie, de la Renaissance aux Lumières: Discours du savoir et représentations romanesques*, ed. Nicole Jacques-Lefèvre and Anne-Pascale Pouey-Mounou (Nanterre, Presses de l'Université Paris X, 2004), 75–93, here 75.

49. François de La Mothe Le Vayer, *Cinq autres dialogues. Faits comme les precedents à l'imitation des anciens. I. De l'ignorance louable. II. De la divinité. III. De l'opiniastreté. III. De la politique. V. Du mariage* (Frankfurt, 1633).

50. Sophie Feller, "De l'ignorance des doctes à la docte ignorance," *op. cit.*, 89–90.

51. La Mothe Le Vayer, *De l'ignorance louable, op. cit.*, 19: "Car notre [the skeptics'] ignorance n'est point de ces stupides & grossieres, que les escholes appellent crasses & supines, *neque est puræ privationis, neque prau & affectionis*, c'est une ignorance honorable, & vrayement philosophique, laquelle s'accommodant à l'obscurité de la Nature, & se mesurant à la portée de l'esprit humain, ne promet rien au-delà de ses forces. C'est

une ignorance discouruë & raisonnable, que je ne veux pas nommer docte, comme le Cardinal Cusan, mais à laquelle neantmoins on ne peut parvenir que par la porte des sciences, qu'elle laisse au dessous de soy, mettant le Sceptique un degré au dessus de tous ces superbes Dogmatiques, & de tous ces Thrasons lettrez."

52. Sophie Feller, "De l'ignorance des doctes à la docte ignorance," *op. cit.*, 90.

53. Marin Mersenne, *Les Questions theologiques, physiques, morales et mathematiques. Où chacun trouvera du contentement, ou de l'exercice* (Paris, 1634), 216: "Il faut icy remarquer que le plus haut sommet de la science où les hommes puissent arriver, sert à les humilier, et à rabattre leur orgueil, d'autant qu'ils voyent clairement qu'apres avoir estudié l'espace de 60 ou 80 ans, qu'ils ont seulement travaillé à descouvrir et à reconnoistre leur ignorance. De là vient que quelques-uns estiment que l'extreme science des hommes a le mesme effet qu'une extreme ignorance, et que toutes les extremitez se rencontrent au mesme but."

54. *Ibid.*, 216.

55. Marin Mersenne, *La Vérité des sciences, contre les Sceptiques ou Pyrrhoniens* (Paris, 1625), 26.

56. *Ibid.*, 37.

57. See in particular Marin Mersenne, *L'impieté des Deistes, Athees et Libertins de ce temps, combatuë et renversee de point en point par raisons tirees de la Philosophie et de la Theologie. Ensemble la refutation du Poëme des Deistes* (Paris, 1624).

58. Marin Mersenne, *Questions Inouyes ou Recreation des Sçavans. Qui contiennent beaucoup de choses concernantes la Théologie, la Philosophie et les Mathématiques* (Paris, 1634), 5–103, Question XXX "Can a man learn philosophy by himself, thanks to reason only, without reading books or conversing with learned men?" (my translation), 83.

59. *Ibid.*, 84.

60. On the specific role of ignorance in one's access to knowledge, according to Descartes and the *libertins érudits*, see in particular part 2.

61. The reception of continental mystical and occult works, in particular Cusanus's, by English radicals during the Civil Wars and Interregnum is analyzed in part 2. On the general reception of Cusanus's philosophy, see Peter J. Casarella, ed., *Cusanus: The Legacy of Learned Ignorance* (Washington, DC: Catholic University of America Press, 2006), as well as Simon J. G. Burton, Joshua Hollmann, and Eric M. Parker, eds., *Nicholas of Cusa and the Making of the Early Modern World* (Leiden: Brill, 2018).

62. Wilhelm Schmidt-Biggeman, "Robert Fludd's Kabbalistic Cosmos," in *Platonism at the Origins of Modernity, op. cit.*, 75–92, here 76.

63. On the reception of Cusanus by Cambridge Platonists, see Burton, Hollmann, and Parker, eds., "Introduction. Nicholas of Cusa and Early Modern Reform," *Nicholas of Cusa and the Making of the Early Modern World, op. cit.*, 1–46, here 24–29. They list the parallels between Cusanus and the Cambridge Platonists: "the idea that reason is 'the Spirit of Man'; . . . an exemplarist metaphysics coupled with an autonomous ethic; the criticism of Aristotelian faculty psychology and the crucial role that self-reflection plays in their philosophical notion of religion; . . . the promotion of man as 'the measure of all things' . . . ; the notion of the world soul as a 'plastick nature' . . . ; and finally,

their efforts to promote universal tolerance" (25–26). See also, in *ibid.*, Eric M. Parker, "'The Sacred Circle of All-Being': Cusanus, Lord Brooke, and Peter Sterry," 257–284 and Derek Michaud, "Varieties of Spiritual Sense: Cusanus and John Smith," 285–306. Finally, Chance Woods has argued that "Henry More can legitimately be regarded as the most authentic heir of Cusanus' legacy of speculative mystical theology in this period," in "Henry More (1614–1687) as Intellectual Heir to Nicholas of Cusa (1401–1464)," *American Cusanus Society Newsletter* 35 (December 2018): 14–23, here 14. But here again, evidence of this legacy is slender at best.

64. Ernst Cassirer, *Die Platonische Renaissance in England und die Schule von Cambridge* (Berlin: Teubner, 1932), 22.

65. Paul Richard Blum, "Nicholas of Cusa in Giles Randall's English Translation: Wisdom and Vision in Language," *Recherches de Théologie et Philosophie médiévales* 83, no. 1 (2016): 201–219, here 202.

66. Neil C. Manson, "Epistemic Restraint and the Vice of Curiosity," *Philosophy* 87, no. 2 (2012): 239–259, here 239. Manson focuses mostly on "epistemic restraint" in a contemporary, nonreligious context.

67. Calvin's *Christianae religionis institutio* (1536) or *Institution de la religion chrestienne* (1541) was translated into English by Thomas Norton and published in 1561 in London under the title *The Institution of Christian Religion, Wrytten in Latine by Maister Iohn Caluin, and translated into Englysh according to the authors last edition*. The quotation given here is found on 319. The 1562 French edition reads: "Ayons donc cela deuant les yeux sur toutes choses, que ce n'est pas vne moindre rage, d'appeter autre cognoissance de la predestination, que celle qui nous est donnee en la Parole de Dieu, que si quelcun vouloit cheminer par des rochers inaccessibles, ou voir en tenebres. Et que nous n'ayons point honte d'ignorer quelque chose en ceste matiere, où il y a quelque ignorance plus docte que le sauoir. Plustost que nous soyons bien aises de nous abstenir d'appeter vne science, de laquelle l'affectation est folle & dangereuse, voire mesme pernicieuse," in *Institution de la religion Chrestienne* (Geneva, 1562), 575.

68. Paul Schuurman, "'Thou Knowest Not the Works of God': Gisbertius Voetius (1589–1676) and John Locke on Learned Ignorance," *Westminster Theological Journal* 72, no. 1 (2010): 59–69, here 60–63. On Voetius, Descartes and the "Utrecht quarrel," which revolved mostly around the use of ignorance in ways of knowing, see part 2.

69. William Perkins, *Lectures upon the Three First Chapters of the Revelation: Preached in Cambridge Anno Dom. 1595* (London, 1604), 98. Perkins also focuses on ignorance in *The First Part of the Cases of Conscience. Wherein specially, three maine Questions concerning Man, simply considered in himself, are propounded and resolved* (Cambridge, 1604), especially 15-18. Perkins was a Church of England clergyman, often labeled a "moderate Puritan." His lectures and writings rejected both the persistence of Catholic influences in the Church of England and all forms of separatism. Michael Jinkins, "Perkins, William (1558–1602), Theologian and Church of England Clergyman," *Oxford Dictionary of National Biography*, September 2004, https://www-oxforddnb-com.janus.bis-sorbonne.fr/view/10.1093/ref:odnb/9780198614128.001.0001/odnb-9780198614128-e-21973. On the history of curiosity from Augustine to the early modern period, see, for example, Line Cot-

tegnies and Sandrine Parageau, "Introduction," in *Women and Curiosity in Early Modern England and France*, ed. Line Cottegnies, Sandrine Parageau, and John J. Thompson (Leiden: Brill, 2016), 1–26.

70. T.W. [Thomas Wilson], *Theologicall rules, to guide us in the understanding and practices of holy Scriptures* (London, 1615), 139.

71. Thomas Wilson, *A commentarie upon the most divine Epistle of S. Paul to the Romanes containing for matter, the degeneration of our nature by Adams Fall; and the Restauration thereof, by the Grace of Christ* (London, 1614), 589.

72. Anthony Burgess, *A Treatise of Original Sin* (London, 1658), 427. Burgess was ejected in 1662 for nonconformity. See E. C. Vernon, "Burgess, Anthony (d. 1664), Clergyman and Ejected Minister," *Oxford Dictionary of National Biography*, September 2004, https://www-oxforddnb-com.janus.bis-sorbonne.fr/view/10.1093/ref:odnb/9780198614128.001.0001/odnb-9780198614128-e-3973.

73. Burgess, *A Treatise of Original Sin*, op. cit., 198.

74. Richard Whitlock, *Zootomia, or, Observations of the present manners of the English: Briefly Anatomizing the Living by the Dead. With an usefull detection of the mountebanks of both sexes* (London, 1654), 222–223. Very little is known about Whitlock, who may have been a parson (see *World Biographical Information System Online*). The title page of *Zootomia* indicates "M. D. Late Fellow of *All-Souls* Colledge in *Oxford*."

75. Whitlock, *Zootomia*, op. cit., 223. See also Julius Caesar Scaliger, *Exotericarum exercitationum* (Paris, 1557), exercitatio 307, para. 29.

76. Whitlock, *Zootomia*, op. cit., 223–224.

77. On the reception of Charron's works in seventeenth-century England, see also the section here on Joseph Glanvill.

78. Locke, *Essay concerning Human Understanding*, op. cit., I, 1, 4, 45.

79. Quoted in David Sytsma, *Richard Baxter and the Mechanical Philosophers* (Oxford: Oxford University Press, 2017), 96–97 (drawing on Dr Williams' Library, London, Ms DWL BT XIX.351, fol. 143r). Locke's and Baxter's interpretations of ignorance have a lot in common, as will appear in part 2 (on Baxter's ignorance of ignorance) and part 3 (on Locke's anthropology of ignorance).

80. Schuurman, "'Thou Knowest Not the Works of God,'" op. cit., 64 and 68–69.

81. Locke, *Essay concerning Human Understanding*, op. cit., III, 10, 10, 495.

82. *Ibid.*, III, 10, 10, 491.

83. *Ibid.*, III, 10, 10, 495–496.

84. *Ibid.*, IV, 12, 12, 647.

85. See also what Locke says of the extent of human ignorance in *ibid.*, IV, 3, 22 (p. 553), a passage analyzed in part 3. The same interpretation of learned ignorance as scholasticism is found for example in Locke's second reply to Edward Stillingfleet: "in Matters of Speculation to *suppose* on, as *others have supposed* before us, is supposed by many to be only a way to learned Ignorance, which enables to talk much and know but little," where learned ignorance is associated with reliance on the authorities and an excessive use of words, in *Mr. Locke's Reply to the right reverend the Lord Bishop of Worcester answer to his second letter* (London, 1699), 266. See also *Conduct of the Understanding* (in *Posthumous*

Works (London, 1706), where Locke denounces again the ill use of words by scholastics: "all that he thinks he knows about them [meaningless Terms], is to him so much Knowledge about nothing, and amounts at most but to a learned Ignorance" (87).

86. Gearing, *The Arraignment of Ignorance*, op. cit., 78.

Chapter 2

1. Stéphane Haffemayer, *Les Lumières radicales de la Révolution anglaise. Samuel Hartlib et les réseaux de l'Intelligence (1600–1660)* (Paris: Classiques Garnier, 2018), 97. Haffemayer argues that the word *learning* was spread mostly by the Hartlib circle.

2. Francis Bacon, *The Twoo Bookes of Francis Bacon. Of the Proficience and Advancement of Learning, Divine and Humane* (London, 1605). The quotations given here are taken from the Oxford Francis Bacon edition of the book: *The Advancement of Learning*, ed. and with introduction, notes, and commentary by Michael Kiernan (Oxford: Clarendon Press, 2000), here 5.

3. *Ibid.*, 6.

4. *Ibid.*, 6, and 34: "As for the knowledge which induced the fall, it was, as was touched before, not the naturall knowledge of Creatures, but the morall knowledge of good and euill, wherein the supposition was, that Gods commaundements or prohibitions were not the originals of good and euill, but that they had other beginnings which man aspired to know, to the end, to make a totall defection from God, and to depend wholy upon himselfe."

5. *Ibid.*, 8–9. This assertion is found in several of Bacon's texts. To a certain extent, this idea echoes Montaigne's denunciation of "mongrels," who are neither utterly ignorant nor completely learned, but, while Montaigne encouraged them to come back to a state of natural ignorance or simplicity, Bacon, on the contrary, pleads for more knowledge. A similar idea is also found in Agrippa's *De incertitudine* (see the introduction to this book).

6. *Ibid.*, 9–12.

7. *Ibid.*, 13.

8. *Ibid.*, 14.

9. On this association, see in particular the analysis of Gauden's denunciation of ignorance and his defense of a learned ministry in part 2.

10. *Ibid.*, 15, 17, 20, and 21.

11. *Ibid.*, 21, 22, 24, 25, 26, and 32.

12. *Ibid.*, bk. 2, 110.

13. *Ibid.*, 110. On this passage and its interpretation along skeptical lines, see Silvia Manzo, "Reading Scepticism Historically: Scepticism, *Acatalepsia* and the Fall of Adam in Francis Bacon," in *Academic Scepticism in the Development of Early Modern Philosophy*, ed. Sébastien Charles and Plinio J. Smith (Cham, Switzerland: Springer, 2017), 81–102, here 97.

14. Bacon, *The Advancement of Learning*, op. cit., 37. On Bacon and the Jesuits, see

also Stephen Gaukroger, *Francis Bacon and the Transformation of Early-Modern Philosophy* (Cambridge: Cambridge University Press, 2001), 128–131.

15. Bacon, *The Advancement of Learning, op. cit.*, 17: "in regard of this, and some other points concerning humane learning, and Morall matters, I may say as *Agesilaus* sayd to his enemie *Farnabasus, Talis quum sis, vtinam noster esses*" (You are so good that I wish you were on our side).

16. Francis Bacon, *The Masculine Birth of Time, Or Three Books on the Interpretation of Nature*, trans. and ed. Benjamin Farrington, in *The Philosophy of Francis Bacon, op. cit.*, 59–72, here 71. See also Andrew Hiscock, *Reading Memory in Early Modern Literature* (Cambridge: Cambridge University Press, 2011), chap. 8, "'This Art of Memory': Francis Bacon, Memory and the Discourses of Power," 219–245, here 226. Yet Hiscock shows that Bacon did also exploit "the medieval discourse of spiritual cleansing and mental catharsis with a secular analogue in mind" (224). Indeed, Bacon sometimes insisted on the necessity to purge one's mind and to "wash [it] clean from opinions," or to "becom[e] again as little children." See *Historia naturalis*, in *The Works of Francis Bacon*, ed. James Spedding, Robert Leslie Ellis, and Douglas Denon Heath (London: Longman and Co., 1857–1874), 5:132–133.

17. Francis Bacon, *Valerius Terminus of the Interpretation of Nature: with the Annotations of Hermes Stella*, in *The Works of Francis Bacon, op. cit.*, 3:215–252, here 3:247.

18. Francis Bacon, *Letter and Discourse to Sir Henry Savill Touching Helps for the Intellectual Powers*, in *The Works of Francis Bacon, op. cit.*, 7:102. More generally, on the reception of Agrippa in England, see Nauert, *Agrippa and the Crisis of Renaissance Thought, op. cit.*, chap. 12.

19. Bacon, *The Masculine Birth of Time, op. cit.*, 70.

20. Montaigne's *Essais* were published in John Florio's translation in 1603 (reprinted in 1613 and 1632), but the French original circulated in England from an earlier date and continued to be read alongside the English translation. Bacon himself read the *Essais* in French. On Montaigne's reception in England in general, see, for instance, Philip Ford, ed., "Montaigne in England," special issue, *Montaigne Studies* 24, nos. 1–2 (2012); Warren Boutcher, "Montaigne in England and America," in *The Oxford Handbook of Montaigne*, ed. Ph. Desan, *op. cit.*, 306–327; and John O'Brien, "Montaigne, Sir Ralph Bankes and Other English Readers of the *Essais*," *Renaissance Studies* 28, no. 3 (2014): 377–391. On Bacon's reception of Montaigne, see Pierre Villey, *Montaigne et François Bacon* (Paris: Revue de la Renaissance, 1913); Kenneth Alan Hovey, "'Mountaigny Saith Prettily': Bacon's French and the *Essais*," *PMLA* 106, no. 1 (1991): 71–82; and Marta Fattori, "Francis Bacon et la culture française," in *Bacon et Descartes: Genèse de la modernité philosophique*, ed. Élodie Cassan (Lyon: ENS Éditions, 2014), 25–47.

21. Montaigne, "*An Apologie of Raymond Sebond*," in *The essayes, op. cit.*, II, 12, 281. This passage was already quoted as directly inspired from Cusanus, according to Pierre Magnard. On the comparison between Montaigne and Bacon made here, see Hovey, "'Mountaigny Saith Prettily,'" *op. cit.*, 74.

22. Hovey, "'Mountaigny Saith Prettily,'" *op. cit.*, 79.

23. Luiz Eva, "On the affinities between Bacon's philosophy and skepticism," trans. Fernando Moraes Barros, *Kriterion, Belo Horizonte* 47, no. 113 (2006): 73–97.

24. Miguel Ángel Granada, "Bacon and Scepticism," *Nouvelles de la République des Lettres* 2 (2006): 91–104, here 95.

25. *Ibid.*, 99.

26. Manzo, "Reading Scepticism Historically," *op. cit.*, 92.

27. Francis Bacon, *Novum Organum*, in Francis Bacon, *The* Instauratio magna *Part II. Novum Organum*, ed. Graham Rees and Maria Wakely (Oxford: Clarendon Press, 2004), bk. 1, aphorism 126, 191.

28. Desiderius Erasmus, *The Praise of Folie. Moriæ encomium, a booke made in latine by that great clerke Erasmus Roterodame, Englished by Sir Thomas Chaloner* (London, 1549), [S1^v].

29. *Ibid.*, [S1^v].

30. *Ibid.*, [S1^v].

31. Agrippa, *The Vanity of Arts and Sciences*, *op. cit.*, 359–360.

32. Replies to this argument were also found in the works of clergymen and theologians who denounced ignorance. See, e.g., the Italian Jesuit Daniello Bartoli, *The Learned Man Defended and Reformed*, trans. Th. Salusbury (London, 1660), 79–88. Bartoli admits that God chose "the rude and ignorant" for apostles, but he argues that God gave them the "gift of the sciences." See also John Gauden, *Hieraspistes. A Defence by Way of Apology for the Ministry and Ministers of the Church of England* (London, 1653), 419–420. Gauden explains that the apostles became learned as soon as they interacted with Jesus: "As for the *blessed Apostles*, who were immediately taught of God, by conversing with the Son of God the Lord Jesus Christ, the Christian world well knowes their miraculous and extraordinary *fulnesse* of all gifts, and powers of the *Spirit*, both *habituall* and *occasionall*; so that they wanted neither any *language* nor *learning*, which was then necessary, to carry on the great work of preaching, and planting the Gospell." Thus, Gauden merely denies that the apostles were illiterate. On Gauden's denunciation of ignorance, see also part 2.

33. Bacon, *The Advancement of Learning*, *op. cit.*, 36.

34. *Ibid.*, 36.

35. The *Oxford English Dictionary* quotes this passage from Bacon's *Advancement of Learning* and defines *learnings* (plural) as "branches of learning" or "sciences."

36. Joseph Glanvill, "The usefulness of real philosophy to religion," in *Essays on Several Subjects* (London, 1676), 38.

37. *Ibid.*, 39.

38. *Ibid.*, 40.

39. *Ibid.*, 40.

40. *Ibid.*, 40–41.

41. The meaning of *integrity* and the condemnation of rhetorical effects in Glanvill's essay echo Proverbs 19.1: "Better is the poor that walketh in his integrity, than he that is perverse in his lips, and is a fool."

42. [Robert Boyle,] *Some Considerations touching the Usefulnesse of Experimental Nat-*

urall Philosophy, Propos'd in Familiar Discourses to a Friend, by way of Invitation to the Study of it (Oxford, 1663), 116.

43. Ibid., 116.

44. Robert Boyle, *The Christian Virtuoso: Showing, that by being addicted to Experimental Philosophy, a Man is rather Assisted, than Indisposed, to be a Good Christian* (London, 1690), 32–33: "*since* God has both given him a Rational Mind, and endow'd it with an Intellect, whereby he can Contemplate the Works of Nature."

45. Ibid., 98.

46. On the fact that experimentalists were surprisingly not much interested in Cusanus's thought, despite the essential role that Cusanus attributed to observation and experimentation, see part 3. On the favorable reception of Cusanus's learned ignorance by mid-seventeenth-century religious radicals in England, see part 2.

47. Joseph Glanvill, *The Vanity of Dogmatizing: Or Confidence in Opinions manifested in a Discourse of the Shortness and Uncertainty of our Knowledge, and its Causes* (London, 1661), "The Preface," [A6^v].

48. Joseph Glanvill, *Scepsis Scientifica: Or, Confest Ignorance, the Way to Science; In an Essay of The Vanity of Dogmatizing, and Confident Opinion* (London, 1665), 4 and 9.

49. Ibid., 48.

50. Ibid., 47–50. The causes of ignorance are given in chapters 9–17 (47–109). The same ideas are also found in Glanvill's *Essays on Several Subjects in Philosophy and Religion* (*op. cit.*), especially in the first essay "Against confidence in philosophy, and matters of speculation," starting at 14.

51. Glanvill, *Scepsis Scientifica, op. cit.*, 50–51.

52. Ibid., 52.

53. Ibid., 55.

54. Ibid., 67–69.

55. Ibid., 70–77.

56. Ibid., 78–85.

57. Ibid., 93.

58. Ibid., 90.

59. Ibid., 48.

60. Glanvill, *The Vanity of Dogmatizing, op. cit.*, 29.

61. Glanvill, *Scepsis Scientifica, op. cit.*, 166. For a similar idea, see Richard Baxter, *A Treatise of Knowledge and Love Compared In two parts: 1. Of Falsly Pretended Knowledge. 2. Of True Saving Knowledge and Love. Written as greatly needful to the Safety and Peace of every Christian, and of the Church. The only certain way to escape false Religions, Heresies, Sects and Malignant Prejudices, Persecutions and Sinful Wars: All caused by falsly pretended knowledge, and hasty judging, by proud Ignorant men, who know not their Ignorance* (London, 1689). There are many similitudes between Glanvill's *Scepsis Scientifica* and Baxter's *Treatise* (on this text, see part 2).

62. Glanvill, *The Vanity of Dogmatizing, op. cit.*, 32.

63. Glanvill, *Scepsis Scientifica, op. cit.*, 52. Glanvill here argues more specifically that

Descartes's method can help correct the errors of the senses, precisely because it consists in questioning all that appears as self-evident.

64. *Ibid.*, 5.

65. *Ibid.*, 57, 83, and 84. Note that Descartes is by far the most frequent reference in *The Vanity of Dogmatizing* (1661) and in *Scepsis Scientifica* (1665). Descartes is often found in the works of Restoration English experimentalists, but he is rarely as omnipresent as in Glanvill's writings.

66. Glanvill, *Scepsis Scientifica, op. cit.*, 53.

67. *Ibid.*, 55. Glanvill even doubts that divesting oneself of all prejudices is actually possible: "But yet this is so difficult in the impartial and exact performance, that it may be well reckon'd among the bare *Possibilities*, which never commence into a *Futurity*: It requiring such a free, sedate, and intent minde, as it may be is no where found but among the *Platonical Idea's*," in *ibid.*, 56.

68. *Ibid.*, 95.

69. Glanvill, "Against confidence in philosophy," *op. cit.*, 24. The same idea is also found in "Modern improvements of useful knowledge," in *Essays, op. cit.*, 51.

70. With *An Exclusion of Scepticks from all Title to Dispute* (London, 1665), in which he defends the possibility of attaining absolutely certain truths, Thomas White entered a debate on skepticism with Glanvill.

71. See, for example, Richard Whitlock's praise of Charron's *liberté d'esprit*.

72. Glanvill, *Scepsis Scientifica, op. cit.*, 172.

73. *Ibid.*, 56.

74. Glanvill, *The Vanity of Dogmatizing, op. cit.*, 186.

75. Baxter, *A Treatise of Knowledge and Love Compared, op. cit.*, 48. On Sanches, see part 2.

76. Glanvill, *Scepsis Scientifica, op. cit.*, 7.

77. This is the definition given by Baxter, for example, in *Treatise of Knowledge and Love Compared, op. cit.*, 181 (the whole passage is quoted and analyzed in part 2).

78. See, for example, Cornel Zwierlein on the terminology of ignorance in *Imperial Unknowns, op. cit.*, 14–15.

79. Glanvill, *Scepsis Scientifica, op. cit.*, 7.

80. *Ibid.*, 1, 56, 93, 85 and 55. "*Antique* Ignorance" is also called "*Pagan* Ignorance" in Glanvill's essay "The usefulness of real philosophy to religion," *op. cit.*, 16.

81. Part 3 shows that Locke also paid a lot of attention to ignorance, but his reception of the learned ignorance tradition was much less favorable. On Glanvill, see also Philippe Hamou, who has underlined the paradoxical character of Glanvill's philosophical stance, or his "skeptical empiricism," which proposed a skeptical description of man's faculties of knowledge, while promoting the ideals of "the new science," in *La Mutation du visible: Essai sur la portée épistémologique des instruments d'optique au XVIIe siècle*, vol. 2, *Microscopes et télescopes en Angleterre, de Bacon à Hooke* (Villeneuve d'Ascq, France: Presses universitaires du Septentrion, 2001), "Glanvill et les antinomies de la 'scepsis scientifica,'" 78–86, here 79 and 82. See also Frédéric Brahami, "Au fil conducteur du scepticisme: science et métaphysique chez Glanvill," *Philosophiques* 35, no. 1 (2008): 207–222; and Richard H. Popkin, *The Third Force in Seventeenth-Century Thought* (Leiden: Brill, 1992), "The Scepticism of Joseph

Glanvill," 246–253; and *The History of Scepticism, op. cit.* (211–215), which gives an entirely different interpretation of Glanvill's philosophy from the one presented here.

Part II

1. See, for example, Cesare Ripa's allegory of ignorance presented in the introduction.

2. Note that there were other forms of internal light in the early modern period, such as the "light of nature" of Restoration English experimentalists, most of whom held that the *lumen naturae*, which was naturally present in all men, had been weakened by the Fall, yet could probably be revived. The main purpose of their work was precisely to show how, on which conditions, and whether it could be entirely revived or not. Locke, whose conception of ignorance differed from most Restoration experimentalists because he did not adhere to the Augustinian-Calvinist interpretation of the Fall, assimilated the light of nature with conscience and knowledge of right and wrong: to him, an "ignorant day-labourer" who could not read was actually not completely ignorant, being endowed with the "light of nature." See Locke's commonplace book in Peter King, ed., *The Life of John Locke with Extracts from his Correspondence, Journals and Common-place Books* (London, 1829), 283.

3. For a short history of the inner light from Greek philosophy to the seventeenth century, see Leif Eeg-Olofsson, *The Conception of the Inner Light in Robert Barclay's Theology. A Study in Quakerism* (Lund, Sweden: CWK Glerrup, 1954), chap. 1, "The Inner Light before Barclay," 19–54.

4. *Ibid.*, 39.

5. Thomas Aquinas, *Summa Theologica*, trans. Fathers of the English Dominican Province (Westminster, MD: Christian Classics, 1981), pt. I, question 12, art. 13. Surprisingly, Eeg-Olofsson does not mention Aquinas in his history of the inner light.

6. Thomas Aquinas, *Aristotle's* De anima *with the Commentary of St. Thomas Aquinas*, trans. Kenelm Foster and Silvester Humphries (New Haven, CT: Yale University Press, 1965), sec. 372, 244–245. See also John Morris, "Descartes' Natural Light," *Journal of the History of Philosophy* 11, no. 2 (1973): 169–187, here 171.

7. Locke, *Essay concerning Human Understanding, op. cit.*, IV, 19, 3, 698.

8. On ignorance and salvation, see also Parageau, "'Papists Make a Direct Profession of This Shamefull Sin,'" *op. cit.*, 102–107.

Chapter 3

1. George Keith, *The Woman-Preacher of Samaria; A Better Preacher and more Sufficiently Qualified to Preach than any of the Men-Preachers of the Man-Made Ministry in these Three Nations* (London, 1674), 6.

2. *Ibid.*, 2.

3. *Ibid.*, 7.

4. *Ibid.*, 3.

5. *Ibid.*, 14–15.

6. George Keith, *The Universal Free Grace of the Gospel Asserted, or, The Light of the*

Glorious Gospell of Jesus Christ, shining forth universally, and enlightening every man that comes into the World, and thereby giving unto every man, a day of Visitation, wherein it is possible for him to be saved (London, 1671), 7.

7. [George Fox], *An Epistle to All People on the Earth; and The Ignorance of all the World, both Professors and Teachers, of the Birth that must be silent, and of the Birth that is to speak, which declares God; and the difference betwixt silence and speaking* (London, 1657), 5.

8. "Christ is the light, Christ is truth," in George Fox, *A Testimony of the True Light of the World. Which is given to every man that comes into the world, and of the true measure of the gift of God, given to every one to profit withal* (London, 1657), 26. The whole book is a commentary on John 3: "He that loves the Light, his deeds are wrought in God, but he that hates the Light his deeds are evil."

9. Fox, *An Epistle to All People, op. cit.*, 5.

10. *Ibid.*, 4: "So every one that cometh into the world being enlightned, which hears not the light, the light which doth enlighten him, he hears not the Prophet which *Moses* prophesied of; so the light condemns him, and he is to be cut off from among the people," and Fox, *A Testimony of the True Light, op. cit.*, 40.

11. Fox, *A Testimony of the True Light, op. cit.*, 10.

12. George Fox, *A Word to the people of the world, who hates the light, to be witnessed by the light in them all; wherein is shewed unto them, what the light is, which is the Condemnation of the world with its deeds, and what the Spirit of truth is, and what it leads them into, who are led by it; and what the spirit of errour is, and what it leads them into, who are lead by it* (London, 1659), 8.

13. Fox, *A Testimony of the True Light, op. cit.*, 40.

14. Fox, *A Word to the people of the world, op. cit.*, 1.

15. *Ibid.*, 2.

16. Jeffrey Dudiak and Laura Rediehs, "Quakers, Philosophy, and Truth," in *The Oxford Handbook of Quaker Studies*, ed. Stephen W. Angell and Pink Dandelion (Oxford: Oxford University Press, 2013), 507–519, here 514.

17. See also Stephen W. Angell, "God, Christ, and the Light," in *ibid.*, 158–171, esp. 160.

18. The work then appeared in a Latin translation in the collection of Descartes's posthumous works, *Opuscula posthuma* (Amsterdam, 1701). The complete original French title reads *Recherche de la vérité par la lumière naturelle qui toute pure, et sans emprunter le secours de la Religion ni de la Philosophie, détermine les opinions que doit avoir un honnête homme, touchant toutes les choses qui peuvent occuper sa pensée, et pénètre jusque dans les secrets des plus curieuses sciences*. See *La Recherche de la vérité par la lumière naturelle*, ed. Ettore Lojacono, Erik Jan Bos, Franco A. Meschini, and Francesco Saita (Milan: FrancoAngeli, 2002); and *The Search for Truth by Means of the Natural Light*, trans. John Cottingham, Robert Stoothoff, and Dugald Murdoch, in *The Philosophical Writings of Descartes, op. cit.*, 2:400–420.

19. René Descartes, *Discours de la méthode pour bien conduire sa raison, & chercher la vérité dans les sciences. Plus la Dioptrique, les Météores et la Géométrie, qui sont des essais de*

cete méthode (Leiden, 1637). The *Discours de la méthode* was translated (anonymously) into English and published in London in 1649 under the title *A Discourse of a Method for the Well-Guiding of Reason and the Discovery of Truth in the Sciences*.

20. André Robinet claims that the expression *lumen naturale* or *lumière naturelle* is found 120 times in Descartes's works, in *Descartes, la lumière naturelle. Intuition, disposition, complexion* (Paris: Vrin, 1999), 26.

21. *The Dioptrics* (*La Dioptrique*), sometimes translated as the *Optics*, is an essay of the *Discourse on Method*.

22. It is argued in part 3 that the dialogue was probably inspired to Descartes by Nicholas of Cusa's *De idiota*, first published in 1450. A comparison between the two texts is drawn, focusing on the "conceptual persona" of the Idiot.

23. René Descartes, *Third Meditation*, in *Meditations on First Philosophy*, in *The Philosophical Writings of Descartes*, op. cit., 2:24. The *Meditations* were first published in Latin in 1641 and then in French in 1647. They were translated into English by William Molyneux (London, 1680).

24. Descartes, *A Discourse of a Method*, op. cit., 2. *Bon sens* is translated as "right understanding" or "understanding," while *raison* is rendered as "reason."

25. *Ibid.*, 16–17. The French original reads: "j'apprenais à ne rien croire trop fermement . . . , et ainsi je me délivrais peu à peu de beaucoup d'erreurs, qui peuvent offusquer notre lumière naturelle, et nous rendre moins capables d'entendre raison," in René Descartes, *Discours de la méthode*, ed. Geneviève Rodis-Lewis (Paris: GF-Flammarion, 1966), 39. In this passage, it seems that the internal light is not the same thing as reason; rather, it is what makes possible the use of reason. The same relation between the light and reason was found later, in works by Cartesians such as Malebranche: "Let him *Retire into himself*, and press near to that *Light*, which perpetually *shines Within*, to the end his *Reason* may be more and more enlightened," in *Father Malebranche his Treatise concerning the Search after Truth*, op. cit., [A3ᵛ]. Here again, the role of the light is to enlighten reason.

26. Descartes, *A Discourse of a Method*, op. cit., 44. Descartes explains here that, thanks to the internal light given by God, he cannot accept other people's opinions without examining them first. See also *ibid.*, 3. John Morris claims that Descartes's natural light cannot be equated with reason or the understanding, and that it is only one function of reason, that of cognition (as opposed to conception), in "Descartes' Natural Light," op. cit., 174–175. Morris further argues that the natural light is a "passive" function, which does not form ideas, but "gives a click of recognition when a true idea is brought before it" (in *ibid.*, 175).

27. Descartes, *Fifth Meditation*, in *Meditations on First Philosophy*, op. cit., 2:47.

28. *Ibid.*, 26.

29. René Descartes, *Author's Replies to the First Set of Objections* [against *Meditations*], in *The Philosophical Writings of Descartes*, op. cit., 2:76.

30. *Ibid.*, 2:76 and Descartes, *Author's Replies to the Third Set of Objections*, in *The Philosophical Writings of Descartes*, op. cit., 2:132.

31. Descartes, *Rules for the Direction of the Mind*, op. cit., Rule III, 14.

32. *Ibid.*, 14.

33. *Ibid.*, 15.

34. *Ibid.*, 13.

35. René Descartes, *Letter to Mersenne*, 16 October 1639, in *Œuvres de Descartes*, ed. Charles Adam and Paul Tannery, vol. 2, *Correspondence, March 1638–December 1639* (Paris: Cerf, 1898), 599 (my translation). Actually, Descartes himself did not translate *intuitus* as "intuition." He rather used the term in its etymological sense of seeing (*intueri*, "to see"). On this subject, see also Robinet, *Descartes, la lumière naturelle, op. cit.*, 30. Despite the assimilation of the natural light with intuition in the letter to Mersenne, John Morris is adamant that they are distinct in Descartes's philosophy, in "Descartes' Natural Light," *op. cit.*, 180–183.

36. As mentioned earlier, in Quaker theology, truth is not exactly accessed directly since the intervention of Christ as teacher (and knowledge simultaneously) in one's heart is required.

37. On the assimilation of Quaker and Cartesian ideas in the seventeenth and eighteenth centuries, see Michael Heyd, *"Be Sober and Reasonable": The Critique of Enthusiasm in the Seventeenth and Early Eighteenth Centuries* (Leiden: Brill, 1995), chap. 4 (on perceptions of Descartes as an enthusiast), 109–143. Heyd studies the reactions to enthusiasm and its medical critique in the early modern period, while the aim here is rather to focus on enthusiasm and ignorance, and on the way they were articulated at the time, an aspect not examined by Heyd. On the whole, Heyd overlooked the role of ignorance and of the internal light as an immediate access to knowledge in his study of enthusiasm and its critics (on Descartes's internal light and its relation to accusations of enthusiasm, see, for example, the brief passage on 132). However, Heyd's examination of early modern enthusiasm presents similitudes—especially methodological ones—with a study of ignorance in the same period: like enthusiasm, ignorance cannot be given a clear and stable definition, yet the reactions to both deserve some attention. As Heyd puts it: "Indeed, the label [enthusiasm] reflects the attitudes of its users rather than describing any particular group which it purports to designate. Hence, what is needed is a systematic study of the social and intellectual carriers of the term and of its various connotations and denotations" (introduction, 5). This applies to the study of early modern ignorance as well.

38. Meric Casaubon, *A Treatise concerning Enthusiasme, As it is an Effect of Nature: but is mistaken by many for either Divine Inspiration or Diabolical Possession* (London, 1655), "The Contents," [A2ʳ] and 1. Although this text has received scholarly attention, its important claims about ignorance have not been studied yet.

39. *Ibid.*, 60.

40. See, for example, *ibid.*, 28–29, on the causes of "Enthusiastick Divination," and 85.

41. On enthusiasm, melancholy and madness, see also Anne Dunan-Page, *Grace Overwhelming: John Bunyan,* The Pilgrim's Progress *and the Extremes of the Baptist Mind* (New York: Peter Lang, 2006); and Claire Crignon–De Oliveira, *De la mélancolie à l'enthousiasme: Robert Burton (1577–1640) et Anthony Ashley-Cooper, comte de Shaftesbury (1671–1713)* (Paris: Honoré Champion, 2006).

42. Casaubon, *A Treatise concerning Enthusiasme, op. cit.*, 3.

43. *Ibid.*, 116.

44. On Denys the Areopagite and his influence from the thirteenth century onwards, see the introduction.

45. Casaubon, *A Treatise concerning Enthusiasme, op. cit.*, 112.

46. *Ibid.*, 116. Casaubon adds in the margin, about the term *ignorance*, that there may be a difference between *ignoratio* and *ignorantia*, but he is at a loss how to render it in English, saying that *ignorance* in this context might perhaps be better translated as "unknowingness."

47. *Ibid.*, 117.

48. *Ibid.*, 116–117: "as though they had been the only wise and godly men of the world, because the most ignorant." Casaubon also says here again that common people are easily manipulated by those who claim inspiration because they are ignorant themselves. See, for example, *ibid.*, 9–10, where he mentions the power of Orpheus over "the poor ignorant multitude."

49. *Ibid.*, 117.

50. *Ibid.*, 124. Casaubon focuses on the case of Sister Catherine of Jesus in Paris.

51. *Ibid.*, 129–130.

52. *Ibid.*, 130–131.

53. [Henry More,] *Enthusiasmus triumphatus, or, A discourse of the nature, causes, kinds, and cure, of enthusiasm, written by Philophilus Parresiastes, and prefixed to Alazonomastix his observations and reply* (London, 1656), 5.

54. *Ibid.*, 37.

55. Henry More, *An Explanation of the Grand Mystery of Godliness, or, A True and Faithfull Representation of the Everlasting Gospel of our Lord and Saviour Jesus Christ, the onely begotten Son of God and Sovereign over Men and Angels* (London, 1660), "To the Reader," ix and xi.

56. *Ibid.*, 528.

57. *Ibid.*, 528.

58. Henry More, *A Plain and Continued Exposition of the Several Prophecies or Divine Visions of the Prophet Daniel, which have or may concern the People of God, whether Jew or Christian* (London, 1681), "The Preface to the Reader," lv. According to Henry More, the knowledge that Quakers and Familists want is that of the Scriptures and "the Records of History" (in *ibid.*, li). See also *ibid.*, xcix.

59. Locke, *Essay concerning Human Understanding, op. cit.*, IV, 19, 8, 700.

60. René Descartes and Martin Schoock, *La Querelle d'Utrecht*, ed. Theo Verbeek, preface by Jean-Luc Marion (Paris: Les Impressions Nouvelles, 1988), 160 (my translation) and 193. At the time of the quarrel, Martin Schoock, a disciple of the Dutch reformed theologian Gisbertus Voetius, was professor of logic and physics at the University of Groningen. The "Utrecht quarrel" started in 1641, when Voetius attacked Descartes's "atheism," an accusation based on the fact that the idea of God was proof of God's existence in Cartesian thought. Voetius argued that not everyone had the idea of God. In his defense, Descartes referred to Socrates's dialogue with the ignorant slave boy in *Meno*,

which shows that the boy had "spontaneous" geometrical knowledge, although he was unaware of it. On this quarrel, see also Popkin, *The History of Scepticism, op. cit.*, 161–162.

61. Descartes and Schoock, *La Querelle d'Utrecht, op. cit.*, 187, 193 and 199.

62. See Martin Schoock, *De scepticismo pars prior, sive libri quatuor* (Groningen, 1652). Sanches's *Quod nihil scitur* was published in 1581 in Lyon. See the translation and edition by Elaine Limbrick and Douglas F. S. Thomson, *That Nothing Is Known* (Cambridge: Cambridge University Press, 1988).

63. Schoock, *La Querelle d'Utrecht, op. cit.*, 189 (my translation) and 307 ("Un adulte qui oublie tout ignore tout; et là où il y a ignorance de tout, là réside le dérangement mental. Car ce qui est, par nature, absolument évident ne peut être ignoré que si l'on éteint la lumière de la raison, de sorte que celui qui est candidat à la sagesse se transforme en prêtre de la bêtise"). Descartes replied again that he did not advocate forgetting all the knowledge that one possessed, but only getting rid of prejudices, in order to establish new knowledge (in *ibid.*, 347).

64. Gauden, *Hieraspistes, op. cit.*, 404.

65. *Ibid.*, 414.

66. Plato, *Timaeus*, 86a–87b and 88b, in *Timaeus and Critias*, trans. Desmond Lee (London: Penguin Classics, 2008), 114–117. Lee translates the two kinds of diseases as "madness" and "stupidity."

67. Schoock, *La Querelle d'Utrecht, op. cit.*, 313–314.

68. *Ibid.*, chap. 2, 312 (my translation). The title of the chapter is "La même méthode conduit directement à l'Enthousiasme." See also 313–314.

69. *Ibid.*, 347 and 351.

70. Denis Kambouchner, "Descartes et le problème de la culture," *Bulletin de la Société Française de Philosophie* (April–June 1998): 1–48. On Descartes, learning and books, see also Arbib, "Le moi cartésien comme troisième livre," *op. cit.*, 162–165.

71. Meric Casaubon, *Generall Learning. A Seventeenth-Century Treatise on the Formation of the General Scholar by Meric Casaubon*, ed. Richard Serjeantson (Cambridge: RTM Publications, 1999), 145.

72. *Ibid.*, 153–154. Intervention in edited text by Richard Serjeantson.

73. Meric Casaubon, *Of Credulity and Incredulity; In Things divine and spiritual* (London, 1670), 151: "The *Puritans* of *England*, I remember were wont to teach, that there is no true Conversion, but through the horrors of a sad kind of desparation, as antecedent to it, or always concomitant; and they made very good use of it, (for I will not say, they had all the same aime and end in it:) many of them. For when they had brought their Disciples as low as they thought fitting; then they were to raise them again by their methods (long prayers, and the like:) until they had put them into a seeming possession of heaven. . . . The Jesuits, some of them (for all, I dare say, are not acquainted with these mysteries), are said to use some such thing, to get to themselves some confidents, whom they may use in time of need. It may be our *Puritans* learned it of them, as they have done many other things."

74. Casaubon, *Generall Learning, op. cit.*, 153.

75. *Ibid.*, 157–158: Casaubon writes that Descartes recommends "that all other bookes

& learning should be layd aside, as needles, but what came from him, or was grounded upon his principles." Descartes's aim, according to Casaubon, is to replace all existing knowledge with his own principles.

76. *Ibid.*, 154.

77. Adrien Baillet, *La Vie de Monsieur Descartes* (Paris, 1691), 2 vols., here 1:81: "s'étant couché *tout rempli de son enthousiasme.*" The English translation (by "S.R.") was published in London in 1693; the dreams are narrated from p. 35 of this edition.

78. [John Sergeant], *The Method to Science* (London, 1696), "Preface dedicatory to the Learned Students of both our Universities," [C2^r].

79. See John Sergeant, *Solid Philosophy Asserted Against the Fancies of the Ideists* (London, 1697). Note that Sergeant also associated Descartes and Locke, whom he accused of favoring skepticism. Locke never replied but his annotated copy of *Solid Philosophy* has survived (on Locke, ignorance, and skepticism, see in particular part 3). Moreover, after the publication of *The Method to Science*, Sergeant entered into a controversy with the Cartesian Antoine Le Grand. See Beverley Southgate, "Sergeant, John (1623–1707), Roman Catholic Controversialist and Philosopher," *Oxford Dictionary of National Biography*, September 2004, https://www-oxforddnb-com.janus.bis-sorbonne.fr/view/10.1093/ref:odnb/9780198614128.001.0001/odnb-9780198614128-e-25095.

80. Sergeant, *The Method to Science*, op. cit., [D1^v]. The assimilation of Quakerism and Cartesianism seems to have been rarer in France. The French Calvinist Samuel Desmarets (Maresius) did explicitly compare Descartes and the Quakers in his *De abusu philosophiae cartesianiae in rebus theologicis et fidei* (Groningen, 1670, 77), but Desmarets, who was professor of theology in Groningen, wrote in the context of the Dutch debate on Cartesianism. Descartes's enthusiasm was denounced in France, especially from the 1690s, but not associated with Quakerism specifically. See, for example, the Jesuit Gabriel Daniel's *Voyage du monde de Descartes* (Paris, 1690); and Pierre-Daniel Huet, *Nouveaux Mémoires pour servir à l'histoire du Cartésianisme* (1692). On this aspect of the reception of Cartesianism, see Heyd, *"Be Sober and Reasonable,"* op. cit., 116–117 and 127–128. In his 1733 *Letters concerning the English Nation*, first published in English in London, Voltaire associated Malebranche and the Quakers, with whom the Cartesian shared the idea of a universal internal light: "After this thou needest only but open thine eyes to that light which enlightens all mankind, and 'tis then thou wilt perceive the truth and make others perceive it. Why this, says I, is *Malebranche*'s doctrine to a tittle" (Letter II, 15).

81. Akihito Suzuki, "Dualism and the Transformation of Psychiatric Language in the Seventeenth and Eighteenth Centuries," *History of Psychiatry* 33 (1995): 417–447, here 418. See also 437: "Madness constructed within the dominant medical systems was *not* conceived as a disease of the mind until the latter half of the eighteenth century. Earlier medical writers conceptualized madness exclusively as a bodily disease, locating the problem in what the body represented to the mind and maintaining that the soul and the higher mental faculties of the patient remained intact. With the shift of emphasis from what the mind received to what the mind did, madness became the disease of the mind *per se.*"

82. *Ibid.*, 429–430.

83. *Ibid.*, 430.

84. Locke, *Essay concerning Human Understanding, op. cit.*, II, 33, 4, 395: "that opposition to Reason deserves that Name, and is really Madness." Yet it should be noted that in II, 11, 13 (*ibid.*, 161), Locke explains that mad people have not lost "the Faculty of Reasoning," but they join incoherent and wrong ideas together. Contrary to idiots, who cannot reason at all, the understanding of mad people can function.

Chapter 4

1. Note that the idea that one should first forgo all previous knowledge in order to reach truth was expressed in other writings in the early modern context of antischolasticism, although it took different forms. See, e.g., Thomas Browne, *Pseudodoxia Epidemica, or, Enquiries into very many Received Tenents, and Commonly Presumed Truths* (London, 1646): "For, what is worse, knowledge is made by oblivion; and to purchase a clear and warrantable body of Truth, we must forget and part with much wee know," "To the Reader," [A3ʳ].

2. Sorel, *De la perfection de l'homme, op. cit.*, 80 (my translation): "*L'ignorance n'engendre ny la Science ny l'Admiration.*"

3. *Ibid.*, 89–90: "Il est certain que tous les Hommes sont naturellement capables de Science & de connoissance; Plusieurs ne sont ignorans ou abusez de l'erreur que pour n'avoir pas receu d'autruy l'instruction qui leur estoit necessaire, ou pource que s'ils l'ont cherchée eux mesmes, ils se sont trompez en leur choix; Aussi des Maistres qui errent ne sont pas une bonne guide pour leur Disciples, & la plupart des Livres où l'on se voudroit instruire tout seul, n'ayans pas le pouvoir d'y servir, l'on peut croire que plusieurs de ceux qui ont employé beaucoup de temps à escouter ou à lire, ne laissent pas d'estre encore dans l'ignorance."

4. *Ibid.*, 90 and 94.

5. *Ibid.*, 80–81 (my translation): "Quelques Sophistes voulans defendre le mauvais party, & empescher que l'Ignorance ne soit entierement mesprisée, la font un principe du Sçavoir, comme si un contraire pouvait engendrer l'autre." This passage inspired the title of the second part of *The Paradoxes of Ignorance*.

6. *Ibid.*, 80–81 (my translation): "Ils disent que l'Ignorance est la cause de l'admiration, & que l'admiration est la cause de la Philosophie, tellement qu'à ce qu'ils croyent, pource que l'on est dans l'Ignorance en admirant tout ce que l'on void, l'on est porté à philosopher, & par ce moyen l'on est rendu sçavant: Mais il ne faut pas leur accorder ce qu'ils pretendent; Ils ne considerent pas que ceux qui sont tout à fait ignorans, n'admirent aucune chose. . . . C'est pourquoy ne demandons point la Science à une Mère si infeconde comme est l'Ignorance."

7. Plato, *Theaetetus*, 155d, in *Theaetetus and Sophist*, ed. Christopher Rowe (Cambridge: Cambridge University Press, 2015), 19: "This wondering of yours is very much the mark of a philosopher—philosophy starts nowhere else but with wondering, and the man who made Iris the offspring of Thaumas wasn't far off with his genealogy." See also Aristotle, *Metaphysics*, trans. and introduction by Hugh Lawson-Tancred (Harmondsworth,

UK: Penguin Books, 1998), 1.2, 982b: "For it was because of wonder that men both now and originally began to philosophize."

8. Montaigne, "*Of the Lame or Cripple*," in *The essayes, op. cit.*, III, 11, 614–615.

9. Giulio Landi, *La vita di Cleopatra . . . con una oratione . . . in lode dell'Ignoranza* (Venice, 1551), 53–54. On Landi, see also Corréard, "Discours, invectives et autres paradoxes 'contre les lettres,'" *op. cit.*, 145–146.

10. Sorel, *De la perfection de l'homme, op. cit.*, 81, and: "Mais il ne faut pas leur accorder ce qu'ils pretendent; Ils ne considerent pas que ceux qui sont tout à fait ignorans, n'admirent aucune chose. . . . C'est pourquoy ne demandons point la Science à une Mère si inфеconde comme est l'Ignorance; si ce n'est que nous entendions une Science modeste & terminée, comme celle des bons Esprits, qui declarant tousjours qu'ils ne sçavent rien, ne cessent de chercher quelque chose de plus que ce qu'ils sçavent" (80–81).

11. Baxter, *A Treatise of Knowledge and Love Compared, op. cit.*, 182.

12. *Ibid.*, 182.

13. *Ibid.*, 128 (Baxter's emphasis).

14. *Ibid.*, 237 and 145. As Barbara Lewalski has underlined, Baxter regularly insisted on the necessity of a learned ministry. He was among the Presbyterians who set forth the "Cambridge Model," a proposal that aimed to promote the education of ministers. See Barbara Kiefer Lewalski, "Milton on Learning and the Learned-Ministry Controversy," *Huntington Library Quarterly* 24, no. 4 (1961): 267–281, here 272.

15. Baxter, *A Treatise of Knowledge and Love Compared, op. cit.*, 237 and 260: "and the most gross and brutish ignorance best serveth the Devils designs and turn."

16. On the ambiguities of Baxter's thought, see also Neil H. Keeble, *Richard Baxter: Puritan Man of Letters* (Oxford: Clarendon Press, 1982), esp. 22–23.

17. Richard Baxter, *The Saints Everlasting Rest; Or, a Treatise of the blessed state of the saints in the enjoyment of God in Glory* (London, 1649), "The dedication of the whole," [A2^v]. The "Ignorant Zealots" Baxter alludes to are Antinomians, Socinians, Arminians, and Anabaptists.

18. *Ibid.*, [A3^v]: "Ignorance is virtually every error."

19. *Ibid.*, [A3^v]. Baxter's wish to encourage poor people's acquisition of knowledge was probably sincere. As Keeble has shown, Baxter made an arrangement with his bookseller, whereby he renounced all profits from the sale of his books in order to make them as cheap as possible, and therefore accessible to a larger part of the population. See Keeble, *Richard Baxter, op. cit.*, 44–45. On the idea that poor people should find the time to acquire knowledge, see also Locke, *Essay concerning Human Understanding, op. cit.*, IV, 20, 2, 707, and this book's part 3.

20. Richard Baxter, *The Arrogancy of Reason against Divine Revelations Repressed, or Proud Ignorance the Cause of Infidelity, and of Mens Quarrelling with the Word of God* (London, 1655), 22.

21. *Ibid.*, 37.

22. Baxter, *A Treatise of Knowledge and Love Compared, op. cit.*, 262: "I confess that *ignorance* is the calamity of our times, and people perish for lack of Knowledge." This reference to Hosea 4.6 is used here again (as it often was in commentaries on ignorance)

to justify a learned ministry. On ignorance of ignorance, see also Jerome R. Ravetz, "The Sin of Science: Ignorance of Ignorance," *Science Communication* 15, no. 2 (1993): 157–165. Ravetz argues that the concept ignorance of ignorance was well known to educated people until the seventeenth century, when "the founders of the modern worldview," mainly Galileo and Descartes, decided to dispense with it, becoming therefore unaware of the limits of human knowledge. With them, humility vanished. *The Paradoxes of Ignorance* tells a very different story.

23. Baxter, *A Treatise of Knowledge and Love Compared, op. cit.*, 117.

24. *Ibid.*, 168–169. See also *The Arrogancy of Reason, op. cit.*: "So that it is the nature of the ignorant, especially half-witted men, that have some little knowledge which may puff them up, to think they have that which indeed they have not" (38–39).

25. Locke, *Essay concerning Human Understanding, op. cit.*, IV, 3, 22, 553. On this passage, see part 3. See also another similar passage in Baxter's *Treatise of Knowledge and Love Compared, op. cit.*: "our knowledg here is so *poor* and *dark* and *low*, that compared with our *Ignorance* it is little; we know not *what* or how *many* or how *great* the things are which we do *not know*; but in general we may know that they are incomparably more and greater than what we *do know*; we know now but as *Children*, and *Darkly*, and in a *Glass* or *Riddle*, 1 *Cor.* 13.11, 12" (13).

26. Baxter, *A Treatise of Knowledge and Love Compared, op. cit.*, 15–25.

27. *Ibid.*, 26.

28. *Ibid.*, 17: "And this is an increasing malady, for new Books are yearly written, containing the said arbitrary notions of the several Authors. And whereas real and organical Learning should be orderly and conjunctly propagated, and *Things* studied for themselves, and *Words* for *Things*, the systems of Arts and Sciences grow more and more corrupted, our Logicks are too full of unapt notions, our Metaphysicks are a meer confused mixture of Pneumatology and Logick, and what part hath totally escaped?"

29. *Ibid.*, 124.

30. *Ibid.*, 191.

31. *Ibid.*, 181.

32. *Ibid.*, 1. See also 12.

33. *Ibid.*, 155.

34. *Ibid.*, 28 and 48.

35. *Ibid.*, 13. See also 113: "And though Teachers are, and must be a great stay to ignorant Learners; yet alas! How can they tell which are the wisest Teachers and whom to chuse?"

36. *Ibid.*, 211.

37. *Ibid.*, 264.

38. This verse is also quoted on the title page of *A Treatise of Knowledge and Love Compared*: "But I fear, lest by any means, as the serpent beguiled Eve through his subtilty, so your minds should be corrupted from the simplicity that is in Christ."

39. *Ibid.*, 4. Also, 1 Corinthians 3.18 reads: "Let no man deceive himself. If any man among you seemeth to be wise in this world, let him become a fool, that he may be wise."

40. *Ibid.*, 270. A similar idea is expressed, for example, in Richard Baxter, *Two Dis-*

putations of Original Sin. 1. Of Original sin, as from Adam. 2. Of Original Sin, as from our Neerer Parents (London, 1675): "I prefer the happiness of many a poor woman that hath *a strong Faith, and cannot define it*, before some Doctors that can define that which they have not" (47).

41. Baxter, *A Treatise of Knowledge and Love Compared*, op. cit., 266. A similar stance on the salvation of Roman Catholics was expressed for example by the clergyman and religious controversialist Hugh Cholmley in his defense of Bishop Hall's *Old Religion*. See Parageau, "'Papists Make a Direct Profession of This Shamefull Sin,'" op. cit., 104–107. See also Keeble, *Richard Baxter*, op. cit., 23–25.

42. Samuel How, *The Sufficiencie of the Spirits Teaching without Humane Learning: Or, a Treatise Tending to Prove Humane Learning to be no Help to the Spirituall Understanding of the Word of God* (London, 1640), "To the Reader," [A4^{r-v}].

43. Ibid., [A5^r]. The argument that Christ chose ignorant apostles, which proves that God wants men to remain ignorant, was examined in part 1, as it was systematically refuted by most English natural philosophers in their defense of the "new science" against doctrines of ignorance.

44. Ibid., [E2^r].

45. Ibid., [B3^r].

46. Ibid., [B1^v–B2^r].

47. Ibid., [B2^v], [B4^r]. How makes a concession and admits that learning is good to repair the loss caused by the Fall, and it is fit for statesmen, physicians, lawyers and gentlemen. But it is nothing but a "detestable filth" when it is used to understand the Word of God [C4^v].

48. Ibid., [B4^r].

49. Ibid., [B4^v].

50. Ibid., [B4^v]. On Pauline folly, which is here referred to, and its reception in the early modern period, see Essary, *Erasmus and Calvin on the Foolishness of God*, op. cit.

51. How, *The Sufficiencie of the Spirits Teaching*, op. cit., [C4^r].

52. Ibid., [E1^r].

53. Thomas Collier, *The Pulpit-Guard Routed, in its Twenty Strong-Holds. Or, a brief Answer, to a large and lawless Discourse, Written by one Tho. Hall of Kings Norton, Intituled, The Pulpit-Guarded, with Twenty Arguments, pretending to prove the unlawfulnesse, and sinfulness of Private mens Preaching* (London, 1651), 2–3. Collier was a traveling lay preacher. In 1647, he gave a sermon at the army headquarters at Putney, which was later included in the Leveller program. See Stephen Wright, "Collier, Thomas (d. 1691), Baptist Preacher," *Oxford Dictionary of National Biography*, September 2004, https://www-oxforddnb-com.janus.bis-sorbonne.fr/view/10.1093/ref:odnb/9780198614128.001.0001/odnb-9780198614128-e-5922.

54. Collier, *The Pulpit-Guard Routed*, op. cit., 38.

55. Ibid., 3. Two replies to Collier's treatise were published as early as 1652, by John Ferriby and Richard Saunders, emphasizing again the importance of the debate on a learned ministry in the Interregnum.

56. Nigel Smith, *Perfection Proclaimed. Language and Literature in English Radical*

Religion, 1640–1660 (Oxford: Clarendon Press, 1989), 11 on Samuel How, 17 on radical Puritans and mystical works, and chap. 3 on the translations and dissemination of those mystical works by John Everard and Giles Randall.

57. Thomas Wilson Hayes, "Nicholas of Cusa and Popular Literacy in Seventeenth-Century England," *Studies in Philology* 84, no. 1 (1987): 80–94, here 90.

58. Gauden, *Hieraspistes, op. cit.*, 395. About the debate on ignorance, learning and inspiration in Church ministry, see in particular sec. VI, "The third Calumny or Cavill: Pretending special Inspirations and extraordinary gifts beyond any Ordained Ministers," 361–393, and sec. VII, "The fourth Cavill or Calumny: Against humane learning acquired and used by Ministers," 395–436. Throughout the 1650s, Gauden published defenses of a traditional Church of England and pleas in favor of the clergy, such as *A petitionary remonstrance presented to O[liver] P[rotector] Feb 4 1655 . . . in behalf of many thousands of his distressed brethren (Ministers of the Gospel, and other good Schollars) who were deprived of all publique imployment, (as Ministers, or Schollars) by His declaration, jan. 1. 1655.* Yet Gauden's views on the political and religious events of the 1640s and 1650s in England are unclear, and may have been ambivalent. He became chaplain to King Charles II and bishop of Exeter at the Restoration. He was elected bishop of Worcester shortly before his death in 1662. He is often known for having played a part in the *Eikon Basilike* of Charles I, but here again, his actual role remains unclear.

59. Gauden, *Hieraspistes, op. cit.*, 396 and 403.

60. *Ibid.*, 396.

61. *Ibid.*, 408.

62. *Ibid.*, 409. Throughout his defense, Gauden refers to learning and knowledge as weapons and "*defensive Arms*" (see, e.g., 412).

63. *Ibid.*, 401: "yea we see, when Christian Religion ran out to much barbarity, illiterate ignorance, and superstition, for *many centuries*, till the last, (for want of the culture, and manuring of learning) it brought forth little *fair fruits*; but much of *Legendary fables*, lying wonders, religious *Romances*, stories of Chivalry in holy warres and Errantries in Religion." Gauden then criticizes the obscurity of scholasticism, a form of ignorance.

64. *Ibid.*, 409–410.

65. See, for example, as early as 1649, in the context of the English Civil Wars, the publication in London of *The Rebellion of Naples, or the Tragedy of Massenello, commonly so called*, by T.B.

66. Gauden, *Hieraspistes, op. cit.*, 400–401. Gauden also speaks of "*illiterate vice*, insolent ignorance, and folly well fed," showing the moral values attributed to ignorance and knowledge respectively (in *ibid.*, "To the Reader," [C2ʳ]).

67. *Ibid.*, 412: "for Ignorance makes men violent, and for want of reason to flye to force."

68. Casaubon, *Generall Learning, op. cit.*, 161–162. Gauden also denounces the fanatics' wish to have but one book left, in *Hieraspistes, op. cit.*, 395, 397, 409 and 414.

69. See the commentary on Casaubon's *Treatise concerning Enthusiasme* in chapter 3. Following Synesius, Casaubon argues that reason is God's temple in man, and neglecting knowledge means neglecting reason.

70. Gauden, *Hieraspistes, op. cit.*, 405.

71. *Ibid.*, 430. The same argument was found, for example, in Edward Waterhouse's *An*

Humble Apologie for Learning and Learned Men, also published in 1653 in London: "The more men are sunk in ignorance, and estranged from Arts and Sciences, the nearer come they to the life of Beasts and Savages; for unless the power of the mind, by which we are distinguished from bruits, be by liberal sciences ordered and modified, all their virtue and nobility will degenerate into not only a likeness to, but into a degree of rudeness beyond beasts" (7).

72. Gauden, *Hieraspistes, op. cit.*, 400. On learning and virtue, as well as the civilizing power of learning, see Richard Foster Jones, "The Humanistic Defence of Learning in the Mid-Seventeenth Century," in *Reason and the Imagination. Studies in the History of Ideas 1600–1800*, ed. J. A. Mazzeo (New York: Columbia University Press; London: Routledge & Kegan Paul, 1962), 71–92, here 79.

73. Gauden, *Hieraspistes, op. cit.*, 410–411.

74. See Bacon, *The Advancement of Learning, op. cit.*, 21.

75. Gauden, *Hieraspistes, op. cit.*, 428. On the definitions of learning in the seventeenth century, see Lewalski, "Milton on Learning and the Learned-Ministry Controversy," *op. cit*. In this article, Lewalski reconciles John Milton's two apparently contradictory stances on learning, by distinguishing two meanings of "human learning" in his works (see in particular 278–279). She argues that learning in the arts, sciences and philosophies is deemed useless in ministers by Milton, whereas learning in the languages is essential to him so as to understand the Scriptures.

76. Gauden, *Hieraspistes, op. cit.*, 398.

77. Gearing, *The Arraignment of Ignorance, op. cit.*, 51–53.

78. Gauden, *Hieraspistes, op. cit.*, 406: "Although the *Mine of Scripture* be rich; yet unlearned men (as the most part of Christians are, in point of humane literature) cannot search it; nor work it; nor try, and refine it; unlesse they have the help of those, who have tooles and instruments, and vessels, and skill, fit for so rich and holy, yet hard and serious a work."

79. *Ibid.*, 413.

80. *Ibid.*, 414.

81. *Ibid.*, 426.

82. Montaigne, "Of vaine subtilties, or subtill devises," in *The essayes, op. cit.*, I, 54, 170.

83. Gauden, *Hieraspistes, op. cit.*, 430 (in the margin: "*Illiteratenesse no reproach or discouragement to humble Christians*").

84. Lewis Griffin, *The Doctrine of the Asse: Or, A Brief Account of their Principles and Practice, in whose behalf the Complaint was written: That it may serve for Advice to others. Whereunto is Added, The Asse's Complaint. Balaam's Reply. And The Authors Apology* (London, 1661), [A1^r].

85. See Leonard Blunt, *Asse upon Asse being a collection of Several Pamphlets written for, and against the Author of the Asses Complaint against Balaam, or the cry of the Country against Ignorant and Scandalous Ministers. Together with some choice Observations upon them all* (London, 1661).

86. John Bunyan, *The Pilgrim's Progress from this World, to That which is to come: Delivered under the Similitude of a Dream Wherein is discovered the manner of his setting out, His dangerous journey; And safe arrival at the Desired Countrey* (London, 1678). Ignorance

first appears on 162. See Roger Pooley, "*The Pilgrim's Progress* and the Line of Allegory," in Anne Dunan-Page ed., *The Cambridge Companion to Bunyan* (Cambridge: Cambridge University Press, 2010), 80–94, here 88. For another figure of religious ignorance which probably inspired Bunyan, see Arthur Dent's popular dialogue, *The Plaine Man's Pathway to Heaven* (London, 1601). On the character of Asunetus in this text, see Christopher Haigh, *The Plain Man's Pathways to Heaven. Kinds of Christianity in Post-Reformation England, 1570–1640* (Oxford: Oxford University Press, 2007), pt. II, "'Asunetus, an Ignorant Man': Knowledge and Neglect," 57–97.

87. Bunyan, *The Pilgrim's Progress*, op. cit., 162.
88. *Ibid.*, 204–206.
89. *Ibid.*, 163–164.
90. *Ibid.*, 199–200.
91. *Ibid.*, 200–201.
92. *Ibid.*, 209–210.
93. *Ibid.*, 211–212.
94. *Ibid.*, 232.

95. Dunan-Page, *Grace Overwhelming*, op. cit., 258. On the possible models for Bunyan's Ignorance, see for example Maurice Hussey, "Bunyan's 'Mr. Ignorance' (1949)," in *Bunyan*, The Pilgrim's Progress. *A Casebook*, ed. Roger Sharrock, London and Basingstoke: Macmillan, 1976), 128–138.

96. Vincent Newey, "'With the eyes of my understanding': Bunyan, Experience, and Acts of Interpretation," in *John Bunyan. Conventicle and Parnassus, Tercentenary Essays*, ed. Neil H. Keeble (Oxford: Clarendon Press, 1988), 189–216, here 213. See also Vincent Newey, "Bunyan and the Confines of the Mind," in The Pilgrim's Progress*: Critical and Historical Views* (Liverpool: Liverpool University Press, 1980), 21–48.

97. Thomas H. Luxon, *Literal Figures: Puritan Allegory and the Reformation Crisis in Representation* (Chicago: University of Chicago Press, 1995), 182.

98. *Ibid.*, 184.

99. Bunyan, *The Pilgrim's Progress*, op. cit., 259.

100. See Henri A. Talon, *John Bunyan. The Man and His Works*, trans. Barbara Wall (London: Rockliff, 1951), 209–212; Richard F. Hardin, "Bunyan, Mr. Ignorance, and the Quakers," *Studies in Philology* 6, 4 (1972): 496–508, here 499; James F. Forrest, "Bunyan's Ignorance and the Flatterer: A Study in the Literary Art of Damnation," *Studies in Philology* 60, no. 1 (1963): 12–22, here 17, and John W. Draper, "Bunyan's Mr Ignorance," *The Modern Language Review* 22, no. 1 (1927): 15–21.

101. John Stachniewski, *The Persecutory Imagination. English Puritanism and the Literature of Religious Despair* (Oxford: Clarendon Press, 1991), 211–212.

102. Dunan-Page, *Grace Overwhelming*, op. cit., 103 and 108. See also 34, where Dunan-Page explains that Bunyan must have been an embarrassment to his colleagues as he "belonged nowhere." See also the anonymous *Dirt Wip'd Off: Or a Manifest Discovery of the Gross Ignorance, Erroneousness and Most Unchristian and Wicked Spirit of one John Bunyan* (London, 1672), 1. There were two separate issues in the controversy on baptism: one was about whether a man baptized in infancy could be admitted as a full member of

a congregation without being re-baptized, and the other, whether a Baptist congregation could share the Lord's Supper with people who had not been rebaptized.

103. Forrest, "Bunyan's Ignorance and the Flatterer," *op. cit.*, 18.

104. Richard Hardin argues that the character of Ignorance reminds the reader of "the primacy of knowledge in Bunyan's worldview," in "Bunyan, Mr. Ignorance, and the Quakers," *op. cit.*, 500.

Part III

1. Gilles Deleuze and Félix Guattari, *Qu'est-ce que la philosophie?* (Paris: Minuit, 1991), 60.

Chapter 5

1. Aristotle, *De anima*, trans. J. A. Smith (Oxford: Clarendon Press, 1931), 430a. Aristotle's word is *grammateion*, which was then translated as "tabula rasa."

2. Cornelius Agrippa, *De incertitudine & vanitate scientiarum declamatio invectiva*, 1539, Caput CI, "De scientiarum magistris," [bbiii^r].

3. Agrippa, *De l'incertitude, vanité, & abus des Sciences*, trans. Louys de Mayerne Turquet, *op. cit.*, 516.

4. See the English editions of Agrippa's *Vanity and Uncertainty of Arts and Sciences* of 1569 and 1575 (183). The seventeenth-century English versions of the text suppressed the second part of the passage ("to the intent to learne")—see editions of 1676, 1684 and 1694 (359), for example.

5. Locke, *Essay concerning Human Understanding, op. cit.*, II, 1, 2, 104. Book I focuses on the refutation of innate principles. The expression "tabula rasa" is found in Drafts A and B of the *Essay*, but not in the final version.

6. On Locke's refutation of innate principles, see, for example, Samuel C. Rickless, "Locke's Polemic against Nativism," in *The Cambridge Companion to Locke's* Essay Concerning Human Understanding, ed. Lex Newman (Cambridge: Cambridge University Press, 2007), 33–66.

7. See Philippe Hamou, *Dans la chambre obscure de l'esprit. John Locke et l'invention du* mind (Paris: Les Éditions d'Ithaque, 2018), 79 and 401–402.

8. John Locke, "Essays on the Law of Nature" (1664), in *Locke: Political Writings*, ed. Mark Goldie (Cambridge: Cambridge University Press, 1997), 96.

9. Boyle, *The Christian Virtuoso, op. cit.*, 112–113. This image was also conveyed by Cambridge Platonists, such as Benjamin Whichcote and Henry More. See Robert Duschinsky, "*Tabula rasa* and Human Nature," *Philosophy* 87, no. 4 (2012): 509–529.

10. To a certain extent, the self-taught philosopher can be seen as a variation on the theme of the noble savage, one of the two doctrines that accompany the blank slate, according to Steven Pinker, in *The Blank Slate: The Modern Denial of Human Nature* (London: Penguin, 2002), 6–11. The other doctrine presented by Pinker is that of "the Ghost in the Machine."

11. "When he came to himself again out of that State of his (which was a kind of spiritual Drunkenness) he conceived that he had no Essence, whereby he differ'd from the Essence of that True Being, the most high," in Ibn-Tufayl, *The History of Hai Eb'n Yockdan, an Indian prince, or, The self-taught philosopher written originally in the Arabick tongue by Abi Jaafar Eb'n Tophail*, trans. George Ashwell (London, 1686), 136.

12. Avner Ben-Zaken, *Reading Hayy Ibn-Yaqzan: A Cross-Cultural History of Autodidacticism* (Baltimore: Johns Hopkins University Press, 2011), preface, xi. On autodidacticism, see also Willem Frijhoff, "Autodidaxies, XVIe–XIXe siècles: jalons pour la construction d'un objet historique," *Histoire de l'Éducation* 70 (1996): 5–27; and Sandrine Parageau, "Autodidacticism and the Construction of Scientific Discourse in Early Modern England: Margaret Cavendish's and Anne Conway's 'Intellectual Bricolage,'" in *Women and Science, 17th Century to Present: Pioneers, Activists and Protagonists*, ed. D. Spalding Andréolle and V. Molinari (Newcastle, UK: Cambridge Scholars Publishing, 2011), 3–18.

13. Ben-Zaken, *Reading Hayy Ibn-Yaqzan*, op. cit., 105.

14. Yet the Latin version was circulated throughout Europe in the late seventeenth century. A French translation was published in 1999 with Éditions Mille et Une Nuits: Ibn Tufayl, *Le Philosophe autodidacte*, trans. Léon Gauthier, with Séverine Auffret and Ghassan Ferzli, Paris.

15. François de La Mothe Le Vayer, *Opuscule ou petit traité sceptique, Sur cette commune façon de parler. N'avoir pas le Sens-commun* (Paris, 1646), 122–123. The weakness of human reason and the comparison between men and beasts are often found in La Mothe Le Vayer's texts. They were a response to the dogmatic discourses of scholastics and Cartesians alike. On La Mother Le Vayer's *Opuscule*, its denunciation of common sense, the role of paradox, and the praise of *bon sens*, see, for example, Rosenfeld, *Common Sense*, op. cit., 101–103.

16. On the influence of Ibn-Tufayl's treatise on Locke's thought, see also Gul A. Russell, "The Impact of the *Philosophus autodidactus*: Pocockes, John Locke, and The Society of Friends," in *The "Arabick" Interest of the New Philosophers in Seventeenth-Century England*, ed. Gul A. Russell (Leiden: Brill, 1994), 224–265.

17. Locke, *Essay concerning Human Understanding*, op. cit., I, 2, 27, 63–64.

18. *Ibid.*, I, 2, 27, 64.

19. See "idiot, n. and adj., 2.a.," *Oxford English Dictionary*.

20. Locke, *Essay concerning Human Understanding*, op. cit., II, 11, 13, 161. See also I, 2, 27.

21. This list of variations on the Idiot comes from Miernowski, "La littérature antiscientifique à la Renaissance," op. cit., 95. *Mechanicus* and *rusticus* should be added to it. If these terms are not considered as synonymous today, their meanings were often conflated in the sixteenth and seventeenth centuries, despite attempts at distinguishing between them over time. See Jacques-Lefèvre and Pouey-Mounou, "Avant-propos: *Le chemin des ânes*," in *Sottise et ineptie*, op. cit., 7–16, here 10.

22. Deleuze and Guattari, *Qu'est-ce que la philosophie?*, op. cit., 60–61 (my translation).

23. Jean-Joseph Surin, *Correspondance*, ed. Michel de Certeau, preface by Julien Green (Paris: Desclée de Brouwer, 1966), Letter 18, 139–145. According to Michel de Certeau, this story may have been fictional, but it is still essential as "a manifesto," in Michel de Certeau, *La Fable mystique 1, XVIe-XVIIe siècle* (Paris: Gallimard, 1982), chap. 7, "L'illettré éclairé," 280–329, here 280 (first published in *Revue d'Ascétique et de Mystique* 44, no. 176 [1968]: 369–412).

24. Certeau, *La Fable mystique, op. cit.*, 280–281. Certeau gives a detailed history of the text, and of its numerous editions and versions, 287–308.

25. Surin, *Correspondance, op. cit.*, 140–141.

26. *Ibid.*, 140 ("simple et grossier en sa parole, sans lettres aucunes").

27. *Ibid.*, 142. Note that the Idiot presented by Surin has most of the qualities of Keith's woman of Samaria, portrayed in part 2.

28. Certeau, *La Fable mystique, op. cit.*, 321–322.

29. *Ibid.*, 323–324. Certeau gives other examples of simple illiterate men and women teaching the learned. See "the Idiot of Egypt," in *ibid.*, chap. 1, "Le monastère et la place: Folies dans la foule," 48–70, in particular "L'idiote (IVe siècle)," 49–58.

30. The whole story is told by A. Chiquot in *Histoire ou légende? Jean Tauler et le "Meistersl Buoch"* (Paris: Champion, 1922), 6–12.

31. Deleuze and Guattari, *Qu'est-ce que la philosophie?, op. cit.*, 61 (my translation).

32. The identity of the translator has not been unequivocally established yet. It has generally been assumed that John Everard or Giles Randall, who translated other Cusan works into English (see part 1), had authored this translation as well, but Paul Richard Blum, for example, expresses doubts, based on an analysis of the language of the text, compared to other English translations of Cusan works, and calls for further investigation, in "Nicholas of Cusa in Giles Randall's English Translation," *op. cit.*, 216–217. For a defense of Everard being the translator of *The Idiot*, see Thomas Wilson Hayes, "John Everard and Nicholas of Cusa's *Idiota*," *Notes & Queries* 28, no. 1 (1981): 47–49; and "Nicholas of Cusa and Popular Literacy in Seventeenth-Century England," *op. cit.*

33. Hervé Pasqua, introduction, 8 (my translation), in Nicolas de Cues, *Dialogues de l'Idiot: Sur la sagesse et l'esprit*, ed. and trans. Hervé Pasqua (Paris: Presses universitaires de France, 2011). The Philosopher is present in the third dialogue only, which deals with the mind. In the other three dialogues, the speakers are the Idiot, the Orator, and the Author.

34. Nicholas of Cusa, *The Idiot in Four Books. The First and Second of Wisdome. The Third of the Minde. The fourth of statick Experiments; Or, Experiments of the Ballance* (London, 1650), 1 and 2.

35. *Ibid.*, 3.

36. *Ibid.*, 4.

37. *Ibid.*, 58.

38. *Ibid.*, 57.

39. *Ibid.*, 1.

40. Certeau is one of the very few commentators who have emphasized the social dimension of the persona of the Idiot. He argues in particular that the fable of the Friend

of God progressively evolved and substituted a confrontation between two social groups (rich and poor) to the initial confrontation between two kinds of religious knowledge, in Certeau, *La Fable mystique, op. cit.*, 326–329.

41. Cusanus, *The Idiot in Four Books, op. cit.*, 170.

42. Richard J. Oosterhoff, "*Idiotae*, Mathematics, and Artisans: The Untutored Mind and the Discovery of Nature in the Fabrist Circle," *Intellectual History Review* 24, no. 3 (2014): 301–319, here 303. Lefèvre d'Étaples's 1514 edition of Cusanus's works played a great part in spreading Cusan ideas throughout Europe. On the reception of Cusanus in sixteenth-century France, see also Richard J. Oosterhoff, "Cusanus and Boethian Theology in the Early French Reform," in Burton, Hollmann, and Parker, eds., *Nicholas of Cusa and the Making of the Early Modern World, op. cit.*, 339–366.

43. Oosterhoff, "*Idiotae*, Mathematics, and Artisans," *op. cit.*, 304.

44. *Ibid.*, 312.

45. See *ibid.*, 312. On the Fabrist circle and the legacy of Cusanus and Denys the Areopagite, see also Jeanneret, "Éloge de l'ignorance," *op. cit.*, 645–647.

46. Descartes, *La Recherche de la vérité, op. cit.*, 5 (my translation). The word "neutral" [*neutre* in French] is here particularly interesting, "neutrality" of the mind being a fictional condition akin to the tabula rasa.

47. On the contrary, Hervé Pasqua argues that, in *De idiota*, wisdom is both an internal light and something that "cries out in the streets," that it is both within and without (in Nicolas de Cues, *Dialogues de l'Idiot, op. cit.*, 8).

48. Cusanus, *The Idiot in Four Books, op. cit.*, 16.

49. *Ibid.*, 36–37.

50. Montaigne, "*An Apologie of* Raymond Sebond," *op. cit.*, 272.

51. Similarly, in Erasmus's prefaces to *Novum Testamentum* (Basel, 1539–1540), the ideal reader of the Bible is an *idiota*, for whom what matters is love, not knowledge. See Jeanneret, "Éloge de l'ignorance," *op. cit.*, 648.

52. Sebastian Brant's *Narrenschiff* was first published in Basel in 1494. Jacob Locher's *Stultifera navis*, also published in Basel, in 1497, was an adaptation of Brant's work, as was also, for example, Pierre Rivière's *Nef des folz du monde*, published in 1497 in Paris.

53. On definitions of the personae of the philosopher in the early modern period, see, for example, Conal Condren, Stephen Gaukroger, and Ian Hunter, eds., *The Philosopher in Early Modern Europe: The Nature of a Contested Identity* (Cambridge: Cambridge University Press, 2006), esp. Stephen Gaukroger, "The *Persona* of the Natural Philosopher" (17–34) and John Cottingham, "Descartes as Sage: Spiritual *Askesis* in Cartesian Philosophy" (182–201). Gaukroger insists on the morality of the natural philosopher and on his intellectual honesty. Those are indeed important characteristics of the persona of the philosopher in the works of Descartes, for example, but Gaukroger neglects the social dimension of the question. The natural philosopher is free from prejudices (29), but this is made possible by the fact that he is free from social expectations and constraints as far as knowledge is concerned.

54. Glanvill, *The Vanity of Dogmatizing, op. cit.*, 1.

55. Glanvill, *Scepsis Scientifica, op. cit*, 4.

56. *Ibid.*, "Advertisement," [d2ʳ].
57. Charron, *Of Wisdome, op. cit.*, 468.
58. Joanna Picciotto, *Labors of Innocence in Early Modern England, op. cit.*, 1.
59. *Ibid.*, 35–39.
60. *Ibid.*, 67.
61. *Ibid.*, 68.
62. *Ibid.*, 155.

Chapter 6

1. Some of the arguments developed here are also presented in Sandrine Parageau, "'Colomb ignorant trouva le nouveau monde': Ignorance, découverte fortuite et expérimentation à la première modernité," *Revue d'Histoire des Sciences* 74, no. 1 (2021): 41–62. © Armand Colin 2021—Armand Colin is a trademark of Dunod Editeur, Malakoff.

2. Mersenne, *La Vérité des Sciences, op. cit.*, bk. 1, "Where the skeptics' opinions are refuted," 26 (my translation): "Certainement celuy qui voudroit soûtenir que les plus ignorans sont plus sages & plus sçavans, que ceus qu'on pense être, les plus sages, & les plus doctes, ne manqueroit pas de raison, car Colomb ignorant trouva le nouveau monde, & neantmoins Lactance docte Theologien, & Xenophanes sçavant Philosophe l'avoient nié: Flavius le Nautonnier, & quelques autres chétifs artisans inventerent l'usage de la boussole aimantée, du canon, & de l'Imprimerie, & les fols, & les ignorans font quantité de merveilles, que les plus scavans ne sçauroient seulement comprendre." Note that, in the early modern period, there was no clear distinction between invention and discovery. See, for example, James Dougal Fleming, ed., *The Invention of Discovery, 1500–1700* (Farnham, UK: Ashgate, 2011), in particular the introduction. See also Brian Copenhaver's introduction to his translation and edition of Polydore Vergil's *On Discovery* (Cambridge, MA: Harvard University Press, 2002), xi: Polydore, whose text, first published in 1499, was influential throughout the early modern period, did not make a distinction between invention and discovery. This was partly due to the ambiguity of the Latin *invenire*, according to Copenhaver.

3. René Descartes, *Optics, First Discourse: Of Light*, in René Descartes, *Discourse on Method, Optics, Geometry, and Meteorology*, trans. and ed. Paul J. Olscamp (New York: Bobbs-Merrill Co., 1965), 65–66 (Cottingham, Stoothoff, and Murdoch, who based their translation on the Adam and Tannery edition of Descartes's works, did not translate this passage, in *The Philosophical Writings of Descartes, op. cit.*, vol. 1).

4. *Ibid.*, 66.

5. Robert Boyle, *The Excellency of Theology, Compared with Natural Philosophy, (as both are Objects of Men's Study.) Discours'd of in a Letter to a Friend* (London, 1671), 168.

6. A number of studies devoted to the notion of ingenuity in the context of the emergence of modern science have been published. See, for example, Rhodri Lewis, "Francis Bacon and Ingenuity," *Renaissance Quarterly* 67, no. 1 (2014): 113–163, and Raphaële Garrod, Alexander Marr, José Ramón Marcaida and Richard J. Oosterhoff, eds., *Logodae-*

dalus. Word Histories of Ingenuity in Early Modern Europe (Pittsburgh, PA: Pittsburgh University Press, 2018).

7. Locke, *Essay concerning Human Understanding, op. cit.*, III, 10, 9, 495. On this quotation, see also the introduction to this book, as well as Montaigne's (imagined) praise of artisans in Matthew Prior's dialogue between Locke and the French "Seigneur."

8. Rob Iliffe, "Material Doubts: Hooke, Artisan Culture and the Exchange of Information in 1670s London," *British Journal for the History of Science* 28, no. 3 (1995): 285–318, here 311. Iliffe's article deals more generally with Hooke's interaction with artisans and laborers.

9. Robert Hooke, *The Diary of Robert Hooke, M.A., M.D., F.R.S. (1672–1680)*, ed. Henry W. Robinson and Walter Adams, with a foreword by Sir Frederick Gowland Hopkins, OM (London: Taylor and Francis, 1935), 100. It appears, though, that Hooke and Tompion would not always agree: on 17 May 1679, for example, Hooke paid Tompion eight pounds for a watch with seconds, but Tompion "would have had more," Hooke says (in *ibid.*, 412). The perusal of Hooke's diary shows that he spent a lot of time with artisans, especially carpenters, whose remarks and advice on practical things he carefully wrote down.

10. See, for example, 27 February 1675, in *ibid.*, 218, but there are many other occurrences. For anecdote's sake, but related to ignorance: on one of the occasions when he was at Tompion's home, Hooke met John Flamstead, the first astronomer-royal, whom he calls "an Ignorant impudent Asse" (17 November 1677, in *ibid.*, 330).

11. Hamou, *La Mutation du visible, op. cit.*, 2:156 (my translation). The reference to the "faithful eye" comes from Robert Hooke's *Micrographia*, where he writes that the reform of philosophy requires only "a *sincere Hand* and a *faithful Eye*, to examine, and to record, the things themselves as they appear," in *Micrographia, Or some Physiological Descriptions of Minute Bodies Made by Magnifying Glasses* (London, 1665), "The Preface," [A2ᵛ].

12. Smith, *The Body of the Artisan, op. cit.*, 8.

13. Shapin, *A Social History of Truth, op. cit.*, chap. 8, "Invisible Technicians: Masters, Servants, and the Making of Experimental Knowledge," 355–407, here 359. Note that technicians were not necessarily illiterate, and some of them were on the contrary highly qualified, for example, Denis Papin (1647–1712?), who worked for Boyle in the late 1670s, or even Hooke himself, who was Boyle's assistant for a while (*ibid.*, 357–359).

14. *Ibid.*, "Noises Off: Technicians' Work as Excuse," 389–391.

15. *Ibid.*, 393.

16. On this "particularly persistent feature of Western culture," see Smith, *The Body of the Artisan, op. cit.*, 6–8 and 17. See also Thomas Sprat's *History of the Royal Society* (London, 1667) for a clear expression of the superiority of natural philosophers over "men of Trade" (396).

17. Shapin, *A Social History of Truth, op. cit.*, 395.

18. Smith, *The Body of the Artisan, op. cit.*, 231.

19. Shapin, *A Social History of Truth, op. cit.*, 395.

20. Boyle, *The Excellency of Theology, op. cit.*, 116.

21. *Ibid.*, 117.

22. Moreover, Boyle had his technicians sign oaths to make sure that they would not reveal the secrets of his experiments, which leaves no doubt as to the fact that he did not trust them. See Shapin, *A Social History of Truth, op. cit.*, 404. On Boyle, see also Malcolm Oster, "The Scholar and the Craftsman Revisited: Robert Boyle as Aristocrat and Artisan," *Annals of Science* 49 (1992): 255–276.

23. André Félibien, *Des principes de l'architecture, de la sculpture, de la peinture, et des autres arts qui en dépendent* (Paris, 1676), preface (unpaginated). The English translation is quoted from Paola Bertucci, *Artisanal Enlightenment. Science and the Mechanical Arts in Old Regime France* (New Haven, CT: Yale University Press, 2017), 14.

24. Bertucci, *Artisanal Enlightenment, op. cit.*, 17.

25. Klaas van Berkel, "Intellectuals against Leeuwenhoek: Controversies about the Methods and Style of a Self-Taught Scientist," in *Antoni van Leeuwenhoek 1632–1723*, ed. L. C. Palm and H. A. M. Snelders (Amsterdam: Rodopi, 1982), 187–209, here 188. Emphasis is often placed on the natural philosophers' conception of artisanal work, but it is interesting to focus on artisans themselves and how they perceived their relations with scholars, and their own alleged illiterateness. In the conclusion to her seminal study of northern Europe, Pamela H. Smith convincingly argues that artisans "began to have a consciousness of their own productive power and . . . claimed a new intellectual and social authority for themselves, based on their relationship to nature. They *knew* nature through the practice of their bodily art, and, like Palissy's *persona* Practice, they asserted their ability, based on this knowledge, to produce works rather than barren words and theories. Their claim of knowing nature was an assertion of authority and certainty in the face of a culture that viewed them as socially and intellectually inferior because of their bodily labor" (in *The Body of the Artisan, op. cit.*, 238).

26. Smith, *The Body of the Artisan, op. cit.*, 18. Smith's point is more precisely that the search for natural knowledge became "active" and now involved the body. Smith also explains how, in this context, philosophers came to be seen as experts, whereas this had been the role of artisans so far (231). On the role of artisans in the emergence of modern science, see also Pamela Long, *Artisans/Practitioners and the Rise of the New Sciences, 1400–1600* (Corvallis: Oregon State University Press, 2011).

27. Boyle, *The Christian Virtuoso, op. cit.*, 73.

28. In Boyle's treatises and essays, sagacity is almost systematically associated with work or "industry," as the natural and spontaneous companion to the effort expected from the experimental philosopher. See, for example, *New Experiments and Observations touching Cold, or an Experimental History of Cold, Begun* (London, 1665), where Boyle explains that the "sagacity and industry" of naturalists can replace instruments of observation. In Boyle's texts, sagacity is attributed to men and animals alike.

29. This idea was often found in the early modern period. See, for example, Montaigne's *Essays*, where the simple and ignorant man is characterized by his proximity to nature, which also accounts for his wisdom. See in particular "*Of the Caniballes*," in *The essayes, op. cit.*, I, 30, 100.

30. For example, Boyle mentions the sagacity of Brazilian botanists in *Some Consider-*

ations Touching the Usefulnesse of Experimental Naturall Philosophy (Oxford, 1663), 416. See also Susan Scott Parrish, *American Curiosity: Cultures of Natural History in the Colonial British Atlantic World* (Chapel Hill: University of North Carolina Press, 2006), chap. 6, "Indian Sagacity"; and Sarah Irving-Stonebraker, "'The Sagacity of the Indians': William Dampier's Surprising Respect for Indigenous Knowledge," *Journal of Early Modern History* 21, no. 6 (2017): 543–564. Irving-Stonebraker argues that Baconian natural history is what encouraged William Dampier to consider Indians as knowledgeable. He believed that their knowledge had been acquired empirically, thanks to their sagacity.

31. Thomas Hobbes, *Leviathan* (1651), ed. J. C. A. Gaskin (Oxford: Oxford University Press, 1996), I, 3, 5, 17. In an article on serendipity, Sean Silver also argues that sagacity is the quality that enables one to make chance discoveries: "Serendipity is ... what happens when someone possessing the right sort of 'sagacity' stumbles across an appropriate 'accident', or, to put it differently, when someone discovers something useful that they did not know they were looking for," in "The Prehistory of Serendipity, from Bacon to Walpole," *Isis* 106, no. 2 (2015): 235–256, here 236.

32. Thomas Hobbes, *Humane Nature, or, The Fundamental Elements of Policy* (1640) (London, 1684), chap. IV, 18–19.

33. Theophilus Gale, *The Court of the Gentiles, or, A Discourse touching the original of human literature, both philology and philosophie, from the Scriptures, and Jewish Church ... Part II. Of Philosophie* (Oxford, 1670), 288. Sagacity was often interpreted as a form of prediction, especially in the sixteenth century. See for example: "For Sagacitie pertayneth to those things which we are about to doo, by smelling them out," in T.R., *A Philosophicall Discourse, Entituled, The Anatomie of the Minde* (London, 1576), chap. 15, 104.

34. Gale, *The Court of the Gentiles, op. cit.*, 6.

35. *Ibid.*, 6.

36. *Ibid.*, 418.

37. *Ibid.*, 288.

38. Bacon, *Novum Organum, op. cit.*, bk. 1, aphorism 82, 129.

39. *Ibid.*, bk. 1, aphorism 129, 195.

40. Bacon, *The Masculine Birth of Time, op. cit.*, 59–72, here 71.

41. Bacon, *Novum Organum, op. cit.*, bk. 1, aphorism 108, 165.

42. Descartes, *Rules for the Direction of the Mind, op. cit.*, Rule V, 20–21 (p. 380 in the Adam and Tannery edition, vol. 10).

43. *Ibid.*, Rule X, 36 (p. 405 in the Adam and Tannery edition, vol. 10).

44. *Ibid.*, Rule X, 34–35. In Cottingham, Stoothoff and Murdoch's English edition of the *Rules*, *sagax* is translated as "discernment." In Laurence Lafleur's translation, *sagax* (i.e., *ut ingenium fiat sagax*) is rendered as "wise," and Lafleur translates *humana sagacitas* later in the text as "human sagacity," in *Rules for the Direction of the Mind*, trans. and introduced by Laurence J. Lafleur (Indianapolis: Bobbs-Merrill Co., 1961), 38.

45. Descartes, *Rules for the Direction of the Mind*, trans. Lafleur, *op. cit.*, Rule X, 38 (p. 403 in the Adam and Tannery edition, vol. 10). Lafleur's translation is here more accurate than "a certain innate discernment," in Cottingham, Stoothoff and Murdoch's edition (*op. cit.*, 35).

46. Descartes, *Rules for the Direction of the Mind*, trans. Lafleur, *op. cit.*, Rule X, 38 (p. 403 in the Adam and Tannery edition, vol. 10).

47. Another interpretation, which is not examined here because it does not deal with ignorance specifically, is that Baconian experimentation aims at *controlling* chance. This has to do in particular with the "experiment by chance," one of the eight modes of *experientia literata*. See Parageau, "'Colomb ignorant trouva le nouveau monde'," *op. cit.*, 56–61. See also Didier Deleule, "L'éthique baconienne et l'esprit de la science moderne," in *Francis Bacon: Science et méthode. Actes du colloque de Nantes*, ed. Michel Malherbe and Jean-Marie Pousseur (Paris: Vrin, 1985), 53–77; Lisa Jardine, "*Experientia literata* ou *novum organum*? Le dilemme de la méthode scientifique de Bacon," in *ibid.*, 135–157; and Didier Deleule, *Francis Bacon et la réforme du savoir* (Paris: Hermann, 2010).

48. The study of *experientia literata* has given rise to many publications. See in particular Dana Jalobeanu, *The Art of Experimental Natural History: Francis Bacon in Context* (Bucharest: Zeta Books, 2015); Sophie Weeks, "The Role of Mechanics in Francis Bacon's Great Instauration," in *Philosophies of Technology: Francis Bacon and His Contemporaries*, ed. Gisela Engel, Claus Zittel, Romano Nani, and Nicole C. Karafilys (Leiden: Brill, 2008), 131–195; Guido Giglioni, "Learning to Read Nature: Francis Bacon's Notion of Experiential Literacy (*Experientia Literata*)," *Early Science and Medicine* 18, nos. 4–5 (2013): 405–434; Laura Georgescu, "A New Form of Knowledge: *Experientia Literata*," *Societate i Politică* 5, no. 2 (2011): 104–120; and Claire Crignon and Sandrine Parageau, eds., "Bacon and the Forms of Experimentation: A Reappraisal," trans. Donald Nicholson-Smith, *Archives de Philosophie* 84, no. 1 (2021): 7–15.

49. Francis Bacon, *Of the Dignity and Advancement of Learning, books IV-IX*, here book V, in *Works*, ed. James Spedding, Robert Leslie Ellis, and Douglas Denon Heath (Boston: Houghton, Mifflin and Co., 1882), 9:71 and 78.

50. Francis Bacon, *Of the Wisdom of the Ancients*, in *The Works of Francis Bacon*, ed. James Spedding, Robert Leslie Ellis, and Douglas Denon Heath (Boston: Houghton, Mifflin and Co., 1860), 13:100.

51. Bacon, *Of the Dignity and Advancement of Learning*, *op. cit.*, bk. III, 8:512–513. A similar idea is expressed in *Novum Organum*: "Now the hard work of the chemists has produced something, but as if by accident and in passing, or by some variation (such as mechanics make) of their experiments and not by any art or theory; for the theory they have fabricated does more to upset the experiments than to promote them" (*op. cit.*, bk. 1, aphorism 73, 117). See also Luc Peterschmitt, "Bacon and the Circle of Experience," trans. Donald Nicholson-Smith, *Archives de Philosophie* 84, no. 1 (2021): 33–49.

52. Michael Witmore, *Culture of Accidents: Unexpected Knowledges in Early Modern England* (Stanford, CA: Stanford University Press, 2001), chap. 5, "Accident and the Invention of Knowledge in Francis Bacon's Natural Philosophy," 116.

53. Bacon, *Novum Organum*, *op. cit.*, bk. 1, aphorism 82, 130: "There remains mere experience which is called accident if it happens by itself, but experiment if it is deliberately sought out."

54. *Ibid.*, bk. 1, aphorism 82, 130.

55. Witmore, *Culture of Accidents*, *op. cit.*, 116 and 3.

56. *Ibid.*, 125: "Experimenting for Bacon is an imitation of what chance does, folding and unfolding different parts of nature, in ways that jostle the imagination and the usual disposition of things."

57. This interpretation echoes that of Guido Giglioni, for whom *experientia literata* is "*empirical awareness*" and *experientia illiterata*, unmediated empiricism, in "Learning to Read Nature," *op. cit.*, 409.

Chapter 7

1. Nathanael Culverwell, *Spirituall Opticks: Or a Glasse, Discovering the weaknesse and imperfection of a Christians knowledge in this life* (Oxford, 1668), 188.

2. On the interpretation of ignorance in England as a deficiency inherited from Adam's Fall, see Harrison, *The Fall of Man, op. cit.*

3. See, for example, Locke, *Essay concerning Human Understanding, op. cit.*, III, 7, 51, 470–471, where he insists on what men have kept from Adam, focusing on language in particular, and *The Reasonableness of Christianity* (London, 1695), where the Calvinistic interpretation of the Fall is explicitly refuted. On Locke's conception of the Fall, see Kim Ian-Parker, *The Biblical Politics of John Locke* (Waterloo, ON: Wilfrid Laurier University Press, 2004), chap. 2, "Reason, Revelation and the Fall," 37–67. Ian-Parker argues that human nature was darker in Locke's earlier writings. See also W. M. Spellman, *John Locke and the Problem of Depravity* (Oxford: Clarendon Press, 1988); and Victor Nuovo, *John Locke. The Philosopher as Christian Virtuoso* (Oxford: Oxford University Press, 2017).

4. Ian-Parker, *The Biblical Politics of John Locke, op. cit.*, 60.

5. Locke, *Essay concerning Human Understanding, op. cit.*, IV, 3, 22, 553. Similar statements are found in Locke's journal. In the entry for 8 February 1677, which deals specifically with the extent of knowledge and ignorance, he wrote: "Our minds are not made as large as truth, nor suited to the whole extent of things; amongst those that come within its reach, it meets with a great many too big for its grasp, and there are not a few that it is fair to give up as incomprehensible. It finds itself lost in the vast extent of space, and the least particle of matter puzzles it with an inconceivable divisibility," in King, ed., *The Life of John Locke, op. cit.*, 84.

6. A similar idea is found for example in Baxter's *A Treatise of Knowledge and Love Compared, op. cit.*: "An ignorant man knoweth but little *parcels* and *scraps* of things: And all the rest is unknown to him: Therefore he fixeth upon that *little* which he *knoweth*, and having no knowledge of the rest, he cannot regulate his narrow apprehensions by any conceptions of them" (169). People tend to focus on what they know, which gives them a wrong conception of knowledge and of their ability to reach truth.

7. Locke, *Essay concerning Human Understanding, op. cit.*, IV, 3, 23, 553–554. The causes of ignorance listed by Locke are similar or even identical to those given by Joseph Glanvill (see part 1).

8. *Ibid.*, IV, 3, 24, 555.

9. *Ibid.*, IV, 3, 26, 556.

10. *Ibid.*, IV, 3, 28, 558–559.

11. *Ibid.*, IV, 3, 30, 561. In the second book of the *Essay*, Locke also associates ignorance and inadvertency as two "usual *Causes*" of "*wrong Judgment*" (II, 21, 67, 278).

12. *Ibid.*, I, 1, 5, 46. See also Locke's correspondence with Edward Stillingfleet. On Locke and skepticism, see, for example, G. A. J. Rogers, *Locke's Enlightenment. Aspects of the Origin, Nature, and Impact of his Philosophy* (Hildesheim, Germany: Georg Olms Verlag, 1998), 33–48; and more recently, Matthew Priselac, *Locke's Science of Knowledge* (New York: Routledge, 2017).

13. King, ed., *The Life of John Locke, op. cit.*, 85.

14. See *ibid.*, 105: "We are here in the state of mediocrity; finite creatures, furnished with powers and faculties very well fitted to some purposes, but very disproportionate to the vast and unlimited extent of things." This passage from 6 March 1677 in Locke's journal is the continuation of the text on the extent of knowledge and ignorance quoted above (from 8 February 1677). See also Locke's draft letter (to Mr. Herbert, according to Peter King): "I have often thought that our state here in this world is a state of mediocrity, which is not capable of extremes" (*ibid.*, 112). Surprisingly, Locke adds that this idea of human mediocrity is "but an odd notion of [his]," whereas it had been developed since the sixteenth century at least. See, for instance, Emmanuel Naya and Anne-Pascale Pouey-Mounou, eds., *Éloges de la médiocrité: Le juste milieu à la Renaissance* (Paris: Éditions de la Rue d'Ulm, 2005). On Locke and mediocrity, see also Giuliana Di Biase, "A Gentleman's 'Moderate Knowledge': Mediocrity as the Appropriate Measure of Learning in John Locke's *Some Thoughts concerning Education*," *XVII–XVIII* 72 (2015): 57–80.

15. King, ed., *The Life of John Locke, op. cit.*, 86 and 115.

16. Locke, *An Essay concerning Human Understanding, op. cit.*, I, 1, 7, 47 and I, 1, 4, 45. See Spellman's analysis of this passage in *Locke and the Problem of Depravity, op. cit.*, 105.

17. Locke, *An Essay concerning Human Understanding, op. cit.*,"The Epistle to the Reader," 6. An example of "invincible" ignorance given by Locke is that of the nature of substance, about which the philosopher writes: "I know not: nor shall be ashamed to own my Ignorance" (II, 13, 17, 17).See also Greg Forster, "'Sit Down in Quiet Ignorance': Locke's Epistemology of Limits," in *John Locke's Politics of Moral Consensus* (Cambridge: Cambridge University Press, 2005), 40–83.

18. King, ed., *The Life of John Locke, op. cit.*, 107.

19. *Ibid.*, 105–106.

20. The quotation from Cicero is "Quam bellum est velle confiteri potius nescire quod nescias, quam ista effutientem nauseare, atque ipsum sibi displicere!" ("How delightful it would be, Velleius, if when you did not know a thing you would admit your ignorance, instead of uttering this drivel, which must make even your own gorge rise with disgust!"), *De natura deorum*, 1.84. For an analysis of those epigrammatic quotations, see Zachary Sng, *The Rhetoric of Error from Locke to Kleist* (Stanford, CA: Stanford University Press, 2010), 24-27. On the influence of Cicero on Locke's philosophy, in particular the insistence on the limits of reason, see Tim Stuart-Buttle, *From Moral Theology to Moral Philosophy. Cicero and Visions of Humanity from Locke to Hume* (Oxford: Oxford University Press, 2019).

21. D. G. James, *The Life of Reason: Hobbes, Locke, Bolingbroke* (London: Longmans, Green & Co., 1949), 92.

22. Locke, *An Essay concerning Human Understanding*, op. cit., IV, 16, 4, 660.

23. *Ibid.*, V, 17, 20, 686.

24. See Charles L. Hamblin, *Fallacies* (London: Methuen and Co., 1970), 43. Hamblin is here quoting from Irving M. Copi, *Introduction to Logic* (1953; New York: Macmillan, 1961), 57.

25. Locke, *Essay concerning Human Understanding*, op. cit., IV, 17, 20, 686.

26. *Ibid.*, IV, 17, 19–22, 685–687. The other three arguments are the *argumentum ad verecundiam*, which relies on authority, the *argumentum ad hominem*, a personal attack on the adversary, and the *argumentum ad judicium*, based on judgment.

27. Hamblin, *Fallacies*, op. cit., 11.

28. Douglas Walton, *Arguments from Ignorance* (University Park: Pennsylvania State University Press, 1996), 37.

29. *Ibid.*, 94.

30. *Ibid.*, 14–15.

31. *Ibid.*, 18.

32. *Ibid.*, 21.

33. *Ibid.*, 21.

34. That Descartes excluded ignorance from science, for example, is highly debatable, as parts 1 and 2 show.

35. See John C. Biddle, "John Locke's Essay on Infallibility: Introduction, Text, and Translation," *Journal of Church and State* 19, no. 2 (1977): 301–327, here 321.

36. *Ibid.*, 312. In this essay, Locke affirms that, when it comes to indifferent matters of worship, the magistrate should impose his viewpoint in order to secure religious peace. He no longer held that stance in his *Letter on Toleration* (1689).

37. Locke, *Essay concerning Human Understanding*, op. cit., I, 4, 24, 101–102. See also IV, 18, "*Of Faith and Reason, and their distinct Provinces*," 688–696.

38. *Ibid.*, IV, 19, 8, 699–700.

39. G. A. J. Rogers, "Locke and the Latitude-Men: Ignorance as a Ground for Toleration," in *Philosophy, Science, and Religion in England, 1640–1700*, ed. Richard Kroll, Richard Ashcraft, and Perez Zagorin (Cambridge: Cambridge University Press, 1992), 230–252. Rogers also shows that the argument from ignorance had already been used from the 1630s by latitudinarians and Cambridge Platonists, but Locke was more radical than all of them in his use of this argument and in the conclusions he drew from it.

40. [John Locke,] *A Letter concerning Toleration, Licensed Octob. 3, 1689*, Second Edition Corrected (London, 1690), 32.

41. *Ibid.*, 34.

42. Locke, *Conduct of the Understanding*, op. cit., 47.

43. *Ibid.*, 29. See also 6. Whether Locke held that men's understandings were naturally equal or not has often been discussed. See, for example, Spellman, *John Locke and the Problem of Depravity*, op. cit., 109. See also *Essay concerning Human Understanding*, op. cit., IV, 20, 5, 709: "Only this is evident, that there is a difference of degrees in Men's

Understandings, Apprehensions, and Reasonings, to so great a latitude, that one may, without doing injury to Mankind, affirm, that there is a greater distance between some Men, and others, in this respect, than between some Men and some Beasts."

44. Locke, *Conduct of the Understanding*, op. cit., 19.

45. Locke, *Essay concerning Human Understanding*, op. cit., IV, 20, 2, 707.

46. Locke, *Conduct of the Understanding*, op. cit., 35.

47. *Ibid.*, 36. In the *Essay*, Locke also states that even laborers must find the time to get knowledge (of religion, in particular), in *op. cit.*, IV, 20, 3, 708.

48. Locke, *Conduct of the Understanding*, op. cit., 36.

49. *Ibid.*, 6.

50. *Ibid.*, 108.

51. *Ibid.*, sec. 19 on reading, 60–63. See also sec. 23 on partiality, 72–74: "There is nothing almost has done more harm to Men dedicated to Letters, than giving the name of Study to Reading, and making a Man of great Reading to be the same with a Man of great Knowledge, or at least to be a Title of Honour. . . . there is no part wherein the Understanding needs a more careful and wary Conduct, than in the use of Books."

52. King ed., *The Life of John Locke*, op. cit., 107. See also in the same article: "converse with books is not, in my opinion, the principal part of study." The main parts of study are meditation and discourse, according to Locke in this passage.

53. John Locke, *Some Thoughts concerning Education* (London, 1693), 137–138.

54. *Ibid.*, 138.

55. Locke, *Conduct of the Understanding*, op. cit., 8: "We see but in part, and we know but in part, and therefore 'tis no wonder we conclude not right from our partial Views. This might instruct the proudest Esteemer of his own Parts how useful it is to talk and consult with others, even such as came short of him in Capacity, Quickness and Penetration: For since no one sees all, and we generally have different Prospects of the same things, according to our different, as I may say, Positions to it, 'tis not incongruous to think, nor beneath any Man to try, whether another may not have notions of things which have 'scaped him, and which his Reason would make use of if they came into his Mind."

56. *Ibid.*, 9.

57. *Ibid.*, 13–14.

58. *Ibid.*, 10.

59. *Ibid.*, 10.

60. Montaigne, "*An Apologie of* Raymond Sebond," in *The essayes*, op. cit., II, 12, 274.

61. On the role of travel literature in Locke's anthropology, see for example Rogers, *Locke's Enlightenment*, op. cit., "Locke, anthropology, and models of the mind," 79–91.

62. See Boutcher, "Montaigne in England and America," op. cit., 210–311. In his journal for 14 February 1685, Locke describes Montaigne's essays as "a texture of strong sayings and sentences and ends of verses" put together so that they have "an extraordinary force upon men's minds," in King ed., *The Life of John Locke*, op. cit., 160. Montaigne was indeed read in late seventeenth-century England mostly as a purveyor of *sententiae* and sayings, which was reinforced by Florio's italicization of chosen passages in his English

translation (see Boutcher, *ibid.*, 318 and 324). On the principle of *libertas philosophandi* in Montaigne's works, see Richard Scholar, *Montaigne and the Art of Free-Thinking* (Oxford: Peter Lang, 2010). See also John Harrison and Peter Laslett eds., *The Library of John Locke* (Oxford: Oxford University Press, 1965): Charron, 105–106, items 672–674a; Montaigne, 191, items 2029 and 2029a.

63. Douglas John Casson, *Liberating Judgment. Fanatics, Skeptics, and John Locke's Politics of Probability* (Princeton, NJ: Princeton University Press, 2011), 77–78 and 80.

Conclusion

1. Jeanneret, "Éloge de l'ignorance," *op. cit.*, 651 (my translation).
2. *Ibid.*, 651 (my translation).
3. Charron, *Of Wisdome, op. cit.*, 467 ("qui est fort sçavant n'est guiere sage: & qui est sage n'est pas sçavant," in *De la sagesse, op. cit.*, 642).
4. Science is also considered synonymous with "learning," in *ibid.*, 470.
5. *Ibid.*, 467.
6. Montaigne, "*Of Pedantisme*," in *The essayes, op. cit.*, I, 24, 63.
7. Bacon, *The Advancement of Learning, op. cit.*, 33.
8. In Bacon's *The Wisdom of the Ancients*, written between 1605 and 1608, *sapience* is defined as the wisdom of prelapsarian Adam. See Francis Bacon, *La Sagesse des anciens*, trans. with introduction and notes by Jean-Pierre Cavaillé (Paris: Vrin, 1997), introduction, 45–46.
9. On this subject, see, for example, Gaukroger, "The *Persona* of the Natural Philosopher," *op. cit.*, 26.
10. Sorel, *De la perfection de l'homme, op. cit.*, 72 (my translation).
11. *Ibid.*, 74 (my translation).
12. *Encyclopédie ou Dictionnaire raisonné des sciences, des arts et des métiers* (Neuchâtel, 1765), 8:549–550. For a systematic presentation of medieval theological conceptions of ignorance as a sin, which throws light on the article on "moral ignorance" in the *Encyclopédie*, see Odon Lottin, "La nature du péché d'ignorance. Enquête chez les Théologiens du XIIe et du XIIIe siècle," *Revue Thomiste: Questions du temps présent* 37 (1932): 634–652, and 723–738.
13. *Encyclopaedia Britannica*, ed. William Smellie (Edinburgh, 1771), vol. 2 on "fool" and "ignorance" (613 and 833); vol. 3 on "metaphysics" (194–195 on ignorance). On the presence of Locke in eighteenth-century encyclopedias, see, for instance, Paul Schuurman, "Locke's Modest Impact on Eighteenth-Century Natural Science: The Encyclopedic Evidence," *Eighteenth-Century Thought* 3 (2007): 189–206.
14. On the reception of Locke's philosophy in eighteenth-century France, see Jørn Schøsler, *John Locke et les philosophes français: La critique des idées innées en France au dix-huitième siècle* (Oxford: Voltaire Foundation, 1997); Ross Hutchison, *Locke in France 1688–1734* (Oxford: Voltaire Foundation, 1991); and John W. Yolton, *Locke and French Materialism* (Oxford: Clarendon Press, 1991).

15. Charles Dédéyan, *Le Retour de Salente ou Voltaire et l'Angleterre* (Paris: A.-G. Nizet, 1988), esp. pt. 5, "Voltaire et la philosophie anglaise," 143–184.

16. Voltaire, *Letters concerning the English Nation, op. cit.*, Letter XIII, 100.

17. Voltaire, *Poèmes sur le désastre de Lisbonne, et sur la loi naturelle* (Geneva, 1756), 40. The contemporary English translation of the poem given in Voltaire's complete works of 1764 misses the idea of "happy boundaries": "Locke who could spirits properties explain, / And understanding's limits ascertain," in *The Works of Voltaire*, trans. T. Smollett, T. Francklin et al., 38 vols. (London, 1764), 33:85.

18. See Voltaire, *Le philosophe ignorant. Avec un Avis au public sur les Parricides imputés aux Calas & aux Sirven*, ([Geneva? London?], 1766). An anonymous English translation was published in London in 1767. See also Voltaire, *A Treatise on Toleration; The Ignorant Philosopher; and a Commentary on the Marquis of Becaria's Treatise on Crimes and Punishments . . . translated by the Rev. David Williams* (London, 1779). In this collection, the *Treatise on Ignorance* seems to be replacing the "Avis au public sur les parricides imputés aux Calas et aux Sirven," given as a supplement to *The Ignorant Philosopher* in the French edition. Both texts deal with the Calas Affair of 1761, the mysterious death of a young Huguenot in Toulouse. His father, Jean Calas, was accused of killing him to prevent his alleged impending conversion to Catholicism. Jean Calas was executed on 10 March 1761. Voltaire published his essay on toleration in 1763 with the hope to obtain a new trial.

19. Voltaire, *A Treatise on Toleration; The Ignorant Philosopher, op. cit.*, 37.

20. *Ibid.*, 9. See Locke's *Essay concerning Human Understanding, op. cit.*, IV, 3, 22, 553. On *The Ignorant Philosopher*, see also Dédéyan, *Le Retour de Salente, op. cit.*, 146.

21. Voltaire, *A Treatise on Toleration; The Ignorant Philosopher, op. cit.*, 86. Note that a portrait of Montaigne, with the title page of the *Essais* and the motto "Que sais-je?" inscribed on an urn, is given in the 1779 English edition of Voltaire's text immediately before "the short commentary" (80), in which Montaigne's works are mentioned as the only books available at the time of Henry IV, apart from "wretched treatises of controversy" (81). But the portrait might also present another "ignorant philosopher."

Bibliography

Primary Sources

Agrippa, Henry Cornelius. *De incertitudine & vanitate scientiarum & artium, atque excellentia verbi Dei, declamatio.* Antwerp, 1530.

———. *De l'incertitude, vanité, & abus des Sciences, traduit en français par Louys de Mayerne Turquet, 1582.* Geneva, 1630.

———. *De occulta philosophia libri tres.* Cologne, 1533.

———. *Of the Vanitie and Uncertaintie of Artes and Sciences, Englished by Ja. San. Gent.* London, 1569.

———. *The Vanity of Arts and Sciences.* London, 1676.

Alciato, Andrea. *Emblematum liber.* Augsburg, 28 February 1531.

———. *Emblemes.* Lyon, 1549.

Anonymous. *Dirt Wip't Off: Or a Manifest Discovery of the Gross Ignorance, Erroneousness and Most Unchristian and Wicked Spirit of One John Bunyan.* London, 1672.

Aristotle. *De anima.* Translated by J. A. Smith. Oxford: Clarendon Press, 1931.

———. *Metaphysics.* Translated and introduced by Hugh Lawson-Tancred. Harmondsworth: Penguin Books, 1998.

Augustine, Saint. *The Works of Saint Augustine, Letters 100–150 (Epistulae).* Translated and with notes by Roland Teske, SJ, and edited by Boniface Ramsey. New York: New City Press, 2003.

Bacon, Francis. *The Advancement of Learning*. Edited by Michael Kiernan. Oxford: Clarendon Press, 2000.

———. *The Essayes and Counsels, Civill and Morall*. Edited by Michael Kiernan. 1985; Oxford: Clarendon Press, 2000.

———. *The* Instauratio magna *Part II*. Novum Organum *and Associated Texts*. Edited by Graham Rees and Maria Wakely. Oxford: Clarendon Press, 2004.

———. *The Masculine Birth of Time, Or Three Books on the Interpretation of Nature*. In *The Philosophy of Francis Bacon*, translated and edited by Benjamin Farrington, 59–72. Liverpool: Liverpool University Press, 1964.

———. *La Sagesse des anciens*. Translated, introduced, and with notes by Jean-Pierre Cavaillé. Paris: Vrin, 1997.

———. *The Works of Francis Bacon*. Edited by James Spedding, Robert Leslie Ellis, and Douglas Denon Heath. 15 vols. London: Longman and Co., 1857–1874.

Baillet, Adrien. *La Vie de Monsieur Descartes*. 2 vols. Paris, 1691.

Baker, Thomas. *Reflections upon Learning, wherein is shewn the Insufficiency thereof, in its several Particulars. In order to evince the Usefulness and Necessity of Revelation*. London, 1699.

[Banchieri, Adriano.] *The Noblenesse of the Asse. A Work Rare, Learned, and Excellent*. London, 1595.

Baret, John. *An Alveary or Triple Dictionary, in English, Latin, and French*. London, 1574.

Bartoli, Daniello. *The Learned Man Defended and Reformed*. Translated by Th. Salusbury. London, 1660.

Baudoin, Jean. *Iconologie, ou Explication nouvelle de plusieurs images, emblèmes et autres figures hierogliphiques des vertus, des vices, des arts, des sciences, des causes naturelles, des humeurs différentes, & des passions humaines*. Paris, 1636.

Baxter, Richard. *The Arrogancy of Reason against Divine Revelations, Repressed, or, Proud Ignorance the Cause of Infidelity, and of Mens Quarrelling with the Word of God*. London, 1655.

———. *A Key for Catholicks, To open the Jugling of the Jesuits, and satisfie all that are but truly willing to understand, whether the Cause of the Roman or Reformed Churches be of God; and to leave the Reader utterly unexcusable that after this will be a Papist*. London, 1659.

———. *The Mischiefs of Self-Ignorance, and the Benefits of Self-Acquaintance*. London, 1662.

———. *The Saints Everlasting Rest: Or, A Treatise of the blessed state of the saints in the enjoyment of God in Glory*. London, 1649.

———. *A Treatise of Knowledge and Love Compared In two parts: 1. Of Falsly Pretended Knowledge. 2. Of True Saving Knowledge and Love. Written as greatly needful to the Safety and Peace of every Christian, and of the Church. The only certain way to escape false Religions, Heresies, Sects and Malignant Prejudices, Persecutions and Sinful Wars: All caused by falsly pretended knowledge, and hasty judging, by proud Ignorant men, who know not their Ignorance*. London, 1689.

———. *Two Disputations of Original Sin. 1. Of Original sin, as from Adam. 2. Of Original Sin, as from our Neerer Parents*. London, 1675.

Blunt, Leonard. *Asse upon Asse being a collection of Several Pamphlets written for, and against the Author of the Asses Complaint against Balaam, or the cry of the Country against Ignorant and Scandalous Ministers. Together with some choice Observations upon them all.* London, 1661.

[Boreman, Robert.] *Paideia Thriamous. The Triumph of Learning over Ignorance and of Truth over Falsehood.* London, 1653.

Boyle, Robert. *Certain Physiological Essays.* London, 1661.

———. *The Christian Virtuoso: Showing, that by being addicted to Experimental Philosophy, a Man is rather Assisted, than Indisposed, to be a Good Christian.* London, 1690.

———. *A Discourse of Things Above Reason, Inquiring whether a Philosopher should Admit there are any such.* London, 1681.

———. *The Excellency of Theology, Compar'd with Natural Philosophy.* London, 1674.

———. *A Free Enquiry into the Vulgarly Receiv'd Notion of Nature.* London, 1685.

———. *New Experiments and Observations touching Cold, or an Experimental History of Cold, Begun.* London, 1665.

———. *Of the High Veneration Man's Intellect Owes to God; Peculiarly for His Wisedom and Power.* London, 1685.

———. *Some Considerations touching the Usefulnesse of Experimental Naturall Philosophy.* Oxford, 1663.

———. *The Sceptical Chymist: Or Chymico-Physical Doubts & Paradoxes, Touching the Spagyrist's Principles.* London, 1661.

[Boyle, Robert.] *The Martyrdom of Theodora, and of Didymus. By a Person of Honour.* London, 1687.

Brant, Sebastian. *Das Narrenschiff.* Basel, 1494.

Browne, Thomas. *Pseudodoxia Epidemica, or, Enquiries into very many Received Tenents, and Commonly Presumed Truths.* London, 1646.

[Bruno, Giordano.] *Cabala del Cavallo Pegaseo. Con l'aggiunta dell'Asino Cillenico. Descritta dal Nolano.* Paris [London], 1585.

———. *The Cabala of Pegasus.* Edited and translated by Sidney L. Sondergard and Madison U. Sowell. New Haven, CT: Yale University Press, 2002.

Bruno, Giordano. *Œuvres complètes.* Vol. 4, *Cabale du cheval pégaséen.* Edited by Giovanni Aquilecchia and Nicola Badaloni. Translated by Tristan Dagron. Paris: Les Belles Lettres, 1994.

Bunyan, John. *The Pilgrim's Progress from this World to That Which is to Come.* London, 1678.

Burgess, Anthony. *A Treatise of Original Sin.* London, 1658.

Calvin, John. *Christianae religionis institutio, totam fere pietatis summam et quicquid est in doctrina salutis cognitu necessarium complectens.* Basel, 1536.

———. *Institution de la religion Chrestienne: en laquelle est comprinse une somme de pieté, et quasi tout ce qui est necessaire a congnoistre en la doctrine de salut.* Geneva, 1541.

———. *The Institution of Christian Religion, Wrytten in Latine by Maister Iohn Caluin, and translated into Englysh according to the authors last edition.* Translated by Thomas Norton. London, 1561.

Casaubon, Meric. *Generall Learning. A Seventeenth-Century Treatise on the Formation of the General Scholar, by Meric Casaubon.* Edited by Richard Serjeantson. Cambridge, UK: RTM Publications, 1999.

———. *Of Credulity and Incredulity; In Things Divine and Spiritual.* London, 1670.

———. *A Treatise Concerning Enthusiasme, As it is an Effect of Nature: but is mistaken by many for either Divine Inspiration or Diabolical Possession.* London, 1655.

Charron, Pierre. *De la sagesse. Livres trois.* Bordeaux: Millanges, 1601.

———. *Of Wisdome. Three Bookes Written in French by Peter Charron, Doct. of Lawe in Paris.* Translated by Samson Lennard. London, 1608.

[Cholmley, Hugh.] *The State of the Now-Romane Church Discussed. By way of vindication of the Right Reverend Father in God, the Lord Bishop of Exceter. From the weak cavills of Henry Burton.* London, 1629.

Clark, John P. *The Cloud of Unknowing: An Introduction.* Vol. 1. Salzburg: Institut für Anglistik und Amerikanistik, Universität Salzburg, 1995.

The Cloud of Unknowing. Edited by Patrick J. Gallacher. Kalamazoo: Western Michigan University Institute Publications, 1997. Accessed via Robbins Library Digital Projects, University of Rochester, https://d.lib.rochester.edu/teams/publication/gallacher-the-cloud-of-unknowing.

Collier, Thomas. *The Pulpit-Guard Routed, in its Twenty Strong-Holds. Or, a brief Answer, to a large and lawless Discourse, Written by one Tho. Hall of Kings Norton, Intituled, The Pulpit-Guarded, with Twenty Arguments, pretending to prove the unlawfulnesse, and sinfulness of Private mens Preaching.* London, 1653.

Cotgrave, Randle. *A Dictionarie of the French and English Tongues.* London, 1611.

Cudworth, Ralph. *A Sermon Preached before the Honourable House of Commons, 31 March, 1647.* Cambridge, 1647.

Culverwell, Nathanael. *Spirituall Opticks: Or a Glasse, Discovering the weaknesse and imperfection of a Christians knowledge in this life.* Oxford, 1668.

Cusa, Nicholas of. *De la docte ignorance.* Translated and edited by Jean-Claude Lagarrigue. Paris: Éditions du Cerf, 2010.

———. *Dialogues de l'Idiot. Sur la sagesse et l'esprit.* Translated and edited by Hervé Pasqua. Paris: Presses universitaires de France, 2011.

———. *La Docte ignorance.* Translated and edited by Hervé Pasqua. Paris: Payot, 2011.

———. *The Idiot in Four Books. The First and Second of Wisdome. The Third of the Minde. The fourth of statick Experiments; Or, Experiments of the Ballance.* London, 1650.

———. *Nicholas of Cusa on Learned Ignorance. A Translation and an Appraisal of* De Docta Ignorantia. Translated and edited by Jasper Hopkins. Minneapolis: Arthur J. Banning Press, 1981.

———. *Nicholas of Cusa: Selected Spiritual Writings.* Translated and introduced by H. Lawrence Bond. Preface by Morimichi Watanabe. New York: Paulist Press, 1997.

[Davies, John.] *Nosce teipsum. This Oracle expounded in two Elegies. 1. Of Humane knowledge. 2. Of the Soule of Man, and the Immortalitie thereof.* London, 1599.

Dent, Arthur. *The Plaine Man's Path-way to Heaven.* London, 1601.

Descartes, René. *Discours de la méthode*. Introduction and notes by Étienne Gilson. Paris: Vrin, 1964.

———. *Discours de la méthode pour bien conduire sa raison, & chercher la vérité dans les sciences. Plus la Dioptrique, les Météores et la Géométrie, qui sont des essais de cete méthode*. Leiden, 1637.

———. *A Discourse of a Method for the Well-Guiding of Reason, And the Discovery of Truth in the Sciences*. London, 1649.

———. *Œuvres de Descartes*. Edited by Charles Adam and Paul Tannery. 12 vols. Paris: Cerf, 1897–1913.

———. *Optics, First Discourse: Of Light*. In *Discourse on Method, Optics, Geometry, and Meteorology*, translated with an introduction by Paul J. Olscamp. Indianapolis: Bobbs-Merrill Co., 1965.

———. *Opuscula posthuma, physica et mathematica*. Amsterdam, 1701.

———. *The Philosophical Writings of Descartes*. Translated by John Cottingham, Robert Stoothoff, and Dugald Murdoch. 3 vols. Cambridge: Cambridge University Press, 1985.

———. *La Recherche de la vérité par la lumière naturelle*. Edited by Ettore Lojacono, Erik Jan Bos, Franco A. Meschini, and Francesco Saita. Milan: FrancoAngeli, 2002.

———. *Rules for the Direction of the Mind*. Translated with an introduction by Laurence J. Lafleur. Indianapolis: Bobbs-Merrill Co., 1961.

Descartes, René, and Martin Schoock. *La Querelle d'Utrecht*. Edited, translated, and annotated by Theo Verbeek, with a preface by Jean-Luc Marion. Paris: Les Impressions Nouvelles, 1988.

Encyclopaedia Britannica. Edited by William Smellie. 3 vols. Edinburgh, 1771.

Encyclopédie ou Dictionnaire raisonné des sciences, des arts et des métiers. Vol. 8. Neuchâtel, 1765.

Erasmus, Desiderius. *De la declamation des louenges de follie, stille facessieux et profitable pour congnoistre les erreurs et abuz du monde*. Paris, 1520.

———. *Moriæ encomium*. Paris: G. de Gourmont, 1511.

———. *Novum Testamentum*. Basel: Johannes Froben, 1539–1540.

———. *The Praise of Folie. Moriæ encomium, a booke made in latine by that great clerke Erasmus Roterodame, Englished by Sir Thomas Chaloner*. London, 1549.

———. *The Praise of Folly and Other Writings*. Edited and translated by Robert M. Adams. New York: Norton, 1989.

Farnworth, Richard. *The Priests Ignorance, and Contrary Walkings to the Scriptures*. London, 1655.

[Fox, George.] *An Epistle to All People on the Earth; and The Ignorance of all the World, both Professors and Teachers, of the Birth that must be silent, and of the Birth that is to speak, which declares God; and the difference betwixt silence and speaking*. London, 1657.

Fox, George. *A Testimony of the True Light of the World. Which is given to every man that comes into the world and of the true measure of the gift of God, given to every one to profit withal*. London, 1657.

———. *A Word to the People of the World, who hates the Light to be witnessed by the light in them all; wherein is shewed unto them, what the light is, which is the Condemnation of the* world with its deeds, and what the Spirit of truth is, and what it leads them into, who are led by it; and what the spirit of errour is, and what it leads them into, who are lead by it. London, 1659.

Furetière, Antoine. *Dictionaire universel.* The Hague, 1690.

Gale, Theophilus. *The Court of the Gentiles, or, A Discourse touching the original of human literature, both philology and philosophie, from the Scriptures, and Jewish Church . . . Part II. Of Philosophie.* Oxford, 1670.

Gassendi, Pierre. *Dissertations en forme de paradoxes contre les Aristotéliciens (Exercitationes Paradoxicæ Adversus Aristoteleos).* Books I and II. Translated, edited, and with notes by Bernard Rochot. Paris: Vrin, 1959.

Gauden, John. *Hieraspistes. A Defence by Way of Apology for the Ministry and Ministers of the Church of England.* London, 1653.

[Gearing, William.] *The Arraignment of Ignorance: or, Ignorance. With the Causes and Kinds of it; the mischiefs and danger of it, together with the Cure of Ignorance: as also, the Excellency, Profit, and Benefit of Heavenly Knowledge, largely set forth from Hos. 4.6.* London, 1659.

Glanvill, Joseph. *An Essay concerning Preaching: Written for the Direction of a Young Divine and useful also for the People, or order of Profitable Hearing.* London, 1678.

———. *Essays on Several Subjects in Philosophy and Religion.* London, 1676.

———. *An Exclusion of Skepticks from all Title to Dispute.* London, 1665.

———. *Plus Ultra, or The Progress and Advancement of Knowledge since the Days of Aristotle.* London, 1668.

———. *Scepsis Scientifica: Or, Confest Ignorance, the way to Science; In an Essay of The Vanity of Dogmatizing, and Confident Opinion.* London, 1665.

———. *Some Discourses, Sermons and Remains of the Reverend Mr. Jos. Glanvil.* London, 1681.

———. *The Vanity of Dogmatizing: Or Confidence in Opinions manifested in a Discourse of the Shortness and Uncertainty of our Knowledge, and its Causes.* London, 1661.

Griffin, Lewis. *The Doctrine of the Asse: Or, A Brief Account of their Principles and Practice, in whose behalf the Complaint was written: That it may serve for Advice to others. Whereunto is Added, The Asse's Complaint. Balaam's Reply. And The Authors Apology.* London, 1661.

Hobbes, Thomas. *Humane Nature, or, The Fundamental Elements of Policy* (1640). London, 1684.

———. *Leviathan* (1651). Edited by J. C. A. Gaskin. Oxford: Oxford University Press, 1996.

Hooke, Robert. *The Diary of Robert Hooke, M. A., M. D., F. R. S. (1672–1680).* Edited by Henry W. Robinson and Walter Adams, with a foreword by Sir Frederick Gowland Hopkins, OM. London: Taylor and Francis, 1935.

———. *Micrographia, or some Physiological Descriptions of Minute Bodies made by Magnifying Glasses.* London, 1665.

How, Samuel. *The Sufficiencie of the Spirits Teaching without Humane Learning: Or, a Trea-

tise Tending to Prove Humane Learning to be no Help to the Spirituall Understanding of the Word of God, 1639. London, 1640.

Ibn Tufayl. *An Account of the Oriental Philosophy Shewing the Wisdom of Some Renowned Men of the East and particularly the Profound Wisdom of Hai Ebn Yokdan, both in natural and divine Things*. Translated by George Keith. London, 1674.

———. *The History of Hai Eb'n Yockdan, and Indian Prince, or, The Self-Taught Philosopher Written Originally in the Arabick Tongue by Abi Jaafar Eb'n Tophail*. Translated by George Ashwell. London, 1686.

———. *Le Philosophe autodidacte*. Translated by Léon Gauthier, with Séverine Auffret and Ghassan Ferzli. Paris: Mille et Une Nuits, 1999.

———. *Philosophus autodidactus, sive, Epistola Abi Jaafar ebn Tophail de Hai ebn Yokdham in qua ostenditur quomodo ex inferiorum contemplatione as superiorum notitiam ratio humana ascendere possit*. Translated by Edward Pocock. Oxford, 1671.

Keith, George. *Divine immediate revelation and inspiration, continued in the true church second part*. London, 1685.

———. *The Universal Free Grace of the Gospel Asserted, or, The Light of the Glorious Gospell of Jesus Christ, shining forth universally, and enlightening every man that comes into the World, and thereby giving unto every man, a day of Visitation, wherein it is possible for him to be saved*. London, 1671.

———. *The Woman-Preacher of Samaria a better preacher, and more sufficiently qualified to preach than any of the men-preachers of the man-made-ministry in these three nations*. London, 1674.

King, Peter, ed. *The Life of John Locke, with Extracts from His Correspondence, Journals and Common-place Books*. London, 1829.

La Mothe Le Vayer, François de. *Cinq autres dialogues. Faits comme les precedents à l'imitation des anciens. I. De l'ignorance louable. II. De la divinité. III. De l'opiniastreté. III. De la politique. V. Du mariage*. Frankfurt, 1633.

———. *Dialogue sur les rares et eminentes qualitez des asnes de ce temps*. In *Cinq dialogues faits à l'imitation des Anciens*. Vol. 1, 241–326. Frankfurt, 1716.

———. *Opuscule ou petit traité sceptique, Sur cette commune façon de parler. N'avoir pas le Sens-commun*. Paris, 1646.

Landi, Giulio. *La vita di Cleopatra reina d'Egitto. Con una oratione nel fine, recitata nell'Academia dell'ignoranti; in lode dell'Ignoranza*. Venice, 1551.

Lando, Ortensio. *The Defence of Contraries: Paradoxes against Common Opinion*. Translated by Anthony Munday. London, 1593.

———. *Paradossi cioè, sententie fuori del commun parere novellamente venute in luce*. Lyon, 1543. (Second edition printed in Venice, 1544.)

———. *Paradoxes, ce sont propos contre la commune opinion*. Translated by Charles Estienne. Paris, 1553.

Locher, Jacob. *Stultifera navis*. Basel, 1497.

Locke, John. *An Essay concerning Human Understanding* (1690). Edited by Peter H. Nidditch. Oxford: Clarendon Press, 2011.

———. "Essays on the Law of Nature" (1664). In *Locke: Political Writings*, edited by Mark Goldie, 79–133. Cambridge: Cambridge University Press, 1997.

[Locke, John.] *A Letter concerning Toleration*. London, 1690.

———. *The Library of John Locke*. Edited by John Harrison and Peter Laslett. Oxford: Oxford University Press, 1965.

———. *Mr. Locke's Reply to the right reverend the Lord Bishop of Worcester answer to his second letter*. London, 1699.

———. *Posthumous Works of Mr. John Locke: viz. 1. Of the Conduct of the Understanding. 2. An Examination of P. Malebranche's Opinion of Seeing all things in God. 3. A Discourse of Miracles. 4. Part of a Fourth Letter for Toleration. 5. Memoirs relating to the Life of Anthony first Earl of Shaftesbury, To which is added, 6. His new method of a Common-place book, written originally in French, and now translated into English*. London, 1706.

———. *Some Thoughts concerning Education*. London, 1693.

Locke, John. *The Reasonableness of Christianity*. London, 1695.

Malebranche, Nicolas. *Father Malebranche his Treatise concerning the Search after Truth. To which is added the Author's Treatise of Nature and Grace: being a consequence of the Principles contained in the Search. All translated by T. Taylor*. London, 1700.

Mersenne, Marin. *L'impieté des Deistes, Athees et Libertins de ce temps, combatuë et renversee de point en point par raisons tirees de la Philosophie et de la Theologie. Ensemble la refutation du Poëme des Deistes*. Paris, 1624.

———. *Questions Inouyes ou Recreation des Sçavans. Qui contiennent beaucoup de choses concernantes la Théologie, la Philosophie et les Mathématiques*. Paris, 1634.

———. *Les Questions theologiques, physiques, morales et mathematiques. Où chacun trouvera du contentement, ou de l'exercice*. Paris, 1634.

———. *La Verité des sciences, contre les Sceptiques ou Pyrrhoniens*. Paris, 1625.

Milton, John. "Of Education. To Master Samuel Hartlib" (1644). In *Areopagitica, Of Education*, edited by K. M. Lea, 45–58. Oxford: Clarendon Press, 1973.

Montaigne, Michel de. *The essayes or morall, politike and millitarie discourses of Lo: Michaell de Montaigne* (1580). Translated by John Florio. London, 1603.

———. *Journal de Voyage*. Edited by François Rigolot. Paris: Presses universitaires de France, 1992.

[More, Henry.] *Enthusiasmus triumphatus, or, A discourse of the nature, causes, kinds, and cure, of enthusiasm, written by Philophilus Parresiastes, and prefixed to Alazonomastix his observations and reply*. London, 1656.

More, Henry. *An Explanation of the Grand Mystery of Godliness, or, A True and Faithfull Representation of the Everlasting Gospel of our Lord and Saviour Jesus Christ, the onely begotten Son of God and Sovereign over Men and Angels*. London, 1660.

———. *A Plain and Continued Exposition of the Several Prophecies or Divine Visions of the Prophet Daniel, which have or may concern the People of God, whether Jew or Christian*. London, 1681.

Pascal, Blaise. *Monsieur Pascall's Thoughts, Meditations, and Prayers, touching matters moral and divine as they were found in his papers after his death . . . done into English by Jos. Walker*. London, 1688.

———. *Œuvres complètes*. Edited by Louis Lafuma. Paris: Seuil, 1963.
Pemble, William. *Five Godly and Profitable Sermons concerning 1. The slaverie of sin, 2. The mischiefe of ignorance, 3. The roote of Apostasie, 4. The benefit of God's service, 5. The Christians love*. Oxford, 1628.
Perkins, William. *The First Part of the Cases of Conscience. Wherein specially, three maine Questions concerning Man, simply considered in himself, are propounded and resolved*. Cambridge, 1604.
———. *Lectures upon the Three First Chapters of the Revelation: Preached in Cambridge Anno Dom. 1595*. London, 1604.
Petrarca, Francesco. *On His Own Ignorance and That of Many Others*. Translated by Hans Nachod. In *The Renaissance Philosophy of Man*, edited by Ernst Cassirer, Paul Oskar Kristeller, and John Herman Randall Jr., 47–133. Chicago: University of Chicago Press, 1948.
Plato. *Charmides*. Translated and introduced, and with notes and analysis, by Christopher Moore and Christopher C. Raymond. Indianapolis: Hackett Publishing, 2019.
———. *Parmenides*. Translated by and analysis by R. E. Allen. Oxford: Blackwell, 1983.
———. *The Republic*. Edited by G. R. F. Ferrari. Translated by Tom Griffith. Cambridge: Cambridge University Press, 2000.
———. *Theaetetus and Sophist*. Edited and translated by Christopher Rowe. Cambridge: Cambridge University Press, 2015.
———. *Timaeus and Critias*. Translated and annotated by Desmond Lee. Translation revised, introduced, and further annotated by T. K. Johansen. London: Penguin Classics, 2008.
Prior, Matthew. "A Dialogue between Mr. John Lock and Seigneur de Montaigne" (1721). In *Dialogues of the Dead and Other Works in Prose and Verse*, edited by Alfred R. Waller, 223–246. Cambridge: Cambridge University Press, 1907.
P.P.P.P. [Perrot de la Salle, Paul]. *Le Contr'empire des sciences, et le Mystere des asnes*. Lyon, 1599.
Reynolds, Edward. *A Sermon touching the Use of Humane Learning*. London, 1658.
Ripa, Cesare. *Iconologia: Or, Moral Emblems, by Caesar Ripa. Wherein are Express'd Various Images of Virtues, Vices, Passions, Arts, Humours, Elements and Celestial Bodies. By the Care and at the Charge of P. Tempest*. London, 1709.
———. *Iconologia overo descrittione dell'imagini universali cavate dall'Antichita & da altri luoghi*. Rome, 1593.
———. *Iconology, or a Collection of Emblematical Figures*. Edited by George Richardson. London, 1779.
Rivière, Pierre. *La Nef des folz*. Paris, 1497.
Sanches, Francisco. *Quod nihil scitur*. Lyon, 1581.
———. *That Nothing Is Known*. Edited by Elaine Limbrick. Translated by Douglas F. S. Thomson. Cambridge: Cambridge University Press, 1988.
Scaliger, Julius Caesar. *Exotericarum exercitationum*. Paris, 1557.
Schoock, Martin. *Admiranda methodus novae philosophiae Renati Des Cartes*. Utrecht, 1643.
———. *De scepticismo pars prior, sive libri quatuor*. Groningen, 1652.

[Sergeant, John.] *The Method to Science*. London, 1696.
Sergeant, John. *Solid Philosophy Asserted Against the Fancies of the Ideists*. London, 1697.
———. *Sure-footing in Christianity, Or Rational Discourses on the Rule of Faith*. London, 1665.
Sorel, Charles. *De la perfection de l'homme ou les vrays biens sont considerez, et specialement ceux de l'ame*. Paris, 1655.
———. *La Science universelle. Tome quatriesme. De l'Usage des Idées, ou de l'Origine des Sciences & des Arts, & de leur Enchaisnement, Du Langage, de l'Escriture et des Chiffres*. Paris, 1668.
Sprat, Thomas. *The History of the Royal Society of London*. London, 1667.
Surin, Jean-Joseph. *Correspondance*. Edited by Michel de Certeau. Preface by Julien Green. Paris: Desclée de Brouwer, 1966.
T.B. *The Rebellion of Naples, or the Tragedy of Massenello, commonly so called*. London, 1649.
Thomas Aquinas. *Aristotle's* De anima *with the Commentary of St. Thomas Aquinas*. Translated by Kenelm Foster and Silvester Humphries. New Haven, CT: Yale University Press, 1965.
———. *On Evil*. Translated by Richard Regan, SJ, and Brian Davies, OP. Oxford: Oxford University Press, 2003.
———. *Questions disputées sur le mal—De Malo*. Translated into French by the monks of Fontgombault. Nouvelles Éditions Latines, 1992.
———. *Summa Theologica*. Translated by the Fathers of the English Dominican Province. Westminster, MD: Christian Classics, 1981.
T.R. *A Philosophicall Discourse, Entituled, The Anatomie of the Minde*. London, 1576.
T.W. [Thomas Wilson], *Theologicall rules, to guide us in the understanding and practices of holy Scriptures*. London, 1615.
Vergil, Polydore. *On Discovery*. Edited and translated by Brian P. Copenhaver. Cambridge, MA: Harvard University Press, 2002.
Voltaire, François-Marie Arouet de. *Letters concerning the English Nation*. London, 1733.
———. *Le philosophe ignorant. Avec un Avis au public sur les Parricides imputés aux Calas & aux Sirven*. [Geneva? London?], 1766.
———. *Poèmes sur le désastre de Lisbonne, et sur la loi naturelle*. Geneva, 1756.
———. *A Treatise on Toleration; The Ignorant Philosopher; and a Commentary on the Marquis of Becaria's Treatise on Crimes and Punishments . . . translated by the Rev. David Williams*. London, 1779.
———. *The Works of Voltaire*. Translated by Tobias Smollett, Thomas Francklin, and others. 38 vols. London, 1761–1774.
Waterhouse, Edward. *An Humble Apologie for Learning and Learned Men*. London, 1653.
White, Thomas. *An Exclusion of Skepticks from all Title to Dispute: Being An Answer to the Vanity of Dogmatizing*. London, 1665.
Whitlock, Richard. *Zootomia, or, Observations of the present manners of the English: Briefly Anatomizing the Living by the Dead. With an usefull detection of the mountebanks of both sexes*. London, 1654.
Wilson, Thomas. *A commentarie upon the most divine Epistle of S. Paul to the Romanes*

containing for matter, the degeneration of our nature by Adams Fall; and the Restauration thereof, by the Grace of Christ. London, 1614.

Secondary Sources

Ahbel-Rappe, Sara. *Socratic Ignorance and Platonic Knowledge in the Dialogues of Plato.* New York: SUNY Press, 2018.

Angell, Stephen W. "God, Christ, and the Light." In *The Oxford Handbook of Quaker Studies.* Edited by Stephen W. Angell and Pink Dandelion, 158–171. Oxford: Oxford University Press, 2013.

Arbib, Dan. "Le moi cartésien comme troisième livre: Note sur Montaigne et la première partie du *Discours de la méthode*." *Revue de métaphysique et de morale* 74, no. 2 (2012): 161–180.

Ashworth, William B. "Light of Reason, Light of Nature. Catholic and Protestant Metaphors of Scientific Knowledge." *Science in Context* 3, no. 1 (1989): 89–107.

Attar, Samar. *The Vital Roots of European Enlightenment: Ibn Tufayl's Influence on Modern Western Thought.* Lanham, MD: Lexington Books, 2007.

Barański, Zygmunt G. "The Ethics of Ignorance: Petrarch's Epicurus and Averroës and the Structures of the *De Sui Ipsius et Multorum Ignorantia*." In *Petrarch in Britain. Interpreters, Imitators, and Translators over 700 Years,* edited by Martin McLaughlin, Letizia Panizza, and Peter Hainsworth, 39–59. Oxford: Oxford University Press, 2007.

Bennett, Andrew. *Ignorance: Literature and Agnoiology.* Manchester: Manchester University Press, 2009.

Ben-Zaken, Avner. *Reading Hayy Ibn-Yaqzan. A Cross-Cultural History of Autodidacticism.* Baltimore: Johns Hopkins University Press, 2011.

Bertucci, Paola. *Artisanal Enlightenment. Science and the Mechanical Arts in Old Regime France.* New Haven, CT: Yale University Press, 2017.

Biddle, John C. "John Locke's Essay on Infallibility: Introduction, Text, and Translation." *Journal of Church and State* 19, no. 2 (1977): 301–327.

Blair, Ann M. *Too Much To Know. Managing Scholarly Information before the Modern Age.* New Haven, CT: Yale University Press, 2010.

Blum, Paul Richard. "Nicholas of Cusa in Giles Randall's English Translation: Wisdom and Vision in Language." *Recherches de Théologie et Philosophie Médiévales* 83, no. 1 (2016): 201–219.

Boutcher, Warren. "Montaigne in England and America." In *The Oxford Handbook of Montaigne,* edited by Philippe Desan, 306–327. Oxford: Oxford University Press, 2016.

Brahami, Frédéric. "Au fil conducteur du scepticisme: Science et métaphysique chez Glanvill." *Philosophiques* 35, no. 1 (2008): 207–222.

———. *Le Travail du scepticisme: Montaigne, Bayle, Hume.* Paris: Presses universitaires de France, 2001.

Brunschvicg, Léon. *Descartes et Pascal lecteurs de Montaigne.* 1945; Paris: Pocket, 1995.

Burke, Peter. *Popular Culture in Early Modern Europe.* London: Temple Smith, 1978.

———. *A Social History of Knowledge, 1500–1800.* Cambridge: Polity Press, 2000.

Casarella, Peter J., ed. *Cusanus: The Legacy of Learned Ignorance.* Washington, DC: Catholic University of America Press, 2006.

Cassirer, Ernst. *Die Platonische Renaissance in England und die Schule von Cambridge.* Berlin: Teubner, 1932.

———. *Le Problème de la connaissance dans la philosophie et la science des temps modernes.* Vol. 1, *De Nicolas de Cues à Bayle.* 1910. Translated by René Fréreux. Paris: Cerf, 2004.

Casson, Douglas John. *Liberating Judgment. Fanatics, Skeptics, and John Locke's Politics of Probability.* Princeton, NJ: Princeton University Press, 2011.

Cavaillé, Jean-Pierre. *Les Déniaisés: Irréligion et libertinage au début de l'époque moderne.* Paris: Classiques Garnier, 2013.

Certeau, Michel de. *La Fable mystique, XVIe–XVIIe siècle.* Paris: Gallimard, 1982.

———. "L'illettré éclairé dans l'histoire de la lettre de Surin sur le Jeune Homme du Coche (1630)." *Revue d'Ascétique et de Mystique* 44, no. 176 (1968): 369–412.

Charles-Daubert, Françoise. *Les Libertins érudits en France au XVIIe siècle.* Paris: Presses universitaires de France, 1998.

Chiquot, A. *Histoire ou légende? Jean Tauler et le "Meisters/Buoch."* Paris: Champion, 1922.

Colie, Rosalie L. *Paradoxia Epidemica: The Renaissance Tradition of Paradox.* Princeton, NJ: Princeton University Press, 1966.

Comerford, Kathleen M. "Clerical Education, Catechesis, and Catholic Confessionalism: Teaching Religion in the Sixteenth and Seventeenth Centuries." In *Early Modern Catholicism: Essays in Honour of John W. O'Malley, SJ,* edited by Kathleen M. Comerford and Hilmar M. Pabel, 241–265. Toronto: University of Toronto Press, 2001.

Condren, Conal, Stephen Gaukroger, and Ian Hunter, eds. *The Philosopher in Early Modern Europe.* Cambridge: Cambridge University Press, 2006.

Copi, Irving M. *Introduction to Logic.* 1953; New York: Macmillan, 1961.

Corbin, Alain. *Terra Incognita: Une histoire de l'ignorance, XVIIIe–XIXe siècle.* Paris: Albin Michel, 2020.

Corneanu, Sorana. *Regimens of the Mind: Boyle, Locke, and the Early Modern Cultura animi Tradition.* Chicago: University of Chicago Press, 2011.

Corréard, Nicolas. "Discours, invectives et autres paradoxes 'contre les lettres': Topique, thème ou genre?" *Réforme, Humanisme, Renaissance* 86 (2018): 117–153.

———. "Le paradoxe landien: Une poétique pour la dissidence?" *Bruniana & Campanelliana* 22 (2016): 541–552.

Cottegnies, Line, Sandrine Parageau, and John J. Thompson, eds. *Women and Curiosity in Early Modern England and France.* Leiden: Brill, 2016.

Crignon, Claire, and Sandrine Parageau, eds. "Bacon and the Forms of Experimentation: A Reappraisal." Translated by Donald Nicholson-Smith. *Archives de Philosophie* 84, no. 1 (2021): 7–15.

Crignon–De Oliveira, Claire. *De la mélancolie à l'enthousiasme: Robert Burton (1577–1640) et Anthony Ashley-Cooper, comte de Shaftesbury (1671–1713).* Paris: Honoré Champion, 2006.

Daston, Lorraine, and H. Otto Sibum, "Introduction: Scientific *Personae* and Their Histories." *Science in Context* 16, nos. 1–2 (2003): 1–8.

Dédéyan, Charles. *Le Retour de Salente ou Voltaire et l'Angleterre*. Paris: A.-G. Nizet, 1988.
Deleule, Didier. "L'éthique baconienne et l'esprit de la science moderne." In *Francis Bacon: Science et méthode, Actes du colloque de Nantes*, edited by Michel Malherbe and Jean-Marie Pousseur, 53–77. Paris: Vrin, 1985.
———. *Francis Bacon et la réforme du savoir*. Paris: Hermann, 2010.
Deleuze, Gilles, and Félix Guattari. *Qu'est-ce que la philosophie?* Paris: Minuit, 1991.
Di Biase, Giuliana. "A Gentleman's 'Moderate Knowledge': Mediocrity as the Appropriate Measure of Learning in John Locke's *Some Thoughts concerning Education*." *XVII-XVIII* 72 (2015): 57–80.
Dilley, Roy. "Reflections on Knowledge Practices and the Problem of Ignorance." *Journal of the Royal Anthropological Institute* 16, suppl. 1 (2010): 176–192.
Dilley, Roy, and Thomas G. Kirsch, eds. *Regimes of Ignorance: Anthropological Perspectives on the Production and Reproduction of Non-Knowledge*. New York: Berghahn, 2015.
Dooley, Brendan. *The Social History of Skepticism. Experience and Doubt in Early Modern Culture*. Baltimore: Johns Hopkins University Press, 1999.
Draper, John W. "Bunyan's Mr Ignorance." *Modern Language Review* 22 (1927): 15–21.
Duclow, Donald F. *Masters of Learned Ignorance: Eriugena, Eckhart, Cusanus*. Aldershot, UK: Ashgate, 2006.
Dudiak, Jeffrey, and Laura Rediehs. "Quakers, Philosophy, and Truth." In *The Oxford Handbook of Quaker Studies*, edited by Stephen W. Angell and Pink Dandelion, 507–519. Oxford: Oxford University Press, 2013.
Dunan-Page, Anne. *Grace Overwhelming. John Bunyan,* The Pilgrim's Progress *and the Extremes of the Baptist Mind*. New York: Peter Lang, 2006.
Dunan-Page, Anne, ed. *The Cambridge Companion to Bunyan*. Cambridge: Cambridge University Press, 2010.
Duschinsky, Robert. "*Tabula rasa* and Human Nature." *Philosophy* 87 (2012): 509–529.
Eeg-Olofsson, Leif. *The Conception of the Inner Light in Robert Barclay's Theology: A Study in Quakerism*. Lund, Sweden: CWK Gleerup, 1954.
Eggert, Katherine. *Disknowledge. Literature, Alchemy, and the End of Humanism in Renaissance England*. Philadelphia: University of Pennsylvania Press, 2015.
Esclapez, Raymond. "Montaigne et Nicolas de Cuse: Le thème de la 'docte ignorance' dans les *Essais*." *Littératures* 18 (1988): 25–40.
Essary, Kirk. *Erasmus and Calvin on the Foolishness of God. Reason and Emotion in the Christian Philosophy*. Toronto: University of Toronto Press, 2017.
Eva, Luiz. "On the Affinities between Bacon's Philosophy and Skepticism." Translated by Fernando Moraes Barros. *Kriterion, Belo Horizonte* 47, no. 113 (2006): 73–97. http://socialsciences.scielo.org/scielo.php?script=sci_arttext&pid=S0100-512X2006000200004.
Fattori, Marta. "Francis Bacon et la culture française." In *Bacon et Descartes: Genèse de la modernité philosophique*, edited by Élodie Cassan, 25–47. Lyon: ENS Éditions, 2014.
Faye, Emmanuel. *Philosophie et perfection de l'homme, de la Renaissance à Descartes*. Paris: Vrin, 1998.
Firestein, Stuart. *Ignorance: How It Drives Science*. Oxford: Oxford University Press, 2012.
Fleming, James D., ed. *The Invention of Discovery, 1500–1700*. Farnham, UK: Ashgate, 2011.

Forrest, James F. "Bunyan's Ignorance and the Flatterer: A Study in the Literary Art of Damnation." *Studies in Philology* 60 (1963): 12–22.

Forster, Greg. "'Sit Down in Quiet Ignorance': Locke's Epistemology of Limits." In *John Locke's Politics of Moral Consensus*, 40–83. Cambridge: Cambridge University Press, 2005.

Forster, Michael N. "Socrates' Profession of Ignorance." *Oxford Studies in Ancient Philosophy* 32 (2007): 1–36.

Franke, William, ed. *On What Cannot Be Said. Apophatic Discourses in Philosophy, Religion, Literature, and the Arts*. 2 vols. Notre Dame, IN: Notre Dame University Press, 2014.

Frijhoff, Willem. "Autodidaxies, XVIe–XIXe siècles: Jalons pour la construction d'un objet historique." *Histoire de l'Éducation* 70 (1996): 5–27.

Gaille, Marie, and Didier Torny, eds. "Faire de l'ignorance un objet de connaissance des SHS." *Lettre de l'InSHS* (November 2016): 18–39.

Garrod, Raphaële, Alexander Marr, José Ramón Marcaida, and Richard J. Oosterhoff, eds. *Logodaedalus: Word Histories of Ingenuity in Early Modern Europe*. Pittsburgh, PA: University of Pittsburgh Press, 2018.

Gaukroger, Stephen. *Francis Bacon and the Transformation of Early-Modern Philosophy*. Cambridge: Cambridge University Press, 2001.

Georgescu, Laura. "A New Form of Knowledge: *Experientia Literata*." *Societate și Politică* 5 (2011): 104–120.

Geraldine, M., CSJ. "Erasmus and the Tradition of Paradox." *Studies in Philology* 61, no. 1 (1964): 41–63.

Gierczynski, Zbigniew. "La Science de l'ignorance de Montaigne." *Roczników Humanistycznych* 15 (1967): 1–85.

Giglioni, Guido. "Learning to Read Nature: Francis Bacon's Notion of Experiential Literacy (*Experientia Literata*)." *Early Science and Medicine* 18, nos. 4–5 (2013): 405–434.

Giocanti, Sylvia. *Penser l'irrésolution: Montaigne, Pascal, La Mothe Le Vayer—Trois itinéraires sceptiques*. Paris: Champion, 2001.

Girel, Mathias, ed. "Fauteurs de doute." *Critique* 799 (January 2014).

Granada, Miguel Ángel. "Bacon and Scepticism." *Nouvelles de la République des Lettres* 2 (2006): 91–104.

Gregory, Tullio. *Genèse de la raison classique de Charron à Descartes*. Translated by Marilène Raiola. Preface by Jean-Robert Armogathe. Paris: Presses universitaires de France, 2000.

Grimaldi-Pizzorno, Patrizia. *The Ways of Paradox from Lando to Donne*. Florence: Olschki, 2007.

Gross, Matthias. "The Unknown in Process: Dynamic Connections of Ignorance, Non-Knowledge, and Related Concepts." *Current Sociology* 55 (2007): 742–759.

Gross, Matthias, and Linsey McGoey, eds. *Routledge International Handbook of Ignorance Studies*. London: Routledge, 2015.

Haffemayer, Stéphane. *Les Lumières radicales de la Révolution anglaise: Samuel Hartlib et les réseaux de l'intelligence (1600–1660)*. Paris: Classiques Garnier, 2018.

Haigh, Christopher. *The Plain Man's Pathways to Heaven: Kinds of Christianity in Post-Reformation England, 1570–1640*. Oxford: Oxford University Press, 2007.
Hamblin, Charles L. *Fallacies*. London: Methuen and Co., 1970.
Hamou, Philippe. *Dans la chambre obscure de l'esprit: John Locke et l'invention du* mind. Paris: Les Éditions d'Ithaque, 2018.
———. *La Mutation du visible: Essai sur la portée épistémologique des instruments d'optique au XVIIe siècle*. Vol. 1, *Du* Sidereus Nuncius *de Galilée à la* Dioptrique *cartésienne*. Villeneuve d'Ascq, France: Presses universitaires du Septentrion, 1999.
———. *La Mutation du visible: Essai sur la portée épistémologique des instruments d'optique au XVIIe siècle*. Vol. 2, *Microscopes et télescopes en Angleterre, de Bacon à Hooke*. Villeneuve d'Ascq, France: Presses universitaires du Septentrion, 2001.
———. "Ophtalmie, vision adamique et restauration du savoir dans la pensée anglaise du XVIIe siècle." *Le Temps philosophique* 9 (2003): 81–116.
Hardin, Richard F. "Bunyan, Mr. Ignorance, and the Quakers." *Studies in Philology* 69 (1972): 496–508.
Harrison, John, and Peter Laslett, eds. *The Library of John Locke*. Oxford: Oxford University Press, 1965.
Harrison, Peter. *The Bible, Protestantism, and the Rise of Natural Science*. Cambridge: Cambridge University Press, 1998.
———. *The Fall of Man and the Foundations of Science*. Cambridge: Cambridge University Press, 2007.
———. "Original Sin and the Problem of Knowledge in Early Modern Europe." *Journal of the History of Ideas* 63 (2002): 239–259.
Haydn, Hiram. *The Counter-Renaissance*. New York: Charles Scribner's Sons, 1950.
Hayes, Thomas Wilson. "John Everard and Nicholas of Cusa's *Idiota*." *Notes & Queries* 28 (1981): 47–49.
———. "Nicholas of Cusa and Popular Literacy in Seventeenth-Century England." *Studies in Philology* 84 (1987): 80–94.
Heft, James L., SM, Reuven Firestone, and Omid Safi, eds. *Learned Ignorance: Intellectual Humility among Jews, Christians, and Muslims*. Oxford: Oxford University Press, 2011.
Heyd, Michael. *"Be Sober and Reasonable": The Critique of Enthusiasm in the Seventeenth and Early Eighteenth Centuries*. Leiden: Brill, 1995.
High, Casey, Ann H. Kelley, and Jonathan Mair, eds. *The Anthropology of Ignorance: An Ethnographic Approach*. New York: Palgrave Macmillan, 2012.
Hiscock, Andrew. *Reading Memory in Early Modern Literature*. Cambridge: Cambridge University Press, 2011.
Hobart, Mark, ed. *An Anthropological Critique of Development. The Growth of Ignorance*, London: Routledge, 1993.
Holland, Nancy J. "'If I Know I Can Be Wrong': The Hidden History of Epistemologies of Ignorance." *Philosophy Today* 54, suppl. (2010): 122–127.
Holmes, Jamie. "The Case for Teaching Ignorance." *New York Times*, 24 August 2015.
Hovey, Kenneth Alan. "'Mountaigny Saith Prettily': Bacon's French and the *Essais*." *PMLA* 106 (1991): 71–82.

Hussey, Maurice. "Bunyan's 'Mr Ignorance' (1949)." In *Bunyan, The Pilgrim's Progress: A Casebook*, edited by Roger Sharrock, 128–138. London: Macmillan, 1976.

Hutchison, Ross. *Locke in France 1688–1734*. Oxford: Voltaire Foundation, 1991.

Ian-Parker, Kim. *The Biblical Politics of John Locke*. Waterloo, ON: Wilfrid Laurier University Press, 2004.

Iliffe, Rob. "Material Doubts: Hooke, Artisan Culture and the Exchange of Information in 1670s London." *British Journal for the History of Science* 28 (1995): 285–318.

Irving-Stonebraker, Sarah. "'The Sagacity of the Indians': William Dampier's Surprising Respect for Indigenous Knowledge." *Journal of Early Modern History* 21 (2017): 543–564.

Jacques-Lefèvre, Nicole, and Anne-Pascale Pouey-Mounou, eds. *Sottise et ineptie, de la Renaissance aux Lumières: Discours du savoir et représentations romanesques*, Nanterre: Presses de l'Université Paris X, 2004.

Jalobeanu, Dana. *The Art of Experimental Natural History: Francis Bacon in Context*, Bucharest: Zeta Books, 2015.

James, D. G. *The Life of Reason: Hobbes, Locke, Bolingbroke*. London: Longmans, Green & Co., 1949.

Jardine, Lisa. "*Experientia literata* ou *novum organum*? Le dilemme de la méthode scientifique de Bacon." In *Francis Bacon: Science et méthode: Actes du colloque de Nantes*, edited by Michel Malherbe and Jean-Marie Pousseur, 135–157. Paris: Vrin, 1985.

Jeanneret, Michel. "Éloge de l'ignorance." In *La Philologie humaniste et ses représentations dans la théorie et dans la fiction*, edited by Perrine Galand-Hallyn, Fernand Hallyn, and Gilbert Tournay, 2:637–651. Geneva: Droz, 2005.

Jolley, Nicholas. *Locke: His Philosophical Thought*. Oxford: Oxford University Press, 1999.

Jones, Richard Foster. *Ancients and Moderns: A Study of the Rise of the Scientific Movement in Seventeenth-Century England*. 1936; St. Louis: Washington University Studies, 1961.

———. "The Humanistic Defence of Learning in the Mid-Seventeenth Century." In *Reason and the Imagination: Studies in the History of Ideas 1600–1800*, edited by J. A. Mazzeo, 71–92. New York: Columbia University Press; London: Routledge & Kegan Paul, 1962.

Kambouchner, Denis. "Descartes et le problème de la culture." *Bulletin de la Société Française de Philosophie* (April–June 1998): 1–48.

Keeble, Neil H. *Richard Baxter: Puritan Man of Letters*. Oxford: Clarendon Press, 1982.

Kempers, Bram. "The Fame of Fake, Dionysius the Areopagite: Fabrication, Falsification and the 'Cloud of Unknowing.'" In *How the West Was Won: Essays on Literary Imagination, the Canon, and the Christian Middle Ages for Burcht Pranger*, edited by Willemien Otten, Arjo Vanderjagt, and Hent de Vries, 301–311. Leiden: Brill, 2010.

Kolesnik-Antoine, Delphine, ed. *Qu'est-ce qu'être cartésien?* Lyon: ENS Éditions, 2013.

Lake, Peter. "Anti-Popery: The Structure of a Prejudice." In *Conflict in Early Stuart England: Studies in Religion and Politics, 1603–1642*, edited by Richard Cust and Ann Hughes, 72–106. London: Longman, 1989.

Levine, David Lawrence. *Profound Ignorance: Plato's* Charmides *and the Saving of Wisdom*. New York: Lexington Books, 2016.

Lewalski, Barbara. "Milton on Learning and the Learned Minister Controversy." *Huntington Library Quarterly* 24 (1961): 267–281.
Lewis, Rhodri. "Francis Bacon and Ingenuity." *Renaissance Quarterly* 67 (2014): 113–163.
Long, Pamela. *Artisans/Practitioners and the Rise of the New Sciences, 1400–1600*. Corvallis: Oregon State University Press, 2011.
Lottin, Odon. "La nature du péché d'ignorance: Enquête chez les théologiens du XIIe et du XIIIe siècle." *Revue Thomiste: Questions du Temps Présent* 37 (1932): 634–652, 723–738.
Luxon, Thomas H. *Literal Figures: Puritan Allegory and the Reformation Crisis in Representation*. Chicago: University of Chicago Press, 1995.
Magnard, Pierre. "Une ignorance qui se sait." *Montaigne Studies* 21, nos. 1–2 (2009): 183–189.
Maia Neto, José R. *Academic Skepticism in Seventeenth-Century French Philosophy: The Charronian Legacy 1601–1662*. Heidelberg: Springer, 2014.
Manson, Neil C. "Epistemic Restraint and the Vice of Curiosity." *Philosophy* 87 (2012): 239–259.
Manzo, Silvia. "Reading Scepticism Historically: Scepticism, *Acatalepsia* and the Fall of Adam in Francis Bacon." In *Academic Scepticism in the Development of Early Modern Philosophy*, edited by Sébastien Charles and Plinio J. Smith. Cham, Switzerland: Springer, 2017, 81–102.
Martin, Andrew. *The Knowledge of Ignorance: From Genesis to Jules Verne*. Cambridge: Cambridge University Press, 1985.
McCanles, Michael. "The New Science and the *Via Negativa*: A Mystical Source for Baconian Empiricism." In *Francis Bacon and the Refiguring of Early Modern Thought*, edited by Julie Robin Solomon and Catherine Gimelli Martin, 45–68. Aldershot, UK: Ashgate, 2005.
McGoey, Linsey, ed. *An Introduction to the Sociology of Ignorance: Essays on the Limits of Knowing*. London: Routledge, 2014.
Merton, Robert K. "Three Fragments from a Sociologist's Notebooks: Establishing the Phenomenon, Specified Ignorance, and Strategic Research Materials." *Annual Review of Sociology* 13 (1987): 1–28.
Michaud, Derek. "Varieties of Spiritual Sense: Cusanus and John Smith." In *Platonism at the Origins of Modernity: Studies on Platonism and Early Modern Philosophy*, edited by Sarah Hutton and Douglas Hedley, 285–306. Dordrecht, Netherlands: Springer, 2008.
Miernowski, Jan. *Le Dieu néant: Théologies négatives à l'aube des temps modernes*. Leiden: Brill, 1998.
———. "Ignorance." In *Dictionnaire Montaigne*, edited by Philippe Desan, 911–915. Paris: Classiques Garnier, 2007.
———. "La littérature anti-scientifique à la Renaissance comme réflexion sur les limites d'une culture." *Nouvelle Revue du XVIe siècle* 14, no. 1 (1996): 91–100.
———. "Montaigne on Truth and Scepticism." In *The Oxford Handbook of Montaigne*, edited by Philippe Desan, 544–561. Oxford: Oxford University Press, 2016.
Moore, Wilbert E., and Melvin M. Tumin. "Some Social Functions of Ignorance." *American Sociological Review* 14, no. 6 (1949): 787–795.

Moran, Dermot. "Nicholas of Cusa (1401–1464): Platonism at the Dawn of Modernity." In *Platonism at the Origins of Modernity: Studies on Platonism and Early Modern Philosophy*, edited by Sarah Hutton and Douglas Hedley, 9–29. Dordrecht, Netherlands: Springer, 2008.

Moreau, Isabelle. *"Guérir du sot": Stratégies d'écriture des libertins à l'âge classique.* Paris: Champion, 2007.

Morgan, John. *Godly Learning: Puritan Attitudes towards Reason, Learning, and Education, 1560–1640.* Cambridge: Cambridge University Press, 1986.

Moriarty, Michael. "Montaigne and Descartes." In *The Oxford Handbook of Montaigne*, edited by Philippe Desan, 347–363. Oxford: Oxford University Press, 2016.

Morris, John. "Descartes' Natural Light." *Journal of the History of Philosophy* 11, no. 2 (1973): 169–187.

Muratori, Cecilia, and Gianni Paganini, eds. *Early Modern Philosophers and the Renaissance Legacy.* Dordrecht, Netherlands: Springer, 2016.

Nauert, Charles G. *Agrippa and the Crisis of Renaissance Thought.* Urbana: University of Illinois Press, 1965.

Naya, Emmanuel, and Anne-Pascale Pouey-Mounou, eds. *Éloges de la médiocrité: Le juste milieu à la Renaissance.* Paris: Éditions de la Rue d'Ulm, 2005.

Newey, Vincent. "Bunyan and the Confines of the Mind." In The Pilgrim's Progress*: Critical and Historical Views*, edited by Vincent Newey, 21–48. Liverpool: Liverpool University Press, 1980.

———. "'With the Eyes of My Understanding': Bunyan, Experience, and Acts of Interpretation." In *John Bunyan: Conventicle and Parnassus, Tercentenary Essays*, edited by Neil H. Keeble, 189–216. Oxford: Clarendon Press, 1988.

Nuovo, Victor. *John Locke: The Philosopher as Christian Virtuoso.* Oxford: Oxford University Press, 2017.

O'Brien, John. "Montaigne, Sir Ralph Bankes and Other English Readers of the *Essais*." *Renaissance Studies* 28, no. 3 (2014): 377–391.

Oosterhoff, Richard J. "Cusanus and Boethian Theology in the Early French Reform." In *Nicholas of Cusa and the Making of the Early Modern World*, edited by Simon J. G. Burton, Joshua Hollmann, and Eric M. Parker, 339–366. Leiden: Brill, 2018.

———. "*Idiotae*, Mathematics, and Artisans: The Untutored Mind and the Discovery of Nature in the Fabrist Circle." *Intellectual History Review* 24, no. 3 (2014): 301–319.

Ophir, Adi, and Steven Shapin. "The Place of Knowledge: A Methodological Survey." *Science in Context* 4 (1991): 3–21.

Ordine, Nuccio. *Le Mystère de l'âne: Essai sur Giordano Bruno* (1987). Translated by F. Liffran and P. Bardoux. Preface by Eugenio Garin. Paris: Les Belles Lettres, 2005.

Oster, Malcolm. "The Scholar and the Craftsman Revisited: Robert Boyle as Aristocrat and Artisan." *Annals of Science* 49 (1992): 255–276.

Paganini, Gianni. *Skepsis: Le débat des Modernes sur le scepticisme. Montaigne—Le Vayer—Campanella—Hobbes—Descartes—Bayle.* Paris: Vrin, 2008.

———. "Socrate, Montaigne, Descartes: Sur l'utilisation de l'ignorance socratique dans les *Essais* et dans les *Regulae*." *Montaigne Studies* 21, nos. 1–2 (2009): 169–182.

Parageau, Sandrine. "Autodidacticism and the Construction of Scientific Discourse in Early Modern England: Margaret Cavendish's and Anne Conway's 'Intellectual Bricolage.'" In *Women and Science, 17th Century to Present: Pioneers, Activists and Protagonists*, edited by D. Spalding Andréolle and V. Molinari, 3–18. Newcastle, UK: Cambridge Scholars Publishing, 2011.

———. "'Colomb ignorant trouva le nouveau monde': Ignorance, découverte fortuite et expérimentation à la première modernité." *Revue d'Histoire des Sciences* 74, no. 1 (2021): 41–62.

———. "'Papists Make a Direct Profession of This Shamefull Sin': Denouncing Catholic Ignorance in Seventeenth-Century England." In *Anti-Catholicism in Britain and Ireland, 1600–2000: Practices, Representations and Ideas*, edited by C. Gheeraert-Graffeuille and G. Vaughan, 93–108. London: Palgrave Macmillan, 2020.

———. "Pour une histoire intellectuelle de l'ignorance: Représentations, usages et valeurs de l'ignorance à la période moderne, XVIe–XVIIIe siècles." *Revue d'Anthropologie des Connaissances* 15, no. 4 (2021): https://journals.openedition.org/rac/23570.

———. *Les Ruses de l'ignorance: La contribution des femmes à l'avènement de la science moderne en Angleterre*. Paris: Presses de la Sorbonne Nouvelle, 2010.

Parker, Eric M. "'The Sacred Circle of All-Being': Cusanus, Lord Brooke, and Peter Sterry." In *Nicholas of Cusa and the Making of the Early Modern World*, edited by Simon J. G. Burton, Joshua Hollmann, and Eric M. Parker, 257–284. Leiden: Brill, 2018.

Peels, Rik, ed. *Perspectives on Ignorance from Moral and Social Philosophy*. New York: Routledge, 2017.

Peels, Rik, and Martijn Blaauw, eds. *The Epistemic Dimensions of Ignorance*. Cambridge: Cambridge University Press, 2016.

Peterschmitt, Luc. "Bacon et le cercle de l'expérience." *Archives de Philosophie* 84, no. 1 (2021): 33–49.

Picciotto, Joanna. *Labors of Innocence in Early Modern England*. Cambridge, MA: Harvard University Press, 2010.

Pinker, Steven. *The Blank Slate: The Modern Denial of Human Nature*. London: Penguin, 2002.

Pintard, René. *Le Libertinage érudit dans la première moitié du XVIIe siècle*. 2 vols. Paris: Boivin, 1943.

Popkin, Richard H. "Charron and Descartes: The Fruits of Systematic Doubt." *Journal of Philosophy* 51, no. 25 (1954): 831–837.

———. *The History of Scepticism from Savonarola to Bayle*. Oxford: Oxford University Press, 2003.

———. *The Third Force in Seventeenth-Century Thought*. Leiden: Brill, 1992.

Popper, Karl. *On the Sources of Knowledge and of Ignorance*. Oxford: Oxford University Press, 1961.

Priselac, Matthew. *Locke's Science of Knowledge*. New York: Routledge, 2017.

Proctor, Robert N., and Londa Schiebinger, eds. *Agnotology: The Making and Unmaking of Ignorance*. Stanford, CA: Stanford University Press, 2008.

Ravetz, Jerome R. "The Sin of Science: Ignorance of Ignorance." *Science Communication* 15, no. 2 (1993): 157–165.
Renz, Ursula. *Self-Knowledge: A History.* Oxford: Oxford University Press, 2017.
Rescher, Nicholas. *Ignorance: On the Wider Implications of Deficient Knowledge.* Pittsburgh, PA: University of Pittsburgh Press, 2009.
Ribard, Dinah. *Raconter, vivre, penser: Histoires de philosophes, 1650–1765.* Paris: Vrin-EHESS, 2003.
Rickless, Samuel C. "Locke's Polemic against Nativism." In *The Cambridge Companion to Locke's Essay Concerning Human Understanding*, edited by Lex Newman, 33–66. Cambridge: Cambridge University Press, 2007.
Rigolot, François. *L'Erreur de la Renaissance: Perspectives littéraires.* Paris: Champion, 2002.
Robinet, André. *Descartes, la lumière naturelle: Intuition, disposition, complexion.* Paris: Vrin, 1999.
Rogers, G. A. J. "Locke and the Latitude-Men: Ignorance as a Ground of Toleration." In *Philosophy, Science, and Religion in England, 1640–1700*, edited by Richard Kroll, Richard Ashcraft, and Perez Zagorin, 230–252. Cambridge: Cambridge University Press, 1992.
———. *Locke's Enlightenment: Aspects of the Origin, Nature, and Impact of His Philosophy.* Hildesheim, Germany: Georg Olms Verlag, 1998.
Rosellini, Michèle. "*La Science universelle* de Charles Sorel, monument polygraphique ou 'Vraie philosophie'?" *Littératures classiques* 49 (2003): 157–179.
Rosenfeld, Sophia. *Common Sense: A Political History.* Cambridge, MA: Harvard University Press, 2011.
Russell, Gul A. "The Impact of the *Philosophus autodidactus*: Pocockes, John Locke, and The Society of Friends." In *The "Arabick" Interest of the New Philosophers in Seventeenth-Century England*, 224–265. Leiden: Brill, 1994.
Schmidt-Biggeman, Wilhelm. "Robert Fludd's Kabbalistic Cosmos." In *Platonism at the Origins of Modernity: Studies on Platonism and Early Modern Philosophy*, edited by Sarah Hutton and Douglas Hedley, 75–92. Dordrecht, Netherlands: Springer, 2008.
Schmitt, Charles. *Cicero skepticus: A Study of the Influence of* The Academica *in the Renaissance.* The Hague: Martinus Nijhoff, 1972.
Scholar, Richard. *Montaigne and the Art of Free-Thinking.* Oxford: Peter Lang, 2010.
Schøsler, Jørn. *John Locke et les philosophes français: La critique des idées innées en France au dix-huitième siècle.* Oxford: Voltaire Foundation, 1997.
Schuurman, Paul. "Locke's Modest Impact on Eighteenth-Century Natural Science: The Encyclopedic Evidence." *Eighteenth-Century Thought* 3 (2007): 189–206.
———. "'Thou Knowest Not the Works of God': Gisbertius Voetius (1589–1676) and John Locke on Learned Ignorance." *Westminster Theological Journal* 72, no. 1 (2010): 59–69.
Scott Parrish, Susan. *American Curiosity: Cultures of Natural History in the Colonial British Atlantic World.* Chapel Hill: University of North Carolina Press, 2006.
Shapin, Steven. "The Man of Science." In *The Cambridge History of Science*, edited by Lor-

raine Daston and Katherine Park, 179–191. Cambridge: Cambridge University Press, 2006.
———. *The Scientific Revolution.* Chicago: University of Chicago Press, 1996.
———. *A Social History of Truth: Civility and Science in Seventeenth-Century England.* Chicago: University of Chicago Press, 1994.
Silver, Sean. "The Prehistory of Serendipity, from Bacon to Walpole." *Isis* 106, no. 2 (2015): 235–256.
Smith, Nigel. *Perfection Proclaimed: Language and Literature in English Radical Religion, 1640–1660.* Oxford: Clarendon Press, 1989.
Smith, Pamela H. *The Body of the Artisan: Art and Experience in the Scientific Revolution.* Chicago: University of Chicago Press, 2004.
Smithson, Michael. "Ignorance and Science: Dilemmas, Perspectives, and Prospects." *Science Communication* 15, no. 2 (1993): 133–156.
———. *Ignorance and Uncertainty: Emerging Paradigms.* Dordrecht, Netherlands: Springer, 1989.
———. "Toward a Social Theory of Ignorance." *Journal for the Theory of Social Behaviour* 15, no. 2 (1985): 151–172.
Sng, Zachary. *The Rhetoric of Error from Locke to Kleist.* Stanford, CA: Stanford University Press, 2010.
Spellman, William M. *John Locke and the Problem of Depravity.* Oxford: Clarendon Press, 1988.
Stachniewski, John. *The Persecutory Imagination: English Puritanism and the Literature of Religious Despair.* Oxford: Clarendon Press, 1991.
Stuart-Buttle, Tim. *From Moral Theology to Moral Philosophy: Cicero and Visions of Humanity from Locke to Hume.* Oxford: Oxford University Press, 2019.
Suzuki, Akihito. "Dualism and the Transformation of Psychiatric Language in the Seventeenth and Eighteenth Centuries." *History of Psychiatry* 33 (1995): 417–447.
Sytsma, David. *Richard Baxter and the Mechanical Philosophers.* Oxford: Oxford University Press, 2017.
Talon, Henri A. *John Bunyan: The Man and His Works.* Translated by Barbara Wall. London: Rockliff, 1951.
Tuana, Nancy, and Shannon Sullivan, eds. "Feminist Epistemologies of Ignorance." Special issue, *Hypatia* 21, no. 3 (2006).
———. *Race and Epistemologies of Ignorance.* Albany, NY: SUNY Press, 2007.
Turner, Denys. *The Darkness of God: Negativity in Christian Mysticism.* Cambridge: Cambridge University Press, 1995.
Unger, Peter. *Ignorance: A Case for Scepticism.* Oxford: Oxford University Press, 2002.
Van Berkel, Klaas. "Intellectuals against Leeuwenhoek. Controversies about the Methods and Style of a Self-Taught Scientist." In *Antoni van Leeuwenhoek 1632–1723*, edited by L. C. Palm and H. A. M. Snelders, 187–209. Amsterdam: Rodopi, 1982.
Van der Poel, Marc. *Cornelius Agrippa: The Humanist Theologian and His Declamations.* Leiden: Brill, 1997.
Vanier, Alain. "Passion de l'ignorance." *Cliniques Méditerranéennes* 70, no. 2 (2004): 59–66.

Verbeek, Theo. "From 'Learned Ignorance' to Scepticism: Descartes and Calvinist Orthodoxy." In *Scepticism and Irreligion in the Seventeenth and Eighteenth Centuries*, edited by Richard H. Popkin and Arjo Vanderjagt, 31–45. Leiden: Brill, 1993.

Verburgt, Lukas M. "The History of Knowledge and the Future History of Ignorance." *KNOW: A Journal on the Formation of Knowledge* 4, no. 1 (2020): 1–24. https://doi.org/10.1086/708341.

Verburgt, Lukas M., and Peter Burke, eds. "Histories of Ignorance." Special issue, *Journal for the History of Knowledge* 2, no. 1 (November 2021). https://journalhistoryknowledge.org/collections/special/histories-of-ignorance.

Villey, Pierre. "Montaigne et François Bacon." *Revue de la Renaissance* 11 (July–September 1911).

Vitebsky, Piers. "Is Death the Same Everywhere? Contexts of Knowing and Doubting." In *An Anthropological Critique of Development: The Growth of Ignorance*, edited by Mark Hobart, 100–115. London: Routledge, 1993.

Vitek, Bill, and Wes Jackson, eds. *The Virtues of Ignorance: Complexity, Sustainability, and the Limits of Knowledge*. Lexington: University Press of Kentucky, 2008.

Walton, Douglas. *Arguments from Ignorance*. University Park: Pennsylvania State University Press, 1996.

———. "Nonfallacious Arguments from Ignorance." *American Philosophical Quarterly* 29, no. 4 (1992): 381–387.

Weeks, Sophie. "The Role of Mechanics in Francis Bacon's Great Instauration." In *Philosophies of Technology: Francis Bacon and His Contemporaries*, edited by Gisela Engel, Claus Zittel, Romano Nani, and Nicole C. Karafilys, 131–195. Leiden: Brill, 2008.

Witmore, Michael. *Culture of Accidents: Unexpected Knowledges in Early Modern England*. Stanford, CA: Stanford University Press, 2001.

Woods, Chance. "Henry More (1614–1687) as Intellectual Heir to Nicholas of Cusa (1401–1464)." *American Cusanus Society Newsletter* 35 (December 2018): 14–23.

Yolton, John W. *Locke and French Materialism*. Oxford: Clarendon Press, 1991.

———. *Locke and the Compass of Human Understanding*. Cambridge: Cambridge University Press, 1970.

Zwierlein, Cornel. *Imperial Unknowns: The French and British in the Mediterranean, 1650–1750*. Cambridge: Cambridge University Press, 2016.

Zwierlein, Cornel, ed. *The Dark Side of Knowledge: Histories of Ignorance, 1400–1800*. Leiden: Brill, 2016.

Index

Adam, 15, 17, 56, 69, 130–31, 139, 146, 162–63, 218n8. *See also* the Fall; sin
Admiranda methodus (Schoock), 84
The Advancement of Learning (Bacon), 30, 49–53, 56, 106, 162, 164, 186nn4–5, 187n15
"Against confidence in philosophy, and matters of speculation" (Glanvill), 62
Agrippa, Henry Cornelius, 11, 14–17, 53–55, 83, 98, 119, 162–63, 173n45, 174n57, 175n59, 175n65. *See also De incertitudine* (Agrippa)
Albanzani, Donato, 7
Alciato, Andrea, 12, *13*
"An necesse sit dari in Ecclesia infallibilem Sacro Sanctae Scripturae interpretem? Negatur" (Locke), 152
anthropology, 23, 27, 146–50, 153, 156–58, 162, 165
The Anthropology of Ignorance (High, Kelly and Mair), 23
antischolasticism, 4–5, 10, 18–21, 55, 72–73, 124, 127–29, 198n1. *See also* discourse against letters; epistemic restraint; learned ignorance; scholasticism

The Apology of Socrates, 6
apophaticism. *See* negative theology
the apostles, 16, 26, 55–59, 101, 188n32. *See also* the Bible; Jesus Christ
Aquinas, Thomas, 68, 172n34
Arbib, Dan, 37
Arguments from Ignorance (Walton), 151
argumentum ad ignorantiam, 150–53
Aristotelianism, 7–8, 83
Aristotle, 7–8, 15, 32, 45, 51, 68, 92, 121
The Arraignment of Ignorance (Gearing), 3, 47
The Arrogancy of Reason against Divine Revelations Repressed (Baxter), 95, 200n24
artisans, 27, 30, 107, 116, 126, 129–38, 160, 162, 169n3, 211nn25–26. *See also* illiterateness; simplicity
Ashwell, George, 121
asininity, 17, 176n70
The Asses Complaint against Balaam (Griffin), 108
atheism, 49–50, 195n60
Augustine, 5, 7–8, 43, 47, 60, 66, 68, 146, 191n2

244 *Index*

autodidacticism, 27, 39, 116–17, 121–24, 136, 142, 147, 157, 161. *See also* knowledge; method; the naked mind; tabula rasa

Bacon, Francis: and Agrippa, 53–54; on discovery, 140–44, 213n47, 213n51, 213n53, 214n56; and the Jesuits, 51–52, 102; and learning, 49–56, 106; and Montaigne, 53–54; and Palissy, 39; rejection of ignorance by, 26, 30, 48–49, 56–57, 93, 160, 162, 164; and sagacity, 132, 142; and the scientific discourse, 132; as skeptic, 5, 54–55. *See also The Advancement of Learning* (Bacon); discovery (by chance); *Essays* (Bacon); *Novum Organum* (Bacon)
Baillet, Adrien, 88
Balaam, 16–17
Banchieri, Adriano, 17–18
Baptists, 3, 20, 100–101
barbarism, 84, 104–5
Bartoli, Daniello, 188n32
Baudoin, Jean, 174n54
Baxter, Richard, 46, 63, 84, 93–99, 109–10, 112, 158, 165, 199n14, 199n19. *See also The Arrogancy of Reason against Divine Revelations Repressed* (Baxter); *Treatise of Knowledge and Love Compared* (Baxter)
Ben-Zaken, Avner, 122
Bertucci, Paola, 137–38
"*Be Sober and Reasonable*" (Heyd), 194n37
the Bible, 16–17, 56–57, 68, 81–82, 107–8. *See also* the Fall; God; Jesus Christ; specific books of the bible
Blaauw, Martijn, 22–23
Blum, Paul Richard, 43, 207n32
The Body of the Artisan (Smith), 211n26
Book of Emblems (Alciato). *See Emblematum liber* (Alciato)
books, 4, 39, 97

Boyle, Robert, 18, 58–59, 120–21, 134, 137–38, 156, 176n80, 211n22, 211n28, 211n30
Brant, Sebastian, 129
Browne, Thomas, 198n1
Bruno, Giordano, 16–18, 176n70
Bunyan, John, 26, 70, 108–12, 204n102, 205n104
Burgess, Anthony, 45
Burke, Peter, 24–25, 179n102

Cabala del cavallo pegaseo (Bruno), 16–17
Calvin, John, 43–44, 47, 146, 158, 163, 184n67
Cambridge Platonists, 43, 160, 163, 183n63, 216n39
Cartesianism, 2, 20, 36, 63, 78–94, 106, 119, 121, 152, 194n37. *See also* Quakers
Casaubon, Meric, 79–81, 86–88, 105, 172n34, 195n46, 195n48, 196n73, 196n75, 202n69
Cassirer, Ernst, 43
Casson, Douglas John, 156–57
certainty, 32, 45, 82, 98. *See also* doubt; infallibility; madness
Certeau, Michel de, 124, 207n23, 207n40
charlatanism, 43, 45, 152
Charmides (Socrates), 6–7
Charron, Pierre, 29–31, 35–37, 42, 45–46, 63, 130, 163–65. *See also Of Wisdom* (Charron)
Cholmley, Hugh, 201n41
Christ. *See* Jesus Christ
The Christian Virtuoso (Boyle), 58–59, 120–21, 138
Church of England, 3, 66, 69, 74, 100, 103–6. *See also* the Reformation
Cicero, 5, 7, 150, 171n19, 215n20
The Cloud of Unknowing (anonymous), 6, 9, 35, 160
Colie, Rosalie L., 173n45
Collier, Thomas, 101–2, 201n53, 201n55
Columbus, Christopher, 133–34

common sense, 34, 36–37, 41, 76, 180n14. *See also* reason; simplicity
Conduct of the Understanding (Locke), 154–55, 217n51, 217n55
conscience, 74, 153, 191n2
Copenhaver, Brian, 209n2
Corbin, Alain, 24
I Corinthians (book of the bible), 10, 57, 99, 101, 200n39
Corréard, Nicolas, 173n43, 173n45
The Court of the Gentiles (Gale), 139
craftsmen. *See* artisans
credulity, 3, 45, 64, 87–88
curiosity, 37, 42–45, 47, 51, 57–58, 75, 92, 106, 130. *See also* epistemic restraint
Cusanus: criticisms of, 83; and Descartes, 36–37, 116, 127–30; and ignorance as wisdom, 29; and infinite diversity, 32, 179n2; as influence, 42–43, 45, 59–60, 65–66, 102, 152, 162, 181nn29, 189n46; and learned ignorance, 8–11, 31, 64–66, 151, 189n46; and Montaigne, 31–32, 179n2; and skepticism, 6. *See also De docta ignorantia* (Cusanus); *De idiota* (Cusanus); *The Search for Truth by Means of the Natural Light* (Descartes)

Dampier, William, 211n30
darkness, 67, 73–74, 87. *See also* internal light
The Dark Side of Knowledge (Zwierlein), 21, 24, 177n86, 178n99
De abusu philosophiae cartesianae in rebus theologicis et fidei (Maresius), 197n80
De anima (Aristotle), 68
Dédéyan, Charles, 166
De dignitate et augmentis scientiarum (Bacon), 53, 142–43
De docta ignorantia (Cusanus), 6–10, 25–26, 30–31, 35, 64–66, 160, 171n27
De docta ignorantia (Voetius), 44
Dee, John, 127

De idiota (Cusanus), 10, 36, 43, 116, 125–30, 162, 175n65, 208n47. *See also* the Idiot; *The Search for Truth by Means of the Natural Light* (Descartes)
De incertitudine (Agrippa), 14–17, 32, 53, 56, 63, 98, 119, 175n59
De la perfection de l'homme (Sorel), 38, 91, 165, 198nn2–3, 198nn5–6, 199n10
Deleuze, Gilles, 124–25
democratization of learning, 102
De Mystica theologia (Areopagite), 79–80
Denys the Areopagite, 9–10, 74, 79–80, 172n34
De occulta philosophia libri tres (Agrippa), 53
Descartes, René: criticisms of, 83–84, 86–89, 91, 93–94, 195n60, 196n63; and Cusanus, 181nn29; and foundationalism, 151; and Glanvill, 189n63; and ignorance as wisdom, 29–31, 36–37, 62, 65, 80–81, 127; and the illiterate inventor, 27, 133–34; and the inner light, 26, 37, 75–78, 83, 193nn25–26, 194n35; and Locke, 83; and Montaigne, 37–38; the philosophy of, 68, 86; and reason, 60–61; and sagacity, 132, 141–42; and Sanches, 83–84. *See also Dioptrics* (Descartes); *Discourse on Method* (Descartes); the illiterate inventor; method; radical doubt; *Rules for the Direction of the Mind* (Descartes); *The Search for Truth by Means of the Natural Light* (Descartes)
"Descartes et le problème de la culture" (Kambouchner), 86
Des principes de l'architecture (Félibien), 137–38
De sui ipsius et multorum ignorantia (Petrarch), 7
d'Étaples, Jacques Lefèvre, 31–32, 65, 126
De visione Dei (Cusanus), 43

246   Index

Dictionnaire universel (Furetière), 38
Diogenes Laertius, 5
Dioptrics (Descartes), 75, 133–34. *See also* *Discourse on Method* (Descartes)
Dirt Wip't Off (anonymous), 111
discourse against letters, 10–12, 14–15, 48–49, 53–55, 60, 65, 108, 162. *See also* antischolasticism
Discourse on Method (Descartes), 37, 75–76, 78, 83, 86, 116, 119, 193nn24–26. *See also Dioptrics* (Descartes)
discovery (by chance), 2, 116–17, 132–36, 138–44, 157. *See also* artisans; Bacon, Francis; Descartes, René; Métius, Jacques; sagacity
docta ignorantia. *See* learned ignorance
The Doctrine of the Asse (Griffin), 107–8
dogmatism, 8, 18, 33, 40–42, 46–48, 59–60, 63–64, 102, 152, 177n85
doubt, 5, 9, 22, 38, 51–52, 55, 65, 75, 94–95, 111, 127–28, 163, 178n97. *See also* certainty; radical doubt; skepticism
Draper, John, 111
"Dualism and the Transformation of Psychiatric Language in the Seventeenth and Eighteenth Centuries" (Suzuki), 197n81
Dudiak, Jeffrey, 74
Dunan-Page, Anne, 110, 204n102

Early Modern Philosophers and the Renaissance Legacy (Muratori and Paganini), 176n82
Ecclesiastes (book of the bible), 10, 41, 149–50
education, 3, 20, 23, 38, 50, 52, 61–62, 82–83, 96, 102, 131, 153–55, 199n14. *See also* illiterateness
Emblematum liber (Alciato), 12, *13*
empiricism, 2, 34, 39, 122–23, 143, 146, 157, 177n86, 190n81, 214n57
Encyclopaedia Britannica (1771), 166

Encyclopédie (Diderot and d'Alembert), 165–66
enthusiasm, 26, 67–69, 78–89, 100, 103, 106–7, 194n37. *See also* madness; melancholy
Enthusiasmus triumphatus (More), 81
The Epistemic Dimensions of Ignorance (Peels and Blaauw), 22–23
epistemic restraint, 26, 30, 43–47, 57, 59, 149. *See also* antischolasticism; curiosity; learned ignorance
Epistle to All People on the Earth (Fox), 73
Erasmus, 11, 32, 55, 175n65
error, 61–62, 68, 73, 76, 89, 104–5, 155, 177n87, 199n18
Esclapez, Raymond, 179n2
Essay concerning Human Understanding (Locke): arguments of, 216n26, 216n43; on *argumentum ad ignorantiam*, 151; on artisans, 2, 134–35; on causes of ignorance, 147–48; on the extent of ignorance, 96, 146–47; on the idiot, 124; and innate principles, 123, 156; on knowledge and ignorance, 27, 46–47, 96, 148–50, 154, 214n5, 215n17; on madness, 198n84; on the tabula rasa, 120; and Voltaire, 167
Essays (Bacon), 53
Essays (Montaigne), 31–37, 156–57, 164, 169n3, 187n20, 211n29, 217n62, 219n21; "Apology of Raymond Sebond," 32, 34–35, 37, 53, 169n3; "Of Cannibals," 32, 37; "Of Customs," 37; "Of the lame or Cripple," 92
Essays on the Law of Nature (Locke), 120
Estienne, Charles, 11
Estienne, Henri, 5
Eva, Luiz, 54
Everard, John, 43, 102, 207n32
The Excellency of Theology (Boyle), 137
Exotericarum exercitationum (Scaliger), 45
experimentalism, 18–19, 24–26, 39, 48,

56–59, 64, 116, 122, 126–27, 130–48, 162–63, 191n2
An Explanation of the Grand Mystery of Godliness (More), 81–82

faith, 7, 15, 35, 57, 72
the Fall, 3, 15, 20–21, 49, 55–56, 60, 130–31, 146, 162, 191n2. *See also* Adam; sin
The Fall of Man and the Foundations of Science (Harrison), 19, 177n83
Félibien, André, 137–38
Ferriby, John, 201n55
Firestein, Stuart, 22
Flamsteed, John, 210n10
Florio, John, 187n20, 217n62
Fludd, Robert, 43
foolishness, 16–17, 21, 56–57, 61, 80, 84, 99–103, 112, 129, 133, 174n46, 200n39
Forrest, James, 111
foundationalism, 151–52
Fox, George, 73–74, 192n8, 192n10, 192n12
Franke, William, 9, 172n34
A Free Inquiry into the Vulgarly Receiv'd Notion of Nature Made in an Essay (Boyle), 176n80
Furetière, Antoine, 38

Gale, Theophilus, 139
Gauden, John, 84–85, 103–7, 112, 188n32, 202n58, 202nn62–63, 202nn66–68. *See also Hieraspistes* (Gauden)
Gaukroger, Stephen, 208n53
Gearing, William, 3, 47, 107, 170n5
the gentleman philosopher, 38
Giglioni, Guido, 214n57
Gilson, Étienne, 37
Girel, Mathias, 178n97
Glanvill, Joseph, 26, 30, 57–66, 98, 130–31, 158–65, 188n41, 190n67, 190n81. *See also Scepsis Scientifica* (Glanvill); *The Vanity of Dogmatizing* (Glanvill)
God: as beyond knowing, 8–11, 32, 66; and epistemic restraint, 44–47; and the internal light, 69, 76, 78, 82, 85, 106, 124–25; as knowable, 35, 82; and knowledge, 49–50, 55–59, 98–102, 106, 109, 112; and sagacity, 139; Spirit of, 100–102. *See also* Jesus Christ
Granada, Miguel Ángel, 54–55
Griffin, Lewis, 107–8
Guattari, Félix, 124–25

Haffemayer, Stéphane, 49
Hall, Thomas, 101
Hamblin, Charles, 151
Hamou, Philippe, 136, 190n81, 210n11
Hardin, Richard, 111, 205n104
Harrison, Peter, 19, 177n83
the Hartlib circle, 49
Hayes, Thomas Wilson, 102
Hayy Ibn-Yaqzan (Ibn-Tufayl), 121–23
Heyd, Michael, 194n37
Hieraspistes (Gauden), 103–7, 188n32, 203n78
High, Casey, 23
Hiscock, Andrew, 187n16
Hobbes, Thomas, 139, 142
Holmes, Jamie, 22
honesty, 18, 33–34, 58, 122, 134, 136, 208n53. *See also* modesty; simplicity
honnête homme, 7, 38, 42, 129
Hooke, Robert, 135–36, 210n11, 210n13, 210nn9–10
Hosea (book of the Bible), 4, 96, 103, 199n22
Hovey, Kenneth Alan, 53–54
How, Samuel, 100–102, 105, 201n43, 201n47
humanism, 10–11, 24, 160
Human Nature (Hobbes), 139
An Humble Apologie for Learning and Learned Men (Waterhouse), 203n71
humility, 15–18, 21, 25, 30–31, 45, 94–99,

124–25, 147, 160. *See also* knowledge; modesty; simplicity
Hypotyposes (Sextus Empiricus), 5

Ibn-Tufayl, Abu Bakr, 121–23, 206n11
Iconologia (Ripa), 12, 14, 174n54
the Idiot, 8, 16, 27, 36, 56, 102, 116, 124–30, 157, 171n18, 206n21, 207n40. *See also De idiota* (Cusanus); foolishness; *The Search for Truth by Means of the Natural Light* (Descartes)
ignorance: absolute, 32, 35, 80, 108, 112; and agnotology, 23; and the ass (as an allegory), 12, *14*, 16–18, 56, 104, 107–8, 173n45, 174n54, 175n65, 176n70; as a bat, 12; definitions of, 112; disguised, 26, 49, 51; as a fish, 12; history of, 23–25, 164 (*See also* scholarship); ignorance of, 94–97, 110–12; medieval doctrines of, 6, 8, 11, 19, 30; mongrel, 33–34, 107, 186n5; natural, 33–34, 41–42, 61; quiet, 46, 149; rehabilitation of, 4, 6, 19–20, 150, 161; Renaissance doctrines of, 5–6, 19, 24, 29–30; as a rich man, 12; and *sacra ignorantia*, 10; secularization of, 20–21, 24, 127, 162; Socratic, 6–9, 18, 29; specified, 178n96; as sphinx, 12, *13*; studies, 22–24; synonyms of, 21; vulgar, 1–2, 15, 40, 56–57, 62; as a woman, 11–12, 26, 71–73, 100, 181n26, 201n40. *See also* asininity; autodidacticism; discourse against letters; enthusiasm; the Idiot; innocence; internal light; learned ignorance; the senses (deception of)
the illiterate inventor, 2, 27, 116–17, 132–42, 169n2
illiterateness, 117, 122, 129, 133–34, 138–44, 203n83, 211n25. *See also* artisans; education
imagination, 34, 41, 51, 61, 81, 106
infallibility, 152–53
ingenuity, 134, 139, 209n6

innate principles (innatism), 76–77, 88, 119–23, 128, 152–53, 156, 166–67, 205nn5–6. *See also* autodidacticism; Descartes, René; *Essay concerning Human Understanding* (Locke); tabula rasa
innocence, 21, 24, 58–59, 96, 110, 130–31
inspiration (ignorance as), 13, 20, 26, 67–70, 73, 78–81, 88–89, 95, 102–12
The Institution of Christian Religion (Calvin), 43–44, 184n67
integrity, 58, 162, 188n41
internal light: as Christ, 72–74, 78, 81; criticisms of the, 103, 112, 152; as enthusiasm, 69, 79, 85; as a guide, 74; and ignorance, 26, 66–69, 79, 161; as knowledge, 68; and learning, 68; and Locke, 191n2; natural, 36–37, 68–69, 74–78, 85, 99–100; other forms of, 191n2; and religious sects, 3, 26, 66, 68, 72–74, 78, 81–82, 89; and the uneducated, 37. *See also* darkness; *lumière naturelle*
intuition, 77, 142, 194n35
irony, 18, 21–22, 38, 51. *See also* satire
Irving-Stonebraker, Sarah, 211n30

Jeanneret, Michel, 11, 159–60
Jesuits, 51–52, 80, 87
Jesus Christ, 55–59, 71–74, 81, 99–100. *See also* the apostles; God; internal light; Quakers
Job (book of the bible), 8
John (book of the bible), 72, 192n8
Journal de voyage (Montaigne), 31
Journal for the History of Knowledge (edited by Verburgt and Burke), 24–25

Kambouchner, Denis, 86
Keeble, Neil H., 199n19
Keith, George, 71–73, 99, 121, 207n27
Kelly, Ann, 23
Kiernan, Michael, 186n2

King, Peter, 215n14, 217n52, 217n62
knowledge: an excess of, 86; cultural, 155; in defense of, 52, 103–4; denunciations of, 15, 35–36, 81; external, 35, 41, 68–69, 77, 82, 101, 127; ignorance as a path to, 18, 20, 23–25, 36, 41, 47, 52–53, 59–60, 67, 84, 91–94, 115, 122, 147–50, 160–61; inequality of, 41; limits of human, 19, 22, 43–44, 47, 52, 199n22; and love, 98–99, 129; and the naked mind, 115, 119–23; natural, 49, 55, 57, 84, 112, 116–17, 161, 164; of nature, 139; and perfection, 91; practical, 136–37; pretended, 94–99, 110–11, 129; reasons for, 51; religious, 67, 72, 94–95, 103–7; scholastic theory of, 68; the search for, 40–41, 57–58, 148–50, 154–57; self, 6–9, 25, 33–36, 39–40, 61–62, 122, 125, 129, 148–49, 160, 162; theoretical, 136–37; theories of, 55, 77, 85, 93–94, 97–98, 105–7; as uncertain, 60–63, 76, 97–98, 148, 150; and wisdom, 35. *See also* autodidacticism; dogmatism; epistemic restraint; humility; the senses (deception of); simplicity; truth; vanity; wisdom

Labors of Innocence in Early Modern England (Picciotto), 24, 130–31
Lafleur, Laurence, 212nn44–45
"La littérature anti-scientifique à la Renaissance" (Miernowski), 206n21
La Mothe Le Vayer, François de, 18, 40, 122, 182n51, 206n15
La Mutation du visible (Hamou), 210n11
Landi, Giulio, 92
Lando, Ortensio, 11, 173n45
La Science universelle (Sorel), 22, 182n39
latitudinarians, 216n39
La Vérité des sciences (Mersenne), 41, 133, 182n39, 209n2
laziness, 42, 82–83, 103, 106, 155
learned ignorance: as an insult, 43; and Aristotelian philosophy, 7, 92; and Augustine, 8; and Bacon, 142–44; and Calvin, 43–44; and Charron, 45–46, 65; and Cusanus, 8–11, 31, 42, 44, 59, 64–65, 151, 189n46; and Descartes, 36, 40, 42, 65, 160; distrust of, 38, 40, 116; and the gentleman philosopher, 38; and Glanvill, 60–66, 163; interpretations of, 42, 65; and the limits of religious knowledge, 43–45; and Locke, 46, 185n85, 190n81; and Mersenne, 40–41; and Montaigne, 33, 40, 42, 65; as natural ignorance, 34; and scholasticism, 30; and science, 93; and truth, 69. *See also* epistemic restraint

The Learned Man Defended and Reformed (Bartoli), 188n32
learned ministry, 26, 69, 99–108, 199n22, 201n55
Le Contr'empire des sciences, et le Mystere des asnes (Perrot de la Salle), 17
Le philosophe ignorant (Voltaire), 166–67
Les Questions theologiques, physiques, morales et mathematiques (Mersenne), 183n53
Letter and Discourse to Sir Henry Savill Touching Helps for the Intellectual Powers (Bacon), 53
Letter on Toleration (Locke), 152–53
Letters concerning the English Nation (Voltaire), 166, 197n80
Leviathan (Hobbes), 139
Lewalski, Barbara, 199n14, 203n75
L'Histoire comique de Francion (Sorel), 182n39
libertas philosophandi, 36–37, 40, 45–46, 63, 157, 190n71
libertins érudits, 18–20, 38–42, 65, 93, 160, 163, 177n85, 180n14, 182n39
The Life of John Locke (King), 215n14, 217n52, 217n62
literacy, 3, 102, 138

Locher, Jacob, 129
Locke, John: as Cartesian rationalist, 1–2; and Charron, 156–58; and his philosophies of ignorance, 46–47, 145–57, 161–62, 165–67, 214n5; and the illiterate inventor, 134–35; and innate principles, 120–21, 123, 152; and the internal light, 82–83, 152; and Montaigne, 156–58, 217n62; and the scientific discourse, 115–23, 149, 161. *See also Conduct of the Understanding* (Locke); *Essay concerning Human Understanding* (Locke)
"Locke and the Latitude-Men" (Rogers), 216n39
Lode dell'ignoranza (Landi), 92
love, 9, 17, 61, 129; of God, 98–99, 101; of ignorance, 74, 85, 155; self, 12, 129
Lull, Ramon, 126
lumière naturelle, 75–76. *See also* internal light
Luther, Martin, 51
Luxon, Thomas, 110

madness, 67, 69, 78, 80, 84–85, 89–90, 197n81. *See also* certainty; enthusiasm; melancholy
Magnard, Pierre, 32
Mair, Jonathan, 23
Malebranche, Nicolas, 38, 193n25, 197n80
Manson, Neil C., 43
Manzo, Silvia, 55
Maresius (Samuel Desmarets), 197n80
The Masculine Birth of Time (Bacon), 52–54, 140
Mayerne, Louis Turquet de, 14, 119–20
melancholy, 69, 79, 81, 194n41. *See also* enthusiasm; madness
memory, 35–36, 76–77, 96, 119, 128, 163–64, 187n16
Mersenne, Marin, 40–42, 133, 147, 182n39, 183n53, 209n2
Merton, Robert K., 178n96

Metaphysics (Aristotle), 8–9, 92
method, 2, 8, 35, 37, 53, 55, 62, 75, 86, 131, 138–44, 161, 171n23; Descartes's, 44, 60, 62–64, 78, 80, 84–85, 88–89, 93, 127–28, 190n63; Locke's, 149–51; new, 3–4, 10, 21, 25, 55, 113, 132, 157, 162; scholastic, 4, 51, 72, 92, 96–97
Métius, Jacques, 133–34, 141
Micrographia (Hooke), 210n11
Miernowski, Jan, 32, 206n21
Milton, John, 203n75
modesty, 18, 40, 45, 58, 60, 64–65, 108, 162, 169n2, 176n80–176n81. *See also* honesty; humility; simplicity
modesty topos, 18, 60, 169n2
Montaigne, Michel de: and Agrippa, 32; and Bacon, 53–54; and Cusanus, 31–32, 179n2; and Descartes, 37–38; on ignorance, 29–35, 92, 186n5; and the illiterate inventor, 135; and infinite diversity, 32, 35, 179n2; and *Je ne sçay*, 63; as pragmatic empiricist, 1–2. *See also Essays* (Montaigne)
Moore, Wilbert, 23
More, Henry, 43, 81–82, 183n63, 195n58
Morris, John, 193n26, 194n35
Muratori, Cecilia, 176n82
mysticism, 6, 8–9, 80–81, 102, 125

Nachod, Hans, 171n18
the naked mind, 20, 27, 115–16, 120–21, 123, 127–32, 159, 161. *See also* autodidacticism; tabula rasa
Narrenschiff (Brant), 129
natural philosophy: definition of, 4; and discovery, 117, 136–37; and intellectual freedom, 129–30; and learning, 39, 71; and the naked mind, 3, 115–16; and sagacity, 139, 141–42; and simplicity, 58, 211n25; uses for, 149. *See also* the Royal Society
Nauert, Charles G., 175n65
negative theology, 6, 9–11, 25, 32, 35, 128–29, 160, 172n34

nescience, 64, 97
New Atlantis (Bacon), 52
Nicholas of Cusa. *See* Cusanus
Nicholas of Cusa and the Making of the Early Modern World (Burton, Hollmann, and Parker), 183n63
"The Noblenesse of the Asse" (Banchieri), 17–18
Norton, Thomas, 44, 184n67
Nosologie méthodique (Sauvages), 89
Novum Organum (Bacon), 53, 55, 140, 213n51, 213n53
Numbers (book of the bible), 17

observation, 10, 42, 119–23, 127, 131–32, 147–48, 160
Of Credulity and Incredulity (Casaubon), 87–88, 196n73, 196n75
Of Wisdom (Charron), 35–37, 130, 165, 180n22, 181nn25–26
On Discovery (Vergil), 209n2
On the Sources of Knowledge and of Ignorance (Popper), 177n84
Oosterhoff, Richard, 127
Opera Dionysii (Denys the Areopagite), 10
Opera omnia (Cusanus), 31, 65
Opera omnia (Petrarch), 8
Opuscule ou petit traité sceptique (La Mothe Le Vayer), 122

Paganini, Gianni, 176n82
Palissy, Bernard, 39, 182n42, 211n25
Paradossi (Lando), 11
paradoxical discourses. *See* discourse against letters
Parmenides (Plato), 172n34, 173n37
Pascal, Blaise, 29, 33–34, 65
Pasqua, Hervé, 207n33, 208n47
passions, 61, 80, 84–85
peasants, 30, 32, 35–36, 41, 90, 107, 160. *See also* simplicity
Peels, Rik, 22–23
Pensées (Pascal), 33–34

perfection, 91
Perkins, William, 44, 184n69
Petrarch, 7–8, 171nn18–19
Philosophus autodidactus (Ibn-Tufayl), 121–23
Picciotto, Joanna, 24, 130–31
The Pilgrim's Progress (Bunyan), 26, 70, 108–11
Pinker, Steven, 205n10
A Plain and Continued Exposition of the Several Prophecies or Divine Visions of the Prophet Daniel (More), 82
Plato, 80, 84–85, 139, 172n34, 198n7
Pocock, Edward, 121
Poel, Marc Van Der, 175n65
Poème sur la loi naturelle (Voltaire), 166
Popkin, Richard H., 5, 54, 61, 174n57
Popper, Karl R., 177n84
The Praise of Folly (Erasmus), 11, 55, 173n46, 175n65
Prior, Matthew, 1–2, 135
Proctor, Robert, 23, 178n97
Protestantism, 20, 52
Proverbs (book of the bible), 61–62, 109, 188n41
Pseudodoxia Epidemica (Browne), 198n1
The Pulpit Guarded (Hall), 101
The Pulpit-Guard Routed (Collier), 101–2
Puritans, 86–87, 100, 112, 184n69, 196n73, 202n56
purity, 15, 119, 123–24
Pyrrhonism, 5–6, 128

Quakers: and Cartesianism, 78–79, 83, 85–86, 88–89, 93, 194n37, 197n80; criticism of, 86–89; and ignorance, 3, 20; and the inner light, 26, 66, 68, 72–74, 77–78, 81, 99, 194n36, 197n80; and a learned ministry, 100; the theology of the, 71–72
"Quakers, Philosophy, and Truth" (Dudiak and Rediehs), 74
Questions Inouyes (Mersenne), 41

Questions theologiques (Mersenne), 40–41
Quod nihil scitur (Sanches), 63, 83, 98

Rabelais, François, 32
radical doubt, 78, 84, 86–88. *See also* Descartes, René; doubt
radicalism (religious), 42–43, 86–90, 102, 112, 161
Randall, Giles, 102, 207n32
Ravetz, Jerome R., 199n22
reason, 7–8, 76, 80–86, 105–6, 128, 139–41, 155
Rediehs, Laura, 74
the Reformation, 3, 5, 24, 69–70, 81, 103–4, 112, 160. *See also* Church of England
revelation, 44, 47, 68, 82–83
Richardson, George, 174n54
Ripa, Cesare, 12, *14*
Rochot, Bernard, 182n47
Rogers, G.A.J., 153, 216n39
Roman Catholic Church, 3, 82, 87, 97, 104, 152
Rosenfeld, Sophia, 180n14
Routledge International Handbook of Ignorance Studies, 22
the Royal Society, 26, 58–60, 64, 131, 135–38, 146, 156, 162. *See also* experimentalism; natural philosophy
Rules for the Direction of the Mind (Descartes), 37, 75, 77, 86, 141–42, 212nn44–45

sagacity, 27, 132, 139, 141–42, 144, 161, 211n28, 211nn30–31. *See also* discovery (by chance); illiterateness; the illiterate inventor; wisdom
The Saints Everlasting Rest (Baxter), 95
Salle, Paul Perrot de la, 17
salvation, 69–73, 94–95, 99, 106, 108–12, 153, 201n41
I Samuel (book of the bible), 7
Sanches, Francisco, 63, 83–84, 98
Sandford, James, 14

satire, 10–11, 176n70. *See also* irony
Saunders, Richard, 201n55
Sauvages, François Boissier de, 89–90
Scaliger, Julius Caesar, 45
Scepsis Scientifica (Glanvill), 60–64, 98, 130–31, 189n46. *See also The Vanity of Dogmatizing* (Glanvill)
scepticism. *See* skepticism
Schiebinger, Londa, 23
scholasticism, 15, 46–47, 96–97, 127–29, 185n85. *See also* antischolasticism
Schoock, Martin, 83–86, 88, 196n63
Schuurman, Paul, 44, 46
science. *See* Bacon, Francis; experimentalism; knowledge; Locke, John; method; the naked mind; nescience; observation; tabula rasa; truth; wisdom
Scientific Revolution, 4–5
Scriptures. *See* the Bible
The Search for Truth by Means of the Natural Light (Descartes), 36, 75, 78, 86, 116, 127–30
Sebonde, Raymond de, 126
sectarianism, 26, 69, 94, 100
self-knowledge. *See* knowledge
the senses (deception of), 60–62
Sergeant, John, 88–89, 197n77
Sextus Empiricus, 5–6
Shapin, Steven, 4, 136–37
Silver, Sean, 212n31
simplicity, 15–18, 21, 25, 30–31, 34, 38–39, 58, 95, 124, 129, 156. *See also* artisans; common sense; honesty; humility; knowledge; modesty; peasants
sin, 74, 94, 103, 109, 129, 146, 157. *See also* Adam; the fall
skepticism: academic, 5; and Agrippa, 174n57; ancient, 4–6, 11, 19, 32, 54, 160; and Bacon, 54; constructive, 5; criticisms of, 89, 98, 182n39; definition of, 5; and Descartes, 197n77; and Glanvill, 63–64, 190n81; and Locke,

148, 150, 197n77; mitigated, 60, 112; radical, 63–64, 84; rediscovered forms of, 5–6; Renaissance, 11, 19, 54; and science, 63, 133; semiscepticism, 5; superscepticism, 5; and wisdom, 41
Smith, John, 43
Smith, Nigel, 102
Smith, Pamela H., 136–38, 211nn25–26
social status, 125–26, 129, 136, 154–56
sociology, 23, 178n96
Socrates, 5, 16, 25, 32–36, 39–40, 51, 64, 128, 181nn26. *See also* wisdom
Solomon, 49
Sorel, Charles, 22, 38–40, 42, 91–93, 164–65, 182n39. *See also* De la perfection de l'homme (Sorel)
Sprat, Thomas, 210n16
Stachniewski, John, 111
Sterry, Peter, 43
Stillingfleet, Edward, 185n85
St. Paul, 11, 49, 57, 99, 201n50
Stultifera navis (Locher), 129
The Sufficiencie of the Spirits Teaching without Humane Learning (How), 100, 201n43, 201n47
Sullivan, Shannon, 23
Surin, Jean-Joseph, 124, 207n27
Suzuki, Akihito, 89, 197n81
Synesius of Cyrene, 80, 202n69

tabula rasa, 27, 52, 62, 116–23, 142, 147, 157, 161. *See also* autodidacticism; the naked mind
Talon, Henri A., 111
technicians, 136–37, 210n13, 211n22
Terra Incognita (Corbin), 24
Tertullian, 43, 45, 66, 68
Theaetetus (Plato), 198n7
Third Meditation (Descartes), 75–76
Thoughts concerning Education (Locke), 155
Timaeus (Plato), 85, 172n34
toleration (religious), 150, 152–53, 157, 167, 216n36

Tompion, Thomas, 135–36, 210nn9–10
translations: and altering the original text, 15; Dutch, 37, 75; English, 11–12, 14, 35, 43, 102, 116, 120–22, 167, 169n3, 187n20, 195n46, 212nn44–45, 217n62, 219n18; French, 11–12, 14, 119–20, 122; Latin, 5, 121, 192n18
A Treatise concerning Enthusiasme (Casaubon), 79–80, 105
Treatise of Knowledge and Love Compared (Baxter), 93–99, 109–10, 199n22, 200n28, 200n35, 200nn24–25, 200nn38–39, 214n6
Treatise on Toleration (Voltaire), 167, 219n18, 219n21
truth: divine, 67, 69, 113, 129, 161; ignorance as a path to, 3, 18, 26, 30, 32, 34–35, 63, 67, 75, 78, 87–88, 92, 116, 125; and knowledge, 60, 63, 68, 73, 77, 148; and learning, 127–28; and mathematics, 126; models of, 27, 78; and natural light, 75, 127–29; and the rehabilitation of ignorance, 20; religious, 45. *See also* knowledge; wisdom
Tuana, Nancy, 23
Tumin, Melvin, 23
Two Disputations of Original Sin (Baxter), 200n39

The Universal Free Grace of the Gospel Asserted (Keith), 72–73
"The Usefulness of Real Philosophy to Religion" (Glanvill), 57–58
Utrecht quarrel, 83–84, 86, 184n68, 195n60, 196n63

Valerius Terminus (Bacon), 52–53
vanity, 51, 103, 110, 128. *See also* dogmatism; knowledge
The Vanity of Dogmatizing (Glanvill), 59–63, 130, 190n65
van Leeuwenhoek, Antoni, 136, 138, 211n25

Verburgt, Lukas M., 24–25, 179n102
Vergil, Polydore, 209n2
Vie de Monsieur Descartes (Baillet), 88
Villey, Pierre, 53
virtue, 6–8, 11, 17, 26, 34–35, 43, 65, 87, 104, 203n72
Voetius, Gisbertus, 44, 195n60
Voltaire, 166–67, 197n80, 219n18, 219n21

Walton, Douglas, 151–52
Waterhouse, Edward, 203n71
White, Thomas, 63, 190n70
Whitlock, Richard, 45
Williams, David, 167
Wilson, Thomas, 45
wisdom: as an internal quality, 35–36; embodiments of, 16–17, 30, 35–36; and foolishness, 101; and the idiot, 125–26; ignorance as, 3, 18, 25–26, 29, 31, 53, 115, 127–31, 160; naïve, 10, 126; religious, 164; and sagacity, 139; and science, 36, 163–65; and self-knowledge, 33, 36; Socratic, 6–7, 39–40, 51, 147, 151, 162. *See also* knowledge; sagacity; truth
The Wisdom of the Ancients (Bacon), 142–43
Witmore, Michael, 143–44, 214n56
The Woman-Preacher of Samaria (Keith), 71–72
women, 23, 36, 71–72, 169n2; and ignorance, 11–12, 26, 71–73, 100, 181n26, 201n40
Woods, Chance, 183n63
A Word to the People of the World (Fox), 74, 192n8, 192n10, 192n18

Zwierlein, Cornel, 21, 24, 177n86, 178n99

The authorized representative in the EU for product safety and compliance is:
Mare Nostrum Group
B.V Doelen 72
4831 GR Breda
The Netherlands

www.ingramcontent.com/pod-product-compliance
Lightning Source LLC
Chambersburg PA
CBHW022004220426
43663CB00007B/957